GROUP DECISION MAKING

Drawing out and Reconciling Differences

Thomas L. Saaty
and
Kirti Peniwati

Library of Congress Cataloging-in-Publication Data
Saaty, Thomas L. & Peniwati, Kirti

GROUP DECISION MAKING: Drawing out and Reconciling Differences

ISBN 1-888603-08-9

1. Group Decision Making 2. Priorities 3. Analytic Hierarchy Process (AHP) 4. Analytic Network Process (ANP) 5. Decision Making with Dependence and Feedback 6. Conflict Resolution 7. Retributive Conflicts 8.Structuring Decisions 9. Possibility Theorem 10. Complex Decision Making

Thomas L. Saaty
University of Pittsburgh
322 Mervis Hall
Pittsburgh, PA 15260
Phone: 412-648-1539
Email: saaty@katz.pitt.edu

Published by

RWS Publications
4922 Ellsworth Avenue
Pittsburgh, PA 15213 USA
Phone: 412-414-5984
FAX: 412-681-4510

CONTENTS

Dedicated to Claudio Garuti for his warmth, brilliance and dedication to group decision making

Preface

The world population today is around 6.6 billion people. We are adding 1 billion to this population every ten years. By 2050 the world population is projected to be 10 to 11 billion. The capacity of the earth to support such a large population is quickly being pushed to the limit. Our individuality is lost within the identity of groups to which we belong, the identity of these groups is lost within the regions to which they belong, and the regions are absorbed into nations and nations into the entire world population. The decisions we make for our personal welfare are diluted by the needs of our families and those of the family by those of the neighborhood and so on.

Individual decision making is a silent process of internal communication. A group, however, cannot survive without a modicum of explicit communication between its members. Thus a group must constantly structure a dialogue that represents what is going on within the mind of each of its members. But this has to be done in a persuasive and logical way. We can no longer let instinct run decision making when it is for a group. Interdependence has become the defining characteristic of our modern world.

A new order is needed – one for structured decision making; a system that can be used by many individuals to communicate with each other and form a purposeful group identity. This process, moreover, must be institutionalized and integrated in the many decisions the group has to make to satisfy its objectives. Beyond that, the group's objectives must be integrated within the objectives of the region to which it belongs and so on. In this sense, guided decision making is not a luxury for 10 billion people who must learn to avoid catastrophic conflict. Can we bring about this broad perspective of creative decision making and use it to protect our freedoms and improve the quality of life? In this book we will show what is needed and how to go about doing it.

Psychological experiments have shown that people are sensitive to the suffering of a single person and are willing to respond to individual appeals for help. When they are told about the suffering of many people, however, they are less affected and not so compassionate and willing to help. They can identify better with one person than with many. It is here that a group can help us to act together to help those in need. When confronted by a problem that leaves us feeling unable to act, we need to examine the consequences of not acting. We need to do the same when we feel that we ought to do something we would rather avoid. It does not matter if we ultimately decide to do nothing. Given the circumstances at least we have made it our choice. A group that is committed can do this better than an individual because they can remind each other and hold each other responsible for carrying out a plan.

A number of bestsellers have been written in recent years about choices made by individuals and by groups and about how crowds tend to be wiser than individuals. But there has been no satisfactory theory about how to organize the factors of a decision, how to get people to express their preferences to reach a group decision, and how this decision then differs from what an individual does naturally and intuitively. This book addresses that subject. We believe that complex decisions call for a quantitative way for us to synthesize a series of judgments into a single overall hunch, insight, or guess that is logically defensible and leads to outcomes that work in the real world. The ideas in this book are brought together from a lifetime of experience in decision making. Many applications have been made of these ideas – in business, in government, in individual decision making, in conflict resolution – that are far beyond academic speculation. What we provide in this book is a practical way for a group to make its decisions.

We all agree that some things are more important to us than others. Moreover, the importance can differ from one person to the next. We need to measure relative importance. Measurement on a scale that fixes a value will not help us determine universal importance because it depends on the situation (and also because we each have a different idea of what value of importance to assign to things). Because of our differing sense of importance, we need to interpret the significance of measurements when we have them. Importance is a subjective concern. While hard data in physics are not subjective, our interpretation of their meaning is. To determine overall importance with respect to more than one objective, we need to assess the importance of the several objectives themselves and use that to weight the different grades of importance with respect to each objective so that we can combine them to determine the overall importance. How do we get measures for things that are subjective on scales that we can combine when we have many objectives to deal with?

There are two ways to measure something. One is to apply an existing scale to it (if we are lucky enough to have one); the other is to compare it with other things. In the absence of a scale, the second way is essential. It is a scientific process in which one of the two things being compared serves as the unit and the other is estimated as a multiple of that unit using experienced judgment to compare homogeneous things. If they are not homogeneous, they have to be put into groups with a common element. If we attempt to assign a number to a thing when there is no scale to measure with, the number is arbitrary and makes little sense. In decision making there are usually many criteria and we need to measure their importance and weight them. This means that the numbers under the different criteria must be meaningful so we can do arithmetic on them and combine them into a final overall priority. When there are several people, one will get several answers. How to combine these answers in a scientifically justifiable way is a fundamental concern of this book. The book's protocol is as follows:

1. Structure the problem to include all the factors that can influence the outcome. These factors are then arranged according to the importance of their influence by putting similar ones together in groups at the top of a hierarchy.
2. Discuss the factors in the structure to clarify what influences what. Further discussion can lead to numerous revisions of the structure.
3. Formulate comparison questions carefully and decide how strongly one factor predominates. The process is slow at first but speeds up later. Individual judgments are combined into a group judgment by using the geometric average which is necessary because a reciprocal comparison must have the reciprocal value of the numerical intensity of dominance that is assigned to the original comparison. The arithmetic average can never satisfy this reciprocal relation. The answer is obtained with the help of a computer program that keeps track of the structure and the judgments. Then sensitivity analysis is performed to ensure that the best outcome is chosen.
4. In case of impasse:
   a. Embed the problem in a larger decision. The parties involved must agree on this new context and structure its influences as before.
   b. Invite a mediator to break the impasse by examining each side's offers and counteroffers.
   c. Examine the historical origins, consider the possible actions that can be taken, and insist on positive gestures by the different sides involved to improve goodwill and overcome opposition to the process.

Our collaboration in writing this book was easy. When Kirti Peniwati studied the criteria essential for evaluating group decision-making methods, she found that Thomas Saaty's Analytic Hierarchy Process (AHP) and Analytic Network Process (ANP) ranked highest among the methods used to measure the influence of intangible factors in decision making. Kirti contributed the latter part of Chapters 1, the preponderance of Chapter 3, the early parts of Chapter 6 and two examples in Chapter 4. Because of its reciprocal comparisons, the AHP offers a natural scientific way to derive priorities, combine individual judgments, and obtain representative group judgments without having to rely on consensus or on the statistics of voters whose preferences may differ markedly in intensity.

We are grateful to Professor Luis Vargas for his collaboration with the first author on two published papers that constitute the last two chapters of the book and Professor Jennifer Shang for her collaboration with the first author on a paper that is now Chapter 7. We also thank Ozlem Arisoy, Enrique Mu, Laura Trahan, Rozann Whitaker, and Don Yoder, for their excellent editorial help in bringing the manuscript to its final form.

This book was revised in 2012 by replacing Chapter 14 by an equivalent chapter that is this book's version of the paper "Possibility of Group Choice: Pairwise Comparisons and Merging Functions", (by T.L. Saaty and L.G. Vargas) published in 2011 in the journal *Social Choice and Welfare*. An earlier and different version of it, "The Possibility of Group Welfare Functions," published in 2005 in the *International Journal of Information Technology & Decision Making* (IJITDM), won the Herbert Simon prize early in 2012. It was awarded by a committee that identified it as the best among 30 contending "best papers" among the hundreds published in the journal since 2002.

Thomas L. Saaty, Pittsburgh
Kirti Peniwati, Jakarta
2012

PART I: The Group and the Decision

There is strength in numbers, the saying goes. When a group makes a decision, that decision carries a lot more weight than when just one person does it. Think of the founding fathers of the American constitution and how much power and influence their ideas have had in the entire world for more than two hundred years. Also think of gravity, a universal force brought about by an enormous number of minute particles that band together to make a universal law. Together, they create a massive force, a law of nature; alone they can barely be noticed. That is how our minds work by deciding together to create a power that transcends our individuality. Group decision making is a gift and an opportunity to create greater influence through the working together of many minds.

There exists perhaps no better example of the pressing need for synthesizing a group's decision making into a unified judgment than the American dilemma in Iraq in late 2006 and early 2007. While the president spoke continuously of victory, Iraq suffered the continuous trauma of sectarian violence. Many generals, members of Congress, Iraqi politicians, and the American majority had expressed their opposition to the war – especially in the November 2006 elections. Even the president himself and his advisers advocated new alternatives in Iraq ranging from an immediate and complete withdrawal of troops to increasing the number of American soldiers deployed to Iraq by tens of thousands. The ability to resolve this kind of chaos is not only desirable but essential in our day.

For another example, consider the issue of investment in different securities whose future is projected by numerous people with varied experience using different techniques. How do we combine their different predictions into a credible overall prediction depending on the priorities of the contributors and their techniques? A hierarchical model of portfolio management can include three separate hierarchies: one based on extrinsic factors, one based on intrinsic factors, and a third based on the investor's objectives. The extrinsic factors are the outside economic, political, social, and technical factors or environmental characteristics that affect an industry's (or firm's) performance and on which a firm has no direct influence. The intrinsic factors are the internal factors or operational characteristics of the firm such as profitability, size, technology, and philosophy. They may be considered as a measure of the way the firm is making its decisions or, in general, a measure of the firm's capacity to compete successfully. The investor's objectives include such factors as profitability, security, excitement, and control. Knowledge about the importance of all the factors affects the way the investment is made. Different people have different ideas about what is important and how important it is. Usually we can't say that any one-sided point of view by an "expert" has greater merit than that by another "expert". How do we combine such immense knowledge to take advantage of the diversity and make a better investment?

In this first part of the book we lay out the reasons for the urgency that exists for adopting and implementing group decisions and introduce and illustrate how the Analytic Hierarchy Process (AHP) can be used in making decisions. Chapter 1 describes the challenges of group decision making today. The complexity inherent in having groups manage various processes has been the subject of many years of research and the finding is that having a structured group process is key to success. The general impossibility of aggregating ordinal group judgments was formerly considered an obstacle to finding a structured method. But the AHP with its method for combining group judgments removes this obstacle. The Fundamental Scale of the AHP and its application are introduced using an example. Chapter 2 describes the step by step process of applying the AHP in more detail using an example of choosing the best hospice with many intangible benefits and costs. Several examples are given that validate the use of the Fundamental Scale in estimating different kinds of physical measurements. This scale both makes the AHP less taxing to apply and also makes it possible to combine group judgments scientifically to obtain fully justified representative judgments for the group that include the power and influence of its members.

Chapter 1

The Need for a Structured Approach

This book is about how to measure the intensity of people's feelings and judgments. Scholars and people in general once thought that you cannot construct a quantitative model that represents with reasonable accuracy how strongly a person reacts to influences. Going further, many people still believe that you cannot combine individual judgments into a representative judgment for a group. But in fact you can – and we will show this in detail throughout the book.

To decide is to choose the best course of action. To choose the best course for action calls for knowledge and sound judgments about what objectives are served by the action and how important they are among all the objectives that are served by all the decisions made and actions taken. It also calls for an understanding of what influences the decision's success and what resistance the action might encounter that would frustrate fulfillment of the objectives. Moreover, it takes planning to determine the effects of the decision in the scheme of things. To judge the relative importance of objectives and influences and trade them off is the heart of decision making. Determining what is more important and what is less important – and how much more or less important – is a quantitative concern that calls for careful measurements. In fact judgment and number are intimately related. Is it possible to measure judgments in a scientific way that is sensible and easy so that we can use the outcome to make better decisions? Although we have been told over and over again that it is impossible to quantify how much more important one thing is than another, we need to find an easy way to link judgments and numbers by observing what people actually do in the real world and then find a suitable framework that we can all use without undue exertion.

The purpose of thinking about decision making is to help people make decisions according to their own understanding so that they feel they really made the decision themselves according to their own values, beliefs, and convictions. To make a good decision, people cannot simply rely on their feelings. They have to consider what it is they need to decide on, what influences their decision, and what alternative courses of action are available to them. They also need to think systematically about the impact of different influences on their decision. Finally, to make judgments they need to call on their past experience. Until today there has been no formal way to make a decision except to wait until there is the pressure of an emergency and then react to it impulsively taking the first option that comes to mind. To make

[handwritten: differing thoughts into a collectible judgement that all group members agree on]

use of thinking and judgment in decision making is what we need to learn more about.

[handwritten margin note: prioritize]
[handwritten margin note: assumptions]

This book is about making group decisions with clarity and confidence. It provides a systematic and workable way to make group decisions despite differences of opinion and disagreements. By making explicit a host of hidden assumptions, knowledge can be used in a rational way to prioritize the alternative outcomes of the decision in order to choose the best one among them. When several people who have varying knowledge, judgments, and expectations are involved in making a decision it is even more essential to have a defensible way to combine their knowledge using a single framework on which they all agree. Moreover there need to be ways to combine their different judgments into a collective judgment that takes into account the importance and reliability of each person's judgments. As we learn to make better decisions for a group, of course, we also learn to make better decisions for ourselves as individuals. Making a good decision requires us to get under the hood and study the processes that run the decision-making engine.

[handwritten margin note: Cardinal #s]

The methods presented in this book are unlikely to be found anywhere else in the literature about group decision making. We base our approach on cardinal numbers that belong to an absolute scale. The numbers in an absolute scale cannot be transformed to other numbers like kilograms to pounds and meters to yards and mean the same thing. This way, they are said to be invariant under the identity transformation. A cardinal number is any number that expresses amount, as *one, two, three,* and so on, as distinct from an ordinal number which is a number indicating position or order in a series. People committed to the old ways of thinking find it especially hard to accept the idea that judgments have intensities that can be measured to yield priorities that are then used to make decisions. A.F. MacKay [1] writes that pursuing the cardinal approaches is like chasing what cannot be caught. Moreover, much of quantitative thinking in economics is based on utility theory, which is grounded in lotteries and wagers [2], thus implicitly subsuming benefits, opportunities, and costs within a single framework of risks. But lotteries are deeply rooted in the material exchange of money, and it does not make very much sense to exchange intangibles such as love and happiness with money. The real value of money varies among people and is a utility. Utilities are measured on interval scales like temperature. They cannot be added or multiplied and fall quite short of the kind of thinking people do to make a decision.

Of significance here is Kenneth Arrow's proof of the impossibility of combining individual judgments into a group judgment that satisfies certain conditions [3, 4, 5, 6] shown in Figure 1.1. His thinking was grounded in using ordinals to express preference in order to prove "impossibility." What does this mean? In the ordinal way we can say that A is preferred to B but

Quantify preferences

not by how much. In other words, Arrow's logic follows the dictates of ordinary logic without the use of quantities to define people's preferences. People in academia have assumed that the impossibility of a group working together without making its members unhappy in some way is simply a logical fact. The real world, however, does not seem to work this way. All living things respond with different intensities to different influences. If A is a clear sunny day and B is a dark and gloomy day, we do not just say I prefer A to B, but I prefer A lots more than B. And we need to capture this

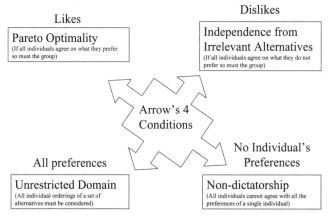

Figure 1.1 Arrow's Four Conditions a Welfare Function Must Satisfy

distinction in our considerations. Readers interested in a proof of the possibility of group decision making that satisfies all of Arrow's conditions should read the last chapter of this book. It shows that we can indeed construct a group preference function in a practical way from individual preferences that satisfies conditions that Arrow's ordinal approach does not. Long after the AHP appeared in the early 1970s, some people perhaps unknowingly, proved the existence of such a cardinal approach without constructing one.

The social sciences have failed to find a way to quantify thinking because the logic we use today, often attributed to Aristotle, is inadequate to deal with the refinements required to handle the complexity of our world. We need a finer logic – one that not only uses words but also numbers and that can synthesize such numbers to show what should be the real output of our thinking and our responses to happenings in the world. Logical thinking as we know it today cannot do this.

The method presented in this book, the Analytic Hierarchy Process (AHP), has been developed over the past thirty years and applied many times by numerous corporations and governments [7, 8, 9]. It involves structuring a decision as a hierarchy whose upper levels are independent of

AHP

the lower levels; providing pairwise-comparison judgments; deriving priorities from these judgments; and synthesizing the priorities to determine the best alternative for a decision. The AHP has been generalized to the Analytic Network Process (ANP). In the ANP the decision structures are networks in which everything can potentially depend on everything else, including itself. There is software called DecisionLens that is very good for making decisions with hierarchies. See www.decisionlens.com. The software for network models is called SuperDecisions. Learn more about it at: ww.superdecisions.com. Of particular interest in group decision making are radio frequency keypads such as the ResponseKey keypads which allow the members of a group to directly enter judgments on one computer. Each participant may respond to posted questions, express preferences or respond to test questions by selecting and pressing one of fifteen keys. The key presses are transmitted to a receiver connected to the computer via a nine-pin connector on the rear panel.

The AHP/ANP is based on making comparisons rather than just assigning numbers off the top of the head. Making comparisons is basically a scientific process that takes a pair of elements and asks how much the larger one dominates the smaller one with respect to a certain property. The two elements must be close so that we can say that one dominates the other by 2 or 3 or 5 or 9 times – but not more than that because there is a limit to our ability to compare the very small and the very large. If they are far apart, we will show a way of putting them into groups then using a common pivot element from one group to the next one to link the measurements of the elements in the groups.

Making Comparisons – an Intrinsic Talent

absolute vs. comparative judgment.

Cognitive psychologists know that making comparisons is an intrinsic human talent and everyone can do this whether educated or skilled or not. Comparisons can then be used to derive relative numbers representing importance or priority. In his book *The Process of Cognition* [10], the Harvard psychologist Arthur Blumenthal tells us that there are two types of judgment: "Comparative judgment, which is the identification of some relation between two stimuli both present to the observer, and absolute judgment, which involves the relation between a single stimulus and some information held in short term memory about some former comparison stimuli or about some previously experienced measurement scale with which the observer rates the single stimulus."

In his book *The Number Sense: How the Mind Creates Mathematics*, the mathematician and cognitive neuropsychologist Stanislas Dehaene [11] writes: "Introspection suggests that we can mentally represent the meaning of numbers 1 through 9 with actual acuity. Indeed, these symbols seem equivalent to us. They all seem equally easy to work with, and we feel that we can add or compare any two digits in a small and fixed amount of time like a computer. In summary, the invention of numerical symbols should have freed us from the fuzziness of the quantitative representation of numbers." Subjectivity of Intangibles

In the past, people talked around intangibles and mostly decided to exclude them, from decision making because they are so subjective. Without measures for the intangibles, however, there is likely to be a lack of agreement on values among the parties in a conflict. While each party can reduce the trade-offs to a single best outcome according to its system of priorities, it is hard to trade off values among several parties because of their differing objectives. In this case we must find an abstract way to define an index for trade-offs among the parties that would be hard to reject on grounds of fairness. In this book, we propose a way to do that. priorities

Comparisons lead to relative thinking and to relative numbers in the form of priorities. People up to now have tended to improvise numbers to capture order without regard to the validity of these numbers in practice. It turns out that relative numbers can be used to estimate all kinds of "objective" measurements that are converted to relative form by dividing by their sum. This is a rather surprising notion for scientists who believe that the truths of the natural world are independent of the human mind. The brain has its own structure that works in certain ways that are not absolute and without constraint. It uses electricity to create feelings, images, aesthetics, and all the things that make us human.

Decision making is a central activity of the human mind; we do it continuously both consciously and unconsciously. For instance, our body continuously and rapidly makes decisions that affect how our immune system will respond to foreign antibodies. Animals and plants are decision makers, too, each in their own way, as a matter of survival. Making better decisions improves our chances of survival and enhances our quality of life. If we know how to use information to make decisions with greater certainty, we can implement them with confidence. Decision making requires a modicum of creativity to develop a structure for the factors and the alternatives of a decision.

Individuals only have to agree with themselves to make a decision; groups, however, generally have trouble coming to a consensus. Therefore all progress in group decision making comes from group members being able to work together. For a good decision, the group needs to be diverse and informed. Its members should hold independent judgments that are not coordinated in advance, to allow for a creative and lively discussion. Above all, the group needs a way to synthesize the judgments of its members into a representative group decision. Decisions can be normative, involving the most desirable outcome, or they can be descriptive, involving what is most

3 step approach to decision-making

likely to happen in view of all the influences at play. There are, of course, ongoing difficulties with decision making. An individual or a group may fail to tackle problems before they occur or fail to recognize them when they occur. They may choose the wrong solution to a problem, or they may make the right choice but it does not work out. Each of these challenges calls for its own kind of remedy.

Often a person must decide whether or not to do something. At other times a person must choose the best of several alternatives. The choice usually depends on many criteria: solving a problem, saving money, putting forth less effort, obtaining favorable influence on the people affected, and so on. Because the criteria may have different levels of importance, we need to establish priorities for discriminating among them. Our approach involves three steps. Step 1: Lay out all the factors of a decision and their interconnections in a hierarchy or network of influences. Step 2: Provide judgments in the form of pairwise comparisons to determine what dominates what and how strongly. Every factor that needs to be considered must be included, and every piece of information must be articulated. Step 3: Synthesize all the judgments about the alternatives and then choose the alternative with the highest priority. When there are resources to allot to a number of alternatives, the allocation must be made according to the priorities.

We live in a world of increasing complexity and accelerating change that forces us to keep learning just to get by. Complexity requires training to cope with it with the emphasis on creative decision making rather than merely following old habits. Technology is the major driver of change today; it speeds things up and increases communication – breaking down the world's boundaries. Technology is intensifying the global economy and sharpening competition, both on the personal and organizational levels. Well-thought-out decisions, especially those involving other people, spell the difference between success and failure.

Although complexity and uncertainty bring challenges, they also bring opportunities and create more possibilities. Technology may make some of our skills obsolete, but it also opens up new ways for us to do more meaningful and productive work. Information technology may cause us to feel overwhelmed with data, but it also enables people thousands of miles apart to work together. Complexity and change make the future less predictable, but they also offer a competitive advantage to those who know how to anticipate situations and impose structure on what seems unmanageable. These challenges may make us feel less competent as individuals, but technology facilitates collective effort. The key is to work with others in striving for common objectives that take into account the aspirations of every member of the group.

data & technology help drive group decision-making

applying knowledge to similar situations

In a stable environment, learning means remembering past experiences and finding new ways to make better decisions as similar situations arise. But can we safely assume that a solution which worked in the past will work in the new situation? Complexity and uncertainty mean that the environment is dynamic – that is, no situation can be assumed to be exactly the same as in the past. Moreover, we cannot assume that an old solution will work when applied to a somewhat similar situation. A dynamic environment adds a new perspective to learning because it is less about acquiring new knowledge and more about knowing how to deepen our understanding and awareness of the assumptions underlying a problem. Working with a group can help with this. If the people know the subject they are trying to make a decision about, their knowledge and expertise will enrich the group's awareness.

Why Use a Structured Approach? *in group decision making*

Let us look at the reasons why we need a structured approach for group decision making. First decision making is contextual. A decision depends on the environment, the objectives, the people who make the decision, and related decisions and problems. These factors must all be considered when making a decision. We may think the outside world is the only source of complexity, but this is not the case. There are internal complexities that can affect a decision and must be considered as well.

Second, we make decisions to satisfy our needs and promote our values. As social beings, we get value from what we do and what those around us do. If we belong to an organization, we increase our personal value indirectly by working with others to increase the organization's value. Working together with people calls for reconciliation of individual and group values with those of the organization.

And third, we need to heighten awareness to make decisions in a complex environment. We can no longer expect to make good strategic decisions in a casual or intuitive way. Complexity is what we find in most of our decisions; and it derives from both internal and external influences on the organization. Complexity can also be traced to the interdependence of the different decisions that people are making in an organization. Now let us turn to the various types of complexity that stem from different sources.

External Complexity *(2 3 sources)*

There are at least three different sources of external complexity. In the first case, not only are there different parties with different values who influence the outcome of a decision and its implementation, but there also are other parties who may not have the power to decide but are nonetheless important stakeholders whose interests must be considered. The second source of complexity comes from how different events are linked to each other. The events may be interconnected in such a way that it is hard to separate the cause (the source of an influence) from the effect. Several events together may cause more than one effect. In some situations there is a long delay between the cause and its effect, or the effect may be experienced by people other than the decision makers. The third source of complexity comes from the discontinuous trend of change over time that makes it so hard to predict the future.

Experience suggests that limiting decision making to the top of the hierarchy is one of the reasons why strategic plans go unimplemented [12]. Organizations do not work like mechanical entities that can be programmed to perform according to predetermined standards. Members who are lower in the hierarchy have brains, too, not simply mechanical muscle. More than ever, people do not merely exist in their world but also participate in creating it. As a product of our thinking, this world cannot be changed without changing our thinking. People need to be given decision-making roles; they may even determine the success or failure of the organization. Involving the right people in a decision may not always be easy but using their knowledge to deal with a complex problem is absolutely essential.

New concepts of leadership are emerging today in successful companies that are fundamentally different from companies that have seen success coming from people at the top with somewhat superhuman characteristics. Research has discovered that today's successful leaders are those who make use of their people's talents. If you study companies that had a high level of growth for fifteen consecutive years, you will find that their leaders have not only a powerful commitment to achieve results but also the skill to bring out the best in subordinates. These leaders set high standards for results – and then share credit for good results and the success of the company. And when failure happens, they take responsibility rather than placing blame elsewhere [13]. Good leaders have high levels of executive intelligence in three dimensions: they seek to excel in their job; they work with and through other people; and they are involved in self-learning [14]. Surely an organization can use many such leaders, not just the one at the top.

Internal Complexity

Daniel Kahneman of Princeton University won the 2002 Nobel Prize in Economics for his groundbreaking research concerning the pathological mistakes and persistent miscalculations made by intelligent people in decision making [15]. He observed that people continue to make irrational choices despite having adequate information. In an automatic, almost

Kahneman: irrational decisions w/o learning from mistakes

Miller — items of information

unconscious, way we often use intuition alone to respond quickly to the world. This kind of behavior is difficult to control and is often emotionally charged. By contrast, reasoning one's way through a decision is a conscious and deliberate way of thinking that often follows rules but takes a great deal more time. Kahneman also noted that organizations make many decisions but do not go back and try to actually understand what they did wrong. He concluded that organizations simply do not care to know. Even when people admit they have made a mistake, it does not mean they have changed their mind and would be able to avoid the same mistake in the future.

The mind is limited in its ability to handle many items of information and the relationships linking those items at any instant. An item may be a word, an idea, or an object in a scene or a group of items called a chunk. George A. Miller [16] has shown that the magic number of items of information the brain can handle at one time is seven plus or minus two. Like a computer, the human mind takes in information, performs operations on it to change its form and content, stores and locates it, and generates responses to it. Thus processing involves gathering and representing information or encoding it; holding information or retaining it; and getting the information when needed or retrieving it. It is reported that working memory sometimes contains over twenty units at one time.

People do not seem to have much control over what information gets stored in their memory. Items in working memory decay over time. The longer it has been since an item was stored, the less likely it is to be currently available; this is why people tend to forget things. The probability of remembering is a function of how many times the information enters the mind, so that articulation, hearing or seeing the item in writing, increases its availability. Losing information from the mind may be a good thing for our mental health – helping us to forget bad memories – but a degree of effort is required to ensure that wanted information is stored and stays in memory. What we need, then, is a decision support system that records the history of a decision with adequate detail. people forget – record decision making process

Classifying and grouping things into chunks is a well-known psychological phenomenon of memory; indeed it is one of the most primitive and common activities of human beings. The limited capacity of the human mind is in a way a blessing because structuring becomes a natural process of organizing the enormous number of information items into chunks, which helps information processing. Grouping things into information chunks enables us to think within the limits of our working memory. Even in nonlinear relations, people naturally build connections between what they have just processed and what they currently are processing and, ultimately, what they expect to process in the near future. Structuring information items into a hierarchy or a network makes this process efficient.

The mind does not work in a seamless continuous way. Rather, the mind is aimless and disconnected. Even when it focuses, the mind is unable to retrieve from its memory storehouse all the information needed. Often the ideas only come to mind later and are added to current information in a patchwork fashion. People, moreover, are forgetful; they remember now but then later behave as if they did not remember. Just as we use language to organize the thoughts behind feelings, we need a systematic way to collect the factors that have bearing on a decision and organize them into a dictionary for easy reference. This systematic approach also would provide a framework for judgments and discussion, helping us to avoid random thoughts and wandering off the subject.

The working memory of experts is no better than that of everyday people. But because of many years of experience, experts have larger and more complex memory chunks. These chunks make it easier for them to recognize complex patterns quickly. Further, they are able to develop commonsense rules to help them solve problems efficiently. The quality of their intuitive decisions is questionable, however, because each decision needs to be thought out carefully due to changing circumstances. The world does not stand still to allow experts to bring their experience to bear on decisions of the future.

We all have mental models of our perceptions and assumptions about the world; they guide our actions and help us in dealing with the world [17]. Such models, however, are inherently subjective and biased toward the past; hence they may not always work in a collective context. Some models may even lose their effectiveness as changes in the environment demand different actions. Aligning the mental models of group members is considered to be one of the key processes in learning organizations [18].

The Problem of Interdependence

One aspect of decision making is consistently underestimated: interdependence. A decision generally does not stand alone. It is usually related to other decisions or is part of a higher-level decision. A business strategy depends on the overall corporate strategy, for instance, while a new product strategy depends on the relative importance of technology in the target market. IBM's Silverlake project is an example of interdependent decision making using the AHP [19]. In Chapter 4 we show an example of successive strategic decisions using AHP – from product and competitor analysis to strategy selection to prioritizing strategic initiatives in order to implement the strategy.

The Need to Sharpen Purpose

[handwritten: subjectivity of decision-making]

What makes decision making largely subjective is that it is driven by the needs and values of the decision makers. This is as true for personal decision making as it is for a group of executives who want to satisfy the needs and values of different units in their organization in a collective decision-making process. Reconciling the needs and values of individuals in a group with those of the organization's makes group decision making especially challenging.

Abraham Maslow [20] classifies seven basic human needs in order of importance from most basic to least basic:

[handwritten: 7 basic human needs]

1. Homeostatic (physiological) needs
2. Safety and security needs
3. Love and belonging needs
4. Esteem needs
5. Self actualization needs
6. The need to know and understand
7. Aesthetic needs

There is overlap from need to need. Each successive need emerges little by little as the previous need is partially satisfied. A need may be 25 percent satisfied when the next one emerges 5 percent. If the previous need is 75 percent satisfied, the following need may emerge 50 percent. Nicholas Rescher [21] argues that people's values guide their deliberations and help us to understand their decisions and actions. A thing has value when it is the object of interest – any interest. Values like the following are related to actions in categorically different ways:

- A motive, habit, or disposition for action (bravery, generosity)
- A physical state (health, good looks)
- A capability, skill, or talent (agility, endurance)
- A state of mind or attitude (indifference toward money, patriotism)
- A character trait (resoluteness)
- A state of affairs (privacy, economic justice)

Within a group, individuals do not give up their personal values but may be willing to trade some of their personal needs and values for certain group values:

[handwritten: self vs. group]

- Physical (health, exercise, sports)
- Educational (learning, communication, information)

- Economic (money, property)
- Social (welfare, cooperation, organization)
- Political (power, influence)
- Moral (order, honesty, trust)
- Ideological (religion, common belief, fervor)
- Technological (innovation, change, problem solving)
- Military (security, force, defense)
- Aesthetic (art, music, theater)
- Competition (quality, reasonable pricing)
- Negotiation (give and take)
- Conflict resolution (reconciliation)

Defining complex problems requires a high level of understanding and needs to be part of the decision-making process. Often it is harder to define a specific problem than it is to decide what to do about it, and it is the decision maker's responsibility to ensure that the decision is consistent with the definition of the problem. Decision making is about finding the question that focuses thinking on understanding the problem; after all, it is useless to find the right answer to the wrong question. Brainstorming techniques to generate questions, rather than the usual preoccupation with generating ideas, have often been used by groups working on complex problems.

A good understanding of a problem and its context is likely to lead to a good decision. Since understanding is inherently tacit, it is essential to articulate the problem carefully in group decision making. Even here a team may only be able to frame the description generally and be forced to leave much of the knowledge tacit in its members' minds. Well-defined problems, as in science, are those that come with well-established ways – or algorithms – for arriving at correct solutions. These problems are manageable because we work within certain boundaries that place limits on the scope of the problem. (This is not to say that such problems are easy to solve.) Complex problems, by contrast, have no known algorithms to solve them because their boundaries are ambiguous and difficult to define. Because we need a boundary if we are to design a solution effectively, we are compelled to define the boundary ourselves. Defining and structuring a decision problem must include all the important goals, objectives, factors, actors, and stakeholders; alternative courses of action must be fully represented; benefits, costs, opportunities and risks must be fully considered.

Two Kinds of Purpose

Influences and values are two basic considerations in decision making. While people do not usually surrender their personal values, they may be willing to trade off some of their lower-level needs listed by Maslow for higher ones. Group decision making is a way to address some of the higher-level needs, such as the sense of love and belonging that comes from being a member of a solid and well-performing group. Members who feel they contribute a lot in producing decisions that lead to group success would certainly feel that their self-esteem and self-actualization needs also are satisfied. There is no sense of belonging or self-actualization to be found in a group decision-making process led by a dictator. *reactive vs. proactive*

One goal of decision making is to find opportunities and courses of action that realize an organization's objectives – a proactive goal. But sometimes the goal in decision making is reactive – solving problems of deteriorating performance, for example, or dealing with threatening events. Research suggests that setting group goals is one of the foundations of successful teamwork. The goal is not only the focus of the group decision-making process but also the reference for evaluating alternative courses of action. The goal must be relevant to the higher-level purpose of the organization. Breaking down an organization's purpose into lower-level objectives ensures that they can be more easily made relevant through implementation. *prioritization process*

Balanced Scorecards, as described by Kaplan and Norton in their series of books [22, 23, 24], have had widespread use as a systematic process for translating an organization's strategy into actions. They serve as a roadmap by breaking down the organization's purpose into clear and specific objectives. The prioritization process enables an organization to allocate resources to different efforts. Mobilizing members toward a set of the organization's strategic objectives calls for aligned actions, and prioritization directs this effort accordingly to ensure more effective and efficient endeavors.

Group decision making does not mean that consensus is always reached. Nor does it mean that all team members have to be involved in every aspect of a decision. Team members are expected to process data and apply their individual expertise to contribute to the outcome. Members also are expected to communicate relevant information and recommendations. If the final authority for a decision rests with a single person, the team members provide the decision maker with assessments that are crucial to the situation. Otherwise how would the decision maker be able to process all the information single-handedly?

Group decision making is a process that requires the participation of every member. Often a group task calls for the application of expertise beyond that of a single person. Individual competence is necessary but not sufficient because accomplishing a group task is not simply a matter of coming up with a decision. The group also needs to work on enhancing its cohesiveness because the quality of its decisions depends on the ability of its members to function collectively as a coherent unit. The group decision-making process needs to bring satisfaction to its members by achieving the task and creating desire to participate in future sessions. In a way, each group session is an investment in developing a long-term collaborative climate.

By involving people with different views, collective decision making widens the perspective of individual decision makers. The challenge of group decision making is how to integrate all the different mental models and diverse perceptions. Moreover, involving other people in decision making creates a new complication because psychological issues of group interaction come into play. Apart from coming up with a decision – called the achievement or content goal – the group also needs to work on preserving good relationships between group members – the maintenance goal. Since these two goals are intertwined, a group leader must simultaneously manage both processes, which means choosing a way to deal with the decision that serves both goals. The structured approach we describe in this book has been used successfully by consultants to facilitate group decision making in complex situations.

When we hear the word "conflict," we may regard it as a negative consequence of group decision making. Often a group is so divided and chaotic that it is a hellish job to bring members together. But conflict can be a productive process, too, because it indicates a diversity of ideas. Research has shown that although managers understand the logic of conflict, they are uncomfortable with the emotional component. Conflicts that keep members focused on relevant differences of opinion tend to improve the team's effectiveness.

Research also shows that the more intense the conflict, the greater the degree of formality needed to manage it. The conflict management method proposed in this book enables a group to approach a decision with an open mind while minimizing conflict-triggering behavior. As ideas become less personalized, egos are less likely to be challenged and the need for time-consuming and distracting conflict management is minimized.

Alignment: The Key to Effective Decision Making

Problem solving is concerned with maintaining the status quo so that performance does not deteriorate. The key process here is finding the cause of deviation from the standard. When we know the cause, action can follow. Problem solving is often associated with finding the right answer – that is, finding the real cause of the problem. Finding the right answer focuses thinking on looking for the best action to bring performance back to normal. Consider, for example, the actions taken to solve quality problems in a complex manufacturing environment. Based on the degree of involvement of people in different management levels [25], the "total quality" movement initiated by Japanese manufacturers makes a distinction between the processes of maintaining standards, making continuous but incremental improvements in the workplace, and innovation. Maintaining standards is mostly in the hands of the shop floor workers who work in teams to solve operational problems. Continuous incremental improvement involves all management levels. Innovation is mostly top management's responsibility.

"Problem solving" may not even be an appropriate phrase for the process of finding an answer to a complex problem, since a complex problem can hardly ever be "solved." Solving it is more a matter of designing a solution (a stream of well-connected or coherent decisions) that we think will be more or less effective, based on how the problem is defined, than of finding an answer that is definite and final. Decision makers need to describe the problem – and the quality of their decision will depend on how well it is defined and how the goal is stated.

Organizational Alignment

In a world of fast change and increasing complexity, organizational decision making is the privilege of those who have the relevant information. A study released by the 3M Meeting Management Institute indicates that people who have the most knowledge about an issue may exert greater influence on decisions than those who have the most power. Clearly, then, an organization will benefit from a system for sharing knowledge among its members.

Some complain that group decision making takes too much time. The 3M Meeting Management Institute says that employees spend about one and a half hours a day in meetings – most of which are called with a 2 hours' notice, and less than half of which have an agenda. It has been reported that a typical meeting of six mid-level managers can cost an organization around $2,000, and this money is often wasted due to poor results or no results at all. Romano and Nunamaker report: "Studies of managers and knowledge workers reveals that they spend between 25%-80% of their time in meetings. Estimates of meeting expenses range from costs of $30 million to over $100 million per year to losses between $54 million and $3.7 billion annually. Self estimates of meeting productivity by managers in many different functional areas range from 33%-47% " [26].

The work of R.M. Belbin [27, 28] is perhaps the most significant piece of research on team effectiveness undertaken so far. His result does not support the common belief that you bring the most intelligent people together, you inevitably get a high-performance team. He discovered that the role people play in a group process is more important than their technical ability in determining the team's success. According to Belbin, there are nine ideal roles that contribute to effective group decision making.

- The *Coordinator* controls team progress toward its objective by making use of the team's strengths and potentials.
- The *Shaper* shapes the group process in an authoritative way with a sense of urgency.
- Creative ideas would come from the *Plant*, who offers new ideas and recommends strategies to solve the problem.
- The *Resource Investigator* with an external network looks for resources or help from outside the group.
- The *Team Worker* improves communication among team members and maintains group spirit.
- The *Monitor-Evaluator* analyzes the problem by evaluating inputs from group members and ensures a balanced decision.
- The *Implementer* translates concepts and plans into practical work procedures and implements the plan systematically and efficiently.
- The *Completer-Finisher* protects the group from making mistakes, looks for things that need special attention and maintains the sense of urgency.
- The *Specialist* shares knowledge and gives professional advice.

Belbin suggests that a group should have a diversity of team roles. It may be easy to establish a group comprised of people who have good understanding, but these people may not be able to use that considerable understanding to reach a good decision. Experts often lack the skill to encourage mutual participation – and therefore fail to elicit the most relevant information that has a bearing on solving the problem collectively in a smooth way by maintaining the high spirit of teamwork. In this book we present a method that helps elicit and organize and utilize collective knowledge. The group decision process we describe helps us refine our initial judgments and determine how stable the outcome is likely to be if the judgments were to change dramatically. With group diversity, a compatibility measure is provided to identify nonhomogeneity in thinking that needs special attention since it may indicate a better perspective. If used by knowledgeable people, this method produces very accurate outcomes.

Forward and Backward Planning

Knowledge and information are usually about the past, which may or may not be useful for looking into the future. Extrapolating past and present trends into the future, as in statistical forecasting, is of little use in a world with rapid change and discontinuous events. It ignores the possibility of a unique event that could alter the pattern of the extrapolation curve. Since the task of management is to create the future, personal perception is more appropriate for making strategic decisions, but we need to balance *analyzing the past o predicting the future*

perception with analysis. The future is better seen as the result of today's actions by all the people involved, rather than an extrapolation of past and present trends. *responses to decisions*

Doing nothing is also a decision. It is then incumbent on us to know what the consequences of doing nothing might be. At the same time, a decision must be evaluated in terms of making a difference compared with doing nothing. One way to do this is to project where we would be by doing nothing, compare it with where we would like to be, and then determine what we must do if the gap between them is not to our liking. Clearly we need to do something to bridge the gap. It is essential that we do both: plan forward to predict what would happen if we do nothing, and plan backward to design a strategy to create the kind of future we want [29]. Perceiving the future as the result of past and present decisions, then predicting the consequences of doing nothing, implies that other people will keep doing what they have always done. But other people will in fact pursue their own desired future, just as we do, and it is fair to assume that they will react to any of our strategies that would hinder the achievement of their objectives, including our doing nothing. Since we cannot ask them what they would do, we can only predict their future actions in yet another backward process representing their interests.

Basically we must ask the following question: If we were in their position, what would we do in response to our strategy? With this hypothetical information, we now need to repeat our forward planning to see how the decisions of others would shape the future. This process leads to viewing strategic planning as an iteration of forward and backward processes. And if we find that the set of backward planning iterations to arrive at a desired future are not really independent, we will need to capture their interactions. This emphasizes, even more, the need for members of the organization to do it themselves. The learning gained from the process will be valuable in implementing the plan. While the process may be carried out as a formal planning process at a designated time, it must be updated regularly to account for the incremental adjustments necessary to keep up with events. To do this effectively, an organization needs a set of records – records that represent its memory of what has been done as well as all the processes that led to the decisions. Essentially, the set of records needs to function as a work-in-progress that can be modified easily.

Advantages of Structured Decision Making

record keeping for decisions

Collective decision making is a necessity. Not only is there a need for diverse perspectives, but gaining the acceptance of those who must implement the decision is as important as making the right decision. To get acceptance means that the psychological problems of working together must be dealt with. Further, in making a decision there are often as many intangible as there are tangible factors, and we need a decision calculus that can handle intangibles simply. What we need is a valid method for eliciting and structuring information from group members in a natural but organized way in order to produce a synthesis. The approach should be scientific but user-friendly.

After an intensive study summarizing more than twenty years of research on teamwork, Dennis A. Romig concluded that "the more systematic or structured the teamwork component was, the better the team's performance" and "the most successful structured approach includes defining the problem clearly" [30]. His first conclusion highlights the systematic process team members use to work together on making a decision; the second highlights the fact that they use a model to capture their understanding of a problem.

Using a Model

The word "model" means different things depending on the context. In decision making, a model means a representation of reality with the intention of gaining understanding about it. A model is a useful way to describe a complex reality that is beyond one's mental ability to comprehend in every conceivable detail. A model is always a simplification. Even so, a model helps us obtain better estimates of reality by channeling our impressions, feelings, and beliefs in a systematic way. Once we have the situation modeled, we can use the model to make judgments on the elements we have agreed on. The goal is to enhance objectivity and downplay subjectivity.

The intention of constructing a model is to capture reality so that one can design a solution that works in the real world. The key question here: how good is the model as a representation? No matter how sophisticated the method and how rigorous the process, it only captures the perception of those who use it. Moreover, simplification in modeling means that its outcome is at best only an approximation. How can we capture a wider perception so that the resulting model is a collective representation of group perception?

Although we have the ability to perceive complexity, it is difficult to communicate our perception using the same language we use in general conversation. Language alone is not enough for communicating a complex problem because it is ambiguous and the same word has different meaning for different people. We need a different kind of language for communicating complexity clearly. We need a language that facilitates articulation of our thinking and offers a productive framework to improve understanding. Above all, the right language can help us synthesize the

Common language

diversity into a unified outcome to which everyone subscribes. By using a structure, we can relate many things to many others and express the relative strength of influences in the structure that when synthesized give a very accurate idea of what is likely to happen. The totality of judgments has a synergy that is lacking in individual judgments.

In developing a model there is always a trade-off. A model is a simplification of reality, certain details are inevitably excluded. The question is what to include and what to exclude. If key components are excluded, there is a chance that the model will be too simple and fail to contribute to understanding. But if too much detail is included, the model may become so complicated that, again, it fails to reach the deeper levels of understanding that we seek. *Models are simplifications*

Apart from complementing the mind to manipulate numbers, the computer is useful for organizing information in a complex problem. In a group setting, the computer becomes a tool for collaboration. In modeling a structured decision problem, there is no limit on the information that a computer can process, but it is reasonable to expect that a user would process only between five and nine chunks of information at a time. To group small numbers of elements together improves the structure and enhances understanding. It also results in a neater display on a computer screen to facilitate group interaction.

Without the aid of a decision-making model for systematically structuring a problem, decisions are often made intuitively. A group of executives learned this lesson when they worked on a problem using different approaches. First they were asked to find a solution via the usual group discussion. Then they were introduced to the AHP for a systematic approach along with some brainstorming and synectics [31] to generate alternative courses of action. They were surprised to find that the solution they had agreed on via the traditional discussion process came out as the worst. *model — clear, comprehensive framework*

A decision-making method with computer support is invaluable. It is mostly useful with group decision making, where a lot of information needs to be organized. People tend to have trouble seeing the big picture and looking at the problem from different perspectives. A model, however, synthesizes all the different perspectives in a comprehensive yet clear framework.

It is useful to consider the way a model is constructed as a special language for describing complexity. As a language, it is a means to articulate a person's mental model in order to be understood by others. When we construct a model, the aim is to represent reality; but the best a model can do is represent the mental model of its developer. The way to construct a model that is a closer representation of reality is by inviting diverse perspectives

individual models are biased
↳ group models are more realistic

from other people and integrating them into a single model. Having a good modeling language helps a group construct a collective model.

What we refer to as reality is simply our description of what we perceive. It is actually a simplified version of a "true" reality, of course, because of the screening and filtering process that takes place in the mind. Our very perception is a mental model itself: subjective and tacit, not clearly and precisely articulated. Constructing a model makes a tacit understanding explicit, but subjectivity remains. Four steps are involved using a decision methodology: structuring the problem by using a hierarchy or network; deriving priorities from the judgments; checking the results for logical consistency; and performing sensitivity analysis to ensure the stability of the outcome to changes in judgments. These steps become the principles that underpin the AHP decision method described in this book.

At this point an important question arises: Does the method produce an outcome that is useful? To answer this question we need to answer two more specific questions. The first is: What is the standard we are going to compare the result with? In general, there is no standard for judging whether or not we have arrived at a good decision. Otherwise we would simply use the standard instead of going to all the trouble of striving for the best decision we can possibly make. In this case, the best thing we can do is to build confidence in the method by testing its power of prediction in a host of situations. These applications not only serve to validate the method but also emphasize the need to have credible decision makers and experts to come to a close approximation. Once we have confidence in the method, we simply need to make sure that all important elements of a decision are considered.

The second question is: What is the maximum deviation from the standard that will allow us to say that two outcomes are close? This question may seem as irrelevant because we do not have standards. Nevertheless, it is a useful question in the context of group decision making to assess the diversity of group judgments. The AHP/ANP has a concept – measuring the compatibility of two ratio scales – that is useful for evaluating how close individual judgments are to those of the group.

Creating a Structure

We have the ability to perceive things and generate ideas. Our minds structure complex reality into its constituent parts, then their subparts, and so on hierarchically. If some feedback or dependence is perceived, it can be structured as a network. By breaking down the description of a situation into homogeneous clusters (with five to nine elements in each cluster), the human mind can integrate large amounts of information to form a picture of the entire system.

A typical decision problem requires us to choose the best among several alternatives with respect to a set of criteria. Take, for example, the problem of selecting the house that gives us the most satisfaction. We have six criteria and three alternatives. Unless we simply jump to a conclusion intuitively, this could be a taxing problem. With the method advocated here, however, it is a simple decision. Figure 1.2 is our house selection model.

The hierarchy is constructed from the top down. The best choice is made on the basis of the criteria at the top, which may be thought of as representing the forces acting to shape the possible outcomes. The object is, given the goals and values, to find the best alternative with the given criteria that represent the decision maker's values. To do this, we distribute the forces downward from the most general to the most particular. Values precede the alternatives in importance. We determine the relative strength of each alternative in satisfying the criteria.

In this problem the decision maker considers only criteria relating to benefits – implying either that cost is not a decisive factor or that the difference in cost among the houses is considered insignificant. The problem would be more complex if costs need to be considered as well. We might intuitively argue that costs are not comparable with benefits. In this case, we would want to represent them in a separate hierarchy with a set of criteria representing costs and other pains, such as purchase cost and maintenance requirements, but with the same alternative houses: A, B, and C. Depending on how the decision maker relates benefits and costs, the two hierarchies may or may not be aggregated into one larger hierarchy with benefits and costs as the two main criteria, each with its own subcriteria. As we will make clear later, with examples, that decision makers can relate benefit and cost considerations in several ways and also include opportunities and risks.

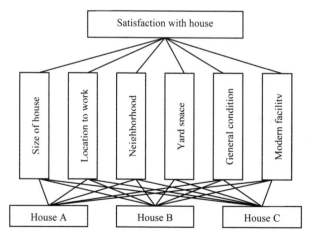

Figure 1.2 Simple Hierarchy for Selecting a House

Dominance and the Scale of Comparisons

preference

Decision making is essentially arriving at a judgment on your preference for
one alternative over another. We may say that the preferred alternative
"dominates" the less preferred one. Consider this simple example: A person
is given a choice of an apple or an orange to eat. Say that he picks the apple,
which means that he regards the apple as dominating the orange in his
mind. Then suppose that, given the same choices next time, he takes the
orange instead. What happened? Is he being inconsistent? It appears he is
not. Instead, his explanation illustrates the contextual nature of a decision.
He might say that in the first situation he took the apple because he was
hungry and he thought that an apple would satisfy him more than an
orange. In the latter situation he was thirsty and took the orange because it
was juicier than the apple. He made the decision by considering the relative
importance of the properties of the fruit with respect to his need. Assuming
that he maintains his relative preference between apple and orange with
respect to substance and juiciness, it is the change of their relative
importance that alters the decision. Structuring this problem like the one for
selecting a house in Figure 1.1, we would have a simple multicriteria
hierarchy: satisfaction with fruit as the goal at the top; the two criteria of
substance and juiciness in the middle level, and the alternatives of apple and
orange at the bottom.

When the articulation of judgments about relative dominance is
reasonable and accurate, and the calculations are credible, we should get the
same outcome from the model as the actual decision. Our fruit selection
example indicates that we need to quantify not only the judgments of
relative importance of substance and juiciness with respect to satisfying the
physical need, but also the relative preference of apple and orange with
respect to substance and juiciness. We may assume here that the relative
preferences between apple and orange with respect to substance and
juiciness are the same for both situations. But how are we going to represent
the comparison judgments when we do not have any physical scales?
Furthermore, how can we be sure that our model has represented the
problem in terms of structure and priorities with reasonable accuracy? What
feedback can be used to indicate the need for improvement? How can we
make such improvements efficiently? In collective decision making, how can
we aggregate group judgments in a credible and meaningful way?

Many people think that measurement demands a physical scale with a
zero and a unit of measure. This is not true. In the AHP we use relative
scales that do not have a zero or a unit and we get them by using our
understanding and judgments – which are, after all, the fundamental
determinants of what the measurements mean. We interpret readings from
physical scales all the time without thinking about it. Physical scales are

relative scales

useful to have for things we know how to measure. But even after we obtain readings from a physical scale, they still need to be interpreted. And the number of things we do not have scales for is infinitely larger than the things we know how to measure. *Fundamental Scale*

The AHP/ANP uses a scale with absolute numbers from 1-9 called the Fundamental Scale, to express pairwise-comparison judgments. If we were to use judgments instead of ratios, we would estimate the ratios as numbers using the Fundamental Scale shown in Table 1.1. A judgment is made on a pair of elements with respect to a property they have in common. The smaller element is considered to be the unit, and we estimate how many times more important, preferable, or likely – more generally "dominant" – the larger is using a number from the Fundamental Scale. Dominance is often interpreted as importance when comparing the criteria and as preference when comparing the alternatives with respect to the criteria. Dominance can also be interpreted as likelihood – as in the likelihood of a person getting elected president – or other terms that fit the situation. *dominance*

Using a universal measurement scale implies that people's perception is linear and homogeneous. But the real world and our perception of it are nonlinear and not homogeneous. Scales are simply indicators of quantity, and it is deceptive to think there is direct meaning in quantity. People need to interpret what a certain quantity on a scale means to them. We can capture meaning via judgments made precise through numbers, and the only way to do this is through comparisons with respect to a common property or goal. Scales of measurement have no intrinsic meaning in themselves.

Moreover, there are many people in the world who know very little about numbers and the arithmetic of numbers. Nevertheless, their judgments lead them to make good decisions with the feelings and understanding they have. It is not the manipulation of quantity but the synthesis of piecemeal understanding of influences that leads them to make good decisions. Quality itself is interpreted according to its effects and not according to some precise numerical value on a linear scale. This observation about the untutored mind is important. People derive meaning from broad and closely connected experiences that they combine to form their overall understanding, not from readings they observe on instruments of measurement. In the house selection example, the criteria are ranked according to their relative importance to satisfying the overall goal: satisfaction with a house. The relative priority of the criteria is not influenced by the alternatives being evaluated. Judgments regarding the houses will be about preference – that is, which house is preferred with respect to a certain criterion.

Table 1.1 The Fundamental Scale of Absolute Numbers

Intensity of Importance	Definition	Explanation
1	Equal importance	Two activities contribute equally to the objective
3	Moderate importance	Experience and judgment slightly favor one activity over another
5	Strong importance	Experience and judgment strongly favor one activity over another
7	Very strong importance	An activity is favored very strongly over another; its dominance is demonstrated in practice
9	Extreme importance	The evidence favoring one activity over another is of the highest possible order of affirmation
2,4,6,8	For compromise between the preceding values	Sometimes we need to interpolate a compromise judgment numerically because there is no good word to describe it
Reciprocals	If activity i has one of the above nonzero numbers assigned to it when compared with activity j, then j has the reciprocal value when compared with i	A comparison mandated by choosing the smaller element as the unit in order to estimate the larger one as a multiple of that unit
Rationals	Ratios arising from the scale	If consistency is to be forced by obtaining n numerical values to span the matrix
1.1-1.9	For tied activities	When elements are nearly indistinguishable; moderate is 1.3 and extreme is 1.9

The process of synthesizing judgments involves numbers. Decision making, however, involves comparing intangibles for which no scale is available. Moreover, judgments about intangibles are expressed more naturally in everyday language than in quantitative terms. Hence using the verbal explanation from the Fundamental Scale that discriminates between our feelings is especially useful because its values have some kind of familiarity and help us to make the correspondence between our qualitative judgments and these absolute numbers of the scale.

People often say that a person is inconsistent if he changes his mind – illustrated here by the example of selecting fruit. This kind of change in preference is a consequence of a shift in context, however, which is different from being inconsistent. We have the ability to establish coherent relationships among objects or ideas – that is, to relate them to each other so that their relation exhibits consistency. Given three different geometric shapes to compare with respect to area, a circle, a square, and a triangle, if we judge the circle to have approximately five times the area of the square, and the square twice that of the triangle, then the area of the circle must be ten times that of the triangle. This would be consistent. But the human mind does not work as precisely as an objective scale. Even a consistent person may not judge the circle to be exactly ten times the triangle. Judging the circle to be seven or eight times the area of the triangle may be considered acceptably consistent, however, while judging it as only three times the area would show great inconsistency, indicating that the comparison process would need to be repeated for more accuracy.

The mind that estimates the relative size of physical objects is the same as the one that compares intangibles. This suggests that there is an underlying scale that operates in the mind which we can also use in a decision theory. The Fundamental Scale needs to be validated to ensure its usefulness. If we have a way of measuring inconsistency, we can use it to find out the decision maker's consistency level – and the judgment that fits least well and contributes most to the consistency – and revise it to ensure a valid outcome. *consistency in decision-making*

Our inconsistency in making judgments may appear to set a limit on how many things we should deal with. Most decision theories disregard this phenomenon and even forbid it as unnatural. Yet inconsistency has not only been proved to be inherent in how the mind works but is a necessary capability of the mind to enable learning and growth. The mind has a screening mechanism to select only meaningful information from the environment. This screening process helps us to be effective by putting all the relevant information before us. Being able to be inconsistent is fundamental in developing our perception as it enables the mind to take in information that does not seem to bear full relevance to the issue we are thinking about at the time. But it leads to inconsistent judgments that may make a decision less reliable. The ability to measure the degree of consistency in our judgments is as critical as the development of a valid scale. Our maxim is: It is better to be approximately right than precisely wrong. Our method strives for validity and accuracy as checked against observable phenomena; it is not satisfied with a decision that comes up with a formally logical and precise outcome that has no relation to what is observed. In the following section we explain how a group of people working together on a decision can deal with judgments and their inconsistency.

Creating a Synthesis of Group Judgments

Group decision making takes advantage of the plurality of its members. The process needs to be managed, however, because decision making is about striving for agreement [32]. Disputes may arise regarding values, beliefs about the consequences of a decision, and preferences for certain alternatives. We need to capture as much diversity of thinking as possible and to process agreement and disagreement in a systematic, efficient, and credible way. The more disagreement can be tolerated, the more actual conflicts can be reduced. Hence we need a method of synthesis that tolerates some level of disagreement without affecting the validity of the outcome.

Different people may have different levels of authority and expertise that need to be considered because they affect the outcome differently. Thus the method must be able to incorporate this situation in such a way that it shows in the outcome. Different people, moreover, may have different strengths of opinion. It is essential to quantify these intensities numerically in order to combine them and trade them off.

And finally, we will need a support system to facilitate the process. When it comes to complex problems, a systematic approach that is also comprehensive is both tedious and taxing. Relying strictly on the human mind aided by language is not only a slow process; it is not very reliable, either, because it does not really capture the different intensities of preference. The need for a support system is therefore inevitable. Our era of information technology and the internet makes it unnecessary for everyone to be present together in a room to make a collective decision. With the appropriate software, it is possible to distribute the tasks for the decision while keeping the whole process coherent.

The AHP/ANP: A Credible Method

The AHP/ANP we use in this book was constructed over a period of more than thirty years to meet the needs described in the previous section. Its well validated Fundamental Scale enables us to articulate judgments in a pairwise- comparison fashion to ensure accuracy. Decision making is inherently subjective because it involves intangible knowledge and tacit preferences. Although the human mind is inherently inconsistent, good decisions need a consistent mind. The AHP/ANP acknowledges this fact and incorporates it in its methodology deriving an inconsistency index that can be used to revise judgments for better accuracy. Its way of aggregating group judgments ensures that the principle of rationality described later is maintained. The generalized way to synthesize judgments enables a group to structure a model that is as elaborate as desired. It also enables a group to integrate its knowledge collaboratively by structuring the problem together. It allows a group to acknowledge the disparate "power" of its members when eliciting their judgments. Further, it enhances the validity of the outcome by incorporating the importance of people's knowledge, the quality of their experience, and other factors. We will also describe ways to make group meetings more efficient — by reducing redundancy in judgments, for example, and not striving for perfect agreement and perfect consistency.

Collectively structuring the problem is a way for a group to aggregate its knowledge. Group members brainstorm the factors involved in the problem and consider how they influence each other. In this early stage, all inputs are accepted without conflict. The group may then decide how elaborate the model should be and tries to reach some kind of consensus. Since there is no rule as to how elaborate a structure should be, there is no harm in following a strong opinion. Constructing a model is an iterative process that the group can improve along the way. Synthesizing judgments, however, calls for a much higher level of agreement.

How the AHP/ANP Supports Group Development

In 1965, Bruce Tuckman introduced the four stages model of group development that has implications for decision making [33]. Group meetings may go through these stages several times in a cycle.

First Stage: Forming

The forming stage is the period when a group is just being established. They may or may not know each other well with respect to the task at hand. They explore each other's level of commitment as well as level of expertise and authority. They are not yet in the position to make a significant decision because they are still learning about each other. They will assess their relative importance with respect to guiding the decision-making process and offering judgments. Here people need to pay attention to the common problem of stereotyping based on first impressions.

Second Stage: Storming

The storming stage – also called the conflict stage – is where relationships and the power structure are challenged. The group may make poor decisions because of personality issues and self-oriented behavior. People may go along with decisions but not really support them. This is the "My position is ..." stage. It may be the most challenging stage for the group facilitator because it is often highly emotional and competitive. Some people may behave self-righteously and refuse to listen to what others have to say. Cliques may be formed with an "us against them" attitude. All this is bound to reduce rationality and objectivity in group decision making. With creativity suppressed and solutions reached by vote or compromise, it is difficult for the group to come up with the best decision. The method we propose here offers a way for the facilitator to orchestrate the group process and prevent the negative effects just described.

Third Stage: Norming

The norming stage is also called the conflict resolution stage. Members coalesce around shared beliefs, values, and norms. This is the "I understand everybody's position and expect to be communicated with" stage. The group makes progress toward objectives by being constructive, open-minded, and less controlling. Group members trust each other to be candid and show creativity. Individual roles are better identified. The method we propose here advances the group to this stage faster by reducing the intensity of the storming stage. At this norming stage, group leadership may rotate from time to time. Thus a method that tracks the group's decision making reminds the group of its progress.

Fourth Stage: Performing

The performing stage is also called the "smoother-sailing" stage. Trust is now high among group members, who have aligned themselves to their common goal. This is an "OK, now we can get to work" stage, where information is shared freely and disagreement is acceptable. Later the group will enter the adjourning stage when the task is done and the group is formally terminated. The group has gone through a learning process that will prove invaluable when they work together again.

Any issue addressed by a group involves objectives, goals, criteria, a diversity of interests, influences, and multiple outcomes. All these need to be defined carefully and arranged within a structure that shows the flow of influences. This structure with influences flowing from top to bottom may be a hierarchy or a network – a hierarchy is simply a special case of a network. By including all the factors, one major problem of settling differences of opinion is solved: nothing has been excluded.

Another problem is how to determine what is more important than what. Usually people have an idea of what is more and less important, but they need to measure both tangibles and intangibles in relative terms and indicate how much more important one factor is than another. To express this intensity of judgments in a meaningful way, we need numbers. Not only this, but we need to determine who is the more reliable judge because of knowledge and experience. Combining all the judgments to produce reliable priorities is the final step. We need a way to do all this. In fact we have such a way: the Analytic Hierarchy Process.

Resolving Conflicts

So far our discussion has proceeded along the lines of a group working together. Here we will talk about individuals or groups that may oppose each other – a situation that leads to conflict rather than harmony [34]. Most discussions on conflict start with the premise that there will always be winners and losers in any situation where people have opposing desires. Sometimes this is true. But it is often possible to find a compromise that will work, if only in the short run; in the long run, of course, it is usually necessary to remove the underlying source of the conflict. The best outcome will almost certainly fall short of each party's desired outcome. How can we persuade each party to accept the compromise solution? It is particularly necessary that people in conflict should use reason to make progress. But the two parties also need to develop a broader framework that offers benefits to both sides.

There are certain steps to be taken to understand the nature of a conflict:

1. Identification of the parties to the conflict
2. Identification of the objectives, needs, and desires of each party
3. Identification of possible outcomes of the conflicts or possible solutions
4. Assumptions about the way in which each party views its objectives and, in particular, its view of the relative importance of these objectives
5. Assumptions about the way in which each party would view the outcomes and the way in which a certain outcome might meet the objectives

An effective model of a conflict must include the emotional factors along with the rational. One major problem in modeling a conflict is to deal with intangibles. Attempts to apply rigorous logic to conflict are not new. Since the publication of Theory of Games and Economic Behavior (von Neumann and Morgenstern) in 1944, game theory has been an important tool for the study of conflict analysis. Indeed there have been many efforts to put conflict analysis on a rigorous and quantifiable foundation.

All conflicts require trade-offs for their solution. The method advanced in this book is unusually appealing because it can combine negatives like costs and risks with positives like benefits and opportunities. At the heart of the process, participants agree on the major issues involved in a conflict even if they disagree about their relative importance. Here we look at conflict in two ways. One approach is to determine the best outcome from the standpoint of representing each party's interests as articulated in a

rational/constructive vs. retributive
Conflict resolution

decision structure of benefits, opportunities, costs, and risks that are then combined to produce an overall best outcome from the standpoint of the diverse interests. We call this type of conflict resolution constructive or rational. The other approach to conflict resolution is retributive. In this case each party considers as a gain not only its benefits from the proposed solution but also the perceived costs to the other party. It is not concerned with the idea of fairness as in the rational approach. In many conflicts in which emotion and hatred are involved, parties aim to punish the other side by increasing its costs, perhaps to deter it from continuing the conflict.

References

1. MacKay, A.F. *Arrow's Theorem: The Paradox of Social Choice - A Case Study in the Philosophy of Economics.* New Haven: Yale University Press, 1980.
2. Keeney, R.L. and Raiffa, H., *Decisions with Multiple Objectives: Preferences and Value Tradeoffs,* New York: John Wiley & Sons, 1976.
3. Barbut, M. "Does the Majority Ever Rule? The Curious Operations of Processes of Rational Decision in Games and Practical Elections." *Portfolio and Art News Annual* 4 (1961):161-168.
4. Arrow, K.L. *Social Choice and Industrial Values.* New haven: Yale University Press, 1963.
5. Mirkin, B.G., *Group Choice.* New York: John Wiley & Sons, 1985.
6. Plott, C. Axiomatic Social Choice Theory: An Overview and Interpretation. *American Journal of Political Science* 20 (1976); **20**:511-596.
7. Saaty, T.L., *Fundamentals of Decision Making with the Analytic Hierarchy Process.* Pittsburgh: RWS Publications, 2000.
8. Saaty T.L. *Theory and Applications of the Analytic Network Process.* Pittsburgh: RWS publications, 2005.
9. Basak, I and T.L. Saaty, "Group Decision Making Using the Analytic Hierarchy Process", *Journal of Mathematical Modeling.* **17** (1993): 415.
10. Blumenthal, A. *The Process of Cognition.* Englewood Cliffs, N.J.: Prentice-Hall, Inc., 1977.
11. Dehaene, S., *The Number Sense: How the Mind Creates Mathematics.* Oxford: Oxford University Press, 1997.
12. Haines, S.G. *The Systems Thinking Approach to Strategic Planning and Management.* St. Lucie Press, 2000.
13. Collins, J. *Good to Great: Why Some Companies Make the Leap ... and Others Don't.* Collins, 2001.
14. Menkes, J. *Executive Intelligence,* Harper Collins World, 2005.
15. Tversky, A and D. Kahneman, "The Framing of Decisions and the Psychology of Choice", *Science* 211 (1981): 453-458.

16. Miller, G. A., "The Magical Number Seven Plus or Minus Two: Some Limits on our Capacity for Processing Information." *Psychological Review.* **63** (1956):.81-97.
17. Dweck, C.S. *Mindset: The New Psychology of Success.* New York: Random House, 2006.
18. Senge, P. *The Fifth Discipline: The Art & Practice of the Learning Organization.* Currency, 2006.
19. Bauer, R.A., E. Collar, and V. Tang. *The Silverlake Project.* New York: Oxford University Press, 1992.
20. Maslow, A. *Motivation and Personality.* New York: Harper & Row, 1954.
21. Rescher, N. *Introduction to Value Theory.* Englewood Cliffs, N.J.: Prentice-Hall, 1969.
22. Kaplan, R.S. and D.P. Norton *Balanced Scorecard: Translating Strategy into Actions.* Cambridge Harvard Business School. Press, 1996.
23. Kaplan, R.S. and D.P Norton *Strategy Maps: Converting Intangible Assets into Tangible Outcomes.* Cambridge: Harvard Business School Press, 2004.
24. Kaplan, R.S. and Norton, D.P., *Alignment: Using the Balanced Scorecard to Create Corporate Synergies.* Cambridge: Harvard Business School Press, 2006.
25. Imai, M. *Kaizen: The Key to Japan's Competitive Success,* New York: McGraw Hill/Irwin, 1986.
26. Romano, N.C. Jr. and J.F Nunamaker Jr. "Meeting Analysis: Findings from Research and Practice." *Proceedings of the 34th Annual Hawaii International Conference on System Sciences,* 2001.
27. Belbin, R.M., *Management Teams: Why They Succeed or Fail.* London: Butterworth-Heinemann, 1981.
28. Belbin, R.M. *Team Roles at Work,* London: Butterworth-Heinemann, 1993.
29. Saaty, T.L. and K.P. Kearns. *Analytical Planning: The Organization of Systems;* Oxford: Pergamon Press, 1985.
30. Romig, D.A. *Breakthrough Teamwork: Outstanding Results Using Structured Teamwork.* Irwin Professional Publisher, 1996.
31. Couger, J.D. *Creative Problem Solving and Opportunity Finding.* Boyd & Fraser, 1995.
32. Rescher, N. *Pluralism: Against the Demand for Consensus.* Oxford: Clarendon Press, 1993.
33. Tuckman, B.W. "Developmental Sequence in Small Groups." *Psychology Bulletin* **63** (1965):384-399.
34. Saaty, T.L. and J.M. Alexander *Conflict Resolution: The Analytic Hierarchy Approach.* New York: Praeger, 1989.

Chapter 2

How to Make a Decision

Decision making is the most important thing we do in life. We decide on whom to marry, what college to attend, what job offer to accept, what city to live in, what stocks to invest in, what service our corporation should sell, how best to advertise, how to resolve a conflict and so on. A complex decision involves many factors all of which play a role in bringing that decision about. But not all the factors are equally important. Our challenge is to find a way to determine their priorities so we can mix them in the right proportion to make a successful decision. How do we do that?

Decisions are made from well thought out judgments about all kinds of influence. To develop well thought out judgments we need to break a decision problem down into smaller judgments about the criteria and alternatives of that decision. Then we must represent these judgments with numbers, derive priorities from the numbers and finally synthesize the priorities to get an overall outcome for the alternatives. Hierarchic and network structures are the only ways we have to break a decision down in this way. In this chapter we develop and illustrate with an example some of the details of setting priorities and synthesizing them to make a decision.

Thus to make a decision we need to develop priorities of importance of the different factors in that decision by comparing them as to how strongly they influence the fulfillment of our goal. The most accurate way to do comparisons is to make them in pairs. For each pair we identify the less important factor and estimate how strongly (how many times more) the other factor is more important or more preferred with respect to the goal. Similarly, for each factor we need to determine which of two alternatives is more preferred than the other and how strongly it is preferred. The final overall decision reflects a combination of all the priorities of the factors and of the alternatives with respect to each of the factors. Later we will show how to combine their separate judgments into a single representative judgment.

It is rare that the knowledge and judgment of one person is adequate to make a decision about the welfare and quality of life for a group. To broaden understanding and improve the accuracy of the judgments and the quality of the outcome, participation and debate are needed by all the people involved. Here two aspects of group decision making have to be considered to capture the diversity of knowledge, understanding, and specialized knowledge and experience within the group. The first is a rather minor complication, namely, the discussion and exchange within the group to reach some kind of consensus

[handwritten: decomposing problem into smaller problems]

on the given problem. The second is of much greater difficulty. The holistic nature of the given problem necessitates that it be divided into smaller subject-matter areas within which different groups of experts determine how each area affects the total problem. A large and complex problem can rarely be decomposed simply into a number of smaller problems whose solutions can be combined into an overall answer. Peter Senge, in his award winning book The Fifth Discipline: The Art and Practice of the Learning Organization used the phrase "Dividing an elephant in half does not produce two small elephants" as one of the laws in systems thinking [1]. Review and iteration are needed to improve the outcome of a strategic decision. We need a process that is simple enough to do all the above credibly and without the assistance of an expert in the method invited in to help. In sum, a decision-making approach should have the following characteristics:

[handwritten: decision-making approach characteristics]

- be simple in construct
- be adaptable to both groups and individuals
- be natural to our intuition and general thinking
- encourage compromise and consensus building
- not require inordinate specialization to master and communicate
- the details of the processes leading up to the decision-making process should be easy to review

We must answer such questions as the following: Which objectives are more important and how important are they? What is likely to be gained? What are the pains and costs involved? What are the risks? After we get the answer the next question would be: What should we plan for and how do we bring it about? These questions demand a multicriteria logic. It has been demonstrated over and over by practitioners who use the process discussed in this chapter, that multicriteria logic gives different and often better answers to these questions than ordinary logic, and does it efficiently.

To make a decision one needs various kinds of knowledge, information, and technical data:

- details about the problem for which a decision is needed
- the people or actors involved
- their objectives and policies
- the influences affecting the outcomes
- time horizons, scenarios, and constraints

[handwritten: items needed to make decision]

The set of potential outcomes and the alternatives from which to choose are the essence of decision making. In laying out the framework for making a decision, one needs to sort the elements into groups or clusters that have similar influences or effects. One must also arrange them in some

[handwritten: essence of decision making]

[handwritten: arranging elements into rational order]

rational order to trace the outcome of these influences. Briefly, we see decision making as a process that involves the following steps:

[handwritten: decision-making steps ↓]

(1) Structure a problem with a model that shows the problem's key elements and their relationships
(2) Elicit judgments that reflect knowledge, feelings, or emotions
(3) Represent those judgments with meaningful numbers
(4) Use these numbers to calculate the priorities of the elements of the hierarchy
(5) Synthesize these results to determine an overall outcome
(6) Analyze sensitivity to changes in judgment

The AHP [2] is about breaking a problem down and then aggregating the solutions of all the sub-problems to arrive at a conclusion. It facilitates decision making by organizing perceptions, feelings, judgments, and memories into a framework that exhibits the forces that influence a decision. In the simple and most common case, the forces are arranged from the more general and less controllable to the more specific and controllable.

What we have described so far may be called a rational approach to making decisions. By rational we mean:

[handwritten: "rational" defined]

- Focusing on the goal of solving the problem
- Knowing enough about a problem to develop a complete structure of relations and influences
- Having enough knowledge and experience and access to the knowledge and experience of others to assess the priority of influence and dominance (importance, preference, or likelihood to the goal as appropriate) among the relations in the structure
- Allowing for differences in opinion with an ability to develop a best collective representation

How to Structure a Hierarchy

Perhaps the most creative part of decision making that has a significant effect on the outcome is modeling the problem. In the AHP, a problem is structured as a hierarchy. It is then followed by a process of prioritization, which we describe in detail later. Prioritization involves eliciting judgments in response to questions about the dominance of one element over another when compared with respect to a property. The basic principle to follow in creating this structure is always to see if one can answer the following question: Can I compare the elements on a lower level using some or all of the elements on the next higher level as criteria or attributes of the lower level elements?

[handwritten: question to ask when creating hierarchy]

A useful way to proceed in structuring a decision is to come down from the goal as far as one can by decomposing it into the most general and most easily controlled factors. One can then go up from the alternatives beginning with the simplest subcriteria that they must satisfy and aggregating the subcriteria into generic higher level criteria until the levels of the two processes are linked in such a way as to make comparison possible. In Chapter 4 we give a variety of examples of hierarchies and networks and discuss the process of structuring decisions in greater detail. In addition, there are two important references with hundreds of examples: The Hierarchon for hierarchic models [3] and the Encyclicon for network models [4].

The Hospice Problem

Westmoreland County Hospital in Western Pennsylvania, like hospitals in many other counties around the nation, has been concerned with the costs of the facilities and manpower involved in taking care of terminally ill patients. Normally these patients do not need as much medical attention as do other patients. Those who best utilize the limited resources in a hospital are patients who require the medical attention of its specialists and advanced technology equipment, whose utilization depends on the demand of patients admitted into the hospital. The terminally ill need medical attention only episodically. Most of the time such patients need psychological support. Such support is best given by the patient's family, whose members are able to supply the love and care the patients most need. For the mental health of the patient, home therapy is a benefit. Most patients need the help of medical professionals only during a crisis. Some will also need equipment and surgery.

"the problem"

The planning association of the hospital wanted to develop alternatives and to choose the best one considering various criteria from the standpoint of the patient, the hospital, the community, and society at large.

In this problem, we need to consider the costs and benefits of the decision. Cost includes economic costs and all sorts of intangibles, such as inconvenience and pain. Such disbenefits are not directly related to benefits as their mathematical inverses, because patients infinitely prefer the benefits of good health to these intangible disbenefits. To study the problem, one needs to deal with benefits and with costs separately.

To keep matters simple we give an example of a decision made by considering benefits and costs only. No opportunities and risks were included as one usually must do in a more complex decision. The first author met with representatives of the planning association for several hours to decide on the best alternative. To make a decision by considering benefits and costs, one must first answer the question: In this problem, do the benefits justify the costs? If they do, then either the benefits are so much more important than the costs that the decision is based simply on benefits, or the two are so close in value that both the benefits and the costs should be considered. Then we use two hierarchies for the purpose and make the choice by forming the ratio from them of the (benefits priority/cost priority) for each alternative. One asks which is most beneficial in the benefits hierarchy of Figure 2.1 and which is most costly in the costs hierarchy of Figure 2.2.

If the benefits do not justify the costs, the costs alone determine the best alternative, that which is the least costly. In this example, we decided

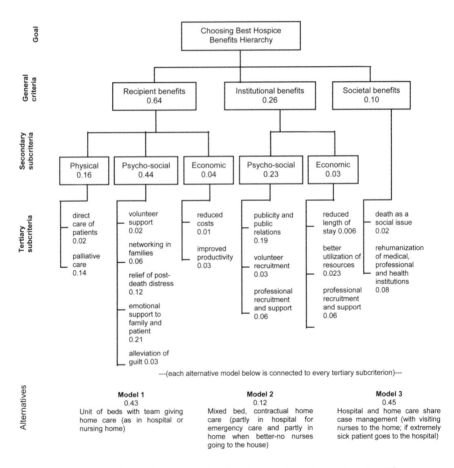

Figure 2.1 Benefits Hierarchy to Choose the Best Hospice Plan

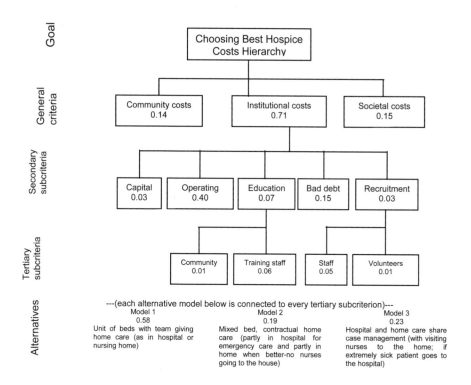

Figure 2.2 Costs Hierarchy to Choose the Best Hospice Plan

that both benefits and costs had to be considered in separate hierarchies. In a risk problem, a third hierarchy is used to determine the most desired alternative with respect to all three: benefits, costs, and risks. In this problem, we assumed risk to be the same for all contingencies. Whereas for most decisions one uses only a single hierarchy, we constructed two hierarchies for the hospice problem, one for benefits or gains (which model of hospice care yields the greater benefit) and one for costs or pains (which model costs more). *2 hierarchies*

The planning association thought the concepts of benefits and costs were too general to enable it to make a decision. Thus, the planners further subdivided each (benefits and costs) into detailed subcriteria to enable the group to develop alternatives and to evaluate the finer distinctions the members perceived between the three alternatives. The alternatives were to care for terminally ill patients at the hospital, at home, or partly at the hospital and partly at home. *alternatives*

For each of the two hierarchies, benefits and costs, the goal clearly had to be choosing the best hospice. We placed this goal at the top of each hierarchy. Then the group discussed and identified overall criteria for each hierarchy; these criteria need not be the same for the benefits as for the costs. *goal*

The two hierarchies are fairly clear and straightforward in their description. They descend from the more general criteria in the second level to secondary subcriteria in the third level and then to tertiary subcriteria in the fourth level on to the alternatives at the bottom or fifth level.

At the general criteria level, each of the hierarchies, benefits or costs, involved three major interests. The decision should benefit the recipient, the institution, and society as a whole and their relative importance is the prime determinant as to which outcome is more likely to be preferred. We located these three elements on the second level of the benefits hierarchy. As the decision would benefit each party differently and the importance of the benefits to each recipient affects the outcome, the group thought that it was important to specify the types of benefit for the recipient and the institution. Recipients want physical, psycho-social and economic benefits, while the institution wants only psychosocial and economic benefits. We located these benefits in the third level of the hierarchy. Each of these in turn needed further decomposition into specific items in terms of which the decision alternatives could be evaluated. For example, while the recipient measures economic benefits in terms of reduced costs and improved productivity, the institution needed the more specific measurements of reduced length of stay, better utilization of resources, and increased financial support from the community. There was no reason to decompose the societal benefits into third level subcriteria and hence societal benefits connects directly to the fourth level. The group considered three models for the decision alternatives, and they are at the bottom (or fifth level in this case) of the hierarchy: in Model 1, the hospital provided full care to the patients; in Model 2, the family cares for the patient at home, and the hospital provides only emergency treatment (no nurses go to the house); and in Model 3, the hospital and the home share patient care (with visiting nurses going to the home).

In the costs hierarchy there were also three major interests in the second level that would incur costs or pains: community, institution, and society. In this decision the costs incurred by the patient were not included as a separate factor. Patient and family could be thought of as part of the community. We thought decomposition was necessary only for institutional costs. We included five such costs in the third level: capital costs, operating costs, education costs, bad debt costs, and recruitment costs. Educational costs apply to educating the community and training the staff. Recruitment costs apply to staff and volunteers. Since both the costs hierarchy and the benefits hierarchy concern the same decision, they both have the same alternatives in their bottom levels, even though the costs hierarchy has fewer levels.

The question now is how to use pairwise comparison judgments and derive priorities and synthesize them to obtain the overall benefits and costs of each of the three alternatives, and then again for the costs and combine the two outcomes into a single overall outcome. To do that we need to first explain in simple terms how the process of prioritization is carried out.

Judgments and Comparisons

A judgment is an expression of an opinion. A comparison is an expression of an opinion about the dominance (importance, preference or likelihood) of one thing over another. Dominance represents the intensity of strength. It is done every day through verbal expression that has some quantitative significance that we need to use to combine the many dominance judgments involved in a decision. The set of all such judgments in making comparisons with respect to a single property or goal can be represented in a square matrix in which the set of elements is compared with itself. It is a way of organizing all the judgments with respect to that property to be processed and synthesized along with other matrices of comparison judgments involved in that decision. Each judgment represents the dominance of an element in the column on the left of the matrix over an element in the row on top. It reflects the answers to two questions: which of the two elements is more important with respect to a higher level criterion, and how strongly. Let us show how by taking a very simple example of how the mind perceives and prioritizes physical objects that have measurements [5].

Assume that we have three apples A, B, C, and wish to compare them in pairs according to their size. Their sizes are known to be 12 cubic inches, 6 cubic inches and 2 cubic inches respectively. Figure 2.3 shows how the actual numerical relative values are used in comparing an apple on the left with an apple at the top of the matrix.

Size Comparison	Apple A	Apple B	Apple C
Apple A	12/12=1	12/6=2	12/2=6
Apple B	6/12=1/2	6/6=1	6/2=3
Apple C	2/12=1/6	2/6=1/3	12/12=1

Figure 2.3 Reciprocal Structure of Pairwise Comparison Matrix for Apples

reciprocal rule

inverse relationship of matrix ratings

rules of matrix

We have the number one on the main diagonal of the matrix, and the values below the diagonal are reciprocals of the corresponding inverse comparison values above the diagonal. Of course it is possible that the apples are not listed in a descending order but we still apply the reciprocal rule. The numbers on the right in each cell tell us how many times an apple on the left dominates an apple at the top with respect to the property of size. If an element on the left is less important than that on the top of the matrix, we enter the reciprocal value in the corresponding position in the matrix. It is important to note that the lesser element is always used as the unit and the greater one is estimated as a multiple of that unit. From all the paired comparisons we calculate the priorities and exhibit them on the right of the matrix. For a set of n elements in a matrix one needs $n(n-1)/2$ comparisons because there are n 1's on the diagonal for comparing elements with themselves and of the remaining judgments, half are reciprocals. Thus we have $(n^2-n)/2$ judgments. In some problems one may elicit only the minimum of $n-1$ judgments.

If we do not have the measurements we would have to estimate the relative sizes. The more expert we are the better the estimates. But still our estimates may not fully conform (be consistent) with the values obtained from the ratios of the measurements. Here we used the sizes of the apples which are visible to the eye to make the comparisons, but what if the property is not a physical one how would we make the comparisons and ensure their validity? It is clear that experience and knowledge are necessary to make the comparisons reliable. A child would not be able to make accurate comparisons of the apples. Not only does a decision involve factors that have numbers which need to be interpreted in terms of satisfying our needs, but also involves factors for which there are no measurements that we can only evaluate with our feelings. Whatever meaning and feeling we have, in the end we need to articulate them numerically so we can combine them on the different factors into an outcome. When a decision is complex with conflicting tradeoffs, our minds are usually unable to perform the synthesis of feelings to produce a credible overall outcome. In a group setting we need to combine our feelings and understanding with those of others to arrive at a credible collective outcome.

feelings made into numerical decisions

The first observation is that we can only compare things accurately when they are close or homogeneous, thus it is enough to have a numerical scale that is within this acceptable range but can be extended when we need to in some way that maintains its credibility. We can use scientific knowledge from psycho-physics to develop the numbers used in the comparison scale. This we will do in Chapter 5. We will now show how the fundamental scale of absolute numbers in Table 1.1 is used in our hospice example, a complex decision with several people involved. Its use in this example involves consensus. More satisfying uses of this scale with reciprocal values will be discussed and used in some examples later that involve not only different judgments by different people, but also including the priority of importance of the people themselves. We note that in making pairwise comparisons it is often easier to get people to reach agreement because it is very specific response to a well defined question of dominance.

If we apply this scale directly to the comparisons of the apples and derive the priorities on the right in Figure 2.4 from any column by dividing an entry by the total of the column.

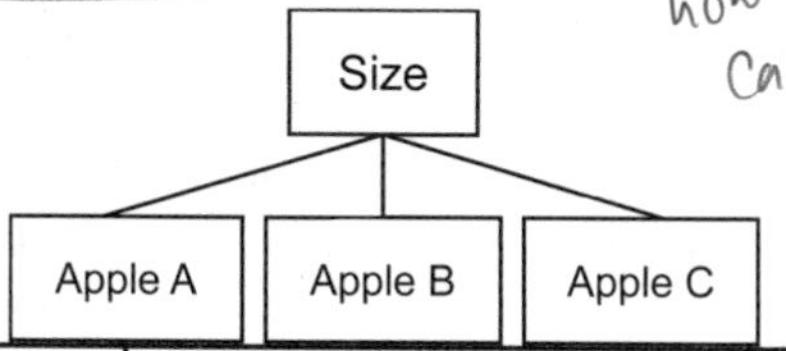

how to Calculate priorities

Size Comparison	Apple A	Apple B	Apple C	Priorities
Apple A	1	2	6	6/10 = 0.6
Apple B	1/2	1	3	3/10 = 0.3
Apple C	1/6	1/3	1	1/10 = 0.1

Figure 2.4 Pairwise Comparison Matrix for Apples Using Judgments

Using the columns or adding each row and dividing by the total to derive the priorities is what we do when the matrix is consistent which means for example that since apple A is twice larger than B and six times larger than C, then apple B must be three times larger than C . When that is not the case because judgments can never be so perfect, if the inconsistency is not too large, one can obtain the priorities by performing operations on this matrix (raising it to large enough power and then adding each row elements and dividing by the total). The inconsistency of the matrix can be measured and which comparison value causes the greatest inconsistency can be modified by examining the thinking involved to determine by how much one is willing to change it and so on to the next most inconsistent judgment. If the inconsistency is high and one is unable or unwilling to change the

inconsistency

inconsistency can lead to indecision.

judgments, particularly on the important criteria, one cannot make a decision.

Here are two examples of a different kind to show that this scale, despite its transparent simplicity, gives back known answers rather accurately. There are enough such examples and more complicated ones that would fill a book.

Table 2.1 shows how an audience of about 30 people, using consensus to arrive at each judgment, provided judgments to estimate the *dominance* of the consumption of drinks in the United States (which drink is consumed more in the US and how much more than another drink?). The derived vector of relative consumption and the actual vector, obtained by normalizing the consumption given in official statistical data sources, are at the bottom of the table.

Table 2.1 Relative Consumption of Drinks

Which Drink is Consumed More in the U.S.?							
An Example of Estimation Using Judgments							
Drink Consumption in the U.S.	Coffee	Wine	Tea	Beer	Sodas	Milk	Water
Coffee	1	9	5	2	1	1	1/2
Wine	1/9	1	1/3	1/9	1/9	1/9	1/9
Tea	1/5	2	1	1/3	1/4	1/3	1/9
Beer	1/2	9	3	1	1/2	1	1/3
Sodas	1	9	4	2	1	2	1/2
Milk	1	9	3	1	1/2	1	1/3
Water	2	9	9	3	2	3	1

The derived scale based on the judgments in the matrix is:

Coffee	Wine	Tea	Beer	Sodas	Milk	Water
.177	.019	.042	.116	.190	.129	.327

with a consistency ratio of .022.
The actual consumption (from statistical sources) is:

.180	.010	.040	.120	.180	.140	.330

Very early in the history of the subject, T.L. Saaty and M. Khouja did the following exercise on an airplane in 1973. They simply used their common knowledge about the relative influence and standing of these countries in the world and without referring to any specific economic data related to GNP values. The two results are close and demonstrate that the general understanding an interested person has about a problem can be used to advantage to make fairly good estimates through paired comparisons [6].

good estimates

Table 2.2 gives the judgments using the AHP 1-9 scale and Table 2.3 provides the derived priorities, the actual and relative GNP values.

Table 2.2 Paired Comparisons of the Relative Dominance in wealth of
Seven Nations

	U.S	U.S.S.R	China	France	U.K	Japan	W.Germany
U.S	1	4	9	6	6	5	5
U.S.S.R	1/4	1	7	5	5	3	4
China	1/9	1/7	1	1/5	1/5	1/7	1/5
France	1/6	1/5	5	1	1	1/3	1/3
U.K	1/6	1/5	5	1	1	1/3	1/3
Japan	1/5	1/3	7	3	3	1	2
W.Germany	1/5	1/4	5	3	3	1/2	1

Table 2.3 Outcome of Estimated Relative Wealth and the Actual and Relative
Values

	Normalized Eigenvector	Actual GNP (1972)	Normalized GNP Values
U.S	.427	1,167	.413
U.S.S.R	.23	635	.225
China	.021	120	.043
France	.052	196	.069
U.K	.052	154	.055
Japan	.123	294	.104
W. Germany	.094	257	.091

Judgments and Priorities for the Hospice Example

As usual with the AHP, in both the cost and the benefits models, we
compared the criteria and subcriteria according to their relative importance
with respect to the parent element in the adjacent upper level. For example,
the entries in the matrix shown in Table 2.4 are responses to the question:
which general criterion is more important with respect to choosing the best
hospice alternative and how strongly? Here recipient benefits are
moderately more important than institutional benefits and are assigned the
absolute number 3 in the (1,2) or first-row second-column position. Three
signifies three times more. The reciprocal value is automatically entered in
the (2,1) position, where institutional benefits on the left are compared with
recipient benefits at the top. Similarly a 5, corresponding to strong
dominance or importance, is assigned to recipient benefits over social
benefits in the (1,3) position, and a 3, corresponding to moderate dominance,

is assigned to institutional benefits over social benefits in the (2,3) position with corresponding reciprocals in the transpose positions of the matrix.

Judgments in a matrix may not be consistent. In eliciting judgments, one makes redundant comparisons to improve the validity of the answer, given that respondents may be uncertain or may make poor judgments in comparing some of the elements. Redundancy gives rise to multiple comparisons of an element with other elements and hence to numerical inconsistencies.

[handwritten margin note: inconsistent judgements are resolved with repetition]

Table 2.4 Judgment Matrix for the Criteria of the Benefits Hierarchy

Choosing best hospice	Recipient benefits	Institutional benefits	Social benefits	Priorities
Recipient benefits	1	3	5	.64
Institutional benefits	1/3	1	3	.26
Social benefits	1/5	1/3	1	.11

C.R. = .033

[handwritten: measuring inconsistency]

For example, where we compare recipient benefits with institutional benefits and with societal benefits, we have the respective judgments 3 and 5. Now if $x = 3y$ and $x = 5z$ then $3y = 5z$ or $y = 5/3\ z$. If the judges were consistent, institutional benefits would be assigned the value 5/3 instead of the 3 given in the matrix. Thus the judgments are inconsistent. In fact, we are not sure which judgments are the accurate ones and which are the cause of the inconsistency. Inconsistency is measured by the inconsistency ratio (C.R.) that compares the inconsistency of the set of judgments in that matrix with what it would be if the judgments and the corresponding reciprocals were taken at random from the scale. For a 3-by-3 matrix this ratio should be about five percent, for a 4-by-4 about eight percent, and for larger matrices, about 10 percent. Inconsistency is inherent in the judgment process. Inconsistency may be considered a tolerable error in measurement only when it is of a lower order of magnitude (10 percent) than the actual measurement itself; otherwise the inconsistency would bias the result by a sizable error comparable to or exceeding the actual measurement itself. These ideas will be further explained in detail in Chapter 5.

[handwritten margin note: < 10%; inconsistency is tolerated]

When the judgments are inconsistent, the decision-maker may not know where the greatest inconsistency is. The AHP can show one by one in sequential order which judgments are the most inconsistent, and that suggests the value that best improves consistency. However, this *tweaking the model for consistency*

recommendation may not necessarily lead to a more accurate set of priorities that correspond to some underlying preference of the decision-makers. Greater consistency does not imply greater accuracy and one should go about improving consistency (if one can, given the available knowledge) by making slight changes compatible with one's understanding. If one cannot reach an acceptable level of consistency, one should gather more information or reexamine the framework of the hierarchy. *priorities*

Priorities are numerical ranks measured on an absolute scale. The reader will remember that absolute numbers cannot be changed to other numbers and mean the same thing by forming ratios as one does by using a yard or a meter for two readings of the same measurement. An absolute scale cannot have more than one set of readings. The object of evaluation is to elicit judgments concerning relative importance of the elements of the hierarchy to create scales of priority of influence. *selecting the alternative*

To derive the answer we divide the benefits priority of each alternative by its costs priority. We then choose the alternative with the largest of these ratios. It is also possible to allocate a resource proportionately among the alternatives. There is another way to synthesize benefits and costs by weighting their relative importance with respect to strategic criteria and use these weights to synthesize the alternatives by subtracting the weighted costs from the weighted benefits. This will be illustrated in other examples later on.

We will explain how priorities are developed from judgments and how they are synthesized down the hierarchy by a process of weighting and adding. Judgments are used to derive local priorities for a set of nodes (alternatives, say) with respect to a single criterion. Global priorities are obtained by multiplying these local priorities by priority of the criterion. The overall priorities for an element (an alternative) are obtained by adding its global priorities throughout the model. The local priorities are listed on the right of each matrix. Repeating what was said before, if the judgments are perfectly consistent, that is, the inconsistency ratio equals zero, we can obtain the local priorities by adding the values in each row and dividing by the sum of all the judgments in the entire matrix, or by normalizing the judgments in any column by dividing each entry by the sum of the entries in that column. If the judgments are inconsistent but have a tolerable level of inconsistency, we obtain the priorities by raising the matrix to large powers, which is known to take into consideration all intransitivities between the elements, such as those we showed above between x, y, and z. Again, we obtain the priorities from this matrix by adding the judgment values in each row and dividing by the sum of all the judgments. To summarize, the global priorities at the level immediately under the goal are equal to the local priorities because the priority of the goal is equal to one. The global priorities at the next level are obtained by weighting the local priorities of this level by the global priority at the level immediately above and so on. The overall priorities of the alternatives are obtained by weighting the local priorities by the global priorities of all the parent criteria or subcriteria in terms of which they are compared and then adding. (If an element in a set is not comparable with the others on some property and should be left out, the local priorities can be augmented by adding a zero in the appropriate position.)

The process is repeated in all the matrices by asking the appropriate dominance or importance question. For example, the entries in the judgment matrix shown in Table 2.5 are responses to the question: which subcriterion yields the greater benefit with respect to institutional benefits and how strongly?

Here psycho-social benefits are regarded as very strongly more important than economic benefits, and 7 is entered in the (1, 2) position and 1/7 in the (2,1) position.

Table 2.5 Judgment Matrix of Subcriteria with Respect to Institutional Benefits

Institutional benefits	Psycho-social	Economic	Priorities
Psycho-social	1	7	.875
Economic	1/7	1	.125

In comparing the three models for patient care, we asked members of the planning association which model they preferred with respect to each of the covering or parent secondary criterion in level 3 or with respect to the tertiary criteria in level 4. For example, for the subcriterion direct care (located on the left-most branch in the benefits hierarchy), we obtained a matrix of paired comparisons in Table 2.6 in which Model 1 is preferred over Models 2 and 3 by 5 and 3 respectively and Model 3 is preferred by 3 over Model 2. The group first made all the comparisons using semantic terms for the fundamental scale and then translated them to the corresponding numbers.

Table 2.6 Relative Benefits of the Models with Respect to Direct Care of Patients

Direct care of patient	Model I	Model II	Model III	Priorities
Model I unit team	1	5	3	.64
Model II mixed/home care	1/5	1	1/3	.10
Model III case management	1/3	3	1	.26

C.R.=.003

For the costs hierarchy, we again illustrate with three matrices. First the group compared the three major cost criteria and provided judgments in response to the question: which criterion is a more important determinant of the cost of a hospice model? Table 2.7 shows the judgments obtained.

Table 2.7 Judgment Matrix for the Criteria of the Costs Hierarchy

Choosing best hospice (costs)	Community	Institutional	Societal	Priorities
Community costs	1	1/5	1	.14
Institutional costs	5	1	5	.71
Societal costs	1	1/5	1	.14

C.R. = .000

The group then compared the subcriteria under institutional costs and obtained the importance matrix shown in Table 2.8. The entries are responses to the question: which criterion incurs greater institutional costs and how strongly?

Finally we compared the three models to find out which incurs the highest cost for each criterion or subcriterion. Table 2.9 shows the results of comparing them with respect to the costs of recruiting staff.

Table 2.8 Judgment Matrix of Subcriteria Under Institutional Costs

Institutional costs	Capital	Operating	Education	Bad debt	Recruitment	Priorities
Capital	1	1/7	1/4	1/7	1	.05
Operating	7	1	9	4	5	.57
Education	4	1/9	1	1/2	1	.01
Bad debt	7	1/4	2	1	3	.21
Recruitment	1	1/5	1	1/3	1	.07

C.R. = .000

Table 2.9 Relative Costs of the Models with Respect to Recruiting Staff

Institutional costs for recruiting staff	Model I	Model II	Model III	Priorities
Model I unit team	1	5	3	.64
Model II mixed/home care	1/5	1	1/3	.10
Model III case management	1/3	3	1	.26

C.R.=.08

As shown in Table 2.10, we divided the benefits priorities by the costs priorities for each alternative to obtain the best alternative, model 3, the one with the largest value for the ratio.

Table 2.10 shows two ways or modes of synthesizing the local priorities of the alternatives using the global priorities of their parent criteria: The distributive mode and the ideal mode. In the distributive mode, the weights of the alternatives sum to one. It is used when there is dependence among the alternatives and a unit priority is distributed among them. The ideal mode is used to obtain the single best alternative regardless of what other alternatives there are. In the ideal mode, the local priorities of the alternatives are divided by the largest value among them. This is done for each criterion; for each criterion one alternative becomes an ideal with value one. In both modes, the local priorities are weighted by the global priorities of the parent criteria and synthesized and the benefit-to-cost ratios formed. In this case, both modes lead to the same outcome for hospice, which is model 3. As we shall see below, we need both modes to deal with the effect of adding (or deleting) alternatives on an already ranked set.

Table 2.10 Global and Ideal Modes of Synthesizing the Local Priorities of the Alternatives

Benefits	Priorities	Distributive Mode			Ideal Mode		
		Model 1	Model 2	Model 3	Model 1	Model 2	Model 3
Direct Care of Patient	.02	0.64	0.10	0.26	1.000	0.156	0.406
Palliative Care	.14	0.64	0.10	0.26	1.000	0.156	0.406
Volunteer Support	.02	0.09	0.17	0.74	0.122	0.230	1.000
Networking in Families	.06	0.46	0.22	0.32	1.000	0.478	0.696
Relief of Post Death Stress	.12	0.30	0.08	0.62	0.484	0.129	1.000
Emotional Support of Family and Patient	.21	0.30	0.08	0.62	0.484	0.129	1.000
Alleviation of Guilt	.03	0.30	0.08	0.62	0.484	0.129	1.000
Reduced Economic Costs for Patient	.01	0.12	0.65	0.23	0.185	1.000	0.354
Improved Productivity	.03	0.12	0.27	0.61	0.197	0.443	1.000
Publicity and Public Relations	.19	0.63	0.08	0.29	1.000	0.127	0.460
Volunteer Recruitment	.03	0.64	0.10	0.26	1.000	0.156	0.406
Professional Recruitment and Support	.06	0.65	0.23	0.12	1.000	0.354	0.185
Reduced Length of Stay	.006	0.26	0.10	0.64	0.406	0.406	1.000
Better Utilization of Resources	.023	0.09	0.22	0.69	0.130	0.130	1.000
Increased Monetary Support	.001	0.73	0.08	0.19	1.000	1.000	0.260
Death as a Social Issue	.02	0.20	0.20	0.60	0.333	0.333	1.000
Rehumanization of Institutions	.08	0.24	0.14	0.62	0.387	0.226	1.000
Synthesis		0.428	0.121	0.451	0.424	0.123	0.453
Costs							
Community Costs	.14	0.33	0.33	0.33	1.000	1.000	1.000
Institutional Capital Costs	.03	0.76	0.09	0.15	1.000	0.118	0.197
Institutional Operating Costs	.40	0.73	0.08	0.19	1.000	0.110	0.260
Institutional Costs for Educating the Community	.01	0.65	0.24	0.11	1.000	0.369	0.169
Institutional Costs for Training Staff	.06	0.56	0.32	0.12	1.000	0.571	0.214
Institutional Bad Debt	.15	0.60	0.20	0.20	1.000	0.333	0.333
Institutional Costs of Recruiting Staff	.05	0.66	0.17	0.17	1.000	0.258	0.258
Institutional Costs of Recruiting Volunteers	.01	0.60	0.20	0.20	1.000	0.333	0.333
Societal Costs	.15	0.33	0.33	0.33	1.000	1.000	1.000
Synthesis		0.583	0.192	0.224	0.523	0.229	0.249
Benefit/Cost Ratio		0.734	0.630	2.013	0.811	0.537	1.819

Model 3 has the largest ratio of benefits to costs in both the distributive and ideal modes, and the hospital selected it for treating terminal patients. This need not always be the case. In this case, there is dependence of the personnel resources allocated to the three models because some of these resources would be shifted based on the decision. Therefore the distributive mode is the appropriate method of synthesis. If the alternatives were sufficiently distinct with no dependence in their definition, the ideal mode would be the way to synthesize. marginal analysis

We also performed marginal analysis to determine where the hospital should allocate additional resources for the greatest marginal return. To perform marginal analysis, we first ordered the alternatives by increasing cost priorities and then formed the benefit-to-cost ratios corresponding to the smallest cost, followed by the ratios of the differences of successive benefits to costs. If this difference in benefits is negative, the new alternative is dropped from consideration and the process continued. The alternative with the largest marginal ratio is then chosen. For the costs and corresponding benefits from the synthesis rows in Table 2.10 we obtained:

Costs: .20 .21 .59
Benefits: .12 .45 .43

From these values we compute the marginal ratios as the final priorities:

$$\frac{.12}{.20} = 0.60 \qquad \frac{.45 - .12}{.21 - .20} = 33 \qquad \frac{.43 - .45}{.59 - .21} = -0.051$$

The third alternative is not a contender for resources because its marginal return is negative. The second alternative is best. In fact, in addition to adopting the third model, the hospital management chose the second model of hospice care for further development.

Absolute Measurement — Rating Alternatives One at a Time

People are able to make two kinds of comparisons - absolute and relative. In absolute comparisons, people compare alternatives with a standard in their memory that they have developed through experience. In relative comparisons, they compared alternatives in pairs according to a common attribute, as we did throughout the hospice example.

People use absolute measurement (sometimes also called rating) to rank independent alternatives one at a time in terms of rating intensities for each of the criteria. An intensity is a range of variation of a criterion that enables one to distinguish the quality of an alternative for that criterion. An intensity may be expressed as a numerical range of values if the criterion is measurable or defined in qualitative terms.

For example, if ranking students is the objective and one of the criteria on which they are to be ranked is performance in mathematics, the mathematics ratings might be: excellent, good, average, below average, poor; or, using the usual school terminology, A, B, C, D, and F. Relative comparisons are first used to set priorities on the ratings themselves. If desired, one can fit a continuous curve through the derived intensities. This concept may go against our socialization. However, it is perfectly reasonable to ask how much an A is preferred to a B or to a C. The judgment of how much an A is preferred to a B might be different under different criteria. Perhaps for mathematics an A is very strongly preferred to a B, while for physical education an A is only moderately preferred to a B. So the end result might be that the ratings are scaled differently. For example one could have the scale values for the ratings as shown in Table 2.11:

Table 2.11 Examples of Scale Values for Ratings

	Math	Physical Education
A	0.50	0.30
B	0.30	0.30
C	0.15	0.20
D	0.04	0.10
E	0.01	0.10

The alternatives are then rated or ticked off one at a time using the intensities. We will illustrate absolute measurement with an example. A firm evaluates its employees for raises. The criteria are dependability, education, experience, and quality. Each criterion is subdivided into intensities, standards, or subcriteria (Figure 2.5). The managers set priorities for the criteria by comparing them in pairs. They then pairwise compare the intensities according to priority with respect to their parent criterion (as in Table 2.12) or with respect to a subcriterion if they are using a deeper hierarchy. The priorities of the intensities are divided by the largest intensity for each criterion (second column of priorities in Figure 2.5).

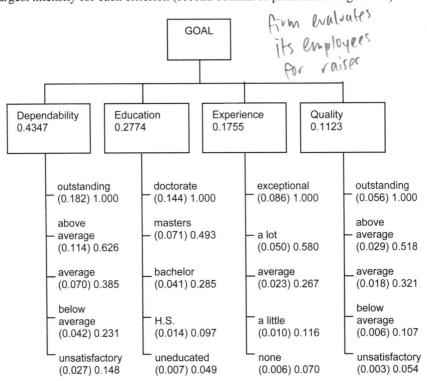

Figure 2.5 Hierarchy with Absolute Measurement

Table 2.12 shows a paired comparison matrix of intensities with respect to dependability. The managers answer the question: which intensity is more important and by how much with respect to dependability. The priorities of the intensities for each criterion are divided by the largest one and multiplied by the priority of the criterion. Finally the managers rate each individual (Table 2.13) by assigning the intensity rating that applies to him or her under each criterion. The scores of these intensities are each weighted by the priority of its criterion and summed to derive a total ratio scale score for the individual (shown on the right of Table 2.13). These numbers belong to an absolute scale, and the managers can give salary increases precisely in proportion to the ratios of these numbers. Adams gets the highest score and Kesselman the lowest. This approach can be used whenever it is possible to set priorities for intensities of criteria; people can usually do this when they have sufficient experience with a given operation. This normative mode requires that alternatives be rated one by one without regard to how many there may be and how high or low any of them rates on prior standards. Some corporations have insisted that they no longer trust the normative standards of their experts and that they prefer to make paired comparisons of their alternatives. Still, when there is wide agreement on standards, the absolute mode saves time in rating a large number of alternatives.

Table 2.12 Ranking Intensities: Which intensity is preferred most with respect to dependability and how strongly?

Depend-ability	Outstanding	Above Average	Average	Below Average	Unsatis-factory	Priorities
Outstanding	1.0	2.0	3.0	4.0	5.0	0.419
Above Avg	1/2	1.0	2.0	3.0	4.0	0.263
Average	1/3	1/2	1.0	2.0	3.0	0.160
Below Avg.	1/4	1/3	1/2	1.0	2.0	0.097
Unsatisfactory	1/5	1/4	1/3	1/2	1.0	0.062

C.R. = 0.015

Table 2.13 Rating Alternatives

Employees	Dependability .4347	Education .2774	Experience .1775	Quality .1123	Total
1. Adams, V	Outstanding	Bachelor	A Little	Outstanding	0.646
2. Becker, L	Average	Bachelor	A Little	Outstanding	0.379
3. Hayat, F	Average	Masters	A Lot	Below Average	0.418
4. Kessel, S	Above Average	H.S.	None	Above Average	0.369
5. O'Shea, K	Average	Doctorate	A Lot	Above Average	0.605
6. Peters, T	Average	Doctorate	A Lot	Average	0.583
7. Tobias, K	Above Average	Bachelor	Average	Above Average	0.456

Homogeneity and Clustering

[handwritten: when comparisons require a range larger than 1-9 ⤷ cluster; pivot]

Think of the following situation: we need to determine the relative size of a blueberry and a watermelon. Here, we need a range greater than 1-9. Human beings have difficulty establishing appropriate relationships when the ratios get beyond 9. To resolve this human difficulty, we can use a method in which we cluster different elements so we can rate them within a cluster and then rate them across the clusters. We need to add other fruits to make the comparison possible and then form groups of comparable fruits. In the first group we include the blueberry, a grape, and a plum. In the second group we include the same plum, an apple, and a grapefruit. In the third group we include the same grapefruit, a melon, and the watermelon. The AHP requires reciprocal comparisons of homogeneous elements whose ratios do not differ by much on a property, hence the absolute scale ranges from one to nine. When the ratios are larger, one must cluster the elements in different groups and use a common element (pivot) that is the largest in one cluster and the smallest element in the next cluster of the next higher order of magnitude. The weights of the elements in the second group are divided by the priority of the pivot in that group and then multiplied by the priority of the same pivot element (whose value is generally different) from the first group, making them comparable with the first group. The process is then continued. The reason for using clusters of a few elements is to ensure greater stability of the priorities in face of inconsistent judgments. Comparing more than two elements allows for redundancy and hence also for greater validity of real-world information. The AHP often uses seven elements and puts them in clusters if there are more than seven. (Elaborate mathematical derivations are given in the AHP to show that the number of elements compared should not be too large in order to obtain priorities with admissible consistency.)

[handwritten: use 7 elements or cluster]

Problems with Analytic Decision Making

At this point you may wonder why we have three different modes for establishing priorities, the absolute measurement mode and the distributive and ideal modes of relative measurement. Isn't one enough? Let us explain why we need more than one mode.

A major reason for having more than one mode is concerned with this question. What happens to the synthesized ranks of alternatives when new ones are added or old ones deleted? With consistent judgments, the original relative rank order cannot change under any single criterion, but it can under several criteria.

Assume that an individual has expressed preference among a set of alternatives, and that as a result, he or she has developed a ranking for them.

[handwritten: how deleting or adding alternatives changes rankings.]

Can and should that individual's preferences and the resulting rank order of
the alternatives be affected if alternatives are added to the set or deleted
from it and if no criteria are added or deleted? What if the added alternatives
are copies or near copies of one or of several of the original alternatives and
their number is large? Rank reversal is an unpleasant property if it is caused
by the addition of truly irrelevant alternatives [7, 8]. However, the addition
of alternatives may just reflect human nature: the straw that broke the
camel's back was considered irrelevant along with all those that went before
it. Mathematically, the number and quality of newly added alternatives are
known to affect preference among the original alternatives.

Most people, unaided by theory and computation, make each
decision separately, and they are not very concerned with rank reversal
unless they are forced for some reason to refer to their earlier conclusions.
We think it is essential to understand and deal with this phenomenon.

An Example of Rank Reversal

Two products A and B are evaluated according to two equally important
attributes P and Q as in the matrices in
Table 2.14 below:

Table 2.14 Preference Matrices of Products A and B with Respect to Equally
Important Attributes P and Q

P	A	B	Priorities
A	1	5	.83
B	1/5	1	.17

Q	A	B	Priorities
A	1	1/3	.25
B	3	1	.75

We obtain the following priorities: $W_A = .542$, $W_B = .458$, and A is preferred
to B.

A third product C is then introduced and compared with A and B as
shown in Table 2.15:

Table 2.15 Preference Matrices with Product C Added

P	A	B	C	Priorities
A	1	5	1	.455
B	1/5	1	1/5	.090
C	1	5	1	.455

Q	A	B	C	Priorities
A	1	1/3	2	.222
B	3	1	6	.666
C	1/2	1/6	1	.111

[handwritten: evolution, not determinism]

Synthesis yields W_A = .338, W_B = .379, and W_C = .283. Here B is preferred to A and there is rank reversal. *[handwritten: fundamental AHP assumption]*

For a decision theory to have a lasting value, it must consider how people make decisions naturally and assist them in organizing their thinking to improve their decisions in that natural direction. Its assumptions should be tied to evolution and not to present day determinism. This is the fundamental concept on which the AHP is based. It was developed as a result of a decade of unsuccessful attempts to use normative theories, with the assistance of some of the world's best minds, to deal with negotiation and trade-off in the strategic political and diplomatic arena at the Arms Control and Disarmament Agency in the Department of State. In the early 1970s, the first author asked the question, how do ordinary people process information in their minds in attempting to make a decision and how do they express the strength of their judgments? The answer to this question led to considering hierarchies and networks, paired comparisons, absolute scales, homogeneity and consistency, priorities, ranking, and the AHP.

R. Corbin and A. Marley [9] provide a utility theory example of rank reversal. It "concerns a lady in a small town, who wishes to buy a hat. She enters the only hat store in town, and finds two hats, A and B, that she likes equally well, and so might be considered equally likely to buy. However, now suppose that the sales clerk discovers a third hat, C, identical to B. Then the lady may well choose hat A for sure (rather than risk the possibility of seeing someone wearing a hat just like hers), a result that contradicts regularity." Utility theory has no clear analytical answer to this paradox or to famous examples having to do with phantom alternatives and with decoy alternatives that arise in the field of marketing [10].

[handwritten: Corbin & Marley → hat example for preference]
[handwritten: ↳ utility theorm – phantom/decoy alternatives]

added

ideal mode resolves alternatives issues

Because of such examples, it is clear that one cannot simply use one procedure for every decision problem because that procedure would either preserve or not preserve rank. Nor can one introduce new criteria that indicate the dependence of the alternatives on information from each new alternative that is added. In the AHP, this issue has been resolved by adding the ideal mode to the normalization mode in relative measurement. The ideal mode presents an alternative that is rated low or "irrelevant" on all the criteria from affecting the rank of higher rated alternatives.

Resolution of Rank Reversal

In the AHP, we have one way to allow rank to change, and two ways to preserve rank.

(1) We can allow rank to reverse by using the distributive mode of the relative measurement approach of the AHP.

(2) We can preserve rank in the case of irrelevant alternatives by using the ideal mode of the AHP relative measurement approach.

(3) We can allow rank to reverse by using the distributive mode absolute measurement of the AHP.

As a recap, in relative measurement, we use normalization by dividing by the sum of the priorities of the alternatives to define the distributive mode. In this mode, we distribute the unit value assigned to the goal of a decision proportionately among the alternatives through normalization. When we add a new alternative, it takes its share of the unit from the previously existing alternatives. This mode allows for rank reversal because dependence exists among the alternatives, which is attributable to the number of alternatives and to their measurements values and which is accounted for through normalization. For example, multiple copies of an alternative can affect preference for that alternative in some decisions. We need to account for such dependence in allocating resources, in voting and in distributing resources among the alternatives.

We conducted an experiment with our colleague L. G. Vargas involving 64,000 hierarchies with priorities assigned randomly to criteria and to alternatives to test the number of times the best choice obtained by the distributive and ideal modes coincided with each other. It turns out that the two methods yield the same top alternative 92 percent of the time. We obtained similar results for the top two alternatives [11].

Decision Making in Complex Environments

The essence of the AHP is the use of absolute scales in elaborate structures to assess complex problems. An absolute scale uses numbers that can't be changed. For example in physics one uses a ratio scale to measure weight in pounds (P) or kilograms (K) approximately related by the formula $P = 2.21K$ or length with inches and with centimeters related by another ratio scale formula centimeters = 2.54 inches. In both formulas the ratio of the weight of two objects measured in pounds or measured in kilograms is the same and similarly for lenghts. Temperature is measured with a Fahrenheit scale (F) and a Celsius scale C, related by the formula $F = \dfrac{9}{5}C + 32$ known as an interval scale. Absolute scale numbers can't be measured with different scales. For example if we compare two apples according to size and determine that one apple is three times larger than another, we can't change the number three to another number by another scale to obtain a meaningful number. Here the number three is an absolute number. In decision making we use absolute numbers whose magnitudes are always the same. The AHP well fits the words of Thomas Paine in his Common Sense, "The more simple anything is, the less liable it is to be disordered and the easier repaired when disordered."   absolute scale ⊕ magnitude

The AHP makes group decision-making possible by aggregating judgments in a way that satisfies the reciprocal relation in comparing two elements. When the group consists of experts, each works out his or her own hierarchy and the AHP combines the outcomes using the geometric mean of the judgments. If the experts are ranked according to their expertise in a separate hierarchy, we can raise their individual evaluations to the power of their importance or expertise priorities before taking the geometric mean. We have also used special questionnaires to gather data in the AHP.

Practitioners have developed multicriteria decision approaches largely around techniques for generating scales for alternatives. But we believe that making decisions in real life situations depends on the depth and sophistication of the structures decision makers use to represent a decision or prediction problem rather than simply on manipulations - although they are also important. Decision making and prediction must go hand-in-hand if a decision is to survive the test of the forces it may encounter. If one understands the lasting value of a best decision, one will want to consider feedback structures with possible dependencies among all the elements. These would require iterations with feedback to determine the best outcome and the most likely to survive. We believe that ratio scales are mathematically compelling for this process. The AHP is increasingly used for decisions with interdependencies (the hierarchic examples we have described are simple special cases of such decisions). We describe applications of feedback later in the book.

[handwritten: People make decisions w/o framework - do we need one?]

The Benefits of Analytic Decision Making

Many good decision-makers do not rely on a theory to make their decisions. Are their good decisions accidental, or are there implicit logical principles that guide the mind in the process of making a decision, and are these principles complete and consistent? We believe that there are such principles, and that in thoughtful people, they work as formalized and described in the analytic hierarchy process. Still academics differ about how people should and should not make decisions. Experiments with people have shown that what people do differs from the theoretical and normative considerations the experts consider important. This may lead one to believe that analytical decision making is of little value. But our experience and that of many others indicate the opposite.

Analytic decision making is of tremendous value, but it must be simple and accessible to the lay user, and must have scientific justification of the highest order. Here are a few ideas about the benefits of the descriptive analytical approach. First is the morphological way of thoroughly modeling the decision, inducing people to make explicit their tacit knowledge. This leads people to organize and harmonize their different feelings and understanding. An agreed upon structure provides ground for a complete multisided debate. Second, particularly in the framework of hierarchies and feedback systems, the process permits decision makers to use judgments and observations to surmise relations and strengths of relations in the flow of interacting forces moving from the general to the particular and to make predictions of most likely outcomes. Third, people are able to incorporate and trade off values and influences with greater accuracy of understanding than they can by using language alone. Fourth, people are able to include judgments that result from intuition and emotion as well those that result from logic. Reasoning takes a long time to learn, and it is not a skill common to all people. By representing the strength of judgments numerically and agreeing on a value, decision-making groups do not need to participate in a prolonged argument. Finally, a formal approach allows people to make gradual and more thorough revisions and to combine the conclusions of different people studying the same problem in different places. One can also use such an approach to piece together partial analyses of the components of a bigger problem, or to decompose a larger problem into its constituent parts. This is an exhaustive list of the uses of the AHP. To deal with complexity we need rationality, and that is best manifested in the analytical approach.

[handwritten left margin: pros for using framework]

References

1. Senge, P. *The Fifth Discipline: The Art & Practice of the Learning Organization"*, 2nd edition, Doubleday, 2006.
2. Saaty, T.L. *Decision Making for Leaders*, Pittsburgh: RWS Publications, 1982.
3. Saaty, T.L. and Forman, E.H., *The Hierarchon, a Dictionary of Hierarchies*, Pittsburgh: RWS Publications, 1993.
4. Saaty, T.L. and Ozdemir, M., *The Encyclicon: a Dictionary of ANP Applications*, Pittsburgh: RWS Publications, 2005.
5. Saaty, T.L. "A Scaling Method for Priorities in Hierarchical Structures."*Journal of Mathematical Psychology*. **15** (1977): No. 3, pp. 234-281.
6. Saaty, T.L. and Khouja, M., "A Measure of World Influence." *Journal of Peace Science*, Spring, 1976
7. Grether, D.M. and Plott, C.R. 1979, Economic theory of choice and the preference reversal phenomenon, *The American Economic Review*, **69**, No. 4, pp. 623-638.
8. Tversky, A.; Slovic, P; and Kahneman, D. "The Causes of Preference Reversal." *The American Economic Review*, **80** (1990): No. 1, pp. 204-215.
9. Corbin, R. and Marley, A.A.J. "Random Utility Models with Equality: An Apparent, but not Actual, Generalization of Random Utility Models." *Journal of Mathematical Psychology*. **11** (1974):No. 3, pp. 274-293.
10. Saaty, T.L. *Fundamentals of the Analytic Hierarchy Process*. Pittsburgh: RWS Publications, 2000.
11. Saaty, T.L. and Vargas, L.G. "Experiments on Rank Preservation and Reversal in Relative Measurement." *Mathematical and Computer Modelling*. 17 (1993): No. 4/5, pp. 13-18.

Additional Reading

Hershey, J.C. and Schoemaker, P.J.H. "Prospect Theory's Reflection Hypothesis: A Critical Examination." *Organization of Behavioral Human Performances*. 25 (1980): No. 3, pp. 395-418.

Luce, R.D. and Raiffa, H., *Games and Decisions*. New York: John Wiley and Sons, 1957.

PART II: Drawing Out Differences about Issues

The Structure of a Decision with Hierarchies and with Networks; Yes-No Voting vs. Intensity of Preference; Planning Forward-Backward

In this part we begin by examining ideas and criteria to be met in group decisions and show that the AHP/ANP provides the best means to meet these criteria. We then go on to show how decision problems are structured as hierarchies, discuss some of the major technical aspects of the AHP and how to combine individual judgments into a representative group judgments and how to apply the ideas with group participation and illustrate them many examples. This is then followed by a chapter about yes-no voting versus voting according to intensity of preference. The role of the AHP in forward-backward planning is examined and illustrated and finally a chapter is dedicated to presenting the ANP. Complex decisions involve four kinds of merits with their own separate structures: Benefits (B), opportunities (O), costs (C) and risks (R) to which we often refer collectively as BOCR. Later we show how to obtain a single overall outcome by rating the top ranked alternative for each of these merits with respect to strategic criteria to derive weights for the BOCR and use them to weight and synthesize the final priorities of the alternatives that are derived separately in the substructures.

Chapter 3

Why the AHP Is Essential

Of all participative management tasks, ensuring reliable and efficient group decision making may be the most difficult. There are several theories and techniques to support individuals and groups in making decisions. We show in this chapter that the AHP is the only group decision support process that does it in an integrated way. We develop criteria from the requirements for successful group decision making and show that the AHP meets each of them all in a remarkable way. We go through the challenges faced by group leaders and indicate the technique of the AHP that can be used to deal with them. The outcome of the group process is a set of priorities for the alternatives. These priorities can be used to choose a best one or to distribute resources proportionately to fund the alternatives when they are projects to be implemented.

The twenty years of Dennis Romig's research on teamwork suggests that using a systematic and structured approach and having a clear definition of the problem are necessary but not sufficient to ensure success [1]. An organization can have more effective meetings by promoting team communication and using a method to manage the conflicts that may arise in the process. The more open the communication, the less likely a conflict will cause a breakdown. It has also been shown that a team's creativity often leads to breakthrough ideas when team roles and responsibilities are clarified. There may be nothing new about this, but Romig's results are significant because they validate the work of many experts who have been trying to find ways to improve group decision making.

People in organizations spend an enormous amount of time in meetings [2]. Some researchers have estimated in the late 1990s that:

- There are 11 million meetings in the U.S. per day
- Most professionals attend a total of 61.8 meetings per month
- Research indicates that over 50 percent of this meeting time is wasted
- Professionals lose 31 hours per month in unproductive meetings, or approximately four work days

Having an effective process to record the objectives, criteria, and alternatives and structure the decision is one sure way to prevent wasting time – our scarcest resource. This is why a systematic approach to decision making is so essential. The method we use here, the AHP, is a solid and rigorously validated approach [3, 4]. By using the AHP and its supporting software, a group leader has a record of the group's results as the discussion progresses, and when the process is finished there is a tangible outcome – a best alternative or a best allocation of resources. The model captures both the problem and the logical step-by-step history of the information given by the group. The model's level of detail is at the user's discretion. The leader can obtain feedback from the system that may prompt him to go back and review previous judgments – or even change the structure if necessary. One of the most important revisions is to add key elements that may have been missed. The group might not even realize that something is missing until the support system produces an outcome that differs from their expectations. People can make the division by relying on either rational thinking or intuitive thinking alone. The following examples illustrate this.

Ideas that appear reasonable in mathematics can lead to surprising paradoxes that may be logically valid but fail to match the reality we experience. Two of the twentieth century's foremost mathematicians, Stefan Banach and Alfred Tarski, proved "a most ingenious theorem" that seems to be a paradox derived from well-known assumptions in mathematics. It is possible they proved, to dissect a solid sphere into a finite number of pieces and then rearrange these pieces so that each forms a ball exactly the same size as the original ball [5]. The only thing done to the pieces is that they are moved around in space like the pieces of a jigsaw puzzle. Their idea can be extended to three or four or any number of balls or a single ball can be formed that is twice as big as the original ball – or as one author put it, you can transform a ball the size of a pea into a ball the size of the sun. Thus logic can lead to ridiculous results that are unobtainable in reality. The outcome of logical thinking is conditioned by the assumptions we make, and these assumptions are often hidden and also very subtle.

Here is another example of the shortcomings of intuition. Imagine you are given a cup of coffee and a cup of milk with equal amounts of liquid in the two cups. A spoonful of milk is transferred from the milk cup to the coffee cup, the mixture in the coffee cup is stirred, and then a spoonful of this mixture is returned to the milk cup so that at the end the amount of liquid in the two cups is still the same. Is there more milk in the coffee cup or more coffee in the milk cup or what? Most people say there is more milk in the coffee cup; a few say the reverse; and fewer still say they are equal. Intuition tells us that the first transfer of milk to the coffee cup so dilutes the milk in the coffee that the best transfer of the mixture cannot take back much of it, hence leaving more milk in the coffee cup than coffee in the milk cup. Of course, not being able to take back much of it should make it possible to take a lot more coffee in the spoonful. But people do not think of it that way. Notice that whatever amount of milk is missing from the milk cup is replaced by an equal amount of coffee (and vice versa), because at the end each cup has the same amount of liquid with which it started. It is therefore obvious that there are equal amounts of coffee in the milk and milk in the coffee. We can verify this with an example. Suppose that we have 5 teaspoons of milk in the milk cup M and 5 teaspoons of coffee in the coffee cup C. One teaspoon of milk from M is transferred to C. After having stirred cup C adequately, one teaspoonful from C is transferred back to M. Cup C, after the first transfer, has 1/6 milk and 5/6 coffee. The teaspoonful transferred to M also contains the proportion 1/6 milk and 5/6 coffee. Therefore, the composition of the two cups will be as follows: M has 4 1/6 milk and 5/6 coffee; and C has 5/6 milk and 4 1/6 coffee. Thus, there is as much milk in the coffee cup as there is coffee in the milk cup.

We need to use both logic and intuition to deal with the world and the AHP helps us do this. The AHP/ANP processes have been rigorously designed and validated so that its users can be assured that with valid inputs the system will produce valid outcomes. If the result produced by the system differs from expectation, however, which is generally based on intuition, it does not necessarily mean that the intuition is wrong or the logical synthesis is wrong. The group needs to review the model to look for causes of deviation. They might find that the model itself needs revision or that their intuition is biased and needs to be changed. Perhaps the difference was caused by the alternatives simply being too close to be sensitive to small changes in judgment or maybe the group failed to recognize an important factor. When a group of executives in an engineering company used the AHP to make a decision about whether or not to go on with a troubled project, they did not feel the outcome of the AHP was correct and found that they had misplaced technology in their model. After some study, the group restructured the model and put technology at a higher level in the hierarchy so that it received more importance. They learned from the model that they had failed to appreciate the influence of technology.

When a group of MBA students tried to model a decision problem faced by the local government, their result differed from the decision announced by the decision makers (with whom they intuitively agreed). The students found that they had considered the benefits, costs, and risks of the project but not the opportunities. When they added opportunities and recalculated their results, they got what they expected. The Analytic Hierarchy Process is not free from the garbage in/garbage out phenomenon.

The AHP does not require a group to reach full consensus at every step along the way, but the group does need to show a certain level of coherence in their thinking to reach a credible outcome. They can ensure this by closely monitoring incremental results from the model as they proceed: Are the pairwise-comparisons sufficiently consistent? Do the priorities that result from a set of pairwise-comparisons look reasonable? The time to revise is part of the process as it moves along. The leader can also use the system to measure how much one person's judgments differ from those of the group as a whole. A wide gap may indicate a diversity in knowledge that the group may be able to make use of; that one person may have new information the group was not aware of. Now is the time to present it, then-revote. If the differences are not great, the group can proceed to the next set of judgments. Now let us see how a systematic and structured approach contributes to success.

The Need for a Structured Decision

To make a good decision, we need to understand the problem. A model is a concise way to describe a complex idea; therefore it is a most effective tool for a group because it offers them a quick way to grasp the situation. Not only does structuring a model together help them to gain a collective understanding of the problem, but it can also be the means by which a diverse group of people with different backgrounds and aspirations can pass information back and forth and develop a consensus. One way to deal with disagreements is to use creativity techniques such as allowing group members to play roles. More and more people in organizations find themselves working in different groups doing project-based assignments. Because of the interdependency in objectives and tasks of today's cross-project teams, there needs to be intergroup coordination. We need to advance from group collaboration to intergroup collaboration [6]. The AHP helps with this by specifying and prioritizing organizational objectives that are common to every team.

Identifying problems as they appear – and taking action to solve them – is a major decision-making activity. Failures may happen for several reasons. Why is it that we often do not anticipate a problem to prevent it from happening? When a problem arises, why do we still fail to perceive it? Similarly, why do we fail to see opportunities before other people do? Why do we fail to see threats? Even when we see the opportunity, why do we repeatedly fail to benefit from it? And when we finally do something to solve a problem or seize an opportunity, why do we often fail to succeed?

How can we become more sensitive to the signs of problems or opportunities? First, we need a way to help us see by providing contrast that forces us to pay attention [7]. Scenario planning is a way to direct our attention to scenarios that might be emerging from our current situation. There are two kinds of scenario planning. In the first kind, a composite scenario emerges as a result of different objectives of the various parties operating in the same environment. The AHP's forward and backward planning has been applied to this kind of scenario planning [8]. The second kind involves predicting a drastic shift in the environment should a certain event occur. This is the process of considering a set of possible changes in the environment with the purpose of promoting understanding of each scenario. The objective is to be prepared with strategic decisions for each scenario [9]. Once the future scenarios are identified and understood, the AHP can be used for articulating the collective understanding and then producing strategic decisions for each of them.

Although we now can see problems and opportunities and realize that we need to change our strategy, we may still be reluctant to make the shift. We refuse to do new things because we do not know exactly how we should change our current best practices. And even if we do know, we are worried that we might do them poorly and wonder how they will affect our performance. We need to know how the new strategy translates into much clearer objectives – and, more importantly, what new actions are needed. Balanced Scorecards offer a systematic way to identify strategic objectives and actions along with their respective lag and lead performance indicators [10, 11]. But there are still two important issues that must be addressed. The first is ensuring the validity of the cause-effect relationships between objectives and actions. Even when this issue is properly addressed, the process tends to produce a lot of seemingly independent initiatives that may lead to uncoordinated actions within the organization. The second issue involves prioritization. Cause-effect relations have different intensities; not all initiatives have the same influence on the achievement of objectives; moreover, not all objectives have the same impact. Thus the second issue becomes a question of prioritizing the actions for the most effective way of implementing our strategy and then allocating resources accordingly.

In his books, Hubert Rampersad [12, 13] stretches the need for alignment even further by formulating frameworks for integrating Balanced Scorecards with several other management ideas in organizational change and learning. He introduces the Personal Balanced Scorecard, which promotes the alignment of an organization's scorecards with its members' personal scorecards. Striving for alignment requires a series of decisions. The challenge in implementing the AHP lies mostly in determining the objective of each decision and getting a group of people to work together to construct the hierarchy or network and provide the judgments.

The AHP/ANP is a great help in strategic decision making [14] and problem solving because it establishes a performance measurement record to track our progress and let us know how well we are doing. An excellent example of using the AHP for resource allocation is how IBM Rochester in Minnesota used it in the development of its successful new computer AS400 [15]. In IBM's example, groups from different levels of management worked one after another using an elaborate framework of AHP to prioritize their processes. IBM Rochester also used the AHP to map its performance relative to its competitors with respect to the key factors for success in computer-integrated manufacturing [16]. IBM Rochester attributed in part its winning the prestigious Malcolm Baldrige Award to its use of the AHP.

Now we know where to go and what to do. Using our new map, we are ready for our journey. We may need to establish new standards and will surely need to improve the way we do problem solving, but now with the new objectives and perspectives in mind.

An example of a model is shown in Figure 3.1. A model can be considered as a special language for communicating complex and abstract ideas. This diagram tells a story about a person's decision to buy a new car. The selection will be based on three criteria – style, reliability, and fuel economy – with four alternatives to choose from: Civic, Saturn, Escort, and Miata. The boxes and arrows show the structure of the problem; the numbers are the derived or synthesized priorities from a number of judgments systematically elicited. The priorities of the criteria indicate their relative importance, and the priorities for the alternatives are the final preferences for the cars. Having a model as a language is particularly useful if the problem is complex. In a decision problem, obtaining numbers that represent relative priority is particularly important. For a decision model to be valid, all the key decision elements must have been considered and the numbers must accurately represent the underlying order in the decision maker's mind.

Finding Consensus in a World of Pluralists

The same models used for individual problem solving and decision making can be used for groups as well. Involving people who will be in charge of implementing the decision in the decision-making process will enhance the likelihood of success because of the tacit knowledge they obtain from the process and because they are more likely to be committed to implementing a decision they contributed to shaping. Not only does an effective group decision create a sense of ownership, but having a structure is a way to align the participants' understanding of a complex decision and its underlying assumptions leading to more coordinated collective actions after the decision is made.

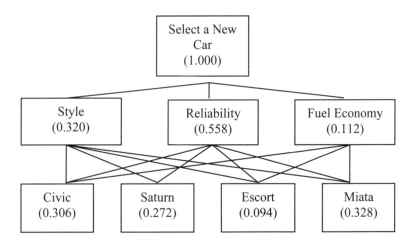

Figure 3.1 A Model as a Special Language

Group decision making is about process. Since disagreement is inevitable, it is essentially a process to come up with alternative ideas and then to work on reaching agreement on the best policy or action. The group may disagree on what values should drive the decision process, on the consequences of a certain policy or action, or on the best policy or action among the set of alternatives being evaluated. The three types of differences are interdependent – a group cannot really resolve one type effectively without addressing the other two differences in an integrated way.

There are two ways to deal with group disagreement: the consensualist approach and the pluralist approach. Consensualists always work for consensus and do whatever it takes to avoid disagreement. A well-known modern philosopher of science, Nicholas Rescher, is a proponent of the pluralist approach. Rescher argues that working toward consensus is not about doing whatever it takes to reach agreement [17]. He maintains that pluralists: "Accept the inevitability of dissensus in a complex and imperfect world. Strive to make the world safe for disagreement. Work to realize processes and procedures that make dissensus tolerable if not actually productive." Pluralists do work toward consensus, because decision making is about agreement, but they do not avoid disagreement or conflict. Consensus is not the same as unanimity.

Rather than being forced to accept plurality as a necessary evil we should seek out diversity in a group because this is the way to capture the complexity that will make our collective decision both relevant and useful. A group whose members have diverse knowledge, experience, values, and preferences has a better chance of arriving at a decision that is acceptable to all. Surely such a decision will have a better chance of being supported in its implementation. The more diverse the group, however, the harder it is to come to a decision in a democratic way because people will inevitably react differently to the same circumstances. The group's leader must feel confident, therefore, that he will be able to manage this diversity to produce a useful outcome.

As Rescher has suggested, resolving disputes in group decision making means identifying exactly what has been agreed upon and disagreed about. Working in a group assigned a specific task does not mean that all members start with the same perception regarding the objective of the decision or know exactly what outcome is expected from them. A group needs to begin by setting a goal. The goal must be relevant to the problem at hand and formulated in such a way that makes clear what kinds of options are to be evaluated. In other words, we have to be sure that implementing the group's decision will solve the problem. Having set its goal, the group then must collaborate to list the set of feasible alternatives and evaluate them to find the best one.

Generating alternatives is not always an integrated part of the group decision-making process; sometimes they are given with the task. But if the group has to generate the alternatives say for a new product, they may call on people with a additional kinds of expertise to do special research. Or, given a set of alternative courses of action, a group may have to choose the factors to consider and they may value the relative importance of the alternatives differently on these factors. Disputes may arise because they have different values or believe there are consequences that must be considered. Ultimately these differences may cause them to differ on what alternative is the best.

The AHP/ANP supports the plural decision makers in their quest to overcome their differences and converge to a solution.   It is the means to address differences in values, consequences, and preferences in an integrated and systematic way within the context of the problem.   Differences in values are addressed by determining what objectives are important; differences in consequences by determining the costs or risks involved in a decision; and differences in preferences by evaluating the alternatives with respect to each criterion. With this process the final preference is not discussed directly, and this should reduce the chances of a dispute regarding the final overall decision. Since it will be the logical outcome of what has been agreed to during the process, disagreement on the outcome would be settled by reviewing the process to find out why their expectations differed.

Collaborating to Produce Tangible Outcomes

Organizations that experience confusion and conflict in decision making often attribute their problems to poor communication. They then try to overcome their problems by conducting employee training programs in communication or by investing in internal communication systems.   Often, despite all the training and investment, the problems remain.

Collaboration aims at producing a tangible outcome; communication aims at the accurate transmission of tacit information from a sender to a recipient. The former is what we need for group decision making. Would better communication ensure better collaboration?   We cannot be sure. Collaboration surely needs communication, but better communication does not always improve collaboration. In fact it may sharpen conflict because a side effect of improving communication is to make differences clear.   Building collaboration is the goal for teamwork, rather than merely improving communication because it aims at collectively producing tangible outcomes [18]. A group of artists may collaborate to craft a statue for example, and a management team may work together to produce a model that describes its competitive environment and can be used to find the best strategy.

In a pluralist world that values diversity, collaboration in decision making happens when two or more people with complementary knowledge and experience working together create something neither of them could have done alone. They work together to focus their attention on the same problem even though they may perceive it differently. Despite their differences, they can think together as a unit, contributing their individual strengths to construct a model that represents their collective understanding of the problem. A decision aid should help people to both expand and sharpen their understanding. It does not necessarily mean that it must reproduce their hunches for answers. It should, however, make it possible for them to see what sort of judgments they need to espouse in order for their hunches to come about. This way they can deal with their differences as they arise, but they need only focus on those that are relevant and would affect the outcome. They would resolve conflicts regarding the model and ignore any trivial disagreements – a different process from compromise. There are differences that can be incorporated, differences that need to be discussed to build consensus, and differences that must be dealt with by allowing team members to express their views according to their expertise, authority, and perhaps power.

Aligning Mental Models

Mental models are sets of beliefs that involve certain assumptions about the world. They shape our perceptions and may lead us to see the world in a biased way. Our mental models not only play an important role in how we interact with the world but also contribute to forming our expectations [19]. Our brains interpret the reality we sense, filling the gaps by making assumptions based on our accumulated experience. Our minds are influenced too by our own genetics. Finally we base our responses on stimuli selected according to our own assumed reality. All these influences make people unique: we all see the same problem in our own way and hence react differently. As much as our differences may become the source of conflicts, they are also the source of the diverse knowledge we need in order to make better decisions.

Learning can be viewed as a conscious process of making mental models explicit so they can be developed and refined to respond to the world [20]. Interaction with other people helps. Although mental models are tacit, they drive behavior that is observable by other people. Group members can help each other to make their mental models more visible so that they can be questioned in order to validate the underlying assumptions of certain opinions or actions – especially when they deal with differences. As our mental models are developed and refined, they become aligned in the context of the problem at hand. Aligning the mental models can establish common descriptions to a useful commonly created description of the problem, opportunities, or systems that are of collective concern. Obviously this alignment calls for a group culture that values differences and does not attempt to squelch them. All this takes time and commitment to carry out.

Modeling for Group Collaboration

Collaboration involves a medium that the team members share to combine their contributions and produce a tangible outcome. This medium may be as simple as a piece of paper (where people draw together), a whiteboard (where people analyze a problem together), or a theater (where actors perform their roles in a play). The use of a common medium makes the process more productive because it depends less on perfect communication. The product of their collective effort practically speaks for itself. People can represent their ideas in the form of explicit and direct contributions that often convey their meaning and relevance better than words. With the AHP, the medium is a decision model on a computer.

A group involved in a collective decision-making task first needs to create a structure to represent their common understanding of the problem. Participants contribute their ideas systematically by proposing the elements of the problem such as criteria and the alternative courses of action. Setting a goal at the beginning and agreeing on the specific outcome they need to produce makes this process easier. They could start, for example, by using one of the brainstorming techniques to generate the set of alternatives they will evaluate [21]. They may write their suggestions on cards or post-it notes, to make them easy to organize, and then work together at the beginning to structure the elements on a whiteboard or flip chart [22]. The group facilitator can lead the process by asking specific questions to group elements that belong to the same cluster in the structure.

Up to this stage, there is no opportunity for conflict because it is not necessary to discard any ideas. When it comes to eliciting judgments on priorities, some agreement should be possible. If not, the group should go back and expand the model. The structure will help them make a series of specific judgments and will minimize unnecessary conflict due to misunderstanding (though there may, of course, be legitimate differences of opinion on specific judgments). When such disagreement occurs, the first step is to make sure the parties have the same understanding of the elements to be compared. The opposing parties can then present their reasoning. If this does not resolve the dispute, find out which party's judgment is more consistent with the rest of the judgments using the AHP consistency check. Or, finally, leave the two opposing judgments in place and perform sensitivity tests at the end. Maybe it will turn out that the disputed judgment does not affect the outcome.

The resulting structured decision model – with priorities derived through the judgments of the group – represents the collective understanding of the issue quite clearly, even to those who did not participate in the process.

If top management produces a strategic map of business objectives, with their priorities explicitly stated, lower level managers should be able to translate them into more specific sub-objectives, actions, and so on throughout the organization.

The development of electronic media has opened wide opportunities for enhancing group collaboration. Today somebody who joins the group in the middle of the process can easily catch up with the group's thinking. And being able to represent the team's thinking process is important because what we learn during the process often contributes more to our understanding than just learning the final conclusion.

Using the same medium for collective work moves the center of attention from individual team members to the problem itself. It minimizes the problem of disagreements that might be perceived as personal attacks. Since conversation often creates confusion, having a visual object (a model in the case of group decision making) can reduce the confusion. The model is an object that can be manipulated, arranged, polished, reorganized, and improved by the group. As collaboration finishes, the model becomes a group creation that can be shared and documented for later review. Because a model tells a story better than a detailed narrative, it conveys more information to top management, making it easier to gain their support or for the issue to be reviewed and revised as the need arises.

The AHP/ANP, with its supporting DecisionLens software or SuperDecisions software, facilitates the collaboration process all the way from structuring the decision problem to presenting its outcome. It is a systematic process that helps a group leader orchestrate the process of engaging people so they can contribute their ideas to produce the best results.

Effective Decision Making

Effective group decision making addresses both task-oriented goals and relationship goals by managing the group process [23]. An effective method needs to address the following major issues:

1. *The goals may be ambiguous.* Telling a group to solve a certain problem does not mean they will know exactly what they are expected to deliver at the end of the process. This is the first thing to be discussed and agreed upon. With the AHP it may take the form of specifying the goal and the kind of alternatives to be evaluated.

2. *It may be hard to ensure perfect attendance,* especially when team members are separated by great distances. The AHP/ANP, with its supporting software, can allow people to work in virtual teams that transcend distance, time zones, and organizational boundaries.

3. *Task-oriented goals (content) and members' relationship goals (process) are inextricably linked.* The AHP/ANP provides a tool to enhance the

collaborative relationship.   It shifts the focus of attention from individual members talking about the problem to the problem itself and helps prevent ego issues from distracting the process.

4. *Although a team leader sets the agenda and shepherds the process, the leadership often actually rotates.* The systematic process of structuring an AHP/ANP model helps a group leader to guide the rotation of leadership roles in line with progress on the task at hand.

5. *Any group decision making takes a lot of time.* Applying the AHP/ANP takes time, too, but it makes group decision making on a complex problem intrinsically efficient. It actually will take less time than an unstructured process of discussion that goes on and on without closure.

6. *It is hard to keep a group focused.* The model, however, is both a record for the status of the task and the means to bring the group back on track should they get derailed in a discussion.

7. *The group fails to learn by reflecting on the group process.* Reviews of the model together with careful documenting can provide the group with highly summarized information for learning.

8. *Personal agendas get in the way of group consensus.* With the AHP/ANP, a decision emerges from pairwise-comparison judgments on each of which it is usually easier to get agreement.

Group Decision Making with the AHP/ANP

The AHP/ANP, with its supporting software, is helpful to a group leader in many ways. First, the group should generally be excited about their new assignment. Everybody should be committed to making a contribution, and many may have some idea as to how to do it. Some may be knowledgeable about the problem but feel overwhelmed by it.   Group passion can be both exciting and tiring, however, because in the early stages the group may have neither a clear common objective nor any structure in the discussion. The group needs to set clear objectives and milestones to measure progress. The leader needs to focus on the objectives but at the same time must be open to different viewpoints and try to involve everyone in the process – promoting a non-threatening environment that stimulates the free flow of ideas and minimizes conflict as the group is encouraged to look for common ground to resolve its differences.

The AHP/ANP makes group decision making intrinsically efficient for at least three reasons. First, it provides a framework for group collaboration and tools that systematize the group process. Second, it enables the group to break the task into a set of subtasks and distribute them to the appropriate members or subgroups.   Each can then work almost independently – minimizing the manpower required and allowing various group techniques to be used such as brainstorming and morphological analysis while still keeping them integrated within the larger unifying model. And third, it provides feedback measures to help the group improve their judgments while allowing a certain degree of inconsistency. The group may also decide to do a quick and cursory evaluation to explore what the likely outcome will be or to streamline the number of judgments. Accepting a certain level of inconsistency will also save time. It is important to run a sensitivity analysis to ensure that the final priorities of the favorite alternatives are not too close.

Consider the following case. A team of consultants was asked to give advice on restructuring a company with a head office located in the state and operations throughout the state. Working with a team of counterparts from the organization, the consultants agreed that the general idea of establishing several branch offices would lead to more effective operations. They realized, however, that they had to clarify the main roles of these branch offices with respect to the head office before moving on to details of the company's structure. The consultants and the counterparts identified two separate strategies for the role of the branch offices and agreed on the criteria for selecting the best one. After analyzing the options they seemed to agree on the trade-offs needed to make the selection. When it came to judging which strategy was the best, however, the consultants and the counterparts differed. Even more troublesome was the fact that the consultants' opinion, although it had been reasoned objectively and independently, happened to align with the inclination of the company's top management. This situation raised a potential conflict as the counterparts began to wonder whether the consultants were really giving an independent recommendation.

At this stage the consultants suggested using the AHP to arrive at a group outcome. First they structured the decision problem in a hierarchy with the goal at the top, criteria at the middle level, and the two alternatives at the bottom. The process of providing judgments was rather easy since there were no significant differences between the two parties with regard to the relative importance of the criteria and their relative preference of the alternatives with respect to each criterion. The counterparts, who represented the decision makers in the organization, were given more say in the judgments regarding the relative importance of the criteria. The consultants served as experts by evaluating the alternative strategies with respect to each and every criterion; the counterparts had the decisive say in judging the relative priority of the criteria. Despite the apparent bias in the deliberations, this exercise produced an outcome that was ultimately the same as the one the consultants had recommended

One problem was that the method had been applied without adequately introducing the theory to the counterparts. They were not familiar with the method and were suspicious about how the judgments were synthesized to get the outcome and to what extent the outcome was valid. The consultants addressed their concern by inviting them to estimate the relative areas of different shapes. After their judgments were processed by the software and they could see a reasonable estimation of the actual areas, the counterparts gained confidence in the method and trusted its outcome regarding the best role for the branch offices. They now supported the consultants' earlier conclusion.

Now that they had the decision model, the consultants could present the reasoning behind the choice and explain how they arrived at that outcome, which improved top management's confidence in the decision. The process of structuring the model promoted common understanding between the consultants and their counterparts, validated top management's inclination, and contributed to a more productive consultation overall.

Group Leadership Techniques

Along with the AHP/ANP models, there are group leadership techniques that a skilled facilitator can apply.

1. *Have the group defer judgments on controversial issues, or use structured communication techniques.* The AHP automatically employs the concept of deferred judgment. In its use of brainstorming it separates the process of problem structuring (which in turn consists of listing the elements of the problem and deciding which level things belong on) from judgment elicitation, evaluation, and analysis. The group can conduct brainstorming, use the structured communication process known as NGT (nominal group technique), or conduct Delphi sessions [24] to identify alternatives and criteria efficiently. During problem structuring, differences with regard to the hierarchy do not need to be resolved. This is a win/win disagreement. The group should be focused on locating elements in the hierarchy rather than arguing too early whether or not an element in fact belongs in the hierarchy. If some elements do not fit logically in a hierarchy, consider adding another hierarchy. (Sometimes a single problem may have separate benefits, opportunities, costs, and risks hierarchies.)

2. *Construct a simple but comprehensive model.* Using the right size of hierarchy, not too large and not too small, can smooth the judgment elicitation process. If the structure is too deep, the leader needs to encourage the group to remove some of its levels – as long as ambiguity does not result that might create difficulties in eliciting judgments. Agreeing on a pairwise-comparison judgment signals the end of the discussion. Members do not have to agree on the reasoning behind the judgment.

3. *Use the appropriate techniques when there are differences.* Conventional group decision making is often demanding because people expect to

decide on alternatives through discussion alone. Such discussions may turn into a kind of win/lose argument where group members take sides and dig in.

The AHP's systematic approach lets the group see where the problems lie so they can be addressed at different stages of the process using different techniques. Structuring the hierarchy captures the group's understanding of different elements of the problem and hence the possible source of differences. Using the structure and the pairwise- comparison method to elicit judgments narrows the possible source of differences considerably. Clearly it is easier to reach consensus on comparing two things than on many things at once. The AHP makes it even easier to compare two things by not requiring a group to reach total consensus on a judgment. Instead, a combined judgment can be produced by taking the geometric mean of the individual judgments, though prudence suggests that discussion is needed when the judgments are widely disparate and that automatic use of the geometric mean should be avoided.

If there are relatively small differences, the leader may use one of the following techniques:

- Obtain the composite of individual judgments by taking their geometric average, the only credible way to aggregate judgments with the AHP.
- Take a judgment that is most consistent with the rest of the judgments that are agreed on.
- Look at each individual set of judgments and see if they make a difference in the outcome, possibly by using the AHP's compatibility measure.

Larger differences may indicate that there are other sources of difference and the solution may be to expand the hierarchy. If the difference concerns matters of value, the group can use one of the following techniques:

- Select judgments that fit the organization's values.
- Select the judgments of people with the appropriate authority, knowledge, or power. The AHP offers a credible way to aggregate judgments of people with different power.

Discussing the differences first and then appointing certain people to vote can help narrow the range of judgments. The majority is not always right.

Challenges to a Group Leader

The major role of a group leader in this context is to manage the intertwined goals of achieving content and having a smooth process. Although the leader is generally not expected to be an expert in the problem, this person must be an expert in keeping the goal in focus and managing the group process. The group is expected to fulfill its mission and, while doing so, strengthen the bond between team members. A group leader faces several challenges:

1. *Planning meetings.* Studies point out a discouraging trend: Professionals agree that as much as 50 percent of their meeting time is unproductive and that up to 25 percent of meeting time is spent discussing irrelevant issues. Typically they complain that meetings are too long, are scheduled without adequate time to prepare, and end without any clear result. We have all been to seminars that left us feeling inspired and revitalized, but rarely do we leave everyday meetings feeling the same way. The reason is simple: good seminars are organized to engage us while most office meetings are not. Meetings should be the most interesting and productive part of our working day. We can make them interesting and productive by being well prepared and having a well-managed facilitation process to yield inspired and creative results.

    Being well prepared means that our meeting must have a clear, stated purpose and an agenda; participants must be chosen carefully, invited in a professional way, and given sufficient prior information. Preparation also means attention to such details as meeting place, equipment, refreshments, and reminders. Having a well-managed process means that someone is responsible for guiding the meeting, that the plan for the meeting is reflected in the agenda, and that the leader keeps things on track. Inspiration is probably the most overlooked aspect of everyday meetings. Getting people inspired means that we have to allow spontaneity and enthusiasm. We should build in activities that engage participants, use strategies to generate discussion, and rely on visual aids to capture attention. To get a creative result, every meeting should be directed toward certain outcomes that make a difference. We need to feel that something has been accomplished and see how this particular meeting is part of a bigger strategy for the future of the organization. Achievements at one meeting should be useful for the next.

2. *Preventing the group from coming to a conclusion too soon or from getting stuck in endless discussion.* When a group is established, their task is usually stated in terms of an unfavorable situation that needs to be

corrected – such as declining revenue – or the need to seize an opportunity such as expanding the business geographically. The first step is to define the problem carefully, including the goal to be met when the group's decision is implemented.

In a good decision process, the group's spirit of inquiry can drive a divergent mode of thinking. In this case the group examines the situation in terms of what influences a certain outcome and the systemic impact of events. Encouraging this kind of thinking ensures that the group addresses the right problem and can find the most effective strategy for solving it. This process is itself a broad decision problem that can also be addressed using the AHP/ANP.

Once the problem is identified, the questioning spirit can again drive a divergent mode of thinking, but now toward the specific problem. Thoughtful questions from the group leader or others can also move the discussion forward, particularly when the group is trapped in a circular discussion. The systematic process of the AHP/ANP prevents such a deadlock in thinking.

The conclusion needs to emerge from an adequate set of alternatives using careful analysis. Group methods such as brainstorming or brainwriting are called for that generate ideas and elicit questions. The group can then apply the AHP/ANP to structure and evaluate these ideas and converge to an outcome.

3. *Maintaining group focus on the problem and keeping track of the progress.* Without a strong leader guiding the process, it is easy for a group to wander away from the core issue. The AHP/ANP and its SuperDecisions software strongly supports group collaboration because the progress of the discussion can be tracked by everyone involved, which helps the leader control the pace and focus of the meeting. SuperDecisions provides a structured and informative record of the group's progress. Whenever the discussion begins to wander, the leader can simply call attention to the model and ask the group to proceed. By the end of the process, the software model has captured the details and outcome of their collective work.

4. *Managing the balance between team members working together and individually.* The group does not have to work together all the time. In fact, doing so may even hinder the process. Separation gives members a chance to gain perspective and efficiency. Certainly the group needs to work together to structure a problem and develop a strategy to distribute tasks. But then the group can break up to carry out their assignments. In this way the group maintains coherence and the whole

process remains integrated.

One important aspect to consider in allocating tasks is to make a distinction between parts of the problem that require special expertise and those that lie within the domains of the decision makers in the group. The structure intrinsic in the AHP/ANP helps a group leader to distribute tasks and establish smaller groups if necessary. For example, the whole group may want to work together to structure the problem, establish small groups only to elicit judgments for subproblems, assign research for information to people in the small groups, assign somebody to integrate the subgroup judgments into the overall model, and then finally gather the whole group again to study the overall outcome and reflect on whether their model needs to be improved.

5. *Promoting learning during and after the group process.* Group members value the knowledge they derived from a group process more than they value general knowledge. Guided interaction, in structured collaboration with the AHP/ANP, gives members a chance to learn from each other and builds a synergy that enhances the knowledge they gained. The AHP/ANP involves feedback to refine the model and judgments and produce a more reliable outcome. The software can produce a combined group outcome by using the combined group judgment in every case, or an individual outcome by working only with that individual's judgments. This allows each member to examine his perception of the problem if the outcome does not meet his expectations. This is an important feature: An outcome that meets expectations generates support for its implementation; one that does not is not likely to be supported. Learning also increases people's capacity to contribute. Reflection allows the group to evaluate what they have achieved so far and to question whether they are on the right track. Doing so for the whole process may lead to ideas for improving future projects. Finally, sensitivity analysis can be made to find out how stable the final outcome is.

The tangible outcome of the AHP/ANP is information about priorities – not only for the alternatives but for other elements of the problem – and this provides the material needed to facilitate learning for a wider audience beyond those participating in the decision process. It also helps by surfacing and questioning mental models. A well-known beer company was so successful in their business in the home country that they thought it was only a matter of time before they introduced their product in a neighboring country. Just as they had been successful in getting the necessary permits to expand their business in their own country, they were certain they would be able to do the same elsewhere. After spending a couple of days using the AHP with representatives of top management, however, they learned that for many reasons, political and otherwise, their government was not eager to help them expand to foreign markets. They immediately ended the meeting and went home to work on persuading the government to grant them greater cooperation – something they had only given a passing thought. They simply assumed that things would work out the same way as in the past.

6. *Ensuring fair decision making.* A decision-making process that is fair is satisfying to members and keeps morale high. Fairness does not mean each member has to be treated equally all the time; after all, they are not equal in terms of expertise and authority. The AHP/ANP assigns different priorities to the people providing judgments. Having a way to recognize the relative importance of expertise and authority is fairer for ensuring the quality of the group's work and thus fairer to the members themselves.

7. *Seeing that the group works in the best possible surroundings.* Group thinking is enhanced by having excellent resources, physical and social, made available to them. Working in a beautiful new location can inspire ideas.

Types of Decision Problems

There are different kinds of decision problems – selection, prediction, and resource allocation, for example. Most decision-making methods are designed for a *selection* problem: choosing the best among a set of alternatives. But there are other kinds of decision problems – predicting what the future holds, for example. With regard to the measurement scale used to make the judgments, only methods such as the AHP/ANP that use cardinal measurement can produce meaningful outcomes. With the AHP/ANP, the process involves the following basic steps:

1. State the problem. Frame the problem in as broad a context as possible. State the goal to be met by implementing the decision.
2. Identify the criteria that influence the problem.
3. Structure a hierarchy of the criteria, subcriteria, properties of alternatives, and the alternatives themselves from the general down to the particular. To remove ambiguity, define every element in the hierarchy carefully.
4. Prioritize the primary criteria with respect to their impact on the overall goal. State the question for pairwise comparisons clearly for

each set of comparisons, that is, for each matrix. Pay attention to the orientation of each question – for example, costs go down, benefits go up. When one element is more costly than another, normally it will be less preferred. Prioritize the subcriteria with respect to their criteria.

5. Elicit judgments of relative preference for the alternatives with respect to the lowest level of subcriteria and calculate the overall priority of the alternatives. Select the alternative with the highest priority.

6. Study the results. If they seem questionable, go through the model again to find out why and improve the model if necessary.

Prediction in a stable environment, viewed as "estimating future events," has been approached using forecasting methods that extrapolate from past data using techniques such as regression analysis. Forecasting calls for subjective judgments from the group or experts with a method such as Delphi [25]. It has been shown that the AHP/ANP predicts future events better when they are viewed as the effect of actions taken by the different parties involved. It is a problem in a many-party environment. Hence the model must relate to the environment – comprised of people, their objectives, their policies, and outcomes – from which we derive the composite outcome (the state of the world).

Ensuring a Valid and Useful Outcome

In the previous section we saw how the AHP/ANP with its supporting software addresses group process goals such as enhancing leadership effectiveness, facilitating learning, allowing for prioritizing judgments of group members, and helping resolve conflict. But a reliable theory for group decision making must also satisfy certain content goals to ensure valid and useful outcomes, particularly when predicting [26].

Create a Sensible Decision Structure

The entire AHP/ANP model can be viewed as a description of the problem – which may be to find the best solution, to assess a situation, or to predict the likely outcome of current forces and influences. The AHP/ANP, at least in theory, poses no constraints on how broad and how deep to go with a structure. For effective decision making, though, the model should be neither too broad nor too detailed.

There are many creativity techniques that can be used to generate alternatives for the AHP/ANP model. The process of structuring the model and making the factors explicit, can trigger thinking about what the alternatives should be. Thus with the AHP/ANP the very process of defining and structuring the problem is integrated with designing a solution. After the process is completed, reflection may lead the group back to refining the problem's definition. The AHP/ANP does not impose limits on how groups structure their thinking. A decision making method is essentially about eliciting tacit preferences from the decision makers. The AHP/ANP does not require physical measurements as inputs though such information can be used if it is available.

Use a Reliable Way to Make Judgments

A multicriteria decision making method should make it possible to elicit judgments that faithfully represent the real world and give credible results when synthesized for the complete problem. The group should be able to incorporate differences in status and power among its members and draw on their special expertise to enhance the validity, accuracy, or implementability of the outcome. Having a synthesis rule that produces credible results also means that the mathematical aggregation of judgments must satisfy the rational condition of group aggregation. Finally, there needs to be a way to conduct sensitivity tests evaluating how changes in judgments might alter the results.

Achieve Valid Outcomes

Ultimately the method should generate an outcome that is valid and generally useful for two fundamentally different types of decision – either simply taking the alternative with the highest number (as in the "select the best" kind of problem) or interpreting the numbers as a distribution used in resource allocation or predicting the likelihood of a different future scenario. Validity of the outcome is the bottom line requirement for group decision making. Since the AHP/ANP is a theory of priority measurement the outcome can be used in either type of decision. With the AHP/ANP knowledgeable people can build models, enter judgments, and produce outcomes that match those in the real world.

Find a Credible Way to Aggregate Group Judgments

Consider a voting situation where three people A, B, and C select in a democratic way the best among three candidates X, Y, and Z. The votes enable the people to order the three candidates from the first choice to the third one. Let A, B, and C order the candidates as XYZ, YZX, and ZXY respectively. The winner is determined by the majority of votes. Two voters prefer X to Y, two voters prefer Y to Z, and two voters prefer Z to X. We are generally rational creatures, so if we prefer X to Y, and Y to Z, then we must prefer X to Z.

Unfortunately, majority voting does not produce a rational outcome when relative preferences are expressed in ordinal terms [27]. This phenomenon mentioned in Chapter 1, and with a little more detail here, was formalized by Kenneth Arrow as Arrow's Impossibility Theory which says that it is impossible to derive a rational group choice from individual ordinal preferences with more than two alternatives [28]. Given a group of individuals, a set of alternatives that includes A and B, and the individuals' judgments of preference between A and B, Arrow's four conditions are as follows:

1. Decisiveness: The aggregating procedure must produce a group order.
2. Pareto optimality (unanimity): If all individuals prefer A to B, then the aggregating procedure must produce a group order indicating that the group prefers A to B.
3. Independence from irrelevant alternatives: If all individuals, given a set of alternatives, prefer A to B and, given another set of alternatives, also prefer A to B, then the aggregating procedure must produce a group order indicating that the group, given any of the two sets of alternatives, prefers A to B.
4. No dictator: No single individual determines the group order.

The generality of Arrow's impossibility statements makes any method of ordinal aggregation problematic. Consequently, the outcome of such aggregation depends on the method. In other words: There are many ordinal aggregation methods to choose from, and different methods may give different outcomes. It has been shown that the AHP/ANP, using absolute scales, removes the impossibility once and for all.

Select Knowledgeable Participants

James Surowiecki, author of *The Wisdom of Crowds*, observes: "While big groups are often good for solving certain kinds of problem, big groups can also be unmanageable and inefficient. Conversely, small groups have the virtue of being easy to run, but they risk having too little diversity of thought and too much consensus" [29]. We agree with him that "diversity and independence are important because the best collective decisions are the product of disagreement and contest, not consensus or compromise."

We assume that the group is composed of people who are knowledgeable about the problem. Given a task, the different perspectives of the group need to be elicited and then represented in terms of consensus on a specific goal. The group leader needs to understand the method. The members need to understand at least the basics and trust its validity. Collaboration is a process of producing something tangible, so the group should know what to expect. Numerous AHP/ANP examples can be shown before the group starts its deliberations. If there is a model that addresses a similar problem, they may want to use it as a template. The group may also learn about the problem by examining similar examples. Being familiar with the whole process and accepting it creates a sense of harmony from the start and builds mental alignment.

Stay Open to New Ideas

Every decision requires having alternatives to choose from. A single alternative leaves no room for choice because then the decision is already made. Listing a comprehensive set of alternatives is therefore a critical step in making a good decision. Otherwise, making a decision is like gambling with the unknown. Implementing the scientific method to select the best choice when there are not enough choices will not be of much help. Indeed the best decision may not even be among those alternatives being evaluated.

Not only is devising a set of alternatives essential, but encouraging creativity at this stage makes a breakthrough decision more likely. *Brainstorming* enables a group to generate more alternatives than the traditional way. Brainstorming means that any judgment which may inhibit creativity must be deferred. Despite its wide use, the technique does have limitations and has been modified over the years. One of its modifications is *brainwriting* or *ideawriting* because the use of writing is considered to be better than presenting ideas orally as there is less danger of domination by certain participants. It also encourages people to participate who have trouble expressing their ideas orally. Participants have a chance to phrase their ideas clearly in writing beforehand or allowing them to be recorded. The method will not work, however, if people are unwilling to express their ideas in writing. It works best with small groups, so big groups need to be broken into smaller groups in parallel sessions. After a proper introduction is given and a stimulating question is asked, group members write their initial response on a given form. They then react in writing to each other's forms. After each participant reads the comments, the small group discusses the principal ideas that emerge from the written interactions and summarizes the discussion in writing.

Other modifications of brainstorming include *bug lists* and *negative brainstorming* (generating complaints to identify weaknesses), the *Crawford blue slip* method (independently brainstorming in response to a number of questions that are related to a problem), and free discussion among group participants. Brainstorming has been used in complex problems to generate questions rather than solutions. The outcome is a list of questions that the group decides to pursue to move the process forward.

Assign Roles

Decision making is the art of managing the iterative process of divergent and convergent thinking aimed at doing the right things right. *Divergent* thinking needs knowledge and creativity; *convergent* thinking needs organized thought with purpose and direction. This focused outcome may again be subject to the next divergent thinking process. Too much divergence breaks collaboration down, and too much convergence leads to narrow and short-term actions. Thus the group needs a strong leader and a structured method to balance the two.

Belbin [30, 31] argues that a group should have diversity in its team roles. Interestingly, his finding suggests that having more than one creative Plant in a group or having a Shaper as the group leader may actually reduce the group's effectiveness. It is not always easy for an organization to establish a team whose members have both the relevant knowledge regarding the task at hand and complementary characteristics so they can take on the necessary team roles. The AHP reduces the need for such diversity. While most people have a strong tendency toward a certain role, many also have the flexibility to take on different roles. The AHP/ANP can be used to help people shift roles. The ideal person to apply the AHP may be the participative Coordinator, for example, as opposed to the more directive Shaper, since the AHP is usually applied when the group is not pressed to make an urgent decision. Even so, a Shaper may find that using the AHP can help him to be more of a Coordinator. He can use his directive strength to help the group succeed rather than driving it to a certain outcome. A Shaper is usually more content-oriented, so he can learn to clarify issues as the group structures the task at hand. The problem of having more than one Plant is reduced because having more alternatives is generally a good thing. Moreover, with the AHP/ANP the decision is derived from the collective judgments, not by following some strong individual directly to a certain conclusion. The systematic process of the AHP helps a person with flexibility to pick the proper role at the proper time.

Seek Outside Expert Assistance

A group may think that it needs an expert's assistance to come to a better decision. Experts are outsiders who do not belong to the group, although they may come from within the organization. The advantage of using experts is that it improves the quality and reliability of the decision without burdening the group with too many specialists or having to worry about how they relate personally to a particular expert.

A group usually invites experts to evaluate alternatives or elements in the model that have already been identified by the group. These evaluations may include quantitative or qualitative judgments. For example, a multinational company may want to open a new branch in a foreign country and therefore establishes a group to recommend which country. The group may be able to make a short list of preferred countries together with a set of selection criteria and their relative importance, but they may not have enough information or experience to judge how well the alternatives meet the criteria. Or perhaps they have made some initial evaluations but are not so sure about them. In this case, they may want to invite experts to make the judgments for them or to validate their initial judgments. Although two experts in the same field may not necessarily have the same judgments about things in their domain of expertise, we can hope that their judgments will not differ by much.

The group may also seek help from experts to develop alternatives by constructing different objectives or suggesting courses of action. The group may ask the experts not only to establish alternatives but to evaluate them as well. The group itself must develop the criteria and judge their relative importance, however, because they represent what the organization values most.

Given a set of alternatives to be evaluated, the group may then face the problem of deciding whom to invite. They may already have a list of reliable people they have worked with in the past. If not, the group has to make the decision – a simple example of interdependence in group decision making. The experts they choose will depend on the problem they have, and the outcome of the problem will depend on the judgments of the experts. The group may select experts based on their experience, the quality of their past work, and suggestions from members or other people. The group must be aware, however, that even the most qualified expert may not know it all.

Effectiveness and Reliability

A general method for group decision making must give a facilitator the means to lead the group and achieve its goals. The method must enhance individual and group learning. It should enable the group to solve problems and make incremental improvements based on past performance and knowledge. It should also urge them to question their assumptions for a breakthrough in knowledge. Systematic development of alternatives means that the group must not view a problem too narrowly to ensure a meaningful solution or too broadly to ensure controllable actions. It also means that the group must be able to define a set of distinct alternatives with the proper degree of abstraction. A group of top executives, for example, would view a problem from a higher level of abstraction than a group of operational managers. Analysis of alternatives means that the group must have a model with the appropriate breadth (for relevance) and depth (for precision). Successful analysis depends on faithfulness of judgment elicitation, psychophysical applicability, and the depth of the analysis. In some methods, for example, you must first accept the premise that eliciting judgment by comparing two alternatives with respect to a certain property will produce the most faithful representation of your tacit preferences.

A faithful judgment can be obtained if:

- It is expressed directly by the decision maker rather than derived from some other form of judgment.
- The decision maker cannot tell how that particular judgment will ultimately affect the outcome and hence he cannot manipulate it to influence the outcome, thus preventing making mischievous judgments.
- The decision maker has the option to express preference relations numerically (for representing objective measurement), verbally (for representing perception or feeling), or even graphically.

Depth of analysis refers to how well an analytical method guides a decision maker's thinking to ensure the validity of the outcome. It includes, for example, having a feedback mechanism for making adjustments or directing the decision maker to an outside expert. Fairness is addressed not only during group interaction but when information from different individuals must be mathematically aggregated into one judgment for the group. For this criterion, we are only concerned with the method of aggregation, since group discussion is likely to be controlled by the leader.

With regard to resource allocation, a decision theory must allow the group to separate the alternatives with cardinal numbers rather than simply order them. Indeed the members themselves may need to be weighted as to the reliability of their opinions. Other parties who may be affected by the decision often need to be considered, too, and a successful method must have a way to include their judgments.

Most significantly, we add, a method must be generally applicable, valid (capable of being scientifically validated), and reflect the truth advocated by those who provide the judgments. Thus we are concerned with issues like these: Is the method applicable in conflict resolution? Does it apply to intangibles in the same way it does to tangibles? Does it have mathematical validity and generality, and is it supported with axioms and theorems? Can the method be applied to psychophysical measurement? And is the outcome valid – ensuring, for example, reliability in prediction?

To be applicable to conflict resolution the method must provide a way for each party to evaluate the costs and the benefits of giving up something in return for getting something from the other party. Applicability to intangibles refers to measurement of the multidimensionality of the factors involved. Mathematical validity and generality call for a formal mathematical representation of the reasoning behind a theory and economy in the assumptions required for its generalization. Psychophysical applicability means that an analytical method must deal with the measurement of relationships between the physical attributes of stimuli and the resulting sensations reflecting diminishing response to increasing stimulus, such as, that described by the Weber-Fechner law. Validity of the outcome involves the accuracy of the outcome in predictions. We need to be careful, however, to define what constitutes a prediction situation. In an experimental study, Schoemaker and Waid [32] showed that guesswork with direct estimation of the rank of multicriteria objects produces a very different ordinal ranking than that of the cardinal ranking produced by another method. Following are some of the reasons the AHP / ANP are so effective.

Group maintenance: leadership effectiveness. Group leadership ranges from the autocratic to the democratic. We assume that the group works mostly with moderate situational control in terms of leader/member relations, task clarification, and status. The ideal method is one that not only encourages group collaboration but also provides the necessary control mechanism to guide the leader in pursuing the group's goals. It should also offer the means for structuring group knowledge and technical computations that do not involve much interaction or leadership. The highly systematic approach of the AHP/ANP means it satisfies this criterion.

Group maintenance: learning. We assume that objective knowledge is considered less important by the people involved in the group than what they know from their own experience. Learning ranges from acquiring objective knowledge, which has little to do with group members' subjective values, to improving their understanding of cause-effect relations in a problem and questioning the underlying assumptions behind certain decisions or actions. The AHP/ANP provides a compact description of the problem that facilitates learning beyond membership of the group. In an experimental study participants ranked the AHP as the least difficult and most trustworthy method among those studied. And the easier to apply and the more trustworthy a method is, the more we can learn from its application.

Problem abstraction: scope. The need to abstract a problem or define it is at the core of all decision making. Modeling is a common approach to this process. Simplification is inherent in modeling, however, as it is used to promote understanding. An ideal method would broaden the scope of problem abstraction without posing constraints on the complexity of group thinking. The AHP/ANP enhances problem abstraction, but it must be combined with other techniques to broaden it. Morphological analysis, for example, with its systematic search for combinations of attributes, may produce more alternatives and help to uncover the assumptions hindering implementation of the suggested solutions.

Problem abstraction: development of alternatives. Alternatives are not usually given to the group; hence problem structuring must go through a process of selecting alternatives. We assume that multicriteria methods allow a certain degree of interaction among group members. Problem abstraction may or may not lead to a set of alternatives. With the AHP/ANP, however, the level of problem abstraction provides the opportunity to question whether the alternatives are appropriate for that level of abstraction. Applying creativity techniques such as brainstorming can improve the quality of the alternatives for an AHP/ANP model. It has been reported, however, that brainstorming is the least effective technique. Morphological connection has been found to be mostly useful for new product or new system development. The nominal group technique (NGT) and the Delphi method can be used to align group members' perceptions.

Structure: breadth. A structure is said to be broad if it has many distinct elements (criteria) that are assumed to be independent of each other. A problem that is modeled by more than one such structure is considered to be even broader. The AHP/ANP theory does not limit the number of criteria considered in the analysis. This is up to the decision makers. Although too broad a structure with too many elements increases inconsistency in judgments, the AHP/ANP provides a way to deal with this issue.

Structure: depth. A structure is said to be deep if each element is broken down into sub-elements, each sub-element into sub-sub-elements, and so on down to the most detailed elements. The AHP/ANP theory does not limit the level of detail with respect to breaking down criteria into subcriteria, sub-subcriteria, and so on.

Analysis: faithfulness of judgments. A judgment is said to be faithful if it is a valid and accurate representation of the decision maker's sense of order. The AHP/ANP way of deriving priorities is a proven method for eliciting faithful judgments – as shown by the rigorous validation of its Fundamental Scale and its many applications in prediction that produce accurate results. Judgments can be expressed in a way that fits the decision maker best (numerically, verbally, or graphically). Objective measurements can also be used to represent judgments.

Analysis: breadth and depth of analysis. The structural flexibility of the AHP/ANP facilitates in-depth analysis of a problem. It also provides inconsistency and incompatibility measures to indicate whether some improvement in judgments is called for and whether some effort to align perceptions among group members is required. Its supporting software indicates the sources of inconsistency and incompatibility and offers a means to conduct a sensitivity analysis.

Fairness: cardinal separation of alternatives. Cardinal separation of alternatives refers to the aggregation of individual judgments. As we have seen, Arrow's theorem indicates that ordinal preference relations do not treat the alternatives fairly. The AHP/ANP use of an absolute scale, however, removes Arrow's barrier.

Fairness: prioritizing of group members. With group decision making there may be times when the group wants to apply the concept of fairness to its members. For example, the group may wish to assign weights to the members according to the relevance of their expertise, their previous contributions to the goal, or their knowledge about certain criteria. With the AHP, it is up to the decision-maker to determine what concept of fairness is appropriate. A hierarchy can be structured with all the different members at the bottom. The criteria levels may include responsibilities or expertise that can then be used to prioritize the members.

Fairness: consideration of other parties and stakeholders. The AHP is the only well-known method that explicitly includes other parties' concerns in detail as part of the problem structure and then quantifies them.

Scientific and mathematical generality. The mathematical foundation of the AHP with its axioms is generalized in a natural way to the ANP without additional assumptions.

Applicability to intangibles. The fundamental measurement of the AHP/ANP can be applied to intangibles in a natural way, and the user can decide whether to use relative, ideal, or absolute measurement.

Psychophysical applicability. Psychophysical applicability involves the issue of stimulus/response. The AHP/ANP addresses it without adding complexity to a model. It has been shown with many examples that its priority-scales approach has produced measurements of responses to physical stimuli that correspond closely to the normalized values of physical measurement.

Applicability to conflict resolution. A method must offer a way to find the best solution for a group conflict – a solution that is understandable, acceptable, practical, and flexible. The desire to be secretive makes it hard to use such a clear step-by-step approach, however, so people often resort to less structured and less explicit methods. The AHP/ANP makes it possible for them to work out their solutions separately, and then debate, weighting as necessary, to combine their final priorities into a final group outcome.

Validity of the outcome (prediction). We can evaluate the strength of the AHP/ANP and prove its validity. The AHP/ANP's reliance on absolute scales that are derived from paired comparisons enables us to model a problem by ordering its elements and levels in a finely structured way to legitimize the significance of the comparisons. Sometimes, however, a method does not perform as intended. Instead of directing decision makers to profitable investment, for example, a series of experiments indicated that use of the Boston Consulting Group (BCG) matrix increases a person's likelihood of selecting a less profitable investment due to misuse of the method. Several applications of the AHP/ANP to presidential elections, turn-around of the US economy, and to projected values of currencies versus the dollar, and even to the outcome of sports competition, indicate that the details included in the structure and the expertise used to provide the judgments produce surprisingly close numerical outcomes to what actually happened many months later.

Conclusion: Collaboration and the AHP/ANP

Group decision making is essentially a process of turning many individual preferences into a decision by the group. Prior to the AHP, a theory for aggregating people's cardinal preferences was considered unfeasible if not impossible. Arrow's barrier created a distinction between procedures for electoral or social choice and those of decision making in organizations. The former generally use formal approaches (normative, quantitative, axiomatic science) with well-formulated voting questions representing the decision problem and assuming no interpersonal interactions among people in the population. The latter rely on intensive interactions among individual members, depending on the complexity of the problem, and it is here that the term "group decision making" is usually used. Such a group can be considered a synergistic group; its task is to combine the knowledge of its members to come to a collective outcome. Involving practically no quantitative method, it is a synergistic approach that is made possible because the group members come from the same organization – implying the existence of common objectives that make them interdependent.

The AHP has removed Arrow's barrier and hence makes it possible to link the two otherwise unconnected worlds of electoral choice and group decision making. The AHP has been used to integrate voting with discussion and thereby creates a hope that somehow a more synergistic approach can be applied in the formal political decision making that now only uses yes or no voting. Synergistic voting is a formal process that includes representation of common objectives that belong to the same community.

Although it may not be realistic to expect that such a voting process will be implemented in the near future, we can speculate on how the AHP makes it feasible. The AHP opens up a wide range of ways to vote, at least from the methodological point of view. Voting on a set of alternatives can be grouped into three key approaches:

1. *Direct comparison (single-criterion problem).* Rather than assuming that one alternative is preferred infinitely more than the others, as is implied in ordinary election voting, we can elicit voters' pairwise-comparison judgments using the AHP's Fundamental Scale. The procedures range from assuming consistency (by eliciting the minimum number of judgments) to ensuring consistency (by allowing full judgments with inconsistency feedback and revised judgments).

2. *Multicriteria voting (given predetermined criteria and their priorities).* Voters evaluate the alternatives with respect to each of a predetermined set of criteria with given priorities. Aggregation is done at the level of alternatives. The range of procedures is the same as in direct comparison.

3. *Full multicriteria voting.* Voters can be asked either to judge the priority of a given set of criteria by making pairwise-comparison judgments or to specify their own criteria and determine their priorities before evaluating the alternatives. In the first case, aggregation is done at the criteria level; then the resulting priorities are used to obtain the aggregated priority of the alternatives. In the latter case, aggregation is done at the alternative level since the alternatives have been given and are the same for everyone whereas the criteria will probably not be the same.

It seems there will be more and more shifts in the way organizations are managed – from hierarchical structures with a static scope of responsibilities to dynamic team-based structures oriented toward project tasks. At the end of the continuum are collaborative organizations, where effective coordination is designed with shared decision making and then implementation. Collaborative processes are at the heart of this kind of organization: Multiple perspectives are used, synergies are promoted, and commitments are nurtured. Their concerns are how groups of people work and learn together as well as how different groups align themselves and learn from each other.

Implementing a collaboration culture breaks down the vertical and horizontal walls of the traditional organizational silos based on the assumptions that specialization works best and conflict is unproductive and hence needs to be prevented. Traditional organizations are divided into functional units such as marketing, production, and administrative support. Walls are built by having distinct job descriptions for each function that specify responsibilities and authority. Cross-functional coordination is achieved by observing a strict discipline that clarifies who does what to perform every business process.

A look at world-class organizations today will tell us that these assumptions are no longer valid. This is not to say that unique expertise is not important anymore; rather, the rigid boundaries of authority that come with each silo are getting blurrier. People's expertise no longer corresponds exactly to what is required by their jobs. A world-class collaborative organization still focuses on business results – but without breaking jobs down into a set of independent functional responsibilities. Rather, the organization creates value by aligning different units to perform their specific roles. A conscious effort is made to build the employees' sense of ownership and discipline. Flexibility is embedded in the organization's policies, and procedures are put in place that emphasize personal accountability. Organization members learn from managing complex trade-offs and balancing their thinking between broadening their view of a problem and converging to a solution.

In one of the rare fully developed collaborative organizations, core groups of three to eighteen members emerged. They work across the boundaries of disciplines, plants, and countries. Decisions are made at all levels of the organization in a highly disciplined way based on a clear set of priorities and trade-off criteria. The AHP/ANP is an excellent means for deploying priorities down through the organization and communicating trade-offs clearly by providing guidelines for developing similar models for operational decisions and ensuring the alignment of efforts made by different parts of the organization.

References

1. Romig, D.A. *Breakthrough Teamwork: Outstanding Results Using Structured Teamwork*. Irwin Professional Publisher, 1996.
2. Romano, N.C. Jr., and J.F. Nunamaker Jr. "Meeting Analysis: Findings from Research and Practice." *Proceedings of the 34th Annual Hawaii International Conference on System Sciences, 2001*.
3. Saaty, T.L. *Fundamentals of Decision Making with the Analytic Hierarchy Process*. Pittsburgh: RWS Publications, 2000.
4. Saaty, T.L. *Theory and Applications of the Analytic Network Process*. Pittsburgh: RWS Publications, 2005.
5. Wapner, L.M. *The Pea and the Sun: a Mathematical Paradox*. Wellesley, MA.: A.K. Peters, Ltd., 2005.
6. Beyerlein, M.M., S. Freedman, C. McGee, and L. Moran. *Beyond Teams: Building the Collaborative Organization*. Jossey-Bass/ Pfeiffer, 2003.

7. Black, J.S. and H.B. Gregersen. *Leading Strategic Change: Breaking Through the Brain Barrier.* Financial Times Prentice-Hall, 2002.
8. Saaty, T.L. and K.P. Kearns. *Analytical Planning: The Organization of Systems.* Oxford: Pergamon Press, 1985.
9. Schwartz, P. *The Art of the Long View: Planning for the Future in an Uncertain World.* Currency, 1996.
10. Kaplan, R.S. and D.P. Norton. *Balanced Scorecard: Translating Strategy into Actions.* Cambridge: Harvard Business School Press, 1996.
11. Kaplan, R.S. and D.P. Norton. *Strategy Maps: Converting Intangible Assets into Tangible Outcomes.* Cambridge: Harvard Business School Press, 2004.
12. Rampersad, H. *Total Performance Scorecard: Redefining Management to Achieve Performance with Integrity.* Butterworth-Heinemann, 2003.
13. Rampersad, H. *Personal Balanced Scorecard: The Way to Individual Happiness, Personal Integrity, and Organizational Effectiveness.* Information Age Publishing, 2006.
14. Bhushan, Navneet, and Kanwal Rai. *Strategic Decision Making: Applying the Analytic Hierarchy Process.* Springer, 2004.
15. Bauer, R.A., E. Collar, and V. Tang, *The Silverlake Project.* New York: Oxford University Press, 1992.
16. Eyrich, H.G. "Benchmarking to Become the Best of Breed." *Manufacturing Systems*, April 1991.
17. Rescher, N. *Pluralism: Against the Demand for Consensus.* Oxford: Clarendon Press, 1993.
18. Schrage, M. *Shared Minds: The New Technologies of Collaboration.* Random New York: House, 1990.
19. Rouse, W.B. and N.M. Morris. "On Looking into the Black Box: Prospects and Limits in the Search of Mental Models." *Psychological Bulletin* **100** (1986): 349-363.
20. Senge, P. *The Fifth Discipline: The Art and Practice of the Learning Organization.* Rev. ed., Currency, 2006.
21. Moore, C. M., *Group Techniques for Idea Building.* 2nd edition. Applied Social Research Methods Series. Vol. **9**. Sage Publications, 1994.
22. Straker, D., *Rapid Problem Solving with Post-it Notes.* Gower Publishing Limited, 1997.
23. Brightman, H.J. *Group Problem Solving: An Improved Managerial Approach.* Business Publishing Division. Georgia State University, 1988.
24. Delbecq, A.L., A.H. Van de Ven, and D.H. Gustafson. *Group Techniques for Program Planning: a guide to nominal group and Delphi process.* Scott, Foresman, 1975.

25. Linstone, H.A. and M. Turoff (eds.). The Delphi Method: Techniques and Applications. Advanced Book Program. Reading, MA.: Addison-Wesley, 1975.
26. Peniwati, K. "Criteria for Evaluating Group Decision-Making Methods." In *Decision Making with the Analytic Network Process: Economic, Political, Social and Technological Applications with Benefits, Opportunities, Costs, and Risks*, edited by T.L. Saaty and L.G. Vargas. Springer International Series, 2006.
27. Barbut, M. "Does the Majority Ever Rule? The Curious Operations of Processes of Rational Decision in Games and Practical Elections." *Portfolio and Art News Annual* 4 (1961): 161-168.
28. Arrow, K.L. *Social Choice and Industrial Values.* New Haven:: Yale University Press, 1963.
29. Surowiecki, J. *The Wisdom of Crowds.* Anchor Books, 2005.
30. Belbin, R.M. *Management Teams: Why They Succeed or Fail.* Butterworth-Heinemann Ltd, 1981.
31. Belbin, R.M. *Team Roles at Work.* Butterworth-Heinemann Ltd., 1993.
32. Schoemaker, P. J. H, and C. C. Waid. *An Experimental Comparison of Different Approaches to Determining Weights in Additive Utility Models. Management Science.* **28** (2) (1982): 181-196.

Additional Reading:

Castellan, N.J. Jr. (ed.). *Individual and Group Decision Making: Current Issues.* Lawrence Erlbaum Associates, 1993.

Micale, F. *Meetings Made Easy: The Ultimate Fix-It Guide.* Entrepreneur Press, 2004.

Pacanowsky, M. "Team Tools for Wicked Problems." *Organizational Dynamics* **23**(3) (1995): 36-52.

Chapter 4

How to Structure a Decision

Are there useful general guidelines in decision theory that can shed light on the process of structuring a decision problem? What general structures are helpful in human thinking and what are the templates for these structures? Finally, how does one recognize relations of dependence and independence among the elements in a decision? Much thought has been given to using the Analytic Hierarchy Process (AHP) to define and structure decision problems and it has been applied to literally thousands of situations. This chapter provides a broad perspective on the subject and includes a discussion of the use of a network system with dependencies and feedback, and the forward and backward hierarchic process of planning. Here we have the top down distribution of influence in the forward process in which existing policies drive the system toward the outcomes. In the backward process, the desired outcomes or scenarios are at the top and the most promising policies to attain them are the decision alternatives at the bottom.

It is no small coincidence to write about creative thinking side by side with decision making. The two subjects work together and are closely intertwined. For more than a dozen years now the first author has been teaching a graduate course to executive MBAs and to graduate business students about creative thinking and problem solving from his book Creative Thinking, Problem Solving and Decision Making [1]. Although ideas of the AHP and its axioms were developed sometime before their counterpart in creative thinking were recorded [2] and became known to the first author, the parallel between the two is nothing short of amazing and affirms the working of our instincts and thinking along a fairly well defined implicit path. It takes little effort to realize that creative thinking is an essential part of decision making. It helps the subject with its four tenets about creativity. They are to brainstorm all the factors that go into a decision. They are then related (synectics) by putting them into groups clusters or components of homogeneous (close identity) elements with respect to the property or criterion being considered (one axiom of the AHP) and pairwise compared with reciprocal values (another axiom of the AHP). The factors are then arranged into a hierarchic or network structures (morphological analysis in creativity that is also the third axiom of the AHP) that can include the goal, objectives, criteria, influential actors and their objectives and the alternatives of the decision (see later). Finally these structures are constantly polished, revised and expanded as needed in the process of arriving at the final best decision (lateral thinking which is the fourth axiom of the AHP with regard to expectations of the outcome and its reliability). We have applied these four operations of creativity on many occasions in individual decisions, in groups gathered for a special purpose as in our hospice example in Chapter 2, in corporate consulting on numerous occasions and even in government and military policy development in Washington and in other nations. Let it be remembered that these two subjects are inseparable and one cannot make a good decision without involving creative thinking at all levels of a decision.

The experienced decision maker, who has been responsible to others for making decisions and justifying them, usually has acquired an intuitive feeling for laying out factors and criteria and alternative outcomes from which he seeks the best choice. Those who have not been responsible to others in the same way will find useful information here about how to structure their decision problems, where to put future time periods, criteria and alternatives, and an explanation as to why certain forms are more appropriate. While the experienced decision maker may not find much that is entirely new to his intuition, still there may be a benefit in having the formal process written down and spelled out.

Hierarchies and Network Systems

A hierarchy is a linear structure in which influence is distributed from the top down like the Figure 4.1 shown below.

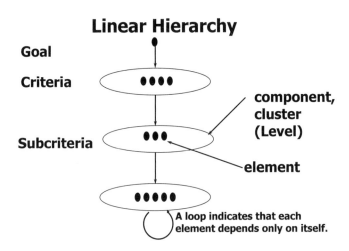

Figure 4.1 A Hierarchic Structure of Components and Elements

The elements of a decision problem are assigned to levels depending on their concreteness, controllability and certainty. Ordinarily the narrower and more concrete are the properties the lower down is the level to which they belong. The less concrete and more general, less controllable, more uncertain and risky are the properties or elements, the higher up is the level to which they belong. In a hierarchy the elements in each level are influenced or controlled by the elements in the level immediately above. Influence is distributed downwards from the top, with the goal having the greatest influence or importance. It has a value of one. This value of one is divided among the elements of the second level, and the values of each of these in turn is divided among those of the third level, and so on down to the level of alternatives of the decision at the bottom.

A hierarchy is an efficient way to deal with complex systems. It is efficient both structurally, for organizing a system, and functionally, for controlling and passing information down the system. Unstructured problems are best grappled with in the systematic framework of a hierarchy or a feedback network which is a generalized form of a hierarchy involving cycles and loops of influence between both elements and levels. Here are two examples that show why a hierarchy is an efficient framework. A person counting 1000 pennies does it more efficiently by arranging them in stacks of ten each and stacks of ten of these stacks and so on. If he makes a mistake or forgets he can recover quickly. Without clustering, a mistake would force him to start again from the beginning. The commander of an army uses a hierarchic organization composed of generals, colonels, majors, captains, lieutenants, sergeants, corporals and privates, to communicate orders throughout his army all the way down to his 100,000 foot soldiers scattered on the battlefield. A hierarchic command structure is what allows the commander to function.

Decision making is a process of planning. To understand the kind of structures that arise in decision making we need to look at planning; using considerable brevity here, but in greater detail and with an in depth example in Chapter 8.

Prediction is a Forward Thinking Process Whereas Decision Making is a Backward Thinking Process

There are two kinds of thinking involved in purposeful decision making: thinking forward and thinking backward [3]. Forward thinking aims at projecting present trends into the future. Given the current forces and influences what is the most likely outcome? By looking backwards we improvise new policies and choose the best among them to help us attain a desired future. Thus decision making is a backward thinking process that must have a clear goal in mind, whether it is preceded by deliberate forward thinking or not. Problems of choice and decision, as opposed to problems of projection, are expressions of desire. They are backward processes in which we set priorities on what is an important goal, and use it to identify the best choice to attain it.

Figure 4.2 illustrates projecting from the present to the likely future and making decisions to overcome difficulties to attain a desired future.

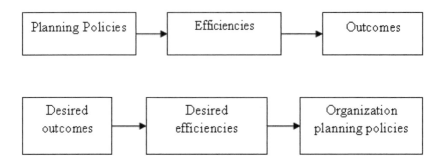

Figure 4.2 Forward Projection and Backward Decision Making

How to Structure a Hierarchy

There are two ways to structure a hierarchy: top down or bottom up as shown in Figure 4.3 below:

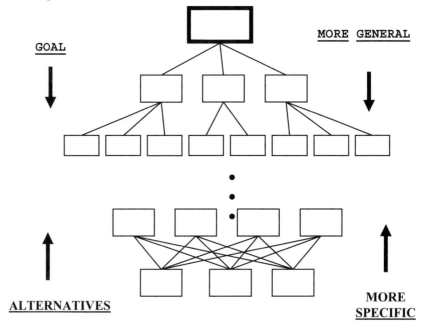

Figure 4.3 How to Structure A Hierarchy: Top Down and Bottom up

The forward process hierarchy takes the general top down form itemized below. To structure it move downward from the universal to the particular, e.g., from criteria to subcriteria; from the uncontrollable to the controllable, e.g., from time horizons and environmental factors to company policies; from the uncertain and risky to the certain and sure, e.g., from scenarios in the upper levels that are broadly drawn as optimistic, status quo and pessimistic to sure, eventual, specific outcomes in the lower levels.

The following is an extensive list of possible levels, in descending order, though the number of levels is usually much abbreviated in practice. It should be noted that each of the levels may itself be subdivided into sublevels as the need arises. For example, a level of criteria may be followed by a level of subcriteria.

The levels of the forward process hierarchy are in the following general top down form:

- Time horizons
- Macro environmental constraints, factors, scenarios or criteria
- Social and political constraints, factors, scenarios or criteria
- The forces which directly influence a system such as a business
- Systems constraints imposed by the forces
- The objectives of the system
- The policies of the system
- The actors who influence those objectives
- The objectives of the actors themselves in case they differ from those of the system
- The policies of the actors
- Stakeholders affected by the policies
- Stakeholder objectives
- Stakeholder policies
- Contrast scenarios for estimating potential outcomes
- Composite or logical scenario which combines features from the various contrast scenarios
- State variables and their measurements to describe the details of the composite scenario from the contrast scenarios.

The levels of the backward process hierarchy are in the following general top down form:

- Anticipatory scenarios, desired or idealized outcomes
- Under the anticipatory scenarios one traditionally includes a level of problems and opportunities.
- Problems involve costs and opportunities involve benefits giving rise to a backward costs hierarchy to allocate effort to policies that solves the problems to attain the desired future, and to a backward benefits hierarchy to assess the benefits of these policies in capturing opportunities
- Actors and coalitions of actors

- Actor objectives
- Actor policies
- Particular stakeholder control policies to attain the desired outcomes; in a simple decision problem these control policies are the alternatives.

To get started on structuring a problem, brainstorm all the elements of the problem from the most general to the most specific, including time horizons, risk competition of actors, stakeholders, and other people and groups affected, and the alternatives of choice. Arrange them in levels according to the following general guidelines:

1. Identify overall objective or goal
2. Identify criteria to satisfy a goal
3. Identify, where appropriate, subcriteria under each criterion
4. Identify alternatives to be evaluated in terms of subcriteria
5. If the subcriteria are too general, immediately above the level of alternatives identify a level of attributes common to the alternatives for their evaluation
6. If the importance of the attributes can be determined in terms of the subcriteria, the hierarchy is finished
7. Otherwise, identify a level of factors above the attributes for evaluation
8. Continue inserting levels until it is possible to link levels and set priorities on   the elements in each level in terms of the elements in the level above it
9. In planning, one can include at the top a level of time horizons and evaluate it in terms of the criteria below and vice versa, a process of interdependence.

Suggestions for learning to structure a decision problem are: 1) Do a simple problem; 2) Look at examples; 3) Look at the two typical hierarchic forms used in planning; 4) Define the overall objective - what question are you trying to answer- 5) Examine your problem as part of several problems under an overall goal; 6) Force a framework. Work from the top down and from the bottom up; 7) Brainstorm the problem by listing every conceivable factor. Organize your ideas hierarchically from the general to the particular; 8) Make certain that you can answer questions about the importance of the elements in a level with respect to the elements in the level above; 9) Formulate written questions you are going to answer in making paired comparisons for each level.

How to Structure a Network

There is a more general way to structure a decision problem involving functional dependence. It consists of components which in turn consist of elements and feedback is allowed between components. A hierarchy is a special case of such a network. In both hierarchies and networks the elements in a component may be dependent on each other. Figure 2 below shows two diagrams which depict the structural difference between the two frameworks. In this figure, a loop means that there is inner dependence of elements within a component.

A nonlinear network can be used to identify relationships among components using one's own free thought associations, relatively unhindered by rules. It is especially suited for modeling dependence relations. Such a network approach makes it possible to represent and analyze interactions and also to synthesize their mutual effects by a single logical procedure

For emphasis we note again that in the nonlinear network diagram or system with feedback of Figure 4.4 below, there are two kinds of dependence: that between components, but in a way which allows for feedback circuits; and the other, the interdependence within a component, in a way which allows feedback loops. We have called these respectively outer and inner dependence.

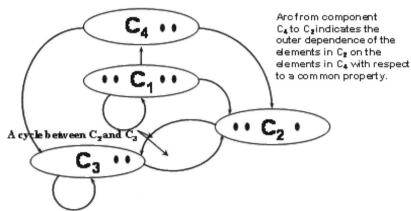

Arc from component C_4 to C_2 indicates the outer dependence of the elements in C_2 on the elements in C_4 with respect to a common property.

A loop in a component indicates inner dependence of the elements in that component with respect to a common property.

Figure 4.4 Feedback Network whose Components Have Inner and Outer Dependence among Their Elements

If the criteria or attributes in a hierarchy cannot be compared with respect to an overall objective because of lack of information about them, they can instead be compared in terms of the alternatives in the level below them by examining each alternative and asking which criterion or attribute is perceived to be more important for the overall integrity well being or behavior of that alternative. The alternatives would naturally be also compared in terms of each attribute as is normally done. The result is a system of two interdependent components.

A holarchy, illustrated in Figure 4.5 is a hierarchy of two or more levels in which the goal is eliminated and what was the second level that used to depend on the goal, now depends on the bottom level of alternatives, thus as a whole the hierarchy is a cycle of successively dependent levels. We have encountered such a form in the analysis of the turn around of the US economy in which the importance of the primary factors is determined in terms of the time periods [4].

Figure 4.5 U.S. Holarchy of Factors for Forecasting Turnaround in Economic Stagnation

Group Structures a Decision Problem

When a group is involved in defining a decision problem as a hierarchy, they can collaborate in constructing the appropriate levels to include all the criteria or attributes anyone suggests including those they think their opponents may want them to include. An elaborate the structure cannot hurt the choice. It is the judgments that determine which alternative is chosen. Thus to construct a rich hierarchy one can invite one's enemies to the process - but not allow them to make the judgments. We include a few illustrations of hierarchies arising in practice and of systems that are self-explanatory.

The purpose is to provide a quick familiarity with decision structures. Many hierarchies have appeared in a coauthored book by the first author called the Hierarchon [5]. It is an extensive dictionary with hundreds of illustrations of decision by different people and of planning hierarchies including portfolio selection and predicting the outcome of chess matches, and other projection processes. Another book coauthored by the first author is known as the Encyclicon [6] which is concerned with network structure of decisions with separate networks for different influence factors (economic, social, political, technical and so on) for benefits, opportunities, costs and risks (BOCR). The many different priority outcomes of the alternatives are then combined into a single overall decision using strategic criteria.

Examples of Structures

Hierarchy for Deciding on Buying or Leasing

The decision regarding company ownership or leasing of a piece of capital equipment (Figure 4.6) depends on its contribution to the company's profitability [7]. This profitability has two dimensions referred to as economic benefits and intangible benefits. The benefits depend on a number of factors that, in turn, depend on certain characteristics of the company. Buying or leasing would promote these characteristics to a varying extent.

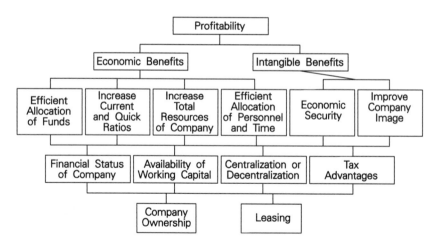

Figure 4.6 Hierarchy for Deciding on Buying or Leasing

By setting priorities for the factors at a certain level with respect to the relevant factors at the previous level and finding the composite priorities, we can find to what extent, relatively speaking, the factors in the same level contribute to the firm's overall profitability. Extending this logic to the question of company ownership or leasing, we can say, in the judgment of the decision maker, which alternative is preferable.

In this example we take the intangible benefits explicitly into consideration for a decision, so the subjective judgments of the decision maker are also considered. This is unlike a conventional exercise where only the hard economic data are considered and then managerial judgment is used in a qualifying manner at the end.

Hierarchy for the Determination of a Strategic Area for the Long-run Growth of a Company

A company aiming at long-run growth needs to decide on a direction to focus their investment [7,8]. The decision hierarchy is shown in Figure 4.7.

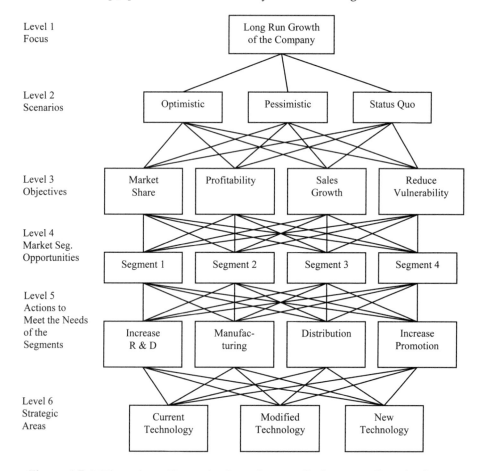

Figure 4.7 A Hierarchy to Determination a Strategy for Long-run Growth of a Company

The alternate strategies are to use current technology, modify current technology or adopt a new technology. They constructed a structure to address the question: What technological direction to follow to ensure the long-run growth of the company? The decision would need to be based on a future scenario of the industry, so they put the three possible scenarios as the most general factors in the structure right below the goal. They specified the long-run growth of the company into four more specific objectives and put them in level 3, to enable them to address the question of which market segments to pursue that is best for achieving the objectives. The actions to meet their needs are located in level 5 that was in turn used to evaluate the strategic areas' three alternatives to support t these actions.

Hierarchy for Choosing a Candidate for Management

To select the proper person to fill a management position, we first identify the four areas of evaluation and then the specific traits to which these areas contribute (Figure 4.8) [7]. Successive stages of priority setting give the overall priorities for the relevant traits in level 3, which represent the relative weights believed to be associated with them for a person to function effectively in that position.

Once all the candidates have been reviewed and the choice has been narrowed down to a few seemingly equal candidates, they may be ranked with respect to each trait. The composite priority for each candidate then represents his or her relative superiority on the basis of overall judgment and is useful in comparing candidates and ranking them in order of preference.

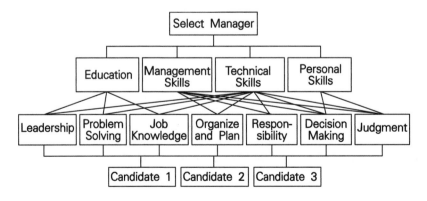

Figure 4.8 Hierarchy for Choosing a Management Candidate

Hierarchy for Evaluating a Division's Performance

There are several dimensions of the performance of a division in a corporation. The principal dimensions to be considered in this evaluation are government dealings, management, imports, and customers (Figure 4.9) [7]. There are several factors for each dimension. Level 3 of the hierarchy shows those pertaining to management alone; other factors can be similarly included for the other dimensions.

The overall priorities of the factors at level 3 are the relative weights by which the evaluators would view performance in that area. Composite priorities of the various divisions with respect to all the factors at this level show the relative performance rating of the division on an overall basis. (This is an example of a complete hierarchy because all the factors at any level relate to all the factors in the next higher level.)

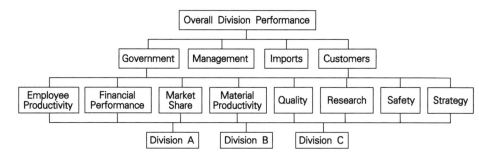

Figure 4.9 Hierarchy for Evaluating Division Performance

Hierarchy to Determine the Level of a Dam: Full or Half-full

The decision on what the level of a dam should be kept can be as elaborate as shown in Figure 4.10 below [7].

This is an example of a structure where different actors are included in the hierarchy. One group of actors is decision makers which is located in the third level of the hierarchy because of their different concerns that affect the outcome of a decision. The other actors are groups who are affected by the decision located in fifth level of the model. The level of the dam need to be determined based on which would serve them the best.

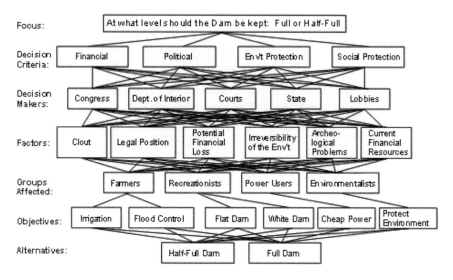

Figure 4.10 Hierarchy for Level of a Dam: Full or Half-Full

Benefit-Cost Hierarchies for Choosing Word Processing Equipment

For the selection of word processing equipment for an office (Figure 4.11), the benefit and cost hierarchies are considered separately and benefit/cost ratios are obtained [7]. The qualities desired of a word processing machine form the second level in the benefits hierarchy, and their priorities represent the relative weights assigned by the user. The equipment characteristics that contribute to these qualities fall in the third level. They are ranked with respect to each desired quality, and the overall priority represents the relative importance of each characteristic. The overall priorities of the brands under consideration represent the relative superiority regarding benefits expected from each.

In the costs hierarchy, likewise, the overall priorities represent the relative weights of the costs. The benefit/cost ratio for each indicates the relative superiority of one machine over the others.

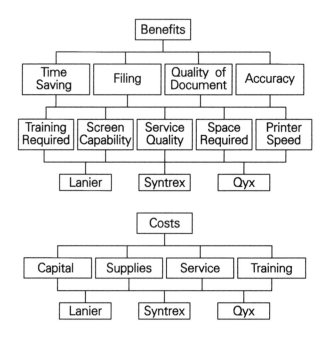

Figure 4.11 Benefits and Costs Hierarchies for Choosing Word Processing
Equipment

**Benefit-Cost Hierarchies for Allocating Resources among R&D
Projects in a Bank**

This decision regarding resource allocation is done as a benefit/cost exercise
involving the benefits expected to accrue from the projects and the costs
expected to be increased thereby (Figure 4.12) [7].

In the benefits hierarchy, the benefits are ranked according to their
impact on the bank's performance. The projects are ranked according to how
far they can generate that benefit. The composite priorities represent their
overall benefit contributions on a ratio scale. In the costs hierarchy, likewise,
the various costs are ranked by their severity (the more costly the higher the
priority) and the projects are ranked with respect to their contribution to that
cost. The resulting composite priorities represent their overall costs. The
benefit/cost ratios measure the superiority of benefit for cost incurred and also
each R&D project's expected attractiveness. Ratios comparing the greatest
marginal benefits to costs are often more useful than simple benefit/cost ratios.
Sometimes discounting of benefits and costs is more realistically done before
forming such ratios.

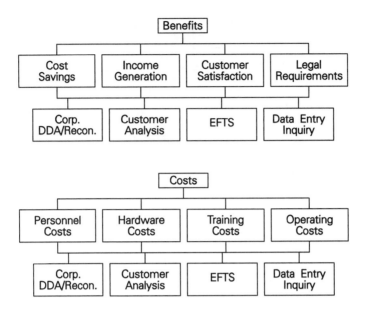

Figure 4.12 Benefits and Costs Hierarchies for Allocating R&D Resources

Benefit-Cost Hierarchies for Making Financial Decisions

To select the best one from a number of financial projects, we may consider the benefits and costs separately (Figure 4.13) [7]. In the benefits hierarchy, three possible scenarios are considered for the future. The company would like to base its decision on a number of considerations whose impact depends on the scenario. Hence the overall priorities will reflect the relative importance of these factors. The projects are ranked according to their contribution to each factor. The composite priorities give relative measures of the benefits accruing from them.

In the costs hierarchy, in a similar way, we find the relative importance of a number of factors the company would like to avoid or minimize, always phrasing the question as, "Which is more costly?" The overall priorities of the projects in this hierarchy, then, give the relative costs of these projects. The benefit/cost ratios give the superiority of the benefits over costs on a ratio scale. The project with the highest marginal benefit/cost ratio is the best selection.

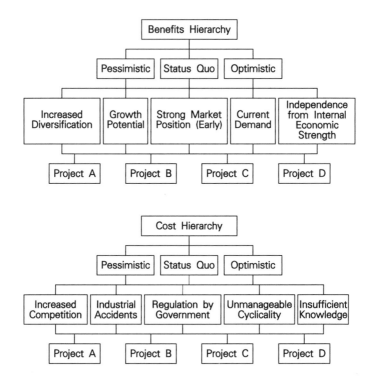

Figure 4.13 Benefits and Costs Hierarchies for Financial Decisions

Hierarchy for Choosing a Mode for Crossing a River

To decide which mode to use for crossing a river would be beneficial to the community as a whole. We consider the nature of benefits envisaged and enlist under each the details (Figure 4.14). Setting priorities for the benefits gives an idea which ones the community regards as important. We can also establish priorities for the costs.

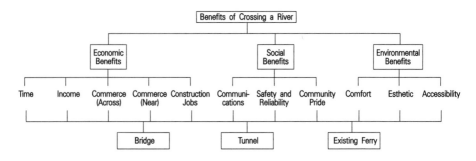

Figure 4.14 Hierarchy for a River Crossing

Hierarchy for Allocating Resources in Juvenile Correction Programs

A group of public officials were interested in juvenile law enforcement and wanted to allocate resources in five programs the staff had suggested. To start with, they considered three principal areas of correction and prioritized them to find out how much attention they should receive (Figure 4.15) [7].

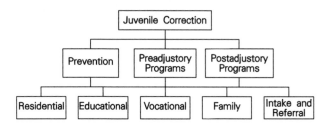

Figure 4.15 Hierarchy for Allocating Resources in Juvenile Correction Programs

Each principal area could be associated with the programs identified, so the programs were prioritized regarding their effectiveness with respect to each area. The overall priorities obtained after weighting by the area priorities show how much relative importance each program commands for the optimum juvenile correction system.

Hierarchy for Analyzing School Busing Conflict

The introduction of busing due to the 1954 Supreme Court ruling has been a source of friction in a certain school district. The minority community wants to introduce complete busing for racial integration at school; the majority community wants segregation to protect the privileged position they now enjoy. To analyze the situation and judge the potential outcome, we rank the stakeholders according to their relative influence on the political scene (Figure 4.16) [7]. Then we prioritize the objectives of each stakeholder to see which objectives weigh more and should thus be pursued in preference to others. The overall priorities give a picture of the relative strengths of the forces at work on the scene.

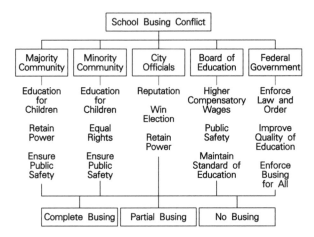

Figure 4.16 Hierarchy for Analyzing School Busing Conflict

The outcomes under consideration here are three scenarios spanning the complete spectrum of possibilities. They are prioritized with respect to each stakeholder objective to find out which outcome is favored by that objective. The overall priorities indicate the relative likelihood that each possible outcome will occur. This exercise shows the interaction of various factors and forces at work, so that if one stakeholder wanted to influence the outcome, he or she could decide accordingly on a course of action such as coalition or persuading others to change their objectives.

Hierarchy for Predicting Likelihood of Technical Innovation

We can investigate the likelihood of technical innovation associated with corporate planning with respect to three forms of corporate control: traditional public ownership, employee ownership, and government ownership. We study the relationship in three representative industries (Figure 4.17) [7].

For each industry, the related corporate factors are prioritized with respect to each form. Next the actors are prioritized with respect to each corporate factor to obtain their relative impact on the factor in question. The objectives of each actor are prioritized to find their relative strengths in influencing decisions, and, finally, the three forms of corporate control are prioritized to indicate how far each would facilitate the objectives in question. Therefore, the overall priorities at this level show the relative likelihood that technical innovation will be fostered by the different forms of corporate control.

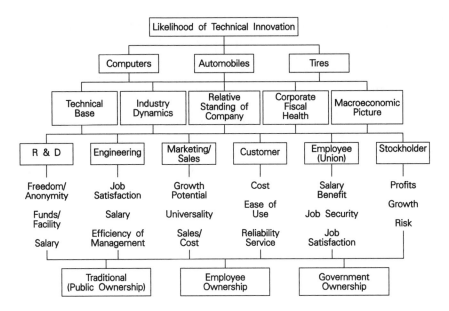

Figure 4.17 Hierarchy for Predicting Likelihood of Technical Innovation

Hierarchy for Predicting the Average Number of Children in a Family

This exercise is carried out to anticipate the average number of children a family is likely to have. Several criteria are considered to influence the number of children in a family: the availability of birth control measures, working mother, older age at motherhood, education of mother, cost of raising children, and social pressure (Figure 4.18) [7].

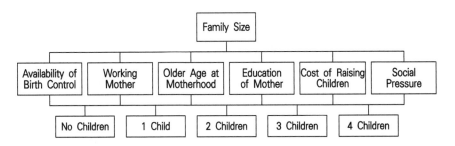

Figure 4.18 Hierarchy for Predicting Average Number of Children

The criteria are prioritized to show the relative degrees of influence they exert. The number of children considered here runs from zero to four. (We assume that the number of families having more children is very small.)

With respect to each criterion, the priority of the number of children is found by ranking on the basis of best judgment. The overall priorities obtained after weighting by the priorities of the criteria reflect the distribution of the number of children in an average family. The expected value of this distribution is the average number of children a family is likely to have.

Network of a Child's Learning System

A child's learning process in the formative years is influenced by many factors. These factors may be classified into certain groups. What is significant, however, is that the various factors interact with and influence one another. Hence we represent them in the form of a system consisting of subsystems and further divisions interacting with one another (Figure 4.19) [7].

By prioritizing the factors in a group with respect to each factor in each group separately, weighting them by the relative importance of the groups themselves, and finding how they influence one another, we can come to a conclusion regarding the intrinsic importance of the various factors bearing upon the child's upbringing.

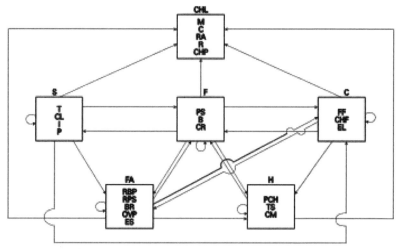

Figure 4.19 Network of a Child's Learning System

The system depicted here consists of five subsystems, which all impact on the child's learning elements (CHL) (motivation, M; creativity, C; reflection ability, RA; retention and assimilation, R; character and personality, CHP).
1. The school (S)
2. The family (F)
3. The community (C)

4. The family atmosphere (FA)
5. The home (H)

The most important components associated with the school subsystem (S) are:
1. Teachers (T)
2. Classmates (CL)
3. Installations (I)
4. Study programs (P)

Those for the family (F) are:
1. Parents (PS)
2. Brothers and sisters (B)
3. Close relatives (those who interact directly with the family) (CR)

Those for the community (C) are:
1. Family friends (FF)
2. The child's friends (CHF)
3. The environmental living characteristics (EL)

Those for the family atmosphere (FA) are:
1. The relation between the parents (RBP)
2. The relation between the parents and the child (RPS)
3. The relation between the child and brothers and sisters (BR)
4. The overprotection of people older than the child (OVP)
5. The family's economic status (ES)

And those for the home (H) are:
1. Physical characteristics (PCH)
2. The child's toys (TS)
3. The communication media (radio and television) (CM)

This model has been evaluated for a certain community, at an average socioeconomic level, in a democratic regime, and for children eight years old with normal psychological characteristics.

Network of a Volleyball Team

Volleyball is a game of teamwork and simple skills, but the players are required to change positions and possess all the skills. Since few players have all the skills to the same extent, the coach has to use players with the proper mix of skills. Thus the coach has to know the relative importance of skills and play the proper combination of players. Since the various skills depend upon one another, we use systems analysis and not hierarchical representation (Figure 4.20) [7].

By prioritizing the skills for a good game of volleyball and prioritizing the players with respect to one another's skills, we get the relative standings of the players and skills in the ultimate analysis. This information helps the coach to select players with basic skills.

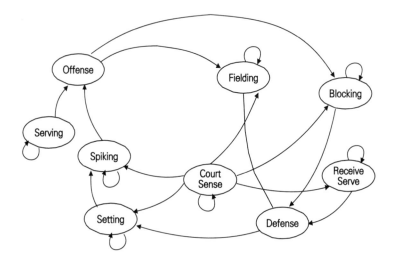

Figure 4.20 Network of a Volleyball Team

Examples: Structures with their Priority Outcomes

Benefit-Cost-Risk Decision Hierarchies for US Sanctioning China

In 1995 ten days before the United States sent a mission to Beijing headed by Mr. Mickey Kantor with the possibility of sanctioning China for copying intellectual property such as videos and compact discs, we did a study to examine the wisdom of sanctioning China for these activities. We constructed three hierarchies one for the benefits to the US to sanction China, one for the costs, and the third one for the risks [4]. They are illustrated in Figure 4.21 below without too much detail. It turned out that while sanctioning China appeared to yield considerably great benefits, the other two hierarchies tended to negate that answer by showing that sanctioning China had the potential of high costs and high risks. This brief analysis was sent to the chief negotiator and several members of Congress for whatever effect it had, the US did not sanction China and we received a telephone call from Mr. Kantor's office congratulating us for the outcome of the study. We exhibit it here along with sensitivity analysis of the outcome in Figure 4.22 which shows that practically in all potential changes in judgments the US should not sanction China.

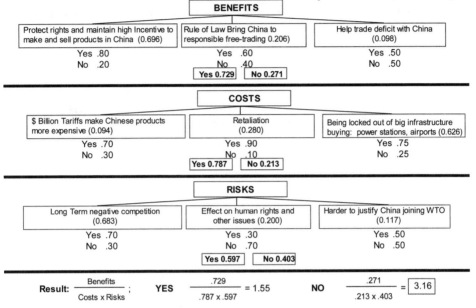

Figure 4.21 Hierarchies for the US sanctioning China

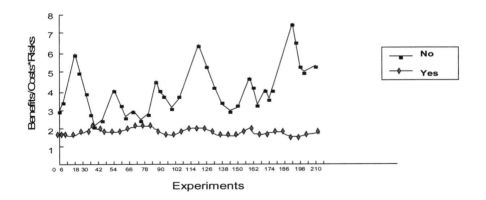

Figure 4.22 Sensitivity of the US Decision on Sanctioning China

Prediction Hierarchy for the Value of Yen/Dollar Exchange

Figure 4.23 shows the hierarchy used to predict the value of the Japanese Yen versus the Dollar. This study was done in the late 1980's [7]. The value of the yen remained stable around the predicted value of 140 for a long period.

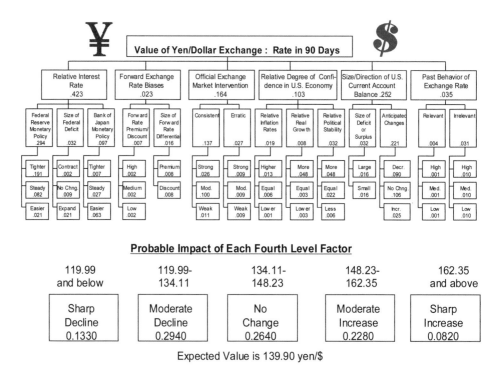

Probable Impact of Each Fourth Level Factor

119.99 and below	119.99- 134.11	134.11- 148.23	148.23- 162.35	162.35 and above
Sharp Decline 0.1330	Moderate Decline 0.2940	No Change 0.2640	Moderate Increase 0.2280	Sharp Increase 0.0820

Expected Value is 139.90 yen/$

Figure 4.23 Predicting the Value of Yen/Dollar Exchange

Prediction Hierarchy for Wins in Chess Matches

Figure 4.24 is an example for predicting the outcome of a world championship chess match. The prediction was that Karpov would win by 6 to 5 games over Korchnoi, which he did [9]. The definitions of the Chess Factors were as follows:

- T (1) Calculation (Q): The ability of a player to evaluate different alternatives or strategies in light of prevailing situations.
- B (2) Ego (E): The image a player has of himself as to his general abilities and qualification and his desire to win.

- T (3) Experience (EX): A composite of the versatility of opponents faced before, the strength of the tournaments participated in, and the time of exposure to a rich variety of chess players.
- B (4) Gamesmanship (G): The capability of a player to influence his opponent's game by destroying his concentration and self-confidence.
- T (5) Good Health (GH): Physical and mental strength to withstand pressure and provide endurance.
- B (6) Good Nerves and Will to Win (GN): The attitude of steadfastness that ensures a player's health perspective while the going gets tough. He keeps in mind that the situation involves two people and that if he holds out the tide may go in his favor.
- T (7) Imagination (IW: Ability to perceive and improvise good tactics and strategies.
- T (8) Intuition (IN): Ability to guess the opponent's intentions.
- T (9) Game Aggressiveness (GA): The ability to exploit the opponent's weaknesses and mistakes to one's advantage. Occasionally referred to as "killer instinct."
- T (10) Long Range Planning (LRP): The ability of a player to foresee the outcome of a certain move, set up desired situations that are more favorable, and work to alter the outcome.
- T (1 1) Memory M: Ability to remember previous games.
- B (12) Personality (P): Manners and emotional strength, and their effects on the opponent in playing the game and on the player in keeping his wits.
- T (13) Preparation (PR): Study and review of previous games and ideas.
- T (14) Quickness (Q): The ability of a player to see clearly the heart of a complex problem.
- T (15) Relative Youth (RY): The vigor, aggressiveness, and daring to try new ideas and situations, a quality usually attributed to young age.
- T (16) Seconds (S): The ability of other experts to help one to analyze strategies between games.
- B (17) Stamina (ST): Physical and psychological ability of a player to endure fatigue and pressure.
- T (18) Technique M: Ability to use and respond to different openings, improvise middle game tactics, and steer the game to a familiar ground to one's advantage.

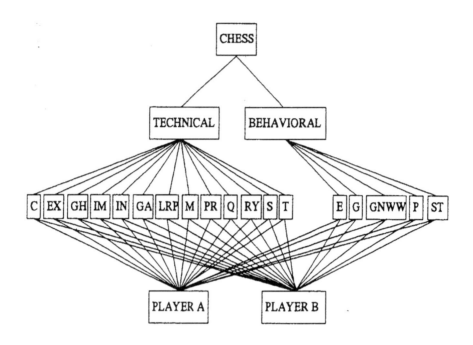

Figure 4.24 Predicting the Outcome of a Chess Games

Decision Network for Determining the Form of Globalization that Best Fits Company X (in 2002)

Many companies face the option to expand their business and venture into a brand new global market. Deciding on entering another market can be very time-consuming and can end up bankrupting a firm if it does not properly choose and execute the correct globalization strategy. When a company is considering globalization, it must properly weigh many key factors in the decision. Some of these factors are tangible and easily identifiable, while others are intangible and more difficult to quantify. The first decision a company has to make is whether it will be beneficial to globalize at all. If a company decides to globalize, it must choose between three alternatives [6]. The approach was to use a complex ANP model with strategic criteria and with separate Benefits, Opportunities, Costs and Risks sub-networks, referred to as the BOCR subnets.

ALTERNATIVES: Globalization, Globalization via acquisition, Joint globalization, No globalization.

BOCR Weight Development

The strategic criteria are given in Figure 4.25. The ratings in Table 4.1 are used to rate the respective highest value alternatives against the strategic criteria and derive the BOCR weights: the b, o, c, and r values in Table 4.2.

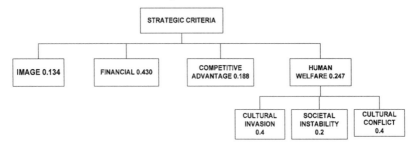

Figure 4.25 Strategic Criteria for BOCR Ratings

Table 4.1 Strategic Criteria and Rating Scale

Image	Financial	Competitive advantage	Cultural invasion	Societal instability	Cultural conflict
high	none	extreme	non-existent	extreme	very high
med	low	high		high	high
low	moderate	moderate	slightly	medium	moderate
	breakeven	neutral	medium	low	low
	high	low	high		non-existent
	extreme	detrimental			

As shown in Table 4.2, the best outcome using either formula is Globalization via acquisition. Note that this is a generalized model that can be tailored for the individual unique needs of a firm. Sensitivity analysis shows that at any priority level above 0.44 for costs, or at any priority level above 0.65 for Risks, the optimal result is Globalization. Figure 4.26 shows the criteria and the networks.

Table 4.2 Overall Outcome

Alternatives	Benefits 0.2803	Oppor-- tunities 0.2850	Costs 0.1978	Risks 0.2368	Outcome BO/CR	Outcome bB + oO −cC - rR
Globalization	0.5919	0.3478	0.4920	0.3114	0.6107	0.1765
Globalization via acquisit.	1.0000	0.4353	0.6223	0.3593	1.0000	0.4919
Joint global.	0.9689	1.0000	0.8125	1.0000	0.6124	0.4766
No global.	0.2834	0.1203	1.0000	0.8172	0.0214	-1.0000

BOCR Networks

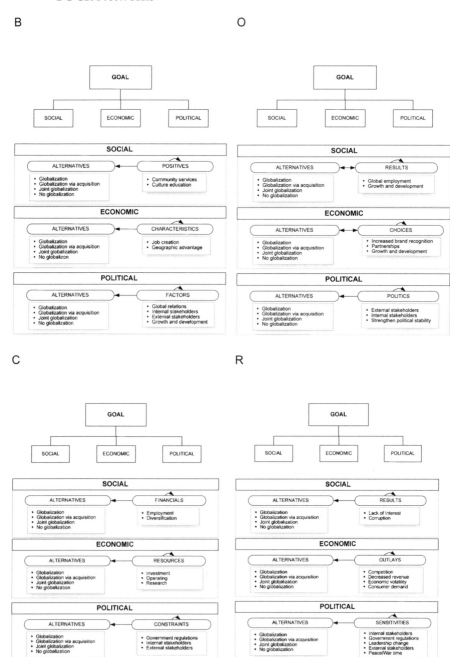

Figure 4.26 Control Criteria and Decision Networks

The Choice of Fiscal Policy to Solve Budget Crisis (in 2002)

Pittsburgh could be facing a deficit of $25 million or more for 2003 if steps are not taken to cut costs or raise revenues. "We are trying to support a growing, vital city (by using) a declining tax base," the Mayor said. "There is a disconnection. It's not that we're not growing. We are growing. But the growth is in people who are exempt from taxes". Proposals to help balance the budget are: Trimming $15 million to $20 million from the public safety budget, proposal to Introduce new taxes, another option on the list, Mayor said, is for Pittsburgh to consider seeking protection under state Act 47 as an "economically distressed" city. That would allow a state overseer to review city revenues and spending and possibly impose layoffs or new contracts on public safety personnel, and finally raise taxes for the people who are currently paying taxes [6].

ALTERNATIVES: File for Act 47, Introduce new taxes, Lower spending, Raise existing taxes.

BOCR Weight Development

The BOCR merits are evaluated against the strategic criteria of Economic, Political, and Social as shown in Table 4.3.

Table 4.3 Strategic Criteria and Rating Scale

	Economic	Political	Social	Priorities
	0.53	0.14	0.33	
Benefits	high	medium	medium	0.27
Opportunities	high	low	medium	0.26
Costs	medium	medium	high	0.24
Risks	medium	low	high	0.23

Table 4.4 shows the overall outcome. Introduce new taxes is the preferred choice. There are a number of things that are somewhat surprising. First, Raise existing taxes is very close in priority to Introduce new taxes. Second, Raise existing taxes is preferred over Lower spending. The fact that the current tax base is diminishing and that the individuals in the current tax base are heavily burdened seems to be in line with the introduction of new taxes, and would allow for the building of a new tax base on different individuals. However the second finding does not seem to be in line because it would be putting a heavier load on already overburdened population. Looking into the details of why this is so, it appears that the risk to public safety and the retention of current businesses are so important that they inhibit a lowering of spending.

Table 4.4 Overall Outcome

Alternatives	Benefits 0.2736	Opportun- ities 0.2358	Costs 0.2642	Risks 0.2264	Outcome BO/CR	Outcome bB + oO – cC - rR
File for Act 47	0.6642	0.5646	0.7129	0.8563	0.6143	-0.4124
Introduce new taxes	1.0000	1.0000	1.0000	1.0000	1.0000	1.0000
Lower spending	0.7019	0.7255	0.7318	0.9225	0.7542	0.0293
Raise existing taxes	0.6066	0.7997	0.7753	0.7320	0.8547	0.3790

Sensitivity Analysis

Carrying out a sensitivity analysis by varying the weights of the BOCR shows that for the majority of situations *Introduce new taxes* would be the optimal choice.

Raise existing taxes is the preferred alternative in some situations: for example, when Benefits and Opportunities are low and Risks and Costs are high. Although *Raise existing taxes* can become the most preferred solution, it is only preferred in extreme situations. One of the surprising findings is how few situations would lend themselves to budget cuts. In order for budget cuts to make sense the Costs have to be high and the Risks have to be very low.

It is found that Act 47 is only appropriate when Opportunities and Risks are low in combination with the high Costs. Because of the extreme nature of Act 47, the city would only use Act 47 in the most desperate times.

In conclusion it is necessary to raise revenue to avoid social and economic risks associated with budget cuts. Hence the most appropriate method for raising revenue would be the introduction of new taxes. These new taxes would hopefully raise revenue from a tax base not already taxed that would lower the burden on the current tax base while maintaining sufficient funds for adequate public safety. Figure 4.27 gives the control criteria and decision networks.

Nettworks and Corresponding Tables

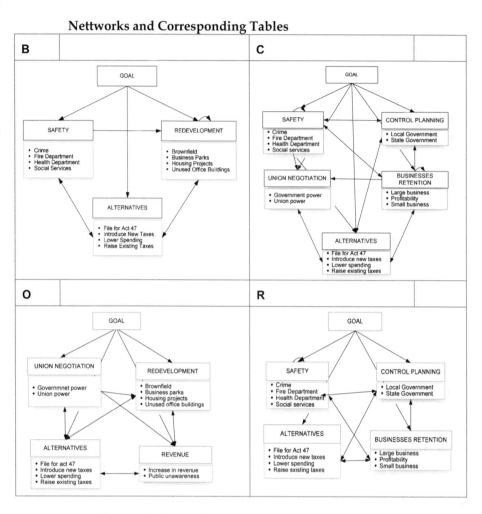

Figure 4.27 Control Criteria and Decision Networks

Should Porsche Introduce a Sports Utility Vehicle? (in 1999)

Porsche is a company that thrives on building cars that go faster than most people can drive and cost more than most people can afford. Because Sports Utility Vehicles (SUVs) are so far up field from Porsche's traditional expertise, the new vehicle could play havoc with the Company's well-established and narrowly defined image. Porsche customers do not like change, and perceive the extension of the product portfolio to be a loss of brand identity. This could result in negative spillover effects into the sports car division, leading to brand dilution. Porsche has failed several times in the past to expand its product line. In the past it has tried to build a mid-engine car with Volkswagen, and then a front-engine car with Audi, both which were eventually discontinued. This study was done before Porsche's decision to make the SUV more than a year later [6].

ALTERNATIVES: Introduce SUV, Do not introduce SUV

BOCR Weight Development

The assessment criteria and their subcriteria are shown in Figure 4.28.

Figure 4.28 Strategic Criteria for BOCR Ratings

The priorities for each merit are shown in Table 4.5.

Table 4.5 BOCR Priorities

Merits	Benefits	Opportunities	Costs	Risks
Weights	0.308	0.209	0.199	0.284

Table 4.6 gives the overall outcome. The study was done in 1999. This determination is validated by Porsche's decision to introduce a SUV, the Cayenne, sometime in 2002 as reported on in Fortune: February 19, 2001, more than two years after the study was done. Porsche has now introduced the first non-sports car in its 53-year history: A four-door, four-seat vehicle with a tailgate and four-wheel drive, a SUV. Porsche is counting on the SUV to boost sales by 50% and secure the company's independence as the world's largest specialty carmaker. Porsche expects to sell 75,000 vehicles by 2003, and has planned their product portfolio out to 2010, while most companies look ahead only 5 years.

Table 4.6 Overall Outcome

Alternatives	Benefits	Opportunities	Costs	Risks	Outcome BO/CR	Outcome bB+oO-cC-rR
Introduce SUV	1.000	1.000	0.385	1.000	1.000	1.000
Do not introduce SUV	1.000	0.282	1.000	0.365	0.039	-0.798

The Structure of the Porsche Model

Table 4.7 indicates the clusters, the control criteria and the clusters and elements in the associated decision subnets.

Table 4.7 Clusters in the Decision Networks and Elements in the Clusters

BOCR	Control Criteria	Clusters	Elements
	Financial	Demographics	Age, Economic status, Gender, Location, Race
		Economic	Price, Sales
		Marketing	Direct mail, Print, Promotions, Radio, TV
Benefits	Social	Trends	Brand, Demographics, Future SUV, Status
	Political	Regulatory	Gas consumption, Safety, Pollution
		Competition	Market demand, Response
	Financial	Demographics	Age, Economic status, Gender, Location, Race
		Economic	Economies of sale, New markets, Reduce risk of takeover
		Marketing	Brand equity
Opportunities	Social	Environmental	Pollution standards
		Trends	Brand, Demographics, Future SUV, Status
	Political	Regulatory	Safety
		Competition	Market demand, Response
	Financial	Economic	After market, Design, Distribution, Labor, Production
		Marketing	Advertising, New product introduction
Costs	Social	Environmental	Pollution, Resources
		Trends	Brand equity

	Financial	Demographics	Unfamiliar market
		Economics	Late arrival, Price, Sales, Spreading too thin
		Marketing	Brand equity
	Social	Environmental	Gas consumption, Pollution, Resources
		Trends	Brand equity, Future of SUV
	Political	Regulatory	Safety
Risks		Competition	Increased chance of takeover, Late arrival, Market demand, Response
All networks		Alternatives	Introduce SUV, Do not introduce SUV

Prediction of Country having the most Severe HIV Epidemic (in 2001)

Worldwide, an estimated 34.3 million people are infected with HIV. Since the early 1980's, when the virus was first detected in Africa, more than 18 million people have died from the disease. The impact of the disease is so widespread in some regions, particularly Sub-Saharan Africa, that they exact a heavy toll on income generation, social structures and educational attainment, all inhibiting economic growth. HIV/AIDS has devastated the developing world but not uniformly. HIV prevalence varies greatly among countries of different economic status and region. This study explores some of the social and economic conditions that allow, or contribute to, the spread of HIV/AIDS in an effort to supply policy options for policy makers at the national and international level. A group of developing Southeast Asian nations in various stages of their HIV epidemic is also compared [6].

ALTERNATIVES: Burma (Myanmar), Cambodia, Indonesia, Malaysia, Thailand, and Vietnam.

The HIV Prediction Model

This model uses an innovative concept. Rather than the typical BOCR merits, a single positive merit of Controlling Factors and a single negative merit of Contributing Factors were used. The current literature on HIV/AIDS in the developing world frames the issue in those terms. Factors that encourage the spread of HIV (Costs) are for more present and persistent in the developing world than conditions (Benefits) that suppress the spread of the virus. The two were weighted accordingly with Controlling at 0.333 and Contributing at 0.667. Table 4.8 gives the overall results. The source of much of the information was from the UN publications: UNAIDS, Global HIV/AIDS and STD Surveillance (June 2000) and their website:
 http://www.unaids.org/epidemic_update/report/index.html

Table 4.8 Overall Outcome

Alternatives	Benefits	Costs	Outcome bB+c(1-C)
Burma	0.772	0.293	1.000
Cambodia	1.000	1.000	0.457
Indonesia	0.425	0.346	0.792
Malaysia	0.336	0.346	0.752
Thailand	0.371	0.385	0.732
Vietnam	0.453	0.488	0.675

Table 4.9 HIV Model Criteria with their Priorities

		Priorities		
Benefits	Economic 0.328	Government health spending 0.333		0.036
		International aid 0.667		0.073
	Social 0.413	Muslim population 0.667		0.092
		Condom use 0.333		0.046
	Government 0.259			0.086
Costs	Economic 0.346	Income inequality 0.249		0.057
		Poverty 0.751		0.173
	Political 0.209	Government 0.547	Corruption 0.667	0.051
			Ineffectiveness 0.333	0.025
		International isolation 0.264		0.037
		War 0.189		0.026
	Social 0.346	Cultural norms / 0.75	Drug use 0.119	0.021
			Prostitution 0.365	0.063
			Sexual promiscuity 0.281	0.049
			Taboo of speaking of Sex/drugs 0.235	0.041
		Education 0.25	Female education gap 0.665	0.038
			Illiteracy 0.333	0.019
	Other 0.099	Geography 0.297		0.020
		Smuggling 0.164		0.011
		Age of epidemic 0.539		0.036

Table 4.9 indicates the criteria and their priorities that led to the outcome given in Table 4.8. Decision sub-networks were created for the main contributing factors Government corruption, Income inequality, Poverty, Prostitution, Sexual promiscuity, Taboo of speaking of Sex/drugs, Female education gap, and Illiteracy. As an example, the actors comprising the network for Prostitution can be given as Consumers, Individual women, Pimp/Traffickers, Police and Tourists. Similar decision networks were created for the other high priority covering control criteria. These included a cluster for the alternatives and major actors or factors.

Market Share of World Car Manufacturers (in 2002)

The aim of this model was to estimate the relative share of the world market possessed by the top automakers. Five car manufacturers were selected as alternatives as shown below. This is a validation model to show that a complex ANP model can be structured using general information from knowledgeable people that will give an outcome that can be compared to actual data. In this case the net income of the companies, normalized to give relative values that would be comparable to the derived priorities, was used. ALTERNATIVES: General Motors, Ford, Toyota, Honda and Others.

The ANP Decision Network

The Categories used in the model are Characteristics, Advertising and Fuel Economy. The Characteristics node includes Emission standards, American made, Foreign made, Price, Styling, Option packages available, and Other. The Advertising node includes Heavily advertised, Normally advertised and Sub-par advertising. It is assumed that for foreign cars Heavy advertising is more important than the other two and that for American made Normal advertising and Heavy advertising are similar. The final criterion is Fuel economy. It is assumed that foreign made cars have better fuel economy overall. The model was similar to those shown above so we do not give the details here. The full model is available in [6]. Table 4.10 shows the estimated and the actual market shares.

Table 4.10 Overall Outcome

Alternatives	Estimated	Actual
General Motors	0.32	0.30
Ford	0.19	0.19
Toyota	0.09	0.11
Honda	0.09	0.10
Others	0.31	0.30

Compatibility index: 1.001

Market Share of Cell Phone Brands (in 2002)

Product characteristics, Advertising, and Others are the main criteria for this model. Design features, Price, Technology and User friendly are the subcriteria under Product characteristics while Advertising has two subcriteria as Global and Spending. Finally Others have Brand recognition, Distribution channels, and Warranty. The alternatives are shown below. Table 4.11 shows the estimated and the actual market shares.

ALTERNATIVES: Nokia, Motorola, Samsung, Sonny Ericsson.

Table 4.11 Overall Outcome

Alternatives	Estimated	Actual
Nokia	0.49	0.52
Motorola	0.19	0.20
Samsung	0.14	0.15
Sony Ericsson	0.18	0.13

Compatibility index: 1.028

Using AHP with Other Techniques in Successive Decisions

An international tool steel company, ASSAB, has applied the AHP for their successive strategic decisions. The AHP was used together with other techniques as appropriate for each particular decision and the AHP outcome from one decision was used for the next one and so on [10]. The process began by predicting the relative viability of the company's products in the next two years, analyzing the competitors to identifying their relative competitiveness in the selected products, selecting the most appropriate strategy, and prioritized strategic actions to implement the strategy. The alternate strategies were developed through a SWOT analysis and the strategic actions were identified using the Balanced Scorecard method.

Product Viability Analysis

Product viability analysis is performed to predict the relative potential for success of the company's three product types of three different quality grades. The structure for Cold Work Steel is presented in Figure 4.29 and the overall results in Table 4.12.

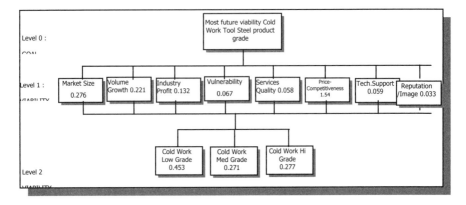

Figure 4.29 The Hierarchy for Cold Work Steel

Table 4.12 Results of AHP for Viability Analysis

	Viability Factors								AHP Results		
	Mkt Share	Vol Growth	Profit	Vulnerability	Svc Quality	Price Competitiveness	Tech Support	Reputation	Lo Grade	med Grade	Hi Grade
Cold Work	0.276	0.221	0.132	0.067	0.058	0.154	0.059	0.033	0.453	0.271	0.277
Hot Work	0.246	0.265	0.143	0.043	0.046	0.168	0.061	0.028	0.391	0.287	0.322
Plastic Mold	0.191	0.201	0.162	0.063	0.086	0.184	0.076	0.037	0.365	0.273	0.362

Competitor Analysis

The next process was to analyze the competitors. There are four other major and prominent players in the Tool Steel industry: Bohler, Thyssen, Hitachi and Daido. The rest are small players that are not considered as potential threat to the company. Three hierarchies were constructed, one for each product type, using the same Critical Success Factor (CSF) but different relative importance. The hierarchy for the Low Grade Steel is presented in Figure 4.30 and the overall results in Table 4.13.

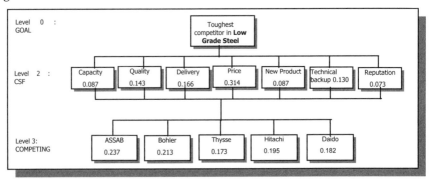

Figure 4.30 AHP Model of Toughest Competitor in Low Grade Steel

Table 4.13 AHP Results of Competitor Analysis

Grades	ASSAB	Bohler	Thyssen	Hitachi	Daido
Low Grade	0.237	0.213	0.173	0.195	0.182
Med Grade	0.217	0.23	0.209	0.168	0.176
Hi Grade	0.251	0.24	0.204	0.161	0.144

The ASSAB company is the industry market leader for low grade and high grade steel and is only a few percentage points lower for medium grade steel. The analysis showed the company was doing quite well for Low Grade and High Grade Steel, but needed to improve for Medium Grade.

Strategy Selection

The next step is the SWOT analysis with four alternate strategies of: Develop Image, Develop Customer Strategic Partnership, Develop New Product, and Improve Customer Service. Pro-Con analysis was conducted to produce the criteria for the hierarchy as shown in Fig 4.31. The same structure was then used to evaluate the benefits, costs, opportunities, and risks of the alternate strategies. The marginal BOCRs as shown in Table 4.14 suggested that the best strategy would be for the company to develop strategic partnership with its customers. Earlier analysis using an ordinal method for strategy selection indicated that introducing new products would be the best. The company executives admitted that introducing new products made sense because of the company's strengths, but they liked the outcome of the AHP better because it would give them a better long term outlook.

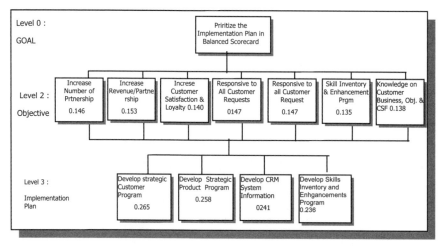

Figure 4.31 Hierarchy for Strategy Selection

Table 4.14 Marginal BOCR Result

	Strategic Partnership	Image Promotion	Better Service Facility	Introduce New Products
COST	0.260	0.271	0.297	0.173
BENEFIT	0.532	0.258	0.130	0.080
RISK	0.430	0.278	0.112	0.181
OPPORTUNITY	0.346	0.254	0.212	0.188
WEIGHTED	**1.646**	**0.870**	**0.829**	**0.480**

Strategic Actions: Identification and Prioritization

Strategic actions to implement the selected strategy were identified using the Balanced Scorecard methodology, which gave fourteen strategic objectives for the four perspectives of Financial, Customer, Business Process, and Learning and Growth; and eight strategic actions to implement. The outcome of the Balanced Scorecard was studied and organized to produce seven objectives and four programs which were then prioritized using the AHP. The hierarchy is shown in Fig 4.32 and the priority outcome in Table 4.15.

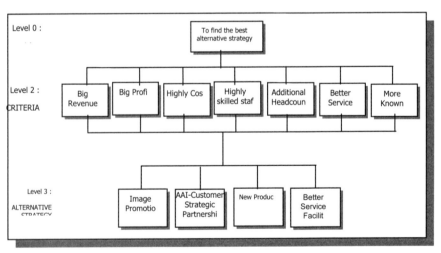

Figure 4.32 Balanced Scorecard Hierarchy

Table 4.15 Priorities of Outcomes for Strategic Programs

Programs	Priority
1. Develop Strategic-Customer Penetration Program	0.265
2. Develop Product Sales Program	0.258
3. Develop CRM System	0.241
4. Develop Sales & Marketing Staff Skill Inventory & Skill Enhancement Program	0.236

An Example of a Model for Integrating Decisions about Human Resource Management

As organizations rely more and more on their intellectual capital as an intangible asset, human resource management increases in importance. For effective collective contributions from their people, organizations need to strive for linking their human resource management systems to their strategy. They need to develop measurement system that provides reliable indicators of how well their people contribute to their organization's performance [11]. The AHP can be used to develop a framework for integrating decisions on human resource management.

This example is a model developed for a multi-business state owned company in Indonesia, PT Wijaya Karya (Limited) - WIKA [12]. A hierarchy is constructed to identify the set of employee competencies required through articulating company objectives. The hierarchy is shown in Figure 4.33 below.

The relative priorities of the competence would differ based on level of responsibility, hence WIKA employees are categorized into seven groups. There are four groups for Junior Staff (JS-1, JS-2, JS-3, JS-4) and three groups for Senior Staff (SS-1, SS-2, SS-3), of which JS-1 is the lowest and SS-3 is the highest. Table 4.16 shows the different priorities (ranked from the highest to the lowest) for JS-2 and SS-1.

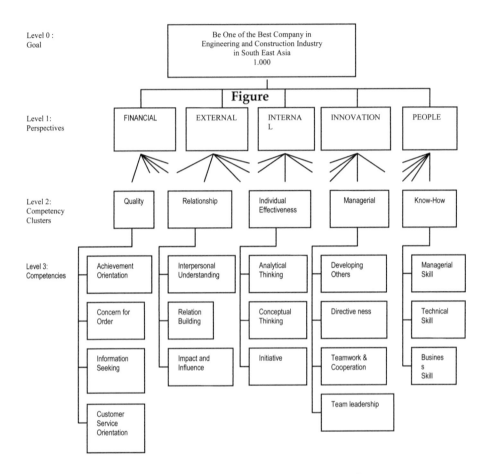

4.33. AHP Model for WIKA HR Competence Based Management

Applying absolute measurement approach of the AHP, six demonstrated levels ranging from no opportunity to always are defined for each type of competence. This model is then used to determine the standard of competence for each employee category and assess the competence profiles of each employee. Figure 4.34 shows an example of the result of performance assessment of an employee from the JS-2 category, which can be used to make decisions regarding a particular member or a group of people in the organization, for example:

- Obtain the employee overall performance score to determine salary or incentive,
- Design training program for the job currently assigned to the employee,

- Assign a new job that uses more of the employee strengths and less of his or her weaknesses.

Table 4.16 Competence Priorities for JS-2 and SS-1

THE SET OF COMPETENCIES FOR			
JS-2		**SS-1**	
COMPETENCY	**PRIORITY**	**COMPETENCY**	**PRIORITY**
Interpersonal Understanding (IU)	0.137	Developing Others (DEV)	0.104
Analytical Thinking (AT)	0.124	Achievement Orientation (ACH)	0.097
Technical Skill (TS)	0.096	Conceptual Thinking (CT)	0.095
Teamwork and Cooperation (TW)	0.095	Managerial Skill (MS)	0.094
Achievement Orientation (ACH)	0.087	Relation Building (RB)	0.084
Business Skill (BS)	0.063	Directive ness (DIR)	0.077
Concern for Order (CO)	0.053	Interpersonal Understanding (IU)	0.075
Initiative (INT)	0.051	Team leadership (TL)	0.075
Team leadership (TL)	0.048	Business Skill (BS)	0.064
Directive ness (DIR)	0.041	Analytical Thinking (AT)	0.045
Impact and Influence (IMP)	0.037	Impact and Influence (IMP)	0.044
Managerial Skill (MS)	0.033	Initiative (INT)	0.034
Developing Others (DEV)	0.032	Technical Skill (TS)	0.030
Relation Building (RB)	0.029	Teamwork and Cooperation (TW)	0.024
Customer Service Orientation (CSO)	0.027	Customer Service Orientation (CSO)	0.021
Conceptual Thinking (CT)	0.025	Concern for Order (CO)	0.020
Information Seeking (INF)	0.022	Information Seeking (INF)	0.017

COMPETENCY	Priority in 1000ths	DEMONSTRATED LEVEL					
		No Opportunity	Never	Seldom	Occasionally	Usually	Always
		080	036	069	132	252	431
Achievement Orientation (ACH)	087		◆				
Concern for Order (CO)	053			◆			
Information Seeking (INF)	022		◆				
Customer Service Orientation (CSO)	027				◆		
Interpersonal Understanding (IU)	137		◆				
Relation Building (RB)	029						
Impact and Influence (IMP)	037			◆			
Analytical Thinking (AT)	124			◆			
Conceptual Thinking (CT)	025			◆			
Initiative (INT)	051		◆				
Developing Others (DEV)	032			◆			
Directive ness (DIR)	041		◆				
Teamwork and Cooperation (TW)	095					◆	
Team leadership (TL)	048		◆				
Managerial Skill (MS)	033		◆				
Technical Skill (TS)	096			◆			
Business Skill (BS)	063				◆		

Figure 4.34 Individual Competence Profiles for JS-2 Employees

Group and Party Effects – What Congress Should Do

One might perceive rightly or wrongly that Congress has been using the buckshot approach in making its decisions that cover the needs of the nation. What else can they do? Can their process of decision making be organized in some way that would not put off the politicians but strengthen their resolve and reward their pride even more in the breadth and depth of their accomplishments? We think so. Let us see how.

The AHP/ANP approach is a very general way to structure a problem holistically as part of a system and relate its parts according to influence. We have chosen the simplest and most direct route to prioritizing most of the bills that have been before Congress recently [13].

The decision criteria were established through in-depth reviews of the functions of the U.S. government as well as some interviews with experts in governmental affairs, and the results are shown in Figure 4.35 and Figure 4.36. We reviewed the committees in the Senate including: the Standing; Special; Select and Joint committees. Additionally we reviewed the committees in the House as well as the Bills before Congress to gain as much insight as possible into its activities. Our goal with the decision criteria was to focus on the highest level and next lower level of purposes of the Government rather than break out every single low level function. The analysis is targeted at providing a coherent and justifiable framework for assisting key senior decision makers in the U.S. Government with prioritizing the issues they should address in 2005 based on their importance in serving the American people. The example is an illustration of what and how one can use comparisons to create priorities in an accurate and justifiable way. One needs to seek further agreement from many more people in government to fine tune the results obtained here.

An essential consideration in using the judgment process to prioritize decisions is the power to be accorded to each of the different contributors to the judgment process. Voting according to party position is different than voting alone or with another group. The judgments on each matter may not be equally important and thus the AHP method of synthesizing judgments would be applied to raise that judgment to the power of its source. The numerical value of the power is obtained from an appropriate hierarchy for the importance of the different parties. It is followed by taking the geometric mean of all the judgments raised to the powers to obtain the single judgment and the process is repeated for all the judgments. The criteria priorities are determined here by comparing them with respect to the goal to determine which is more important. But it would be better to derive their priorities by comparing them using the ANP with respect to some select very important decisions at least to get a rough idea as to their importance in the real situation when decisions are made under pressure to decide on what is more important and how much more important it is. The alternatives were rated with respect to the subcriteria using scale intensities shown below Table 4.17 used to rate them one by one by assigning each alternative the value from the scale that represents its standing with respect to the corresponding criterion. One can allocate resources to projects proportionately to their ratings in a dynamic way as more money and more bills and projects are added. The priorities serve as a measure of performance to determine how much money to allocate to cover the costs of those decisions that are funded completely (zero-one allocation), or in part by specifying levels such as 20%, 40%, and so on.

One way to deal with urgency is to include a special criterion called "urgency" and assign it a priority alongside the other factors and prioritize all the bills past and present with respect to it over regular time horizons and note the change in overall priorities of all the bills. One can then also periodically reassign resources for their implementation.

Decision Goal: To Prioritize Congressional Decisions to be Made
- Transportation and Communication
- International Relations
- Justice and Regulation
- Health
- Learning and Knowledge
• Science
• Education
• Technology
- Security
• Armed Services and Veterans Affairs
• Homeland Security
• Intelligence
- Economic Prosperity
• Availability of Resources
° Appropriations
° Taxation
• Business
• Agriculture/Environment and Resource Management
• International Trade
• Labor
• Social Services
° Social Security
° Welfare
° Indian Affairs

Figure 4.35 Criteria used to Prioritize Congressional Decisions

The priorities of the major criteria which correspond to areas of government concern and their subcriteria are shown with their priorities in Figure 4.36. In Table 4.17 we list the bills and the priorities they received based on these criteria. The priorities are presented as scores obtained by multiplying the rating in each cell times the criterion weight of the column and adding. They could also be presented with their relative weights by normalizing the scores. The highest score a project could achieve if it were perfect would be 1.000.

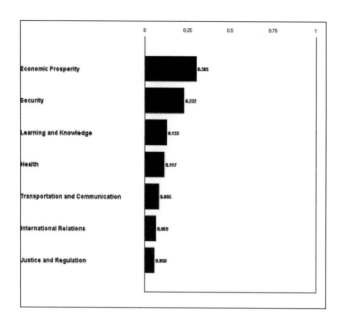

Figure 4.36 Priorities of Major Governmental Areas

Table 4.17 Overall Scores of the Bills along with How They Rated on Some of the Criteria

	Score	Transportation and Communication (0.085)	International Relations (0.07)	Justice and Regulation (0.06)	Health (0.118)	Science (0.034)	Education (0.067)	Technology (0.034)	Services and Veterans Affairs (0.105)	Homeland Security (0.053)
Class action lawsuits, assure fairness	0.391	0.000	0.000	0.800	1.000	0.250	0.250	0.250	0.250	0.000
Allow human embryonic stem cell research	0.299	0.000	0.250	0.800	1.000	1.000	0.800	0.800	0.000	0.000
Continuity of Congress (special elections/appointments in national emergencies)	0.274	0.250	0.250	0.250	0.000	0.000	0.000	0.000	0.500	1.000
Minimum wage increase	0.253	0.000	0.250	0.250	0.000	0.000	0.000	0.000	0.000	0.000
Drivers licenses and security for immigrants	0.245	0.000	0.500	0.250	0.000	0.000	0.000	0.000	0.000	1.000
Social Security overhaul including personal savings accounts	0.243	0.000	0.000	0.250	0.250	0.000	0.000	0.000	0.250	0.000
Make tax cuts permanent	0.238	0.000	0.000	0.000	0.000	0.000	0.250	0.250	0.000	0.000
Protect internet users from unknown transmission of personal data	0.237	0.800	0.000	0.800	0.000	0.250	0.000	0.500	0.000	0.000
Farm Subsidies- Limit Federal Farm Payments	0.236	0.000	0.250	0.000	0.000	0.000	0.000	0.000	0.000	0.000
Clear Skies Act (emissions control for power plants)	0.215	0.000	0.000	0.250	0.500	0.250	0.250	0.250	0.000	0.000
Transportation (TEA-21), Re-authorization of surface transportation programs	0.202	1.000	0.000	0.000	0.000	0.000	0.000	0.000	0.000	0.000
Prohibit discrimination based on genetic health info	0.185	0.000	0.000	0.500	0.250	0.500	0.000	0.250	0.000	0.000
Increase coverage of service members life insurance	0.178	0.000	0.000	0.250	0.000	0.000	0.000	0.000	1.000	0.000
Death gratuity for military, improve	0.177	0.000	0.000	0.250	0.000	0.000	0.000	0.000	0.800	0.000
Improve Death Gratuity for Military	0.175	0.000	0.000	0.250	0.000	0.000	0.000	0.000	1.000	0.000
Senate committee organizing resolutions	0.165	0.000	0.000	0.000	0.250	0.250	0.250	0.250	0.250	0.000
Estate tax, make repeal permanent	0.161	0.000	0.000	0.250	0.000	0.000	0.000	0.000	0.000	0.000
Provide standards for Congressional Gold Medals	0.157	0.000	0.000	0.000	0.000	0.000	0.000	0.000	1.000	0.250
Repeal Estate Tax	0.151	0.000	0.000	0.250	0.000	0.000	0.000	0.000	0.000	0.000
Incapacitated Persons Protection Act	0.149	0.000	0.000	0.800	0.000	0.000	0.000	0.000	0.000	0.000
Enhance privacy of social security numbers	0.136	0.000	0.000	0.250	0.000	0.000	0.000	0.000	0.000	0.500
Amend to marraige between only man and woman	0.134	0.000	0.000	0.800	0.250	0.000	0.000	0.000	0.000	0.000
Prohibit minors having abortions across state lines	0.128	0.000	0.000	0.800	0.250	0.000	0.500	0.000	0.000	0.000
Terry Schiavo bill	0.118	0.000	0.000	1.000	0.500	0.000	0.000	0.000	0.000	0.000
Tsunami Relief, accelerate tax benefits for charitable contributions	0.112	0.000	1.000	0.000	0.000	0.000	0.000	0.000	0.000	0.000
Prohibit same sex marraige	0.104	0.000	0.000	1.000	0.250	0.000	0.000	0.000	0.000	0.000
Prevent sales of abusive life policies to military service members	0.103	0.000	0.000	0.500	0.000	0.000	0.000	0.000	0.500	0.000
Increase FCC indecency penalties	0.069	0.000	0.000	0.800	0.000	0.000	0.000	0.000	0.000	0.000
Gun Liability Bill	0.054	0.000	0.000	0.500	0.000	0.000	0.000	0.000	0.000	0.000
Amendment Prohibiting Flag Desecration	0.015	0.000	0.000	0.250	0.000	0.000	0.000	0.000	0.000	0.000

Ratings: Excellent 1.000, Very Good 0.800, Good 0.500, Marginal 0.200, No Contribution 0.000

Perspective

The hierarchies and networks just presented are only a few of those that have actually been used to make decisions with the AHP/ANP. But they suggest the wide range of problems to which the AHP/ANP can be applied. The AHP can be used for the following kinds of decision problems:

☐ Setting priorities
☐ Generating a set of alternatives
☐ Choosing the best policy alternative
☐ Determining requirements
☐ Allocating resources
☐ Predicting outcomes and assessing risks
☐ Measuring performance
☐ Designing a system
☐ Ensuring system stability
☐ Optimizing
☐ Planning
☐ Resolving conflicts

Different people may have their own idea about how to deal with a problem, and that is how they should carry it out. Only when a group must act together, as in a corporation, do people need to agree on the structure of their problem.

In forming a hierarchy, one should include as much detail as seems to be needed to understand the problem; the prioritization process will eliminate elements that are unimportant. A new level should be added to the hierarchy if it facilitates the comparison and evaluation of the elements in the level immediately below and contributes to improving precision in the judgments. One contribution of a good hierarchy is that it enables people to make better guesses about the effects of the unknown by laying out its components and studying each separately instead of lumping everything together and making one big guess at the consequences of decisions made in the face of that unknown. The hierarchy can provide an effective buffer between reason and worry.

In sum, when constructing hierarchies one must include enough relevant detail to depict the problem as thoroughly as possible. Consider the environment surrounding the problem. Identify the issues or attributes that you feel contribute to the solution. Identify the participants associated with the problem. Arranging the goals, attributes, issues, and stakeholders in a hierarchy serves two purposes: It provides an overall view of the complex relationships inherent in the situation, and it permits the decision maker to assess whether he or she is comparing issues of the same order of magnitude in weight or impact on the solution. When constructing networks one must be particularly paying attention to feedback influences.

The elements should be clustered into homogeneous groups of five to nine so they can be meaningfully compared to elements in the next higher level. The only restriction on the hierarchic arrangement of elements is that any element in one level must be capable of being related to some elements in the next higher level, which serves as a criterion for assessing the relative impact of elements in the level below.

A hierarchy does not need to be complete; that is, an element in a given level does not have to function as a criterion for all the elements in the level below. Thus a hierarchy can be divided into sub-hierarchies sharing only a common topmost element. Further, a decision maker can insert or eliminate levels and elements as necessary to clarify the task of setting priorities or to sharpen the focus on one or more parts of the system. Elements that are of less immediate interest can be represented in general terms at the higher levels of the hierarchy and elements critical to the problem at hand can be developed in greater depth and specificity.

In addition to identifying within a hierarchic structure the major factors that influence the outcome of a decision, we need a way to decide whether these factors have equal effects on the outcome or whether some of them are dominant and others so insignificant they can be ignored. This is accomplished through the process of priority setting. The task of setting priorities requires that the criteria, the subcriteria, the properties or features of the alternatives being compared, and the alternatives themselves are gradually layered in the hierarchy so that the elements in each level are comparable among themselves in relation to the elements of the next higher level. Now the priorities are set for the elements in each level several times, once with respect to each criterion of the upper level. These in turn are prioritized with respect to the elements of the next higher level and so on. Finally a weighting process is used to obtain overall priorities. This is done by coming down the hierarchy and weighting the priorities measured in a level with respect to a criterion in the next higher level with the weight of that criterion. The weighted priorities can then be added for each element in the level to obtain its overall priority.

Finally, after judgments have been made on the impact of all the elements, and priorities have been computed for the hierarchy as a whole, the less important elements can be dropped from further consideration because of their relatively small impact on the overall objective. Now let us examine some of the real-world applications of the hierarchy.

Clearly the design of an analytic hierarchy, like the structuring of a problem by any other method, is now more art than science, making it more and more a science through the Hierarchon and Encyclicon [6, 7]. There is no precise formula for identification or stratification of elements. But structuring a hierarchy does require substantial knowledge about the system or problem in question. A strong aspect of the AHP is that the experienced decision makers who specify the hierarchy also supply judgments on the relative importance of the elements. That brings us to the next topic: establishing priorities.

References

1. Saaty, T.L., *Creative Thinking, Problem Solving & Decision Making,* RWS Publications, Pittsburgh, PA, 2001.
2. Saaty, T.L., Axiomatic Foundation of the Analytic Hierarchy Process, *Management Science,* Vol. 32, No. 7., pp. 841-855. 1986.
3. Saaty, T.L. and K.P. Kearns, *Analytical Planning: The Organization of Systems;* Pergamon Press; Oxford, 1985.
4. Saaty, T.L., Theory and Applications of the Analytic Network Process: Decision Making with Benefits, Opportunities, Costs, and Risks, RWS Publications, Pittsburgh, PA, 2005.
5. Saaty, T.L. and E.H. Forman, *The Hierarchon, a Dictionary of Hierarchies,* RWS Publications, Pittsburgh, PA, 1993.
6. Saaty, T.L. and M. Ozdemir, *The Encyclicon: a Dictionary of ANP Applications,* RWS Publications, Pittsburgh, PA, 2005.
7. Saaty, T.L., Decision Making for Leaders: The Analytic Hierarchy Process for Decisions in a Complex World, RWS Publications, Pittsburgh, PA, 1990.
8. Javalgi, R. and J. Hosseini, The Analytic Hierarchy Process Based Choice Theory in Marketing Research, Working Paper Marquette University Library, 1988.
9. Saaty, T.L. and L.G. Vargas, *Prediction, Projection and Forecasting,* Kluwer Academic Publishers, Boston, Massachusetts. 1991.
10. Kintarso, H. and K. Peniwati, Developing and Selecting Business Strategy, and Prioritizing Strategic Actions for a Tool Steel Company with the Analytic Hierarchy Process, *Proceedings of The 7th Asia Pacific Management Conference Kuala Lumpur, Malaysia,* 2001.
11. Becker, B.E., M.A. Huselid, and D. Ulrich, *The HR Scorecard: Linking People, Strategy, and Performance,* Harvard Business School Press, 2001.
12. Suryo, K.I. and Peniwati, K., HR Development Strategy through Competency Profile Analysis in Wijaya Karya (Limited), *Proceedings of the 7th International Symposium on the Analytic Hierarchy Process (ISAHP2003),* Bali, Indonesia, 2003.
13. Saaty, T.L., Multi-Decisions Decision-Making: In Addition to Wheeling and Dealing, our National Political Bodies Need a Formal Approach for Prioritization, *Mathematical and Computer Modeling special issue on the AHP/ANP,* 2007.

Chapter 5

Turning Individual Judgments into Group Decisions

Decision making is not like measuring something on a scale because it involves human values that are intangible. We cannot make a decision without knowing how important each person's value is in each particular decision and how to combine them all in the appropriate way to get the best decision. How to measure and prioritize these values and trade them off is a primary concern of decision making. In this chapter we delve deeper into the details of the AHP, beginning with more validation examples, stimulus-response derivation of the 1–9 scale, why we should only compare a few elements at a time and the role of inconsistency in that determination. Finally, why the geometric mean, not the arithmetic mean is the only way to combine individual judgments into a group judgment is discussed along with how, when necessary, to include the priorities of the individuals because of their power and expert knowledge.

The greatest test of the validity of a theory of measurement for decision making is the way it deals with judgments of intangible factors. Even the measurements we have for tangibles do not always tell us how accurately the measurements represent our values. The same measurements may not serve all values in the same proportion and may need to be assessed by using new judgments that represent the subjective nature of our values and desires. In other words: rarely do measurements in dollars, tons, yards, and even hours serve all the purposes of decision making. But there are numerous cases where our estimation coincides with the physical dimension being measured. Thus the process we apply to measure intangibles must apply equally well to those tangibles. These values can only be obtained in relative terms because the measurements themselves depend on a unit that is chosen arbitrarily.

As we pointed out in Part I, a credible decision theory should be able to justify its approach in an objective way by producing successful predictions using the judgments of experts – thus demonstrating that the theory does not impose constraints based on its inherent assumptions. We should not argue defensively that decisions are subjective anyway and the numbers obtained by the theory simply have to be accepted in their own right. What the theory does with numbers must meet the reasonable expectations of experts, because meaningful decision making needs to produce meaningful outcomes from meaningful numbers – not just outcomes dictated by the assumptions of the method. The ultimate question is: How do we elicit meaningful numbers and produce meaningful outcomes?

In multicriteria decisions, we need to assign priorities to the criteria that govern the choice of alternatives. These priorities must be derived by making pairwise comparisons with respect to higher objectives by answering this question: Given two criteria, which one contributes more to the objective (and how much more)? We have no other credible way to do it because only we can judge the relative importance of the criteria with respect to the goal. Since most of the criteria are intangible, we cannot use numbers derived on a measurement scale. Moreover we must compare the alternatives in pairs. Pairwise comparison is tried-and-true procedure that elicits judgment about how many times one element is perceived by an expert to dominate another element with regard to influence. Rating one at a time by construct, relies on a perceived ideal to rank an alternative – sometimes by going through an elaborate procedure to give the appearance of realism and rigor but still making a guess as to how desirable that alternative may be.

In the end, to obtain an overall rank for each alternative the priorities must be traded off. Thus decision making depends on numerical representation and how valid it is. Otherwise, as the saying goes, "Garbage in/garbage out" – all in the name of subjectivity and utility, interpreted for each situation in an appropriate and justifiable way.

When applied to estimate physical dimensions, a measurement theory should be able to produce approximate values. If its estimates are found to be sufficiently accurate and reliable, it can then be applied to estimate values that are intangible. In addition to the examples we gave in Chapter 2, here we offer further cases to show that the AHP, when used by knowledgeable people, produces credible outcomes that match known data.

Validation Examples

To validate a set of priorities that are homogeneously derived from pairwise comparisons we use the Saaty Compatibility Index [1]. Given two sets of positive numbers, form the matrix of ratios of all the numbers in one set; then also form the matrix of ratios of all the numbers in the second set. Take the transpose of the second matrix. Multiply the two matrices elementwise (that is perform Hadamard multiplication). Add all the resulting numbers and divide by n^2. If the two sets of numbers are identical, the result will be equal to 1. If after dividing by n^2 the ratio is 1.01 or less, the two sets of numbers are said to be compatible; otherwise not. When all sorts of priority numbers are being considered, some ratios my have a very small number in the denominator, and a different index has been proposed by Dr. Claudio Garuti of Santiago, Chile, who uses $\sum_{i=1}^{n} \frac{a_i+b_i}{2} \cdot \frac{Min(a_i,b_i)}{Max(a_i,b_i)}$ for the compatibility of two vectors a and b.

Relative Sizes of Areas

Figure 5.1 shows five areas. The object is to compare them in pairs to reproduce their relative weights as shown in Table 5.1. The reader can apply the paired-comparison process using the 1–9 scale and find its principal eigenvector and compute the compatibility index using the values given in Table 5.1 to test the validity of the procedure. The actual relative values of these areas are approximately A = 0.47, B = 0.05, C = 0.24, D = 0.14, and E = 0.09. Here A is 47 percent of the overall area of the five figures, B is 5 percent, and so on. Or, putting it another way, A/B = 0.47/0.05 = 9.4, and A is about nine times as large as B. the relative sizes of the other figures can be determined in the same way.

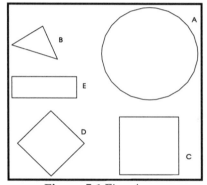

Figure 5.1 Five Areas

Table 5.1 One Individual's Judgment Matrix

Comparisons With Respect to Area Size	Circle	Triangle	Square	Diamond	Rectangle	Eigenvector (priority vector of relative sizes)
Circle	1	9	2.5	3	6	0.488
Triangle	1/9	1	1/5	1/3.5	1/1.5	0.049
Square	1/2.5	5	1	1.7	3	0.233
Diamond	1/3	3.5	1/1.7	1	1.5	0.148
Rectangle	1/6	1.5	1/3	1/1.5	1	0.082

If there is no computer available, there is a shortcut for computing the principal eigenvector: assume the matrix is consistent, normalize each column, and then take the average of the corresponding entries in the columns to obtain the priority vector. The priority vector shown in the right column of the matrix in Table 5.1 is the actual eigenvalue solution, but using the shortcut calculation gives a similar result for this case: A=0.488, B=0.049, C=0.233, D=0.148, E=0.082.

It is easy to make consistent judgments in this exercise because we are dealing with measures that are familiar to most people. If we were to measure the shapes, we would compute the ratios of their areas exactly, and enter these ratios instead of using judgments, the priority vector would give back the exact relative areas of the figures. The point here is to show that judgments can give accurate results. Sometimes people try to measure the shapes and use formulas dimly remembered from high school geometry to verify the results. The errors associated with physically measuring the figures often give worse results than eyeballing the figures and making judgments.

An interesting thing often happens when the exercise is tried with a group. In the AHP the member's judgments on a pair are combined using the geometric mean. When the combined judgments are used in the matrix, often the answer is closer to the actual relative sizes of the figures than most of the individuals' answers are.

Relative Weights of Objects

The matrix in Table 5.2 gives the estimated pairwise comparisons of the weights of five objects lifted by hand by a friend of ours. The two vectors appear to be very close, but are they really? To determine the closeness of the two priority vectors one must again use the Saaty Compatibility Index.

Table 5.2 Pairwise Comparisons of the Weights of Five Objects

Weight	*Radio*	*Type-writer*	*Large Attache Case*	*Projector*	*Small Attache Case*	*Eigen-vector*	*Actual Relative Weights*
Radio	1	1/5	1/3	1/4	4	0.09	0.10
Typewriter	5	1	2	2	8	0.40	0.39
Large attaché case	3	1/2	1	1/2	4	0.18	0.20
Projector	4	1/2	2	1	7	0.29	0.27
Small attaché case	1/4	1/8	1/4	1/7	1	0.04	0.04

An Optics Example

Four identical chairs were placed on a line from a light source at the distances of 9, 15, 21, and 28 yards. The purpose was to see if a person could stand by the light, look at the chairs and compare their relative brightness in pairs, fill in the judgment matrix, and obtain a relationship between the chairs and their distance from the light source. This experiment was repeated twice with different judges. Their judgment matrices are shown in Table 5.3. The judges of the first matrix were two young children, ages 5 and 7, who gave their judgments qualitatively. The judge of the second matrix was the children's mother, who was not present during their judging. The results are shown in Table 5.4.

Table 5.3 Pairwise Comparisons of Relative Brightness of Chairs

Relative visual brightness (1st trial)

	C_1	C_2	C_3	C_4
C_1	1	5	6	7
C_2	1/5	1	4	6
C_3	1/6	1/4	1	4
C_4	1/7	1/6	1/4	1

Relative visual brightness (2nd trial)

	C_1	C_2	C_3	C_4
C_1	1	4	6	7
C_2	1/4	1	3	4
C_3	1/6	1/3	1	2
C_4	1/7	1/4	1/2	1

Table 5.4 Relative Brightness Eigenvectors and Consistency Ratios

Relative brightness eigenvector (1st trial)

0.61
0.24
0.10
0.05

Relative brightness eigenvector (2nd trial)

0.62
0.22
0.10
0.06

$\lambda_{max} = 4.39$, C.I. $= 0.13$, C.R.$= 0.14$ $\lambda_{max} = 4.10$, C.I. $= 0.03$, C.R.$= 0.03$

Table 5.5 Inverse Square Law of Optics

Distance	Distance squared	Reciprocal of distance squared	Normalized reciprocal	Rounded off
9	81	0.0123	0.606	0.61
15	225	0.0044	0.217	0.22
21	441	0.0023	0.113	0.11
28	784	0.0013	0.064	0.06

First-and-second trial eigenvectors should be compared with the last column of Table 5.5, which is calculated from the inverse square law in optics. Observe that the judgments have captured a natural law here. As we shall see, presumably they could do the same in other areas of perception.

Note the sensitivity of the results when the object is very close to the source, for then it absorbs most of the value of the relative index and a small error in its distance from the source yields great error in the values. From this sensory experiment we can see that the observed intensity of illumination varies (approximately) inversely with the square of the distance. The more carefully designed the experiment, the better the results obtained from the visual observations.

Electric Consumption of Household Appliances

Table 5.6 shows paired comparisons done by engineering estimating the consumption of electricity of common household appliances. How compatible are the derived and actual vectors?

Table 5.6 Electric Consumption (Kilowatt-Hours) of Household Appliances

Annual Electric Consumption	Electric Range	Refrigerator	TV	Dish wash	Iron	Radio	Hair dryer	Eigen-vector	Actual Relative Weights
Electric Range	1	2	5	8	7	9	9	.393	.392
Refrigerator	1/2	1	4	5	5	7	9	.261	.242
TV	1/5	1/4	1	2	5	6	8	.131	.167
Dishwasher	1/8	1/5	1/2	1	4	9	9	.110	.120
Iron	1/7	1/5	1/5	1/4	1	5	9	.061	.047
Radio	1/9	1/7	1/6	1/9	1/5	1	5	.028	.028
Hairdryer	1/9	1/9	1/8	1/9	1/9	1/5	1	.016	.003

Note: The hairdryer is of such a small magnitude that it probably should have been left out to make the set homogeneous.

How to Derive the 1–9 Scale

In Chapter 2 we looked at the Fundamental Scale of Absolute Numbers we use to express pairwise-comparison judgments with their justification in Chapter 2. Here we will describe how we use scientific knowledge from psychophysics to develop the numbers used in the comparison scale [2].

First let us note that the human mind cannot respond to stimuli in linear proportion to their intensity. As the intensity of the stimulus increases, our senses become duller and gradually level off to a point where we cannot distinguish between an explosion and a much larger explosion, a distant hill and a mountain or among very large numbers ranging from the millions to the billions. We can describe this dampening effect of response by a mathematical function $w(s)$, which we can derive from an equation that describes the relationship between the response at a distance to a stimulus s that must be proportional to what the response would be at the origin.

To be able to sense objects in the environment, our brains miniaturize them within our system of neurons so that we have a proportional relationship between what we perceive and what is out there. Without proportionality we cannot coordinate our thinking with our actions with the accuracy needed to control the environment. Proportionality with respect to a single stimulus requires that our response to a proportionately amplified or attenuated stimulus should be proportional to what our response would be to the original value of that stimulus. If $w(s)$ is our response to a stimulus of magnitude s, then the foregoing gives rise to the functional equation $w(as) = bw(s)$. This equation can also be obtained as the necessary condition for solving the Fredholm equation of the second kind:

$$\int_a^b K(s,t)\, w(t)\, dt \; = \; \lambda_{max}\, w(s)$$

obtained as the continuous generalization of the discrete formulation $Aw = \lambda_{max} w$ for deriving priorities where, instead of the positive reciprocal matrix A in the principal eigenvalue problem, we have a positive kernel, $K(s,t) > 0$, with $K(s,t)\, K(t,s) = 1$ that is also consistent; that is, $K(s,t)\, K(t,u) = K(s,u)$, for all s, t, and u. The solution of this functional equation in the real domain is given by

$$w(s) = Ce^{\log b \frac{\log s}{\log a}} P\!\left(\frac{\log s}{\log a}\right)$$

where P is a periodic function of period 1 and $P(0) = 1$. One of the simplest such examples with $u = \log s / \log a$ is $P(u) = \cos(u/2\pi)$ for which $P(0) = 1$.

The logarithmic law of response to stimuli can be obtained as a first-order approximation to this solution through series expansions of the exponential and the cosine functions as:

$$v(u) = C_1 e^{-\beta u} P(u) \approx C_2 \log s + C_3$$

where $\log ab \equiv -\beta, \beta > 0$. The expression on the right is known as the Weber-Fechner law of logarithmic response, $M = a \log s + b, a \neq 0$, to a stimulus of magnitude s. This law was empirically established and tested in 1860 by Gustav Theodor Fechner who used a law formulated by Ernest Heinrich Weber regarding discrimination between two nearby values of a stimulus. We have now shown that that Fechner's version can be derived by starting with a functional equation for stimulus response.

The integer-valued scale of response used in making paired-comparison judgments can be derived from the logarithmic response function as follows. For a given value of the stimulus, the magnitude of response remains the same until the value of the stimulus is increased sufficiently large in proportion to the value of the stimulus, thus preserving the proportionality of relative increase in stimulus for it to be detectable for a new response. This suggests the idea, well known in psychology, of just noticeable differences (jnd). Thus, starting with a stimulus s_0, successive magnitudes of the new stimuli take the form:

$$s_1 = s_0 + \Delta s_0 = s_0 + \frac{\Delta s_0}{s_0} s_0 = s_0(1 + r)$$

$$s_2 = s_1 + \Delta s_1 = s_1(1 + r) = s_0(1 + r)^2 \equiv s_0 \alpha^2$$

$$\vdots$$

$$s_n = s_{n-1}\alpha = s_0 \alpha^n \ (n = 0, 1, 2, ...)$$

We consider the responses to these stimuli to be measured on a ratio scale ($b = 0$). A typical response has the form $M_i = a \log \alpha^i$, $i = 1, ..., n$, or one after another they have the form $M_1 = a \log \alpha; M_2 = 2a \log \alpha; ...; M_n = na \log \alpha$. We take the ratios M_i / M_1, $i = 1, ..., n$, of these responses in which the first is the smallest and serves as the unit of comparison, thus obtaining the *integer* values 1, 2, ..., n of the Fundamental Scale of the AHP. It appears that numbers are intrinsic to our ability to make comparisons, and were not just an invention by our primitive ancestors.

The upshot of this approach is to observe that our responses fall into categories involving just noticeable differences from one category into another. Within each category we are unable to tell the difference between a certain value and a slightly larger value. At the very beginning we can compare an object with itself and obtain the value 1 for its dominance over itself with respect to a property. We then compare it with an object that is a little larger. Because of the JND syndrome, we would decide whether the slightly larger object is equal to it or falls in the next category, which is twice its size, and so on, thus obtaining the numbers 1, 2, 3,... and so on. But as we said before we cannot go on with very large numbers because we are unable to compare the object with something that is too large. If we do, we will make such an error that our estimate in the comparison will be very inconsistent and therefore inaccurate and our result will be unreliable. Essentially it amounts to assigning values from the positive integers, by dividing our ability to sense things into high, medium, and low and then dividing each one into three categories so we would get for the largest value (high, high), followed by (high, medium), (high, low), (medium, high), (medium, medium), (medium, low), (low, high), (low, medium), (low, low). The numerical values we assigned to them would range from 9 for the (high, high) pair and so on down to 1 for the (low, low) pair. When we compare the smaller object, with the larger object we use the reciprocal value. If the large apple is three times bigger than the small orange, then the orange is automatically one-third as large as the apple. One can prove mathematically that small changes in the numbers lead to small changes in the final answers that we call priorities. This is one reason why using the fuzzification methods of the recent fad fuzzy sets, has little to contribute in improving the outcome of the AHP. Because the numbers 1-9 are not crisp in the first place, they don't need to be made fuzzy as some fuzzy set zealots want to do to every number they run into. Our advice is never to use fuzzy sets in decision making with the AHP and as found by Buede and Maxwell experimentally [3], never to use it, period.

Because of increases in inconsistency when we compare more than about seven elements, we need to keep in mind no more than seven plus or minus two elements. This was first conjectured by the psychologist George Miller in the 1950s and explained in the AHP in the 1970s [4]. Finally, we note that the scale just derived is attached to the importance we assign to judgments. If we have an exact measurement such as 2.375 and want to use it for our judgment without attaching significance to it, we can use its entire value without approximation.

Priorities, Consistency, and Number of Elements

Although we have not emphasized it here, the AHP has four axioms: reciprocal judgments, homogeneous elements, hierarchic or feedback-dependent structure, and rank-order expectations. The validation examples and numerous applications demonstrate that the axioms provide a valid logical foundation for the morphological structures used to represent complex decisions, the judgments, and how they are elicited to produce a reliable outcome.

Assume that we are given n stones, $A_1, ..., A_n$, with known weights $w_1, ..., w_n$, respectively. Now suppose that a matrix of pairwise ratios is formed whose rows give the ratios of the weights of each stone with respect to all others. Thus we have the equation: $\mathbf{A}w = nw$ where $\mathbf{A}$ is multiplied on the right by the vector of weights w shown in Figure 5.2.

$$
Aw = \begin{array}{c} \\ A_1 \\ \vdots \\ A_n \end{array}
\begin{bmatrix}
w_1/w_1 & \cdots & w_1/w_n \\
\vdots & \cdots & \vdots \\
w_n/w_1 & \cdots & w_n/w_n
\end{bmatrix}
\begin{bmatrix} w_1 \\ \vdots \\ w_n \end{bmatrix}
= n \begin{bmatrix} w_1 \\ \vdots \\ w_n \end{bmatrix} = nw
$$

Figure 5.2 The Consistent Eigenvector Formulation

The result of this multiplication is nw. Thus to recover the scale from the matrix of ratios, we must solve the problem $\mathbf{A}w = nw$ or $(\mathbf{A} - n\mathbf{I})w = 0$. This is a system of homogeneous linear equations. It has a nontrivial solution if and only if the determinant of $\mathbf{A} - n\mathbf{I}$ vanishes, that is, n is an eigenvalue of $\mathbf{A}$. Now $\mathbf{A}$ has unit rank since every row is a constant multiple of the first row. Thus all its eigenvalues except one are zero. The sum of the eigenvalues of a matrix is equal to its trace, the sum of its diagonal elements, and in this case the trace of $\mathbf{A}$ is equal to n. Thus n is an eigenvalue of $\mathbf{A}$, and we have a nontrivial solution. The solution consists of positive entries and is unique to within a multiplicative constant.

To make w unique, we can normalize its entries by dividing by their sum. Thus given the comparison matrix, we can recover the scale. In this case, the solution is any column of $\mathbf{A}$ normalized. Notice that in $\mathbf{A}$ the reciprocal property $a_{ji} = 1/a_{ij}$ holds; thus, also, $a_{ii} = 1$. Another property of $\mathbf{A}$ is that it is consistent: its entries satisfy the condition $a_{jk} = a_{ik}/a_{ij}$. Thus the entire matrix can be constructed from a set of n elements that form a chain across the rows and columns.

In the general case, the precise value of w_i/w_j cannot be given – only an estimate of it as a judgment. For the moment, consider an estimate of these values by an expert who is assumed to make small perturbations of the coefficients. This implies small perturbations of the eigenvalues. The problem now becomes $\mathbf{A}'w' = \lambda_{max}w'$, where λ_{max} is the largest eigenvalue of $\mathbf{A}'$. To simplify the notation, we will continue to write $\mathbf{A}w = \lambda_{max}w$, where $\mathbf{A}$ is the matrix of pairwise comparisons. The problem now is to find how good the estimate of w is. Notice that if w is obtained by solving this problem, the matrix whose entries are w_i/w_j is a consistent matrix. It is a consistent estimate of the matrix $\mathbf{A}$. $\mathbf{A}$ itself needs not be consistent. In fact, the entries of $\mathbf{A}$ do not even need be transitive; that is, stone A_1 may be preferred to stone A_2 and A_2 to A_3, but A_3 may be preferred to A_1. What we would like is a measure of the error due to inconsistency. It turns out that **A** is consistent if and only if $\lambda_{max} = n$ and that we always have $\lambda_{max} \geq n$.

Since small changes in a_{ij} imply a small change in λ_{max}, the deviation of the latter from n is a deviation from consistency and can be represented by $(\lambda_{max} - n)/(n-1)$, which is called the *consistency index* (CI). The consistency index associated with a comparison matrix is compared with a consistency index that represents the average of consistencies of random comparisons at the same matrix order. This index is called the *random index* (RI).

The relations $a_{ji} = 1/a_{ij}$ and $a_{ii} = 1$ are preserved in the matrices to improve consistency. The reason for this is that if stone A_1 is estimated to be k times heavier than stone A_2, one should require that stone A_2 be estimated to be $1/k$ times the weight of stone A_1. If the consistency ratio is significantly small, the estimates are accepted; otherwise, we try to improve consistency by obtaining additional information. Three things contribute to the consistency of a judgment: (1) the homogeneity of the elements in a group, that is, not comparing a grain of sand with a mountain; (2) the number of elements in the group, that is a person cannot hold in mind simultaneously the relations of more than a few objects; and (3) the knowledge and diligence of the decision maker.

To get a feel for what the consistency index might be telling us about a positive n-by-n reciprocal matrix **A**, consider the following simulation. Choose the entries of **A** above the main diagonal at random from the seventeen values $\{1/9, 1/8, \ldots, 1, 2, \ldots, 8, 9\}$. Then fill in the entries of **A** below the diagonal by taking reciprocals. Put 1's down the main diagonal and compute the consistency index. Do this 50,000 times and take the average, which we call the *random index*. Table 5.7 shows the values obtained from one set of such simulations, and also their first-order differences, for matrices of size 1, 2,..., 15, although we always recommend comparing 7 ± 2 elements.

Table 5.7 Random Index with First- Order Differences

Order	1	2	3	4	5	6	7	8	9	10	11	12	13	14	15
RI	0	0	0.52	0.89	1.11	1.25	1.35	1.40	1.45	1.49	1.52	1.54	1.56	1.58	1.59
First-order differences		0	0.52	0.37	0.22	0.14	0.10	0.05	0.05	0.04	0.03	0.02	0.02	0.02	0.01

Figure 5.3 plots the first two rows of Table 5.7. It shows the asymptotic nature of random inconsistency. Since it would be pointless to try to discern any priority ranking from a set of random comparison judgments, we should probably be uncomfortable about proceeding unless the consistency index of a pairwise comparison-matrix is very much smaller than the corresponding random index value in Table 5.7. The consistency ratio of a pairwise-comparison matrix is the ratio of its consistency index to the corresponding random index value in Table 5.7.

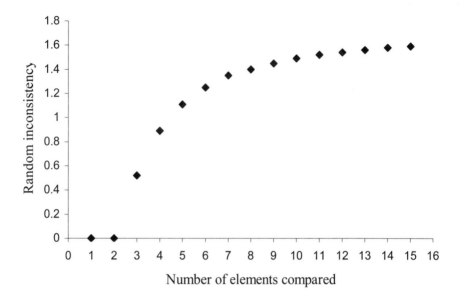

Figure 5.3 Plot of Random Inconsistency

The notion of order of magnitude is essential in any mathematical consideration of changes in measurement. When we have a numerical value, say between 1 and 10, for some measurements and want to determine whether change in this value is significant or not, we reason as follows: A change of a whole integer value is critical because it changes the magnitude and identity of the original number significantly. If the change in value is on the order of a 1 percent or less, it would be so small (by two orders of magnitude) that it would be considered negligible. If this perturbation is a decimal (one order of magnitude smaller), however, we are likely to modify the original value by this decimal without losing the significance and identity of the original number as we first understood it to be. Thus in synthesizing nearly consistent judgment values, changes that are too large can cause dramatic shift in our understanding and values that are too small cause no shift in our understanding. We are left with only values of one order of magnitude smaller that we can deal with incrementally to change our understanding. It follows that our allowable consistency ratio should be no more than about 0.10. The requirement of 10 percent cannot be made smaller without trivializing the impact of inconsistency. But inconsistency itself is important – without it, new knowledge that changes a preference cannot be admitted. Assuming that all knowledge should be consistent contradicts our experience that understanding must be continually revised.

If the consistency ratio is larger than desired, we do three things. First find the most inconsistent judgment in the matrix (for example, that judgment for which $\varepsilon_{ij} = a_{ij} w_j / w_i$ is largest). Second, determine the range of values to which the most inconsistent judgment can be changed to improve consistency. And third, ask the judge to consider, if he can, changing his judgment to a plausible value in that range. If he is unwilling, we try with the second most inconsistent judgment and so on. If no judgment is changed, the decision is postponed until we get better understanding of the stimuli. Judges who understand the theory are always willing to revise their judgments – often not to the full value but partially – and then examine the second most inconsistent judgment and so on. If a judge is unable to improve his consistency, more information may be required.

Before proceeding further, the following observations may be useful. The quality of response to stimuli is determined by three factors: Accuracy (or validity), consistency, and efficiency (or amount of information generated). Our judgment is much more sensitive to large perturbations. When we speak of perturbation, we have in mind numerical change from consistent ratios obtained from priorities. The larger the inconsistency – and hence the larger the perturbations in priorities – the greater is our sensitivity to make changes in the numerical values assigned. Conversely, the smaller the inconsistency, the harder it is to know where the best changes should be made to produce not only better consistency but also better validity of the outcome. Once near consistency is attained, it becomes uncertain which coefficients should be perturbed by small amounts to transform a nearly consistent matrix to a consistent one. If such perturbations were forced, they could be arbitrary and thus distort the validity of the derived priority vector in representing the underlying decision.

The third row of Table 5.7 gives the differences between successive numbers in the second row. Figure 5.4 plots these differences and shows the importance of the number seven as a cutoff point beyond which the differences are less than 0.10 where we are not sufficiently sensitive to make accurate changes in judgment on several elements simultaneously. This is a powerful result. It shows that comparing too many elements reduce sensitivity to an inconsistent judgment. Thus to be safe in deriving reliable priorities from comparisons, we should avoid comparing more than about seven elements.

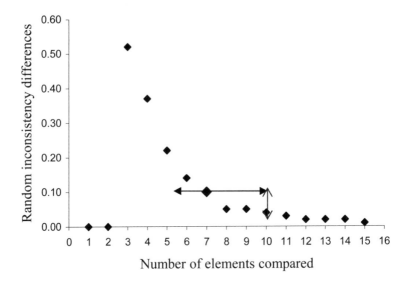

Figure 5.4 Plot of First Differences in Random Inconsistency

Sensitivity of the Eigenvector

Stability of the principal eigenvector also imposes a limit on our mental-channel capacity and highlights the importance of homogeneity. To a first-order approximation, perturbation Δw_1 in the principal eigenvector w_1 due to a perturbation ΔA in the matrix A where A is consistent is given by Wilkinson [5]:

$$\Delta w_1 = \sum_{j=2}^{n} (v_j^T \Delta A \; w_1 / (\lambda_1 - \lambda_j) \; v_j^T w_j) w_j$$

Here T indicates transposition. The eigenvector w_1 is insensitive to perturbation in A, if the number of terms n is small; if the principal eigenvalue λ_1 is separated from the other eigenvalues λ_j, here assumed to be distinct (otherwise a slightly more complicated argument can be made); and, if none of the products $v_j^T w_j$ of left and right eigenvectors is small, or if one of them is small, they are all small. But $v_1^T w_1$, the product of the normalized left and right principal eigenvectors of a consistent matrix is equal to n, which being an integer, is never very small. If n is relatively small and the elements being compared are homogeneous, none of the components of w_1 is arbitrarily small, and correspondingly, none of the components of $v_1{}^T$ is arbitrarily small. Their product cannot be arbitrarily small, w is insensitive to small perturbations of the consistent matrix **A**. The conclusion is that n must be small, and one must compare homogeneous elements.

When the eigenvalues have greater multiplicity than 1, the corresponding left and right eigenvectors will not be unique. In this case the cosine of the angle between them which is given by $v_i^T w_i$, corresponds to a particular choice of w_i and v_i . Even when w_i and v_i correspond to a simple λ_i they are arbitrary to within a multiplicative complex constant of unit modulus, but in this case $|\ v_i^T w_i|$ is fully determined. Because both vectors are normalized, we always have $|\ v_i^T w_i\ | < 1$.

Aggregating Individual Judgments into a Representative Group Judgment

Let us now talk about how to combine different judgments for comparing an apple and an orange in order to obtain a representative judgment for the group. We also want this representative judgment to satisfy the reciprocal relation. Let us note that we cannot use the arithmetic average. Suppose we have three people estimating how many times the apple is larger than the orange. If the first person says it is twice larger, the second three times larger, and the third four times larger, their average is $\dfrac{2+3+4}{3} = 3$ which is the actual value. But the reciprocal of 3 is not equal to $\dfrac{\frac{1}{2} + \frac{1}{3} + \frac{1}{4}}{3}$. Now we know that we will never again mention taking the arithmetic average for this purpose.

Since we cannot add and average numbers, we have one other simple alternative to try — that is, to multiply them and see if their average works. Let us observe using multiplication that if all the people give the same value to obtain the representative value for the group, we have to multiply these values and then take their root, which equals the number of people in the group. By perturbing these equal judgments, we would still have to take the root in order to get their representative judgments. The operation of taking the root n of n numbers multiplied together is known as the geometric mean. We might inquire whether using the geometric mean is the only way to combine group judgments. It turns out that under the fairly general conditions that are needed in group decision making, including the reciprocal property, it is the only way [3, 4, 5]. To take the geometric average of the numbers 2, 3, and 4 we multiply them and take the cube root because there are three people involved which we can write as $(2 \times 3 \times 4)^{1/3}$ .Of course everyone knows that $(2 \times 3 \times 4)^{1/3} = 2^{1/3} \times 3^{1/3} \times 4^{1/3}$. Here the root of each judgment is extracted by 1/3, which is the same for all of them. Now let us note that 1/3 + 1/3 + 1/3 = 1. We need this observation in the next step.

Individuals in a group possess different degrees of power as a result of many variables: formal authority within an organizational context, size and strength of an outside constituency, personal charisma, perceived intelligence, expertise on an issue, and the ability to call in favors owed by other group members. These factors, alone and in combination, make some group members stronger than others. If the people themselves have priorities x, y, and z that indicate their respective importance as judges, then their contribution will be different than the accorded value of 1/3; of course we have $x + y + z = 1$. In this case their judgments would – instead of being raised equally to the power of 1/3 are now raised to the respective powers of x, y, z and their average would be $2^x \times 3^y \times 4^z$.

Thus we have a way to obtain a representative group judgment when the people are equally important: a root or power of their judgments is taken that equals to 1 over their number n. This means that, in the product of the judgments, each judgment is taken to the power $1/n$, which indicates that all the judges have an equal priority of $1/n$. When the judges are not equally important, the root to take of their judgment is equal to their actual priority. Recall that the sum of the priorities of the judges is equal to 1. The product of their resulting judgments, raised to powers as their priorities, is then taken for the representative judgment for the group. How to derive priority for the people can be obtained from a hierarchy like Figure 5.5.

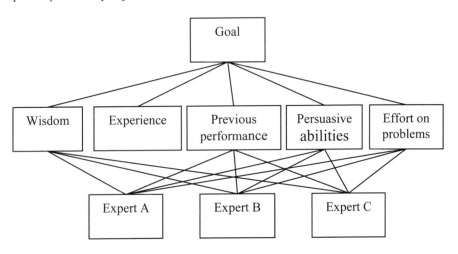

Figure 5.5 Example of a Hierarchy for Ranking Experts

Aggregating Individual Judgments: A Formal Approach

The foregoing results have been derived mathematically and at best we can summarize the findings here. Let the function $f(x_1,...,x_n)$ for synthesizing the judgments given by n judges satisfy the following conditions:

1. The separability condition (S): $f(x_1,...,x_n) = g(x_1)...g(x_n)$ for all $x_1,...,x_n$ in an interval P of positive numbers, where g is a function mapping P onto a proper interval J and is a continuous, associative, and cancellative operation. [(S) means that the influences of the individual judgments can be separated as here.]

2. The unanimity condition (U): $f(x,...,x) = x$ for all x in P. [(U) means that if everyone gives the same judgment x, this judgment should also be the synthesized judgment.]

3. The homogeneity condition (H): $f(ux_1,...,ux_n) = uf(x_1,...,x_n)$, where $u > 0$ and x_k, ux_k (k=1,2,...,n) are all in P. [For ratio judgments, (H) means that if everyone judges a ratio u times as large as another ratio, then the synthesized judgment should also be u times as large.]

4. The power conditions (P$_p$): $f(x_1^p,...,x_n^p) = f^p(x_1,...,x_n)$. [(P$_2$), for example, means that if the kth person judges the length of a side of a square to be x_k, the synthesized judgment on the area of that square will be given by the square of the synthesized judgment on the length of its side.]

5. The special case (R = P$_{-1}$): $f(\frac{1}{x_1},...,\frac{1}{x_n}) = 1/f(x_1,...,x_n)$. [(R) is of particular importance in ratio judgments. It means that the synthesized value of the reciprocal of the individual judgments should be the reciprocal of the synthesized value of the original judgments.]

Aczel and Saaty [6] proved the following theorem:

Theorem The general separable (S) synthesizing functions satisfying the unanimity (U) and homogeneity (H) conditions are the geometric mean and the root-mean-power. If moreover, the reciprocal property (R) is assumed even for a single n-tuple $(x_1,...,x_n)$ of the judgments of n individuals, where not all x_k are equal, then only the geometric mean satisfies all the previous conditions.

In any rational consensus, those who know more should, accordingly, influence the consensus more strongly than those who know less. Some people are clearly wiser and more sensible in such matters than others; others may be more powerful and their opinions too should be given greater weight. For such unequal importance of voters, not all g's in (S) are the same function. In place of (S), the weighted separability property (WS) is now $f(x_1,...,x_n) = g_1(x_1)...g_n(x_n)$. [(WS) implies that not all judges have the same weight when the judgments are synthesized, and the different influences are reflected in the different functions $(g_1,...,g_n)$.]

In this situation, Aczel and Alsina [7] proved the following theorem:

Theorem The general weighted-separable (WS) synthesizing functions with the unanimity (U) and homogeneity (H) properties are the weighted geometric mean $f(x_1, x_2, ..., x_n) = x_1^{q_1} x_2^{q_2}...x_n^{q_n}$ and the weighted root-mean-powers $f(x_1, x_2, ..., x_n) = \sqrt[\gamma]{q_1 x_1^\gamma + q_2 x_2^\gamma ... + q_n x_n^\gamma}$, where $q_1 + \cdots + q_n = 1$, $q_k > 0, k = 1,...,n$, $\gamma > 0$, but otherwise $q_1,...,q_n, \gamma$ are arbitrary constants.

If f also has the reciprocal property (R) and for a single set of entries $(x_1,...,x_n)$ of judgments of n individuals, where not all x_k are equal, then only the weighted geometric mean applies. The following theorem, which is an explicit statement of the synthesis problem that follows from the previous results, applies to the second and third cases of the deterministic approach:

Theorem If $x_1^{(i)},...,x_n^{(i)}$ $i = 1, ..., m$, are rankings of n alternatives by m independent judges and if a_i is the importance of judge i developed from a hierarchy for evaluating the judges, and hence $\sum_{i=1}^{m} a_i = 1$, then

$$\left(\prod_{i=1}^{m} x_1^{a_i}\right), ..., \left(\prod_{i=1}^{m} x_n^{a_i}\right)$$ are the combined ranks of the alternatives for the

m judges.

The power of judge i is simply a replication of his judgment (as if there were as many other judges as indicated by his power a_i), which implies multiplying his ratio by itself a_i times, and the result follows.

Judgments of Experts and Novices

Here is a useful observation for combining group judgments. When the members of a group are all experts who do not wish to participate in the judgment process but prefer to obtain their own answer after the group has structured a decision, we can apply the geometric mean or the mean weighted by the importance of the experts to the different individuals' final outcome to obtain an overall final outcome. If the people think of themselves as novices, however, and are willing to participate in debating and synthesizing individual judgments, then we apply the geometric mean if we wish to treat them as equal in order to derive a representative of a group judgment — or if necessary apply the process of weighting their judgments by their relative importance to derive each representative judgment for the group. When a group is very large and cannot get together, as in statistical sampling of a population, the problem must be organized by consultation with experts. Judgments must then be elicited at random and combined by the geometric mean to obtain representative samples for the population and also an answer for that population. The contacts are made by telephone, by e-mail or even by television via remote control.

And now a final observation: When people make pairwise-comparison judgments, their judgments may be inconsistent. In the AHP the measure of inconsistency is used to show that an inconsistency much beyond 10 percent is undesirable. The DecisionLens and SuperDecisions software programs not only provide the inconsistency index but also indicate the most inconsistent judgment. The person making the judgment can then be invited to change his mind. If judgments remain very inconsistent and there is no way to improve them, however, a decision cannot be made – unless the corresponding criterion has low priority and thus does not seriously affect the overall inconsistency. When all the matrices of several people are consistent or nearly consistent, the corresponding group matrix is also consistent or nearly consistent. When a resulting group matrix is inconsistent, one needs to improve the judgments by consulting with the group about the most inconsistent judgments in the hope of getting them to agree about improving them. Sometimes it is useful to ask an individual, whose judgment is most consistent with the remaining judgments of the group in the matrix, to try and pursue the others judgment. Despite inconsistency, the priority derived from an inconsistent matrix can themselves can be discussed and modified to produce better agreement. A plausible way to deal with the issue of disagreements to present the parties (or different groups) themselves in the structure, have each group provide its more consistent judgments, and let an agreed upon mediator prioritize the importance of the parties relative to various criteria and use these priorities to combine their separate outcomes.   Thus   the   major   ground   for disagreement may be wide variations in judgments.   Although such judgments call for substantial discussion, ultimately the geometric mean is the rational way to combine them into a judgment that is representative of the entire group. We will have more to say on this subject in Chapter 13.

References

1.   Saaty, T.L. *Theory and Applications of the Analytic Network Process.* Pittsburgh: RWS publications, 2005.
2.   Saaty, T.L. *Fundamentals of Decision Making with the Analytic Hierarchy Process.* Pittsburgh: RWS publications, 2000.
3.   Buede, D. and D.T. Maxwell "Rank Disagreement: A Comparison of Multi-criteria Methodologies," *Journal of Multi-Criteria Decision Analysis*, 4, (1995):1-21.
4.   Miller, G. A. "The Magical Number Seven Plus or Minus Two: Some Limits on our Capacity for Processing Information." *Psychological Review* 63 (1956): 81-97.
5.   Wilkinson, J.H. *The Algebraic Eigenvalue Problem.* Oxford: Clarendon Press, 1965.
6.   Aczel, J. and T. L. Saaty "Procedures for Synthesizing Ratio Judgments." *Journal of Mathematical Psychology* 27 (1983) 93-102.
7.   Aczel, J. and C. Alsina "On Synthesis of Judgments." *Socio-Economic Planning Sciences* 20 (1986): 333-339.

Chapter 6

Group Sessions: The Promise and the Problems

In group decision making, sharing ideas and insights often leads to better understanding of the issues. Brainstorming to generate new ideas works better with a group than a single decision maker could hope to achieve. In an ideal situation, the group is small and the participants are well informed, highly motivated, and fully cooperative in responding to the basic question being considered. In reality, such a scenario is the exception. Often the participants are unequal in their expertise, influence, and perspective, and getting them to cooperate may take some coaxing by the leader. Even then, organizing the diverse responses from its individual members to arrive at a group solution could pose a considerable challenge, especially if the issues addressed are complex ones. The group needs a way to structure all the information.

Moreover, group cooperation is far less than ideal. A leader is needed to direct the group process in a systematic way, draw and structure group knowledge and judgments. The leader should be able to identify points of agreement and disagreement and deal with disagreements effectively. He not only needs to lead the group to structure all the information, but also solicit judgments without forcing consensus. When the AHP is used in a group session, the members structure the problem, provide the judgments, debate the judgments, and make a case for their values until agreement or compromise is reached.

Conducting Group Sessions

The process of group interaction cannot be reduced to a set of rules. As in any activity that broadens people's views and stimulates their thinking, flexibility is essential. What we offer here are suggestions based on experience in conducting many group sessions.

Preliminary Steps

First make sure that the participants are comfortable and well provided with writing materials, refreshments, adequate lighting, and so on. If the AHP is being used for the first time, explain how it works and illustrate it with simple applications and then elaborate ones. Show some validation examples, too, and help the group to do one involving aggregation of group judgments. A computer and software will be needed for validation exercises to aggregate judgments because they involve computation. Allow for a question-and-answer period. The objective of this introductory session is to convince the group that they will be free to structure the problem as elaborately as they wish and that their judgments will be aggregated in a credible way. Accepting a variety of different judgments will not change the outcome as much as they fear. Structuring the key elements to represent a problem is only half the story. The other half – equally important – is how individual judgments regarding relative dominance of the elements are elicited and aggregated to produce representative group judgments.   The exercise emphasizes the importance of formulating each question carefully to elicit judgments.

It may be helpful to have two discussion leaders with one or two assistants.   Since the typical session lasts for two days, especially for planning, much of the pressure on one leader is reduced by having the other carry on when necessary. A computer terminal makes it possible to get answers immediately and to test the consequences of judgments with respect to sensitivity and consistency.

A good way to begin the session is by brainstorming the overall focus or goal of the problem. Several suggestions may be made; then one is selected as most representative of the overall concern. The important thing is to define the objective of the discussion clearly at the very beginning.

Brainstorming

Brainstorming, a process of eliciting ideas freely, is based on the premise that deferring judgments enhances creativity and oral criticism diminishes it. Ideas are invited using a well-formulated question. At this stage evaluation is prohibited. Discussion may be allowed for clarification only. Setting the generality of the question is important. A question that is too general will generate diverse ideas that may be difficult to structure later on. A question that is too specific will narrow the scope of ideas and possibly miss important elements or even clusters of elements.

With the AHP, brainstorming will be more efficient if the leader is familiar with its applications and uses the clusters that are commonly used for certain types of problems. For a simple problem it may be enough to have clusters of criteria, perhaps subcriteria, and alternatives. For more complex problems we may need to have clusters of stakeholders, people affected by the decision, and similar concerns with people who are involved, and finally progress to do benefit-cost-opportunity-risk evaluations, brainstorming their elements separately. For even more complex problems that involve higher-level values, a cluster of strategic criteria will be needed. For prediction and planning the group needs to identify all the parties and list their objectives.

There are hundreds of AHP/ANP applications available for a group leader to study.

The group can also use brainwriting – that is, participants write their ideas on sheets of paper, one idea per sheet. Post-it notes are useful because they can be moved around during the structuring process. This technique is also known as the KJ method [1]. Here we will consider an example of using brainwriting to create a *strategy map*, which is a set of an organization's strategic objectives for creating its tangible values, the first step in constructing a Balanced Scorecard [2]. The four perspectives of financial, customers, internal business process, and organization and learning, commonly used to construct a Balanced Scorecard, can be used directly to form the questions in order to draw out ideas. Participants may need to be introduced to the concept before the session. Some of the objectives in the map may be considered uncontrollable and are only achieved after attaining the controllable objectives. Hence after the strategy map is constructed, it is useful to organize the objectives further to produce a set of controllable objectives that can be used as criteria to develop and evaluate action programs later. Here are seven steps to take during a brainwriting session [3]:

Provide the materials and tools for the session. The following materials and tools are needed to conduct the brainwriting session.

- Three large flipcharts or whiteboards. One is for the group's post-it notes, one for arranging the notes for each issue, and one for structuring the brainwriting results of the four issues. The leader draws lines on the third one, dividing the space horizontally into four parts, and labels the parts from top to bottom: Financial, Customers, Internal Business Process, Organization and Learning.
- Post-it notes for all participants, preferably in four colors with one for each issue.
- Pens or pencils for all participants.

State the objective of the session and explain the process. The leader opens the session by stating that today the objective is to produce the organization's strategy map. There are four different issues to be brainstormed that will be discussed and connected later in the structure.

Draw out ideas for an issue. The leader announces the first question: What are the tangible outcomes our organization should strive for? He then asks participants to list their responses to the question on the post-it notes, reminding them to write clearly and concisely, one note per idea. For an example we will start with the financial issue.

Collect and organize group responses. The leader asks the participants to stick their notes on a flipchart or whiteboard so that everybody can study them. The group then discusses and arranges them to produce a small number of tangible outcomes. They do this by moving the notes to another flipchart or whiteboard, stacking notes with the same general idea together as they are moved. They make sure that they empty the first flipchart or whiteboard completely, leaving no ideas behind. The leader then moves the organized notes to the the third flipchart or whiteboard, puts them in the "Financial Space," and tells the group to study the outcome.

Continue drawing out and organizing ideas for the other issues. The leader repeats steps 3 and 4 for the other issues and announces the questions in the following order:

- What expectations do we need to meet for customers to act favorably (by buying our products) so that our organization can achieve the tangible outcomes we brainstormed earlier?
- What internal business processes do we need to master to ensure that we meet the external expectations we brainstormed earlier?
- What organizational and learning objectives do we need to strive for to improve the internal business processes we brainstormed earlier?

The group now has a strategy map with a complete set of strategic objectives.

Identify leverages. The leader may ask the group (or delegate a smaller group) to come up with the leverages or controllable objectives that will be used as criteria for designing and evaluating the organization's action programs.

Follow up. The next step is to brainstorm the strategic actions that will lead to the objectives, which in turn will be synthesized into a small number of action programs.

Figure 6.1 is the strategy map of a steel company that has used the AHP for its decisions (Chapter 4).

Several objectives are considered as leverages; drawing from each of the four areas:

- Increase the number of partnerships.
- Increase the revenue per partnership.
- Increase customer satisfaction and loyalty.
- Be responsive to customer requests.
- Be knowledgeable about customers' business objectives and their key success factors.

The company continues the process by constructing the complete Balanced Scorecard and organizes the strategic actions into a smaller set of action programs:

- Develop a strategic customer program.
- Develop a strategic product program.
- Develop a customer relationship management (CRM) information system.
- Develop a skill inventory and enhancement program.

Constructing the Hierarchy

With the elements identified, the group constructs the hierarchy by connecting elements that influence other elements. The hierarchy can be as detailed as necessary to cover the issues. For the example described here, there would be a three-level hierarchy: the goal on top, the objectives at the second level, and the programs at the third level. After the hierarchy is completed, it should be drawn, typed, and distributed to all the participants. Before proceeding to the judgments, revisions are made and the hierarchy is retyped and redistributed. Such work can also be done on computers.

Breaking down a complex issue into different levels is particularly useful for a group with widely varying perspectives. Each member can present his or her own concerns and definitions, no matter what level they are on. Then the leader helps the group create the overall structure of the issue. In this way agreement can be reached on the higher-order and lower-order aspects of the issue through a clustering and ordering of all the concerns that members have expressed.

The group then agrees on how it will enter judgments. The whole group might start at the top level and then progress downward. It may delegate to subgroups the responsibility of considering, subdividing further, or setting priorities on a particular level. Or it may choose a combination of these ways.

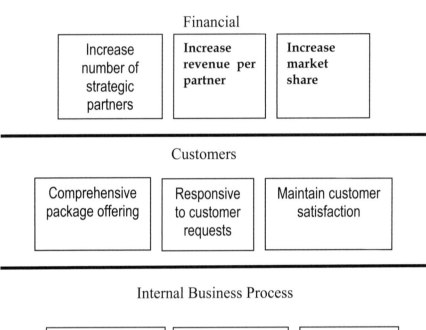

Figure 6.1 Strategy Map of an Organization's Objectives

Setting Priorities and Synthesizing

Setting priorities is by nature interactive and noisy and involves bargaining and persuasion. This lively interaction need not, however, be perfectly orchestrated or the participants may feel regimented and intimidated. Those who have no patience for the process should be allowed simply to observe or, if they wish, to leave the room and return when the hubbub is over. A leader should be sensitive to the unspoken feelings of group members. Some need coaxing and encouragement to participate. In a large group the business of setting priorities is more easily handled by dividing the members into specialized subgroups, each dealing with an issue of particular interest or expertise. When the subgroups rejoin for a final justification, the values in each matrix can be debated and revised if desired.

The debate could be eliminated entirely by gathering individual opinions using a questionnaire, a method that is described later. The final values are derived from the geometric mean of the judgments. Recall that to compute the geometric mean, the values are multiplied and a root equal to the number of people who provided the values is taken. For example, the geometric mean of 2, 3, and 7 is $\sqrt[3]{2\times3\times7}$, which is approximately 3.48. This number is used as the judgment in the matrix.

Taking the geometric mean of individual judgments is the way to resolve a lack of consensus on values only after debate has failed. Another method of resolving conflict is to vote on the proposed values. The final solution can also be obtained as a range of values that represents the range of judgments. The individual judgments are transmitted by radio keypads and collected by the computer and synthesized into the group judgment. Each individual judgment is stored separately so it can be analyzed for its consistency if desired, or at the end of the process, any individual's personal results may be obtained.

The AHP does not subvert human nature. There is no guarantee that dissent can be harnessed, nor should it be. Dissent is a valuable basic process that should not be banned in group interaction. But if anything is to be accomplished, dissent must eventually lead to some kind of cooperation.

Special Problems in Group Sessions

The leader of a group session should be prepared to deal with such problems as inequality of power and expertise among members, varying degrees of interest in certain questions, frequent change of expressed preferences, and unwillingness to reveal the true strength of preferences. The following paragraphs deal with these special problems of group sessions.

Unequal power and expertise. Groups are often composed of people with different levels of status, knowledge, and experience. A superior might be unwilling to participate in a process that treats his judgment as equal to that of subordinates. The chances that such a person will abide by the outcome are slim indeed.

One way to handle this problem is by weighting votes according to the importance or expertise of the participants. The group can design a hierarchy to judge the relative power and merit of the people who will be voting. All factors that bear on the issue at hand should be included, such as power, experience, political favors, fame, wealth, and ability to disrupt or withhold participation. The people can then be compared according to their relative influence with respect to these factors. This will result in the priorities for weighting the respective people's judgments. The final solution is obtained not just by taking the geometric mean, but by raising each person's judgment to the power of his priority. The power and merit of individuals, will shift as the issues change.

But votes do not have to be weighted if the interaction process itself, combined with the participants' knowledge of each other, allows people to exercise their influence through reasoned debate to reach consensus judgment. Shared decision making exposes an organization's leaders to a broader range of views and arguments than is typically filtered up to them. The AHP thus serves a useful intelligence-gathering function.

Variable preferences. In groups that must decide on a host of complex and varied issues, some people may be much more interested in certain questions than others. Such people are often willing to bargain for support on issues of importance to themselves by trading their own votes on less important questions. Bargaining helps a group come to an agreement and speeds the process. But when trading of political favors determines the outcome, not facts or informed judgment, there is little point in using the AHP. The group should have a positive interest in understanding the complexity of the problem and finding approaches to its solution.

Changes in preferences. People may change their judgments as a result of new information or shifts in external factors such as the state of the economy. Such change complicates the business of planning, allocating resources, and predicting the behavior of people and organizations. The question arises whether the AHP can be useful if priorities and the outcome of decisions are subject to sudden change. Of course, the AHP does not change reality. It cannot impose stability on an unstable environment. But the AHP does try to make reality comprehensible. It can also provide an opportunity to find out which variables are especially sensitive to change and to attach certain probabilities to those changes.

The AHP is not a tool for one-time application but a process that has ongoing validity and utility. It permits iterations and adaptations that can incorporate changing environmental factors. Thus the question of the AHP's usefulness in the context of change may reduce itself to the question of whether people are willing to spend the time required to participate in the process. Does the expenditure of personal and organizational resources seem justified? Or would people rather rely on seat-of-the-pants of decision making and problem solving?

Unwillingness to reveal preferences: Sometimes people are not willing to reveal their true preferences and the strength of their attachment. They may even wish to hide their secret agenda item because an explicit statement might expose it as a focus for opposition. If people are unwilling to state their preferences, the definition of issues will be incomplete and the group's analysis and priority setting will be inadequate. One strategy for coping with hidden agendas is to include enough people in the group session to produce a broad range of ideas. In such a situation other people may be able to anticipate hidden agendas and put them out on the table for discussion. Another strategy is to design the rules so that □the list of priorities can emerge only from the set of stated issues.

If a certain person is intent on disrupting the process, perhaps by distorting his or her preferences, that person can be isolated by dividing the group into smaller subgroups so that the majority can proceed without interruption. Clearly, groups should be prepared in advance to use the AHP. If the organization is committed to its use because of the benefits it expects, the group will probably regulate itself.

Getting the Best Results

When applying the AHP in a group session, several factors may affect the quality of the results. Some have to do with the people involved, others with the process itself. In conducting a group session, the leader should be concerned about the problem, be willing to share without dominating, encourage the participants, and set targets to reach on time. This leader should be willing to listen to suggestions and dissent and then, if necessary, modify the approach accordingly. The leader should also encourage the reticent ones to express themselves.

The room should be large and comfortable. Participants should be able to face, hear, and see each other easily. Minutes should be taken and the important points of the debate recorded for the final report. Thus the environment should be the best conceivable place to encourage camaraderie and break down the barriers of formality. The problem and its solution should be seen as the work of all involved.

The number of people in the work group is significant. It helps to have a lot of people participate in constructing the hierarchy. The more ideas offered, the richer the representation of relevant issues. But analyzing the elements of the hierarchy can become unwieldy if there are too many people with diverse points of view. In this case it is better to form smaller sub-groups for priority setting.

The status and expertise of the group leader (or indeed a member) can influence the outcome. Usually this is good because experience and informed judgment contribute to a better understanding of complex situations. But everyone should be encouraged to participate, even if the range of judgments widens. As a group becomes more experienced in using the AHP, consistency should improve. Commitment is another important factor. Generally the AHP should be used for group interaction only when a majority have a genuine interest in the outcome of the process, are willing to be open-minded about the possibilities, and have set aside the necessary time to develop the structure and make the judgments.

In constructing the hierarchy, the number of levels may affect the quality of the results. The levels should relate naturally to each other. If necessary, a level may be expanded into two or more levels or even eliminated. The criteria at each level should be of the same order of magnitude and relate to at least two elements in the level immediately below as it will be necessary to pairwise-compare elements in the level below with respect to an element in the level above.

In applying the AHP, most of the problems occur in the priority-setting stage. Particularly when the process is being used for the first time, the number of elements being compared and the order in which the comparisons are made should be carefully monitored. The more elements in a level, the greater the chance of inconsistency and the more taxing the comparison process is. To represent the issue adequately, however, a sufficient number of elements (7 ± 2) must be listed. As a rule, it is best to compare the strongest and the weakest elements in a level first with respect to an element in the level above. The resulting value serves as a guidepost for the other comparisons; all the other judgments will perforce be less than this one.

Attributes perceived through the senses can be evaluated more precisely than those recalled from memory or abstract ideas. The meaning of the values in the pairwise- comparison scale must be clearly understood. It is best to state the verbal judgment first about what dominates what, and then translate it into its numerical value. It is essential to allow enough time for debating priorities. The more carefully the judgments are made, the more valid the conclusions. Consensus is not essential at the lower levels of the hierarchy, but it is needed at the higher levels where the priorities strongly drive the results.

Using Questionnaires

Participants in group sessions sometimes remark that the process of judging strained their patience when it took too long a time. To remedy this problem, a minimum number of judgments can be required rather than the usual set of all possible comparisons. The minimum number of judgments must interconnect, however, so that every element at each level of the hierarchy is compared, directly or indirectly, with every other element. If one row is used, the element governing that row is related to all the other elements, making it possible to obtain relationships among the other elements indirectly. Thus A = 7B and A = 5C leads to 7B = 5C or B = 7/5C.

One way to make at least the minimum number of comparisons is to use a *spanning tree*. Figure 6.2 shows a spanning tree that connects nine criteria. If, for example, nine elements are being examined, eight comparisons (line segments) are the minimum. Making all the judgments in one row is one way to get the minimum number. In a spanning tree all the elements are connected in one and only one way to prevent ambiguity, and we can travel from any element to any other. Such a connection makes it possible to derive all other comparisons in the matrix from just a few of them. This matrix is consistent because it is entirely derived from a minimal set of judgments.

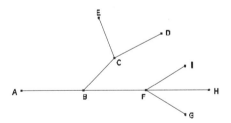

Figure 6.2 Spanning Tree

Another way to get the minimum number of judgments is to travel down the diagonal of the matrix that is immediately above the main diagonal of unit entries. This has the advantage of involving different elements in each comparison in contrast to using, for example, the first row in which the governing element id involved in every one of the comparisons. To get some redundancy which should lead to better accuracy with respect to the real world, take the next diagonal above that.

One may also use questionnaires to collect the judgments. The disadvantage of a questionnaire is that live debate is missing with its opportunity for passing information. For each pair, a questionnaire asks for a judgment expressing the intensity of dominance with respect to the criterion: "Does A dominate B or does B dominate A with respect to this criterion?" Indicate how strongly (See Figure 6.3.) The same process is followed for the remaining pairs. If there are several people, we can ask each of them to provide a minimum number of judgments, but if the spanning tree for each is different it will enrich the results. The spanning tree would be generated by a computer program that randomizes the selection of the elements to be compared.

Questionnaire
Compare X and Y with respect to a criterion

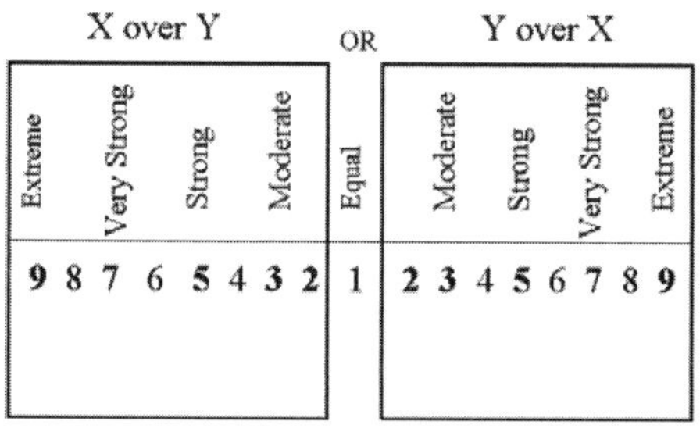

			X over Y			OR			Y over X				
	Extreme	Very Strong	Strong	Moderate		Equal		Moderate	Strong	Very Strong	Extreme		
	9	8	7	6	5 4 3 2	1	2 3	4	5	6	7 8 9		

Figure 6.3 Questionnaire for making a Paired Comparison

The final step is to take all these matrices, each constructed completely from its minimum number of judgments, and develop a single matrix whose entries are obtained by taking the geometric mean of all the entries from the matrices that are in the corresponding position to the entry in question. We then construct another matrix from the entries of the spanning trees and their geometric means and fill in any gaps from the previously constructed matrix. This matrix is generally inconsistent and provides an overall representation of the judgments of the group. With prior preparation, the process can be done rapidly.

Since the questionnaires are prepared in advance and calculations are made after the interviews, little burden is placed on the participants. Nevertheless, it is worthwhile to encourage discussion and debate on issues, even if this means more work for the group. The next chapter shows how a good decision can be reached through the intense participation of group members.

Introducing the AHP in Your Organization

Introducing the AHP in an organization requires the same kind of tact, patience, and fortitude needed in conducting group sessions. The following suggestions may be helpful:

- Persuade the leader of the organization to try the process.
- Ask a large audience how the organization currently does its priority setting, its resource allocation, and its planning.
- Explain the process to interested parties and present simple, practical examples.
- Offer to help people structure their problems in an informal atmosphere.
- Prepare one level of judgments at a time and return to the problem at intervals. Too much pressure may cause people to resist.
- Prepare good examples for presentation.
- Work (perhaps independently) with several departments of an organization and with innovative personnel; try to get the word out about this.
- Leave the arithmetic to specialists.
- Ask the management committee and chief executive officer to participate in defining the organization's overall objectives. They can also supply the judgments for the top objectives. With their interest stimulated in this way, they can be shown the rest of the hierarchies and priorities developed by other groups. This approach reduces tedium for upper management and creates a dynamic interaction on major issues.

Key Concepts

In the systematic framework of the AHP for group decision making, people have an opportunity to define the problem and structure its solution together. They can interact to debate, justify, and modify their personal judgments. They can also test the sensitivity of the chosen alternative to variations in their individual judgments. A few differences of opinion may not have a significant impact on what is the best alternative. The AHP offers an opportunity to represent various interests in a balanced participation. It also enables the participants to use hard data along with their carefully deliberated judgments. If time is limited, it is possible to use a questionnaire to elicit the judgments and obtain a wide representation. The consistency test provides feedback on the coherence of available information. Finally, the process of synthesizing the judgments of many people in order to select an alternative is perhaps the most practical and lasting contribution of the

AHP. To summarize, a superior group decision can be conducted by paying attention to the following key concepts:

- When the AHP is used in a group session, the group structures the problem, provides the judgments, debates the judgments, and makes a case for their values until consensus or compromise is reached. Occasionally people feel so certain about their judgments that they want them documented.
- The ideal group is small. Its members are well informed, patient, and highly motivated.
- The greater the number of people involved in constructing the hierarchy, the greater the range of ideas. If too many people are involved, however, the analysis may become unwieldy and time consuming.
- The objective of the discussion should be clearly defined at the outset. Once the focus has been determined, the group defines the issues and constructs the hierarchy.
- Priorities are established through group discussion or by voting or questionnaires. Although questionnaires can be used to sidestep the heat of debate, discussion often brings more worthwhile results.
- It is best to compare the strongest and weakest elements in a level first. The resulting value can then serve as the limiting range for other comparisons.
- Consensus is reached by taking the geometric mean of individual judgments or by voting on the proposed values. Consensus is not so important at the lower levels of the hierarchy, where averaging can be used to better advantage, but it is essential at the higher levels. Yet, even here ranges of differences can be used to estimate the variability in the outcomes.
- The more careful the judgments, the more valid the conclusions.
- After circulating the results for comment, a wrap-up session is useful for making changes and for testing the sensitivity of the results to changes in criteria weights.

A Practical Example

Usually people need time to identify the real problem. There may be several issues that need to be prioritized before the most important one is selected for consideration. The group then constructs a hierarchy and debates the problem, a process that usually takes two to four hours.

The debate on the judgments begins. All that is said can be recorded. Although people will often accept using the geometric mean of their judgments, sometimes they are adamant in their opinion. It is possible to resolve such differences by selecting the judgments that are most consistent with the judgments on which there is general agreement. Even then, however, there are occasions when people would rather hold their ground than yield to the consistency test. In this case, different priorities are obtained because of the range of differences. In the end people often accept averaging the final priorities rather than insisting on consensus at each step during the process. Participating in the process anyway gives greater confidence that other people's judgments may also be sound despite differences. The following application illustrates some of the highlights of the process in operation.

Setting Priorities for Projects

The Regional Advisory Committee (RAC) of the National Health Care Management Center (NHCMC) met, in two full-day sessions, to identify problem areas for research affecting health care in the United States [4]. They first structured a hierarchy of parties who would influence the research but then decided to focus on those who provide health care rather than those who use it or regulate it or do research.

The major objectives of these providers were separated into two groups as shown in Figure 6.4. Initially RAC members estimated the relative weights of economic and service objectives to be one-third and two-thirds, respectively. As the day progressed, however, members felt that these groups should have equal weights. To corroborate this feeling, RAC members cross-weighted selected objectives from among the two groups. This, however, produced implied weightings of two-thirds (economics) and one-third (service).

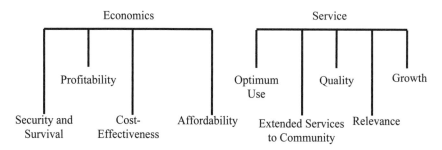

Figure 6.4 Main Objectives of Health Care Providers

Tables 6.1 and 6.2 give the pairwise comparisons of the providers' objectives. In these two tables, the shaded areas represent conflict; in such cases, the reciprocal value was nominated. Conflict is defined as either a four-unit difference between the highest and lowest values nominated by

RAC members (for example: 5 and 1; 1/3 and 1/8) or an integer accompanied by a reciprocal value (for example: 1, 1/3, and 1/7).

Table 6.1 Matrix of Economic Objectives

Economic objectives	1	2	3	4	5	Priority
Security and survival (1)	1	7	3	6	2	0.44
Profitability (2)	1/7	1	1/5	5	1	0.102
Cost-effectiveness (3)	1/3	5	1	7	1	0.237
Growth (4)	1/6	1/5	1/7	1	1/9	0.033
Affordability (5)	1/2	1	2	9	1	0.188

Table 6.2 Matrix of Service Objectives

Service objectives	1	2	3	4	5	Priority
Optimum use (1)	1	1/8	1/4	1/5	5	0.078
Extended services to community (2)	8	1	1*	1	7	0.331
Quality of care (3)	4	1	1	1	7	0.272
Relevance (4)	5	1	1	1	7	0.286
Prestige (5)	1/5	1/7	1/7	1/7	1	0.033

* Three hospital administrators voted together here, assigning a value of 1/3.

The economic objectives were ranked as follows:

Security and survival:	0.44
Profitability:	0.10
Cost effectiveness:	0.24
Growth:	0.03
Affordability:	0.19

Then RAC members assigned priorities to the service objectives:

Optimum use:	0.08
Extended services to the community:	0.33
Quality of care:	0.27
Relevance:	0.29
Prestige:	0.03

Objectives with low priorities were dropped from further consideration, and the priorities of the remaining objectives were renormalized to express their relative importance with respect to one another. This produced the final list of important objectives and their priorities shown in Table 6.3.

Table 6.3 Weighted Objectives

Objective	Original Within-Group Weight	Renormalized Weights Within Each Group
Economic		
Security and Survival	0.44	1
Service		
Extended services	0.33	0.37
Quality of care	0.27	0.31
Relevance	0.29	0.32

Note: Cost-effectiveness, an economic objective with a reasonably high weight (0.24), was omitted because of time considerations.

General Problems

The RAC then developed an extensive list of specific issues in the health care field. These, in turn, were grouped into six general health care management problems:

1. Institutional management/governance
   - Operations management
   - Institutional planning
   - Systems approach
   - Organization, direction, and control
2. Financial management
   - Reimbursement
3. Service delivery
   - Evaluation
4. Environmental control and regulation
5. Consumer behavior/health education
6. Manpower and industry structure
   - Manpower
   - Industry structure

- Medical education

Each of the six areas represented issues that the RAC had noted previously.

Setting Priorities for Problems

The RAC then compared the six problem areas, one at a time against each other, with respect to their relative impact on each of the four objectives. This process produced a set of relative weights for each of the six problem areas (Table 6.4). In Table 6.4, the last two columns indicate the overall relative impact of the six problem areas on the economic and service objectives. (The last column is obtained by multiplying the problem area weight, with respect to each of the three service objective columns, by the weight of that service objective and then adding the results.) From these last two columns we can determine the final weights assigned to each of the six problem areas – specific to the three variations in the relative importance of economic to service objectives (that is, 1: 2, 1:1, and 2:1). Table 6.5 summarizes these findings.

The last column of Table 6.5 records the final weights assigned to each problem area with respect to the values assigned to economic and service objectives. It is noteworthy that irrespective of the value assigned to economic versus service objectives, the rank ordering of problem areas remains unchanged:

Rank	Problem Area
1	Institutional management/governance
2	Financial management
3	Service delivery
4	Environmental control and regulation
5	Consumer behavior/health education
6	Manpower and industry structure

Table 6.4 Relative Weights of Problem Areas

Problem Area	Economic Objectives Security and Survival	Service Objectives			Overall Weight Relative to Economic Objectives	Overall Weight Relative to Service Objectives
		Expanded Services (0.37)*	Quality of Care (0.31)*	Relevance (0.32)*		
Institutional management/governance	0.36	0.09	0.33	0.06	0.36	0.15
Financial management	0.29	0.30	0.16	0.07	0.29	0.18
Service delivery	0.13	0.19	0.27	0.19	0.13	0.21
Environmental control and regulation	0.12	0.15	0.11	0.16	0.12	0.14
Consumer behavior/health education	0.04	0.16	0.03	0.28	0.04	0.16
Manpower and industry structure	0.06	0.11	0.10	0.24	0.06	0.15

* Renormalized weight with respect to the other two service objectives.

Table 6.5 Problem Area Rankings

	Economic/Service Ratio			
Problem Area	1:2	1:1	2:1	Rank
Institutional management/governance	0.22 *	0.26	0.29	1
Financial management	0.22†	0.24	0.26	2
Service delivery	0.19	0.17	0.16	3
Environmental control and regulation	0.13	0.13	0.13	4
Consumer behavior/health education	0.21†	0.10†	0.08	5
Manpower and industry structure	0.12*	0.10*	0.09	6

Note: Before rounding off, ratios marked with an asterisk slightly dominated those marked with a dagger.

It appears that even if cost-effectiveness were returned to the economic objectives, the rank order of problem areas would probably not be changed. Within the service objectives, security and survival was assigned a weight of 0.44.   Cost-effectiveness (which was dropped from further consideration) received a relatively high weight of 0.24.   If we add cost-effectiveness, the renormalized weights of these two would be 0.65 (security and survival) and 0.35 (cost-effectiveness). At most, the weights of institutional management/governance and financial management would probably increase slightly while closing the gap between the relative weights of these top-ranked problem areas. Generally there tended to be greater agreement among RAC members than disagreement with respect to the relative value placed on various problem areas vis-à-vis certain objectives. There was greater disagreement when weighting problem areas with respect to lower-order objectives - such as extending services to the community, relevance, or quality of care – than with respect to high-priority objectives such as security and survival. These lower-order service objectives averaged more conflict zones, and an increased percentage of votes were reciprocals.

Relative Weighting of Projects

To develop the matrices required for the AHP each project was assigned to one of three problem areas: institutional management, financial management, and management of service delivery. One project, work measurement, was assigned to both the first and third categories.

1. Institutional management
    - Conflict in institutional management
    - Fixed-cost analysis
    - Management Information Systems (MIS)
    - Work measurement
    - Long-range planning methodologies
    - Continuing education strategies
    - Interorganizational relationships
    - CEO-CMO relationships
    - Matrix organization
    - Internal/external capability analysis
    - Financial incentives
    - Alternative management styles
    - Governance
2. Financial management
    - Budget development process
    - Present-value analysis
    - Financial feasibility methodology
    - Reimbursement incentives
    - Simplification of reimbursement procedures
3. Management of service delivery
    - Work measurement
    - Quality control measures for patient outcomes
    - Measuring services to patients
    - Service utilization payoff guides

- Analysis of service addition/deletion decisions
- Alternative delivery systems

Matrix I: institutional management. Because so many projects fell into the category of institutional management, the group was divided into two subcategories: structural/interpersonal relations and operations management. The RAC then voted on the relative importance of the areas. One man argued that structure is largely a function of the particular group of personalities in an organization at a given time and that operations management offers more promise for projects and real help for managers. Others took exception to this view – suggesting that structural concerns are dominant for several reasons: importance of structural problems in multi-institutional systems, for example, and greater possibility of learning from experience rather than mechanical classroom education. The range of votes was 1/5 to 7.

	Structural	*Operations*
Structural	1	2
Operations	1/2	1

One person suggested that years of sociological research have not had much effect on improving health care management. Instead, modern management techniques are needed. On the contrary, noted a doctor, social change in hospitals has been far-reaching; certainly health care is much more accessible to the poor.

Matrix IA: operations management. Discussion on the pairing of MIS and fixed-cost analysis revealed two points of view (Table 6.6). The first was that fixed-cost analysis was a greater problem because so little work has been done, whereas considerable effort has been put into MIS. The opposing view held that since management information systems are fundamental to direction and control of organizations, they present more significant problems. Also receiving brief debate was the pairing of MIS and financial incentives. Discussion focused on a definition of financial incentives for employee and medical staff performance. One person noted that the financial incentives of the reimbursement system work against optimum use. Another questioned whether enough was known about this topic to warrant a priority rating. Then someone suggested that fixed-cost analysis is subordinate to MIS because MIS are necessary to determine where financial incentives are needed. Each range follows the geometric mean of judgments.

Matrix IB: structural/interpersonal relations. Matrix IB (Table 6.7) was the last matrix developed during the first meeting. There was no significant discussion of any of the matrix pairings. Unfortunately, one project that had engendered much interest in the morning discussion was inadvertently left out of the institutional management matrices. This project was long-range planning methodologies. While it is impossible to determine through hindsight what relative weighting this project would have obtained, its similarity to several projects that did receive high priorities should be noted. In fact, it could be argued that the following topics are actually subsumed under long-range planning methodologies: management of conflict in institutional planning, management/development of inter-organizational relationships, budget development process, methodologies for analyzing service addition/deletion, and analysis of alternative delivery systems. All in all, it appears that NHCMC should give careful consideration to R&D activities relating to long-range planning for institutions and community-based agencies.

Table 6.6 Matrix IA: Operations Management

	MIS	Fixed-Cost Analysis	Work Measurement	Financial Incentives
MIS	1	2 (1/5-5)*	2 (1/3-5)*	3 (1/7-5)*
Fixed-cost analysis	½	1	3 (1/5-5)*	1 (1/3-3)*
Work measurement	½	1/3	1	1/2 (1/5-7)*
Financial incentives	1/3	1	2	1

* Indicates Range of Values Provided

Table 6.7 Matrix IB: Structural/Interpersonal Relations

	Conflict in Institutional Planning	*Inter-organizational Relationships*	*CEO-CMO*	*Matrix Organization*	*Governance*	*Management Style*
Conflict in institutional planning	1	3 (1/5-7)*	5 (1-9)*	7 (3-9)*	1/2 (1/7-7)*	5 (1/2-9)*
Inter-organizational relationships	1/3	1	7 (5-9)*	7 (3-9)*	1/2 (1/4-1)*	6 (3-9)*
CEO-CMO	1/5	1/7	1	1 (1/5-3)*	11/3 (1/9-3)*	2 (1-5)*
Matrix organization	7	1/7	1	1	1/5 (1/9-3)*	(1/9-3)*
Governance	2	2	3	1/4	1	4 (1-9)*
Management style	1/5	1/6	½	1	1/4	1

* Indicates Range of Values Provided

Priorities among Projects

A computer was used to determine the relative weight of each project within its category. Then the top choices were identified and a composite ranking across categories was prepared. The results are as follows.

Matrix II: financial management. Matrix II (Table 6.8) was originally a four-project matrix. Partway through the voting, however, the two reimbursement-related projects were combined, necessitating some new votes. Only the pairing of budget development versus reimbursement received much discussion. Most RAC members appeared to agree that since an institution's approach to budgeting is a function of the reimbursement system, problems with the latter are more significant than those with the former. One doctor's vote for a reverse weighting stressed the importance of the budget process as a significant planning tool for health care managers.

Table 6.8 Matrix II: Financial Management

	Budget Development	*Financial Feasibility*	*Reimbursement*
Budget development	1	3 (1-5)*	1/4 (1/9-3)*
Financial feasibility	1/3	1	1/5 (1/9-3)*
Reimbursement	4	5	1

* Indicates Range of Values Provided

Matrix III: management of service delivery. Matrix III was then considered. At the outset of the discussion, RAC members agreed that they were not voting on the intrinsic importance of project topics but rather on which areas posed greater problems for health care managers and providers. It was also agreed that the issues of feasibility and NHCMC's competence to address a project would not be considered during the matrix voting. These and other criteria would be decided on after the projects had been ranked for priority. Then the criteria could be chosen and used to select a subset of projects for full-scale development as NHCMC activities utilizing internal or external resources.

Only the first pairing – quality control outcome measures versus measurement of service to patients – received much discussion during the rating. Two divergent points were represented. The first argued that an institution's ultimate survival is a function of patient and staff satisfaction. The opposing view held that the health care system must address needs (because wants are infinite) and that quality is of central importance. The results of the voting on relative weights of project areas are presented in Matrix III (Table 6.9). In almost every pairing in this matrix (and in other matrices as well), a considerable range of values was proposed. The range of votes is indicated next to the geometric mean score in each cell.

Overall Ranking

After project scores were normalized across all three categories, and the seven top projects were selected:

Reimbursement:	0.24
Quality outcome measures:	0.11
Budget development process:	0.08
Conflict in institutional planning:	0.07

Governance	0.07
Inter-organizational relations	0.05
Service use payoff	0.05

Each of these high-scoring projects is related to one of the top three out of six problems defined during the session in June. At that meeting it was recognized that the problems had different impacts on economic and service objectives and that the weights assigned to the problems would depend on the importance assigned to economic and service objectives. Three ratios of the relative importance of economic versus service objectives were proposed - 1:1, 1:2, and 2:1 - and the effect on problem area weight was calculated.

The scores of the projects vary according to the different economic/service ratios. To determine the scores under each of the different ratios, the project scores were multiplied by the appropriate values in Table 6.10 and the results were normalized. Table 6.11 shows that varying the economic/service ratio had a very slight impact on project scores. The overall ranking of the seven projects was not significantly affected.

Table 6.9 Matrix III: Management of Service Delivery

	Quality Control Outcome Measures	Service to Patients	Service Use Payoff	Service Addition/ Deletion	Alternative Delivery Systems	Work Measures
Quality control outcome measures	1	2 (1/3-7)*	6 (5-7)*	3 (1-5)*	2 (1-5)*	4 (1/7-7)*
Service to patients	1/2	1	1/2 (1/5-4)*	1/2 (1/5-1)*	1/2 (1/5-3)*	1/5 (1/7-1/3)*
Service use payoff	1/6	2	1	3 (1/3-5)*	1 (1/5-5)*	3 (1/7-7)*
Service addition/ deletion	1/3	2	1/3	1	1/2 (1/5-3)*	3 (1/7-7)*
Alternative delivery systems	1/2	2	1	2	1	3 (1/5-7)*
Work measures	1/4	5	1/3	1/3	1/3	1

* Indicates Range of Values were Provided.

Table 6.10 Priorities of Projects in Each Area

Institutional management
Operations management (1)*
  MIS $0.43 \times 1/3 = 0.14$
  Fixed-cost analysis $0.25 \times 1/3 = 0.08$
  Work measurement $0.12 \times 1/3 = 0.04$
  Financial incentives $0.20 \times 1/3 = 0.07$
Structural/interpersonal relations (2)*
  Conflict in institutional planning $0.31 \times 2/3 = 0.21$
  Interorganizational relationships $0.23 \times 2/3 = 0.15$
  CEO-CMO relationships $0.06 \times 2/3 = 0.04$
  Programmatic matrix/organization $0.04 \times 2/3 = 0.03$
  Governance $0.31 \times 2/3 = 0.21$
  Management style $0.05 \times 2/3 = 0.03$
Financial management
  Budget development process   0.23
  Financial feasibility   0.10
  Reimbursement   0.67
Management of services
  Quality outcome measures   0.37
  Alternative delivery systems   0.17
  Service use payoff   0.17
  Addition/deletion service analysis 0.11
  Work measurement   0.10
  Service to patients   0.07

* Within the category of institutional management, *structural/interpersonal relations* was given twice the weight of *operations management*. Hence to normalize the project scores in this category, the structural scores are multiplied by 2/3 and the operations management scores by 1/3.

Table 6.11 Project Rankings

Project	Economic/Service Ratio		
	1:1	1:2	2:1
Reimbursement	0.35	0.36	0.36
Quality outcome measures	0.17	0.14	0.12*
Budget development process	0.12	0.12	0.12*
Conflict in institutional planning	0.11	0.12	0.12*
Governance	0.11	0.12	0.12
Inter-organizational relations	0.08	0.09	0.09
Service use payoff	0.08	0.06	0.06

*Before values were rounded off, these projects were ranked in the following order: conflict in institutional planning, quality outcome measures, and budget development process.

The AHP in the Real World

People who are anxious for quick, dependable answers are often concerned whether the same problem structured by the same group more than once leads to the same hierarchy and priorities. The answer clearly is no. Stable results are produced from broad knowledge and understanding derived from experience. People who do not make a process of solving the problem are apt to create too narrow or too broad a hierarchy. They may give judgments conditioned by the emotions, by problems sensed at the time of the meeting, and by the incisiveness of the logic expressed then. To stabilize a process, we need to analyze it according to well-founded experience, to use a variety of criteria, and to take into consideration variations in judgment. Only repetition of the process and continued interaction with the real world can bring the AHP closer to a true representation of the problem - whether it concerns priority setting, planning, or resource allocation - and ensure the quality of the results.

References

1. Jiro, K. *The Original KJ Method*. Tokyo: KJ Method Headquarters, Kawakita Research Institute, 1982.
2. Kaplan, R.S. and D.P. Norton. *Strategy Maps: Converting Intangible Assets into Tangible Outcomes*. Cambridge: Harvard Business School Press, 2004.
3. Straker, D. Rapid Problem Solving with Post-it Notes. Gower, 1997.
4. Saaty, T.L., Decision Making for Leaders: The Analytic Hierarchy Process for Decisions in a Complex World. Pittsburgh: RWS Publications, 1990.

Chapter 7

Group Decision Making:
Head-Count versus Intensity of Preference

This chapter puts forth a framework for reshaping the group decision making process in the area of public policy. The proposed framework extends from the usual one-issue-at-a-time decision making to one that involves several related issues simultaneously, and from the head-count way of voting to one that involves expressing intensity of preference. Weaknesses of the traditional majority voting mechanism are first identified, and then a different voting method that takes each individual voter's sentiment into account is discussed. Specifically, a decision maker is asked to express his/her intensity of preference for the issues encountered. Three hierarchical structures – benefits, costs, and risks – are developed to evaluate the alternatives. Due to the nature of pairwise comparisons and synthesis, the proposed method is amenable to consensus building and has higher reliability and consistency. It can be used for candidate selection, e.g. governmental election, when a large population is involved. It is also effective for resource allocation and prioritization when a small group or business is concerned. We believe the proposed approach has potential for resolving deficiencies of the conventional voting mechanism, and can be applied to many real-world problems. Its implementation on the Internet is also discussed.

Conventional wisdom regarding public policy making is grounded in the widespread majority vote mechanism. That is, either a simple or a two-thirds majority vote determines the final decision, and the minority must unconditionally compromise its position. It is a winner-take-all outcome. The losers' possible strong preferences for the opposite alternative are no longer important, and their cooperation with, and deference to the will of, the majority are expected. While convenient, the current voting system oversimplifies the representation of voter preferences and "drowns out" the true merit of counterarguments. In spite of its fairness, in principle and often in practice, opposing opinions are ignored, and this may be painful to the losers. We wonder if this approach to democracy is ordained by divinity, generated through our biology, or improvised by human rationality. Much attention has been paid by the *utility theory* researchers to study group decision making problems (see [1-4]). However, the absence of a formal, dominating, and widely accepted theory to aggregate cardinal preferences may be a stumbling block that prohibits us from moving beyond the traditional ordinal approach.

Using ballots to solicit the inclination of individuals in a group has been a subject of great interest for nearly 200 years. In *Group Choice*, Mirkin [5] scanned the diverse horizons of the field. He found that much of the research had focused on the ordinal representation of preferences, and on the problems and pitfalls of the ordinal approach. Barbut [6] constructed examples to illustrate paradoxes of the ordinal approach when voting on three alternatives. Several cases were subsequently shown and demonstrated to be contradictory. This eventually led to the development of the well-known Arrow [7] impossibility theorem for ordinal preferences. The theorem states that if the number of alternatives is greater than two, it is impossible to create a group preference ordering that satisfies four seemingly natural conditions that one would expect to hold. These are *non-dictatorship, decisiveness, Pareto optimality (agreement),* and *independence of irrelevant alternatives.*

To remove the contradiction outlined by Arrow, three types of ordinal methods were attempted in the literature: preference scoring, distance-based methods, and statistical methods. These are intended to relax one or the other of the four conditions and, in particular, the fourth one. However, the results are unsatisfactory, at least for addressing the question of the general uniqueness of the outcome regardless of the method used.

In addition to the work of Armstrong et al. [8] and Cook and Seiford [9], Cook and Kress [10] developed a model for aggregating ordinal rankings to express intensity of preference. Mueller [11] and Plott [12] provided an extensive survey for consensus ranking through generalized network formulation. The debate has continued because the roots of impossibility lie in the use of ordinal preferences.

We mentioned in Chapter 1 about what MacKay [13] wrote doubtfully about pursuing the cardinal approaches. The AHP provides a method for aggregating individual cardinal preferences into a unique group preference while removing impossibility, as shown by Saaty and Vargas [16] in Chapter 14. Because it deals with measurement, the AHP facilitates the group process to capture preference intensities of individuals and incorporates them into a final group decision. It ensures the validity of the outcome as it relates to the real world, a question rarely addressed in the ordinal approach.

In this chapter, we illustrate the use of the cardinal approach. It is organized as follows. In the next section, we discuss the deficiency of the traditional decision-making (voting) system; the following section provides the framework for applying the AHP to voting, and for analyzing the sensitivity of the proposed method. In the section following that, we discuss its implementation on the Internet. Summary and conclusions are made in the final section.

Deficiencies of the Traditional Yes-No Voting System

The traditional voting method requires voters to choose between "yes" and "no" for an alternative. Many regard this (1-0) majority voting method as an unchallengeable law of nature. It is because, thus far, we have not found a way of voting that is more practical and better represents the decision makers' true preferences. In this section, we examine the deficiencies of the traditional (1-0) head-count procedure.

First, with a majority vote, individuals are unable to express their true preference for the subject of a debate without eventually taking the most extreme position by either voting for or against it. A person may prefer one issue over its opposite only by a proportion of 51 to 49 percent. Yet, when that person votes, the vote is recorded as definitely for (=1) or definitely against (=0). If many people vote with lukewarm feelings, the outcome indicates a stronger win than is justified in practice. Decision making under such circumstances is subject to extreme bias.

Second, when the issues involved are of public concern, it may not be appropriate to resolve them through the familiar process of competitive voting. The danger of basing decisions on head-count is that the win/lose dynamic may not be good for cases where success depends on cooperation and teamwork. The winner-take-all method may be appropriate for a society facing a war and seeking to win, but, perhaps, is not as suitable when collaborative effort is essential for getting along.

A third flaw of the yes-no voting system is that the decision derived from a majority vote may result in an outcome that is the opposite of what the collectivity wants. For example, suppose there are three people voting on two alternatives, A and B. Two people have intensities of preference of 45% for A, and 55% for B. The third person has preference intensity of 90% for A, and 10% for B. Under the yes-no voting system, B wins by a simple majority 2:1 vote. If the intensities of preference are taken into account, the mean preference intensity for A and B (using either of the two well-known and mathematically advocated methods in the literature, the arithmetic and geometric means) would be $(0.45+0.45+0.90)/3=0.60$ and $(0.55+0.55+0.10)/3=0.40$; and $(0.45*0.45*0.90)^{1/3}=57\%$ and $(0.55*0.55*0.10)^{1/3}=31\%$, respectively. Consequently A wins over B, exactly the opposite of the yes-no approach.

A fourth potential difficulty arises in voting on several issues at the same time (agenda effects). When multiple issues are encountered, the traditional voting approach takes on each issue separately. If the issues are bound together (dependent) to some extent, it can happen that an earlier issue with bearing on what follows is voted out, killing the chance to successfully influence the others, unless the older issue is brought back again for reconsideration.

Such yes-no voting often prevents the decision makers from following a comprehensive view of issues as a whole. It can then lead to a chain of policies that is hard to carry out, or, at best, makes it less efficient to create what the public sentiment is asking for. This opens the floodgate for unsettling and paradoxical results. A better approach might be to discuss all the relevant issues simultaneously and make decisions on them with a ranking of the issues.

Table 7.1 Head-Count Method vs. Intensity Rating of Preference

	Number of Voters For "Yes" or "No"		Geometric Mean Based on the Preference Intensity of the Voters		Outcome Based on Preference Intensity	Majority Outcome
Issue #	Yes	No	Yes	No		
1	19	21	0.55	0.45	Yes	No
2	10	30	0.38	0.62	No	No
3	23	17	0.47	0.53	No	Yes
4	22	18	0.61	0.39	Yes	Yes

The difference between the yes-no head-count method and that of using intensity of preference in decision making is illustrated in Table 7.1. The example includes 40 voters. In terms of issue #1, 19 people voted "yes", while 21 people voted "no" Each of the voters is also asked to express his/her intensity of preference on both the "yes" and "no" alternatives. The geometric mean of all 40 voters' preference intensity for "yes" is found to be 0.55, while that of the "no" alternative is 0.45. Thus, issue #1 has a "yes" outcome when using preference intensity, as opposed to the "no" outcome when applying the majority count (19 "yes" versus 21 "no") criteria. The decisions for issues 1-3 are derived likewise.

The example demonstrates that when various issues are deliberated concurrently, each possible outcome (yes or no alternative) under an issue has different chances of success. The voter must specify intensities of preference for all issues and alternatives and form an ordered set of preferences. Under such circumstances, one cannot exaggerate the importance of a specific alternative without making the others suffer. Since more than just a 1 or a 0 is required, a decision maker is forced to think more about the strength of preference (s)he is asked to provide. Thus, decision making becomes more substantive and less of a "muddling through" process.

Applying the Analytic Hierarchy Process to Voting

Policy making requires inputs of eligible individuals or representatives. Our example in this section focuses on the public policy-making issues encountered by a legislative body. The political example is meant to give a slightly more serious flavor to the analysis and to draw the attention of readers to matters about which the public is usually concerned. Our hope is to invite a broader and strategic look at our approach. The views expressed here are drawn from newspapers, magazines, and Internet articles. They form the basis for constructing the hierarchies and judgments. The variables used in the model and the values assigned to them are purely illustrative. Nevertheless, it would not diminish the importance of the idea we are presenting in this chapter. In the following, we discuss the legislative matters that are important to the US public. Those viewpoints serve as foundation for walking the readers through the new method.

Current Events

Many in today's society wish to lower taxes, eradicate discrimination, and reform the political system. When properly taken into account, these concerns would lead to new policies essential for reshaping society. If mismanaged, they can increase racism, intensify economic class war, and drag the nation into dissatisfaction, negativism and recession. The challenge is to transform the power of national sentiment into realistic, constructive policies that make the government more productive and less costly. To illustrate the situation faced by our AHP model, we focus on the following issues.

Tax Reform

To increase supply of capital as to create jobs, raise living standards, and lay the groundwork for growth and prosperity in the long run, the Bush administration proposed to eliminate the tax on dividends, accelerate income tax cuts, offer investment incentives for small businesses, and provide funds for job re-training [17]. While it makes sense to eliminate the double taxation of dividends, new tax cuts indeed may embroil the nation in deficit and create higher interest rates that cut growth. Critics also argue that tax reform skews the benefits to wealthier taxpayers and that it will not help the middle class, stimulate investment spending, or spur growth.

Affirmative Action Reform

Racial discrimination remains a fact of our society [18]. Should affirmative action continue to exist, or should it be unplugged? Opponents argue that the current policy of employment and college admission based on an applicant's color of skin is discriminatory [19]. Supporters believe that affirmative action is necessary as long as racial discrimination persists, and that our nation functions better when diverse members of the population co-exist harmoniously. Thus, we should balance short-term pressures with long-term sustainability, and continue practicing affirmative action [20].

Legislative Term Limits

Term limits is often regarded as a way to end the unlimited control by a few elites and to create a fairer political system. [21].   But youdebate.com [22] argues that limiting terms restricts citizens' rights to choose, and treats competent or incompetent representatives the same. It may also cause representatives to ignore the needs of the people they represent, since seeking long-term support from their districts is not a concern. Moreover, the goal of eliminating the oftentimes cozy relationship between legislators and special interest groups may not be realized by implementing term limits alone.   Others believe that a strong campaign finance reform would be a better idea as it deprives incumbents of their considerable financial advantage.

Applying AHP to Policy Making

The political opinions assembled later provide the necessary foundation for readers to understand the AHP example to be illustrated in this section. Here, we give details of how the AHP can be used to improve the policy making process. To give a comprehensive view, we divide the above factors that influence decisions into three hierarchies: one for the benefits of implementing certain policies, one for the costs, and a third for the risks and uncertainties that can arise.   Each hierarchy has a goal followed by the criteria that affect the performance of that goal.   The issues are listed at the bottom level of the hierarchy.   Our purpose here is to walk the reader through practical examples, both to improve his/her understanding of the main idea of the chapter, and to show how it can be implemented in real-world decision making.

The Analysis Framework

Figure 7.1 presents a framework for problems dealing with multiple issues and various criteria simultaneously. When applying the model to the national issues discussed above, a decision maker first assesses the relative importance of the issues under the benefits, costs and risks hierarchies. The analysis would be followed by a decision as to whether or not reform is needed. This is done by comparing the two alternatives – to reform or not to reform – with each other under a criterion. Proportionality of the rankings – the three issues among themselves and the two alternatives (reform, no reform) within each issue – makes it possible to integrate all six alternatives into a single rank order under a hierarchy.

Step 1 - Assess the relative importance of each issue

(a) Compute c_{ij} = the weight of criterion j under hierarchy i.
   - pairwise compare the importance of each criterion under each hierarchy (see Figure 3).
(b) Compute w_{ijk} = the relative importance of issue k contributing to criterion j under hierarchy i.
   - pairwise compare the importance of each issue under each criterion (see Figure 4).

$$\sum_{j=1}^{J} c_{ij} = 1 \; (for \; i=1, 2,....I. \quad I \; is \; the \; total \; number \; of \; hierarchies; \; J=the$$

(total number of criteria under hierarchy i)

$$\sum_{k=1}^{K} w_{ijk} = 1 \; (K=the \; total \; number \; of \; issues)$$

Step 2 – Determine the importance of each alternative. SeeFigure 7.5

Step 2 – Determine the importance of each alternativeSee Figure 7.5
(a) Compute the <u>local priority</u>: P_{ijk}^{l}
   - pairwise compare the two alternatives ($l=1, 2$) of issue k, under criterion j in hierarchy i.
(b) Derive the <u>global priority</u>: $g_{ijk}^{l} = p_{ijk}^{l} \times w_{ijk}$
   - multiply the local priority of each alternative with its corresponding issue's weight, w_{ijk}.

(c) Derive the <u>Local Rating</u>: $LR_{ik}^{l} = \sum_{j}^{J} c_{ij} \times p_{ijk}^{l}$ *(for i=1,2...I;*

k=1,2,...K; l=1,2)
   - sum the product of the alternative's local priority with its corresponding criteria's weight, c_{ij}.

(d) Derive the <u>Overall Rating</u>: $OR_{ik}^{l} = \sum_{j}^{J} c_{ij} \times g_{ijk}^{l}$ *(for i=1,2...I; k=1,2,...K;*

l=1,2)
  - sum the product of the alternative's global priority with its corresponding criteria's weight, c_{ij}.

Step 3 - Derive the ratio

For each alternative, use the Overall Rating from each hierarchy and derive the ratio, R:

$$\frac{Benefits}{Costs \times Risks}$$

$$= R_k^l = \frac{OR_{1,k}^l}{OR_{2,k}^l \times OR_{3,k}^l} \quad for\ k=1,2,3\ and\ l=1,2$$

Step 4 – Make decision

Choose the alternative with the highest ratio within each issue k

$D_k = arg\ max_l \{ R_k^l \}$ *for k=1,2,3* The importance (priority) of the issues indicates the relative commitment with which they would each be carried out if they must all be implemented. Our task is to determine which ones may or may not be implemented in an overall consideration of benefits, costs, and risks relative to all the issues involved and not simply in isolation. Of course, for each pair to change, or to preserve the status quo, only one would be chosen. But, the one chosen is then determined as a function of the overall priorities. Details are given below.

Figure 7.1 AHP Voting Procedure for Dealing with Various Issues and Multiple Alternatives

(i) Determining the importance of each issue, w_{ijk}. Figures 7.2a-c display the benefits, costs, and risks hierarchies needed to assess the importance of the three reform issues. The goal is at the top of each hierarchy, followed by the criteria that contribute to attaining that goal. At the bottom of each hierarchy are the issues whose priorities are to be determined. The weights of the criteria, c_{ij}, in the second level of each hierarchy are derived by pairwise comparisons and synthesized as illustrated in the matrices of Figure 7.3a. Each matrix specifies the judgments of the decision maker about the relative importance of each criterion in terms of its contribution to the achievement of the goal of that hierarchy.

     For example, in the benefits hierarchy, a possible question is: How much more important is promoting harmony in society over the importance of stimulating employment? Assume that social harmony is strongly believed to be more of a serious concern vs. stimulating employment; a priority value of 5 is thus assigned. When a group is involved, each individual needs to provide his/her own judgment; members' final judgments are then combined by taking the geometric mean.

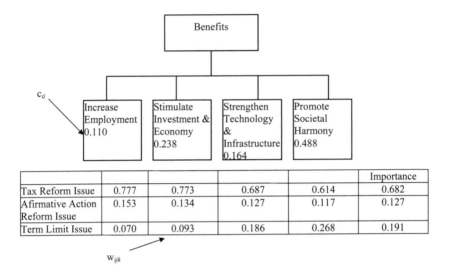

Figure 7.2a Benefits Hierarchy

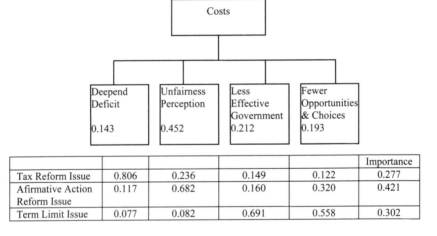

Figure 7.2b Costs Hierarchy

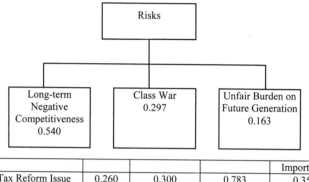

				Importance
Tax Reform Issue	0.260	0.300	0.783	0.357
Afirmative Action Reform Issue	0.413	0.600	0.155	0.426
Term Limit Issue	0.327	0.100	0.062	0.217

Figure 7.2c Risks Hierarchy

(a) Pairwise Comparisons in Each Hierarchy

Benefits	Employment	Investment	Infrastructure	Societal Harmony	Weight (w_{ij})
Employment	1	1/3	1	1/5	0.110 (=c_{11})
Investment	3	1	1	1/2	0.238 (=c_{12})
Infrastructure	1	1	1	1/3	0.164 (=c_{13})
Societal Harmony	5	2	3	1	0.488 (=c_{14})

Costs	Deficit	Unfairness	Less Effic. Gov.	Less Op.& Ch.	Weight
Deficit	1	1/3	1	1/2	0.143 (=c_{21})
Unfairness	3	1	3	2	0.452 (=c_{22})
Less Efficient Government	1	1/3	1	2	0.212 (=c_{23})
Less Opportunity & Choice	2	1/2	1/2	1	0.193 (=c_{24})

Risks	Weak Compet.	Class War	Burden	Weight
Weak Competition	1	2	3	0.540 (=c_{31})
Class War	1/2		2	0.297 (=c_{32})
Burden Future Generation	1/3	1/2	1	0.163 (=c_{33})

(b) Approximating the Weights of the Benefit Factors

Step 1: Sum the values in each column

Benefits	Employment	Investment	Infrastructure	Societal Harmony
Employment	1	1/3	1	1/5
Investment	3	1	1	1/2
Infrastructure	1	1	1	1/3
Societal Harmony	5	2	3	1
Column Sum	10	13/3	6	61/30

Step 2: Divide each element by its column sum

Benefits	Employment	Investment	Infrastructure	Societal Harmony
Employment	1/10	1/13	1/6	6/61
Investment	3/10	3/13	1/6	15/61
Infrastructure	1/10	3/13	1/6	10/61
Societal Harmony	5/10	6/13	3/6	30/61

Step 3: Average the elements in each row

Benefits	Employment	Investment	Infrastructure	Societal Harmony	Weight
Employment	0.100	0.077	0.167	0.098	0.110 (=c_{11})
Investment	0.300	0.231	0.167	0.246	0.238 (=c_{12})
Infrastructure	0.100	0.231	0.167	0.164	0.164 (=c_{13})
Societal Harmony	0.500	0.462	0.500	0.492	0.488 (=c_{14})

Figure 7.3 Deriving the Weights for Factors

For simplicity, Figure 7.3b gives an approximation procedure for generating the priority for the benefits hierarchy. AA Reform stands for Affirmative Action Reform. The third level of the hierarchy in Figure 7.2a shows the importance of each issue, w_{ijk}'s, i.e, how it contributes to each criterion. Its pairwise comparisons are detailed in Figure 7.4. As an example, in the employment matrix in the benefits hierarchy, the tax reform issue is considered to be very strongly more important in contributing to increasing employment over affirmative action reform. The former is thus assigned the value 7 when compared with the latter. The three issues are compared with respect to their contributions to each criterion. Relative importance, or priority, w_{ijk}, is listed in the right-hand column of each matrix.

Benefits

Employment	Tax Reform	AA Reform	Term Limit	Scale
Tax Reform	1	7	8	0.777 $(=w_{111})$
AA Reform	1/7	1	3	0.153 $(=w_{112})$
Term Limit	1/8	1/3	1	0.070 $(=w_{113})$

Investment	Tax Reform	AA Reform	Term Limit	Scale
Tax Reform	1	8	6	0.773 $(=w_{121})$
AA Reform	1/8	1	2	0.134 $(=w_{122})$
Term Limit	1/6	1/2	1	0.093 $(=w_{123})$

Infrastructure	Tax Reform	AA Reform	Term Limit	Scale
Tax Reform	1	4	5	0.687 $(=w_{131})$
AA Reform	1/4	1	1/2	0.127 $(=w_{132})$
Term Limit	1/5	2	1	0.186 $(=w_{133})$

Societal Harmony	Tax Reform	AA Reform	Term Limit	Scale
Tax Reform	1	4	3	0.614 $(=w_{141})$
AA Reform	1/4	1	1/3	0.117 $(=w_{142})$
Term Limit	1/3	3	1	0.268 $(=w_{143})$

Costs

Deficit	Tax Reform	AA Reform	Term Limit	Scale
Tax Reform	1	9	8	0.806
AA Reform	1/9	1	2	0.117
Term Limit	1/8	1/2	1	0.077

Unfairness	Tax Reform	AA Reform	Term Limit	Scale
Tax Reform	1	1/4	4	0.236
AA Reform	4	1	6	0.682
Term Limit	1/4	1/6	1	0.082

Less Efficient Government	Tax Reform	AA Reform	Term Limit	Scale
Tax Reform	1	1	1/5	0.149
AA Reform	1	1	1/4	0.160
Term Limit	5	4	1	0.691

Less Opportunity & Choice	Tax Reform	AA Reform	Term Limit	Scale
Tax Reform	1	1/3	1/4	0.122
AA Reform	3	1	1/2	0.320
Term Limit	4	2	1	0.558

Risks

Weak Competitiveness	Tax Reform	AA Reform	Term Limit	Scale
Tax Reform	1	1/2	1	0.260
AA Reform	2	1	1	0.413
Term Limit	1	1	1	0.327

Class War	Tax Reform	AA Reform	Term Limit	Scale
Tax Reform	1	1/2	3	0.300
AA Reform	2	1	6	0.600
Term Limit	1/3	1/6	1	0.100

Burden	Tax Reform	AA Reform	Term Limit	Scale
Tax Reform	1	8	8	0.783
AA Reform	1/8	1	4	0.155
Term Limit	1/8	1/4	1	0..62

Figure 7.4 Pairwise Comparison Matrices for All Issues

Next, we copy all derived scales into Figures 7.2a-c and weight the importance of an issue by the corresponding c_{ij} to obtain the overall importance of that issue (i.e., the rightmost column). For example, the importance of tax reform in the benefits hierarchy is 0.682, using

$$0.777 \times 0.110 + 0.773 \times 0.238 + 0.687 \times 0.164 + 0.614 \times 0.488 = 0.682.$$

Note that the benefits hierarchy (Figure 7.2a) determines which issue yields the greatest benefits with respect to each criterion. The costs and risks hierarchies (Figures 7.2b-c), respectively, decide the relative costs and risks of each issue. From those, we find that tax reform is likely to generate the most benefits, while affirmative action reform is most costly and has the highest risk.

(ii) Determining the local and overall rating for each alternative, $LR_{ik}{}^l$ and OR_i. This step distinguishes our model from the traditional AHP application. Having developed the priorities of the issues in the respective hierarchies, we return to the third level of each hierarchy in Figure 7.2. The three issues are then replaced by three pairs of alternatives, one pair for the actions of the tax reform issue, another for the actions of the affirmative action issue, and the third for the term limit issue. Each pair represents (i) the status quo, and (ii) the potentially new state obtained by changing from the status quo (see Figure 7.5). A tax reform rating of 0.634 = (0.875 × 0.110 + 0.889 × 0.238 + 0.800 ×0.164 + 0.400 × 0.488) and a no tax reform rating of 0.366 can be derived through step 2(c) of Figure 7.1. The corresponding column in Figure 7.5a is named "Local Rating" (LR) since only one issue is considered at a time. When all issues are considered jointly, its column is named "Overall Rating" (OR). Figures 7.5b-care derived similarly.

The local priority, $p_{ijk}{}^l$, can be converted to global priority, $g_{ijk}{}^l$, by weighting the corresponding issue's priority, w_{ijk}. For example, the local priorities for each of the three (reform, no reform) pairs under the increase employment criterion are: $(p_{111}{}^1, p_{111}{}^2)=(0.875, 0.125)$, $(p_{112}{}^1, p_{112}{}^2)=(0.667, 0.333)$, and $(p_{113}{}^1, p_{113}{}^2)= (0.100, 0.900)$. Weighted by w_{ijk}, the global priority becomes $(g_{111}{}^1, g_{111}{}^2) = (0.680, 0.097)$, $(g_{112}{}^1, g_{112}{}^2) = (0.102, 0.051)$, $(g_{113}{}^1, g_{113}{}^2) = (0.007, 0.063)$. By applying step 2(d) of Figure 7.1, we obtain the overall ratings for each alternative as shown in the rightmost column of Figure 7.5a-c. These numbers are then used to develop the final ratios in Table 7.2.

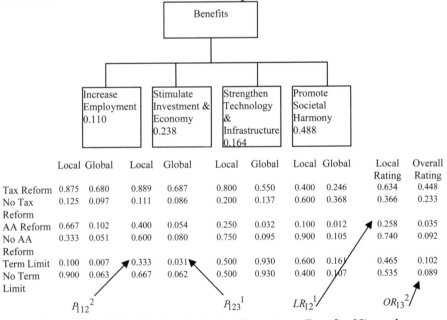

Figure 7.5a Global Rating for Each Alternative - Benefits Hierarchy

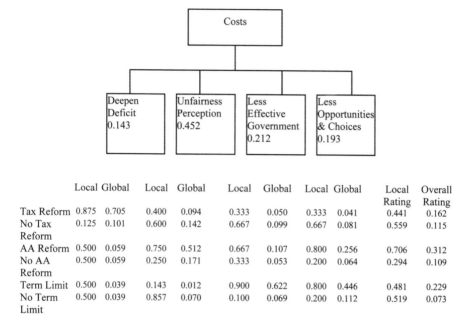

	Local	Global	Local	Global	Local	Global	Local	Global	Local Rating	Overall Rating
Tax Reform	0.875	0.705	0.400	0.094	0.333	0.050	0.333	0.041	0.441	0.162
No Tax Reform	0.125	0.101	0.600	0.142	0.667	0.099	0.667	0.081	0.559	0.115
AA Reform	0.500	0.059	0.750	0.512	0.667	0.107	0.800	0.256	0.706	0.312
No AA Reform	0.500	0.059	0.250	0.171	0.333	0.053	0.200	0.064	0.294	0.109
Term Limit	0.500	0.039	0.143	0.012	0.900	0.622	0.800	0.446	0.481	0.229
No Term Limit	0.500	0.039	0.857	0.070	0.100	0.069	0.200	0.112	0.519	0.073

Figure 7.5b Global rating for Each Alternative – Costs Hierarchy

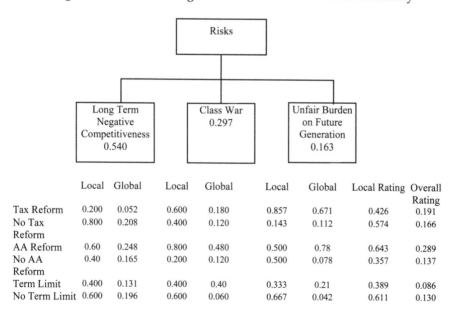

	Local	Global	Local	Global	Local	Global	Local Rating	Overall Rating
Tax Reform	0.200	0.052	0.600	0.180	0.857	0.671	0.426	0.191
No Tax Reform	0.800	0.208	0.400	0.120	0.143	0.112	0.574	0.166
AA Reform	0.60	0.248	0.800	0.480	0.500	0.78	0.643	0.289
No AA Reform	0.40	0.165	0.200	0.120	0.500	0.078	0.357	0.137
Term Limit	0.400	0.131	0.400	0.40	0.333	0.21	0.389	0.086
No Term Limit	0.600	0.196	0.600	0.060	0.667	0.042	0.611	0.130

Figure 7.5c Global Rating for Each Alternative – Risks Hierarchy

Table 7.2 Deriving Ratios for Alternatives

Calculation of Benefits/ (Costs.Risks) Ratio	To Do or Not To Do
Tax Reform $\dfrac{0.448}{0.162\times0.191}=14.48$ No Tax Reform $\dfrac{0.233}{0.115\times0.166}=12.205$	Yes (Tax Reform has higher ratio than No Reform)
Affir. Action Reform $\dfrac{0.035}{0.115\times0.166}=0.388$ No Affirm Action Reform $\dfrac{0.092}{0.109/0.137}=6.161$	No (No Affirmative Action Reform far exceeds Reform)
Term Limits $\dfrac{0.102}{0.229\times0.086}=5.179$ No Term Limits $\dfrac{0.089}{0.073\times0.130}=9.378$	No (No Term Limits dominates Term Limits)

(iii) Deriving the ratio. Because we respond to the question "which is more costly and which is more riskier?" when combining the priorities derived from the three hierarchies to obtain the final outcome we can use, as appropriate, the marginal or the total method of aggregating benefits, costs, and risks. For simplicity, we only illustrate with the simpler marginal formula as it does not require weighting these three different merits of the alternatives. [25, pp. 89, 120]. Thus for our example, we divide the benefit results from the benefits hierarchy by those from the costs and risks hierarchies (see Table 7.2). In our example, we find that the benefits of tax reform are the highest among all alternatives, while its corresponding costs and risks are a little greater than those of the no tax reform alternative. Therefore, the tax reform ratio is higher than that of the no tax reform. The former dominates the latter both when no risk is considered, and also when projected risk is taken into account.

Compared with affirmative action reform, the no affirmative action reform benefits are higher, with costs and risks lower. Thus, the no affirmative action reform overall ratio is much higher than that of the affirmative action reform decision.

Term limits dominates no term limits when costs are not considered. When costs are taken into account, however, no term limits has a higher priority than term limits. We note that including risks by using possible scenarios of the future can be a powerful tool in assessing a decision. The same procedure can be applied if one chooses a different merit system. For example, instead of using benefits, opportunities, costs, and risks for the analysis framework, one may choose strength, weakness, opportunity, and threat (SWOT) to evaluate the alternatives. We find that the proposed approach is useful in either framework.

Linked Issues. If we encounter a situation in which acting on one of the issues requires that we also act on another so that two issues appear together, then we would consider the pair as a single issue. The sum of the B/CR ratios (i.e., Benefits/(Costs×Risks)) for changing the two may exceed the sum of not doing both, even though taken singly, one of them may be rejected. For example, if term limits is required for tax reform, we should add the B/CR ratio of both (14.48+ 5.179=19.659) and compare it with the sum of no tax reform and no term limits (12.205+9.378= 21.5834). Since the latter is larger, we would carry out neither tax reform nor term limits. The object of this process is to integrate the issues so that decision makers would not arbitrarily decide on each issue alone as they do in ordinary voting.

By linking an issue's B/CR ratio to the ratios of the other issues, the decision makers can weight it carefully by assigning the appropriate strength (judgment). Otherwise, exaggerating its value would, in the proportionality and normalization scheme, unduly reduce some other issue of its desired priority. This appears to be a compelling method for determining the relative importance of issues rather than simply giving one of them too high a value and the other a correspondingly very low one, or just voting yes-no the issues.

Sensitivity Analysis. To ensure that the outcome of the above example not be construed as a result of whimsical judgments, we performed a comprehensive sensitivity analysis on the 11 main criteria (4 under benefits- and costs-hierarchy each, and 3 under risks hierarchy). A sensitivity analysis helps determine the robustness of a model. It tests a plausible range of values for each criterion to determine how sensitive outcomes are to changes in the inputs estimates. Through sensitivity analysis, policy makers can discover how changes in judgments or priority about the importance of each criterion might affect recommended decisions. We changed the importance of each criterion by ±30%. That is, we tested each criterion with 70% and 130% of its original priority value.

In the meantime, the minimum priority value is limited to 0 and the maximum to 1. Since each criterion is allowed to vary twice, and we have four criteria for benefits, altogether we have 2×4=8 variations in the benefits hierarchy, 2×4=8 variations in the costs and 2×3=6 in the risks hierarchies. To cover all possible interactions, we generated 8×8×6=384 data points. We found that tax reform dominates no tax reform 95.1% of the time. When the burden on future generations and class war risks are considered much more important, no tax reform dominates. No affirmative action reform dominates affirmative action reform 92.9% of the time, and no term limits is preferred to term limits in about 54.8% of the cases. The results suggest that tax reform is the most pressing issue, while affirmative action reform is not preferred at this time. The implications of term limits are not particularly decisive in the debate due to its low percentage in dominance.

The public policy-making example given above takes into account preference intensity, so that collective priority is not determined merely by head-counting. It accommodates both objective and subjective judgment, and individual shared values, thus allowing all pertinent information to be deliberated. Users can input and modify the data format, and synthesize the results. More importantly, the example considers both winners' and losers' positions. Therefore, the proposed approach can contribute to building consensus and accord.

Internet and Group Decision Making

In this section, we examine two potential useful applications of our proposed framework using computers and the Internet. The first is in public policy voting, and the second in business group decision making.

Public Policy Making through Internet Voting

The idea of using Internet technology to facilitate the voting process has engendered much interest in our society, particularly after the technical glitches in the US presidential election of 2000 [26]. E-voting (electronic voting, Internet voting or online voting) is a method that transmits voters' choices over the Internet through secure encryption. There are three Internet electronic voting models: (*i*) electronic voting at conventional sites, where traditional voting locations are enhanced with Internet technology; (*ii*) remote voting, where voters vote from home or work; and (*iii*) kiosk voting, where Internet terminals are placed at convenient sites such as malls. Remote voting holds the greatest promise due to its convenience and universal access.

In reforming and modernizing the conventional voting system, many have studied the social and technical implications of e-voting [27]. Problems such as how e-voting affects voters' presence, and if different sectors of the population participate differently have drawn much attention [28]. An important concern is that those who have no Internet access from home or work are digitally divided from those who do, and thus they become disadvantaged. In addition to the lack of equal Web access, critics also worry about Internet security. Since computers and the Internet are fundamentally vulnerable, the threat of an election ruined by malicious attack, software glitches and mechanical errors is real and daunting. It is important to protect privacy and safeguard against "hackers" so those with culpable intent cannot disrupt the casting and tallying of the votes through the Internet.

In governmental elections, the need to create a secure process for collecting and counting votes must be addressed satisfactorily before online voting becomes a viable option. Other concerns include verifying accuracy and authenticating voters (is this the only ballot that the voter sent? Is the voter the person that sent this ballot?). Digital signature technology may help accomplish such a verification function. While this type of technology can protect privacy and secrecy, its cost remains high.

Public policy making has, thus far, not taken full advantage of current information technology. With the popularity of the Internet, our framework may well be implemented on the Internet to bring the general public and government closer together. Such implementation would permit wider participation and more careful deliberation within the democratic process than in conventional voting systems. The Internet Policy Institute [29, 30] has been promoting government use of the Web, and is working toward developing an effective e-voting system. However, developments thus far have revolved around the fundamental yes-no type of voting, using the traditionally familiar 0-1 concept in the digital era.

The yes-no method is popular mainly because no convenient way exists to express preference intensities on ballot paper. It is true that putting marks on a ballot is simple and easy to count, whereas synthesizing intensity of preferences is not as straightforward. However, the advance of computer technology and the emergence of software have changed such concerns. Through prudent analysis and design, and improving Internet technology in safety, security, accessibility, integrity, and cost, a wide-ranging Internet application for public voting is foreseeable.

One may safely assume that policies are more likely to be implemented successfully when they are thought through carefully beforehand. Through an internet implementation of our framework, voters would be able to send their preferences using computers, so that individual preferences can be heard, and popular sentiments and choices could be brought together. This promises to be a more proactive and participatory process, and will likely lead to better communication and more efficient governance.

Web-Enabled Framework for Business Application

In addition to governmental elections, businesses and small groups may also benefit from Internet voting and Web-based group decision support systems (DSS). In today's world, every organization should have at its disposal an efficient group decision-making method that permits its members to express their preferences through computers. Since the Internet has become an integral part of our daily life, it offers a valuable opportunity for collecting opinions.

The decision support framework we proposed brings about greater consensus and buy-in, and prevents one person from dominating meetings and promoting his/her own political agenda. It may be useful for a small management team allocating a company's funds or for a 600-person marketing force seeking to contribute ideas to new product design. For example, in reference [31], it is reported that the AHP-based multi-criteria group decision-making approach has been used by Lockheed Martin to select new information technology (IT) products and services; by IBM to benchmark industry competition and to better allocate resources; by the Federal Aviation Agency (FAA) to prioritize R&D projects; by Housing and Urban Development (HUD) to manage their IT portfolio and request funding from Congress; and by the U.S. Army to plan multi-year budgets. Ford has also employed an AHP-based DSS to assess customer satisfaction and to evaluate next-generation vehicle designs [32]. These applications can be adapted for the Internet, allowing for greater and more effective participation in decision making. By allowing users to give critical input from anywhere in the world, the software may eliminate the need for some business travel and face-to-face meetings.

Our web-based DSS can also enable users to establish priorities on criteria that are linked to remote databases. For example, it can help establish criteria for selecting a supplier by linking to each supplier's database with past performance characteristics. The decision maker first sets priorities on performance characteristics relevant to procuring supplies. The system then links to each remote supplier's database and brings supplier data directly to the model. The Internet can thus bring greater value to business decision making.

Conclusions

We have identified some key shortcomings of traditional majority voting, in which public policy makers have little or no way to express the intensity of their preferences. We thus developed a voting procedure that is objective, takes into consideration each individual's sentiments, and allows for reasoning based on a structured evaluation framework. The approach is general and relatively easy to understand, and puts voting in a richer human context to match more closely how people feel about issues. It could have wide applicability in the real world, particularly in business and politics where one needs to know the best outcomes of debate and negotiation. The proposed "cardinal" approach helps ensure that one thinks things through so that he/she can provide fair judgments to derive priorities.

We believe that a voter's true feelings can be elicited because people are generally concerned with (1) moral (conscience) obligation, (2) law requirements, (3) personal credibility, and (4) averting social chaos (if everyone misleads others, society will not achieve harmony). When multiple issues are considered, the proposed AHP method prohibits one from overstating the importance of an issue without sacrificing the priority of the other issues. In life, in business, and in all political decisions, various criteria and multiple issues are often contemplated simultaneously; yet, single issues are regularly considered with their corresponding negations. A comprehensive evaluation approach helps one create more value for the quality of life, for the profit of a company, or for the well-being of society.

A useful approach for dealing with factor dependence and feedback matters within the B/CR ratio framework is the Analytic Network Process (ANP) [25]. Due to the limitation of this chapter's scope, we will leave this consideration for future study.

We do not assume that AHP is the best analytical tool to use. We also understand that the world will not hasten to implement our proposal. Rather, we believe this method, which includes how strongly people feel about their choices (an integral part of their biological and psychological makeup), provides a method for making policies and decisions that is more precise and valid than earlier approaches.

Our method is also sensible in that it explores strength of preference across issues. A limitation is that the procedure does not fully explore the relative strengths and weaknesses of alternative methods. However, such comparisons have been made by Peniwati [33].

Some weaknesses of our proposed method may be:

(1) It is difficult to change the current voting system.
(2) It would take time to implement the approach.
(3) People may be reluctant to use it because they have to justify their own preferences, rather than simply saying yes or no;
(4) It requires employing a new way of making decisions.

Possible strengths of the proposed voting approach includes the following:

(1) It provides a structured decision-making approach and aligns with organizational and strategic goals.
(2) It brings about conditions conducive to better, faster, more justifiable decisions, and helps generate consensus, improve communication, and thus enhance results.
(3) It allows groups to weigh team members' preferences and evaluate outcomes based on demographics, while providing a capability for sensitivity analysis;
(4) Through information technology, it may accept judgments from

multiple stakeholders using wireless keypads or the Internet for same-time, different-time, same-place, and/or remote decision making.

The concept presented in this chapter is preliminary; we hope that the ideas we presented here will help draw attention to the subject.

References

1. Harsanyi J., Cardinal welfare, individualistic ethics, and interpersonal comparisons of utility, *Journal of Political Economy*, **63**:309-321, 1955.
2. Keeney R.L., C.W. Kirkwood, Group decision making using social welfare functions. Management, *Science*; **22**:430-437, 1975.
3. Keeney R.L., Raiffa H.., *Decisions with Multiple Objectives: Preferences and Value Tradeoffs*. New York: Cambridge University Press; 1993.
4. Brock H.W., The problem of "utility weights" in group preference aggregation (in   preference models), *Operations Research*, **28**:176-187, 1980.
5. Mirkin B.G.., *Group Choice*, New York: John Wiley & Sons distributor; 1985.
6. Barbut M., Does the majority ever rule? The curious operations of processes of rational decision in games and practical elections. Portfolio and Art News Annual, **4**:161-168, 1961.
7. Arrow K.L., *Social Choice and Industrial Values*. Yale: Yale University Press; 1963.
8. Armstrong R., D. Wade, D. Cook and L. Seiford, Priority ranking and consensus formation: The Case if Ties. *Management Science* , **28**:638-645, 1982.
9. Cook W.D., Seiford L., On the borda-kendall consensus method for priority ranking problems, *Management Science*, **28**:621-37,1982.
10. Cook W.D. and M. Kress, Ordinal ranking with intensity of preference, *Management Science*, **31**:26-32, 1985.
11. Mueller D., Public choice: A Survey, *Journal of Economic* Literature, **14**:395-433, 1976.
12. Plott C., Axiomatic social choice theory: an overview and interpretation, *American Journal of Political Science*, **20**:511-596, 1976.
13. MacKay A.F., *Arrow's Theorem: The Paradox of Social Choice - A Case Study in the Philosophy of Economics*. New Haven: Yale University Press, 1980.
14. Saaty T.L., A scaling method for priorities in hierarchical structures. Journal of Mathematical Psychology 1977; **15**:234-281.
15. Saaty T.L. *Fundamentals of Decision Making and Priority Theory*. RWS Publications: 4922 Ellsworth Ave. Pittsburgh, PA 15213; 1994.

16. Saaty T.L., Vargas L., The possibility of group welfare functions. *International Journal of Information Technology & Decision Making* 2005; 4:67-76. Also in a more mathematical version: The possibility of group choice: pairwise comparisons and merging functions. Working Paper, University of Pittsburgh. Pittsburgh, PA, 15260; 2007.

17. Barro R.J., Bush's tax cuts: Reaganomics Redux? Business Week online. January 20, 2003.
    http://www.businessweek.com/magazine/content/03_03/b3816046.htm

18. Ferguson L., Racism unfortunately fact of real world. The Penn Online. October 11, 2004.
    http://www.thepenn.org/vnews/display.v/ART/2004/10/11/416b1389a2bcc

19. Cohen, C., Race Preference in College Admissions. Heritage Lecture #611. April 29, 1998.
    http://www.heritage.org/Research/Education/HL611.cfm.

20. Bowen W.G., and D. Bok, The shape of the river: long-term consequences of considering race in college and university. Society, 37:71-80, 2000.

21. Flynn V., *Term Limits*, Pocket Star, 1999.

22. Anonymous, Term Limits Debate and Poll: Do you support Term Limits? 2005.
    http://www.youdebate.com/DEBATES/term_limits.HTM.

23. Aczel J. and T.L. Saaty, Procedures for synthesizing ratio judgment. *Journal of Mathematical Psychology*, 27:93-102, 1983.

24. Aczel J., and C. Alsina, On synthesis of judgments, *Socio-Economic Planning Sciences*, 20:333-339, 1986.

25. Saaty T.L., *Theory and Applications of the Analytic Network Process*, Pittsburgh: RWS publications; 2005.

26. O'Connor E., Technology plays central role in post-election 2000, December 13, 2000.
    http://www.cnn.com/SPECIALS/views/effect/2000/12/oconnor.pres.dec13.

27. Kenski K., To I-Vote or Not to I-Vote?, *Social Science Computer Review*, 23: 293-303, 2005.

28. Stromer-Galley, J., Voting and the public sphere: conversations on internet voting, *Political Science and Politics*, 36 (4): 727-731, 2003.

29. Rose R., A global diffusion model of e-governance, *Journal of Public Policy*, 25: 5-27, 2005.

30. Lee-Kelley L, J. Thomas, E-government and social exclusion: an empirical study. *Journal of Electronic Commerce in Organizations*, 1: 1-16, 2003.

31. Davolt, S., The man who knew too much: For up-and-coming

Georgetown software developer, decision support software adds up. http://www.bizjournals.com/washington/stories/2000/08/07/sm allb1.html

32. Peniwati K., Criteria for Evaluating Group Decision-Making Methods. Chapter 13 in *Decision Making with the Analytic Network Process: Economic, Political, Social and Technological Applications with Benefits, Opportunities, Costs and Risks*, T.L. Saaty and L.G. Vargas Eds., Springer International Series, 2006.

Chapter 8

Planning the Future with Risk and Uncertainty
The Forward Backward Processes of Planning

Serious planning is almost always a group activity in the same way that governments and corporations have to plan the future. This involves many people working together to structure the plan and provide judgments as in any decision.

There is no better way to think about the complexity and uncertainty of the future than through the eyes of creative thinking. In all this there is no better substitute to expert knowledge and understanding except the use of the prioritization process that is not amenable to spontaneous thinking and the use of imagination in guessing what should be included and where in the elaborate structure. Our representation of the relationship between decision making and creative thinking is roughly represented by Figure 8.1.

Risk, Uncertainty and the Unknown

To deal with complexity our mind must model it by creating a structure and providing observations, measurements, and judgments and of course hopefully rigorous analysis to study the influences of the various factors included in the model. How well the model works out depends on several factors having to do with its form or structure whose meaning and purpose are identified and described with language and words and the functions and flows within the structure to serve the goals and purpose of the model. In general the structure is fixed for a given analysis. However, the flows are dynamic and are mostly studied with logic and mathematics. Smets [1] very aptly addresses issues having to do with the goodness of the logical and mathematical aspect of models in terms of three forms of "ignorance": incompleteness, imprecision and uncertainty. Although he does not decompose his discussion about ignorance by making a distinction between structure and flow, we believe that his scheme is useful for that purpose. With his idea of incompleteness we associate the absence of factors such as criteria and alternatives in the structure of a model (the subject of this paper) and perhaps due to insufficient understanding or in an effort to save time not providing a full set of judgments in a decision. With imprecision we associate the fact that we cannot pinpoint exactly the names and identity of the criteria and alternatives or the precise numerical values of variables that in the case of decision-making take the form of numerical judgments. With uncertainty we associate probabilities with the different factors used in the model and with the likelihood that the judgments are what we think they are.

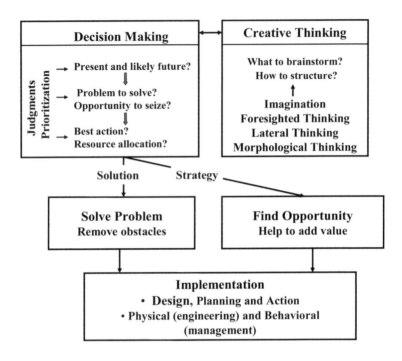

Figure 8.1 Relationships between Decision Making and Creative Thinking

The unknown or "other" [2] that affects our lives is what we usually very much want to know about to cope with uncertainty. We often suspect that it affects us with partial and indefinite evidence that it exists but we only have uncertain feelings about it. Even when we do not know what it is we would like to allow for its influence in our explaining the outcome of a decision. One way to deal with the many factors of a decision is to include the unknown as one of them and then determine its priority of influence on the outcome by comparing it with other factors. We are able to do that to the extent that we are sure of what we know and of the residual that remains outside our understanding that may also have some effect on what we do. Confidence from good understanding and past success are what we need in order to judge the potential significance of what we don't know on the outcome. We can then perform sensitivity analysis to see how much effect unknown factors can have on the stability of the choice we make.

There is concern in the literature about all these three forms of ignorance. O'Connor et al [3] described problems in maintenance arising from imprecision by not having clear criteria and not having robust decisions with which to maintain failing equipment. The object of this work was to develop a dynamic and adaptive maintenance decision-making system using the AHP that utilizes existing data and supports decisions accordingly. Faults identified as others or unknown were approximately 30 percent of the total faults. The maintenance tradesmen decided to examine the faults in greater detail and classify them. In the end unidentified faults became less than 5 percent of the total faults for any machine.

To deal with incompleteness, we show how to include unknown influences as an intangible whose effect is determined through relative measurement. Instead of assigning (guessing) probabilities to the unknown, we derive priorities by performing the more general operation of paired comparisons that involves systematic and reasoned redundancies in all the judgments about the likelihood of influence which then helps improve the validity of the numbers assigned. The unknown is simply a measure of the confidence an expert has about covering all the important criteria that influence the outcome of the decision. This enables one to capture the relative effect of what one "feels" the unknown to have on the outcome of the decision as one of the factors. The process itself diminishes uncertainty about the values of these probabilities. This says nothing about the naiveté and ignorance of the judge. It simply provides a means to remove doubt about the factors and their influence on the decision. With the unknown included as a criterion, the decision maker should no longer have any doubt about the factors included. They are all there. One caveat is that the unknown cannot be too important in priority for then one would be making a decision based on ignorance about other important criteria that should be involved. The main advantage of including a factor called "other" or the "unknown" is that it makes it possible for the decision maker to do sensitivity analysis to test the potential stability of the outcome with respect to the "unknown" according to his belief. It is an alternative that involves the use of uncertain knowledge instead of statistical methods of projection to determine the degree of confidence in the outcome of a decision under uncertainty. It is likely to be of value to an expert known for his care and accuracy in making decisions.

There are two kinds of "other" we can think of. One is to think of "other" as miscellaneous diverse criteria not considered in the decision. Such criteria we believe can and should be included as sub-criteria of a parent criterion designated as for example "miscellaneous". But that is not what we have in mind. We are thinking of residual criteria that one may suspect are there but cannot articulate them explicitly. Residual does not mean central in the sense that they would serve as an alibi for ignorance. Their relative priorities must be commensurate with those of the criteria that are known.

Planning

For the long range planner the important question is not what we should do tomorrow, but what we should do today to prepare for an uncertain future. Some factors of the future, however, need to be converged with various time spans into a decision in the present. Decision making is, in essence, an attempt to synthesize into the present a great number of divergent time spans.

To deal with the future we need to plan ahead. Planning is thinking and a social process of aligning what is deduced to be a likely outcome of a situation, given current actions, policies, and environmental influences, with what is perceived as a desirable outcome that requires new policies and new actions. How to do planning in a scientific way has always been the first author's area of interest having introduced the idea of forward and backward planning by using the AHP all included in his book Analytical planning translated to Russian.

Strategic, adaptive planning is a process of learning and growth. Above all it is an ongoing event kept in the foreground to be seen, studied, used as a guide, and revised as change is seen to happen in the environment. Strategic planning is the process of projecting the likely or logical future-the composite scenario-and of idealizing desired futures. It is the process of knowing how to attain these futures, using this knowledge to steer the logical future toward a more desired one, and then repeating the operation. The backward process of idealization inspires creative thinking. It affords people an opportunity to expand their awareness of what states of the system they would like to see take place, and with what priorities. Using the backward process, planners identify both opportunities and obstacles and eventually select effective policies to facilitate reaching the desired future.

David Cooperrider with his Appreciative Inquiry principles [4] contrasts the problem solving approach of organizational change that focuses on weaknesses by correcting things that do not work, with one that builds on strengths or things that work through envisioning a future in which the strengths become common norms rather than simply accidental. This approach requires the backward planning process with the vision clearly articulated by specifying its key elements and their priorities.

Forward-Backward Planning

Let us elaborate the idea of forward and backward planning process [5]. Planning is an ongoing decision process whose purposes are: (1) to specify the ideals, objectives, and goals an organization desires to obtain in the future; (2) to define the programs that must be undertaken to achieve these ends; and (3) to procure the resources, create the organization, and control the results of planning implementation.

An implicit assumption underlying an organization's long-range strategic planning process is that actions based only on what is best for present-day considerations (that is, tactical decisions) will not be sufficient for getting the organization to where it ought to be in the future. Were this assumption not so, the future could "take care of itself when we get there." However, the process by which an organization determines its strategic decisions is tremendously more complicated than it is for day-to-day tactical decisions. Among the complexities are the following:

1. Performance criteria: Long-range strategies strategic decisions must address a wider range and less quantifiable set of values in determining ends to be achieved than do short-range tactical decisions.
2. Feedback: Long-range strategic planning requires actions now, but the major impact is long term; hence the correctness of strategies and sustainability of the impact is difficult to evaluate because of the lack of feedback.
3. Controllability: In short-term tactical decisions, the factors that are under the organization's control can formally be separated from those that are not; over the long term there is less pure control over any single factor but more potential influence over many other factors.

Many planning processes move only in one direction. That is, they follow a time-sequenced order of events beginning at the present time $t = 0$ and terminating at some future point $t = T$. The first sequence, called the forward process, considers the factors and assumptions of the present state, which in turn generate some logical outcome. The second sequence, the backward process, begins with a desired outcome at time T and then works backward to identify and evaluate the factors and intermediate outcomes required to achieve that desired outcome. Both processes are theoretically sound and practical.

In the forward process, one considers the relevant present factors, influences, and objectives that lead to sensible conclusions or scenarios. The factors/influences/objectives may be economic, political, environmental, technological, cultural, and/or social in nature. The backward process begins with the desired scenarios then examines the policies and factors that might achieve those scenarios. Iteration of the two processes narrows or "converges" the gap between the desired and the logical scenarios. The forward planning process provides an assessment of the state of the likely outcome. The backward planning process provides a means for controlling and steering the forward process towards a desired state.

Scenarios

The key to these processes is the scenario. A scenario is a hypothesized outcome that is conceived and specified by making certain assumptions about current and future trends. The assumptions must be reasonable and should include constraints of nature, time, people, and technology. One must guard against uninhibited imagination.

There are two types of scenarios—exploratory and anticipatory. The former proceeds from the present to the future, whereas the latter takes an inverse path by starting with a future point and works backward toward the present to discover what influences and actions are required to fulfill the desired goal. Each of the scenarios can be reiterated as needed.

The exploratory scenario examines the logical sequence of events generated by the components of the system under study. It is used often as a technique to fire the imagination, stimulate discussion, and attract the attention of people involved in the planning process. Its significance does not lie in answering questions. Its importance may be to force attention on factors formerly unconsidered.

There are two kinds of anticipatory scenario: normative and contrast. The normative scenario determines at the start a given set of objectives to be achieved and then defines a path for their realization. In this case, objectives may be idealized to find if the path truly exists. The contrast scenario, on the other hand, is characterized by both a desired and feasible future. Its main asset is to sharply emphasize claims on which assumptions of feasibility rest.

The combination of normative and contrast scenarios forms a composite scenario, which in turn retains the properties of the specific scenario. This scenario allows for a synthesis of a wider range of considerations.

Rationale for the Forward-Backward Planning Process

One may question whether either the forward or the backward process is the most effective method of planning. Depending on the circumstances, one might be totally acceptable while the other is impractical. More importantly, each one alone may be inadequate to generate a good plan. Combining the two into a single forward-backward process can effectively overcome the problem. In this manner we conscientiously attempt to unite desired goals with logical goals, thereby providing a framework for the convergence of the two outcomes.

Perhaps the best reason for using the forward-backward planning process is classical planning theory itself. The theory states that there are essentially two planning goals. One is a logical or reachable goal that assumes the assumptions and factors affecting the outcome will remain substantially unchanged from the present state of affairs. Marginal changes in strategy and inputs will affect output only slightly or not at all. The other planning goal is a desired one whose attainment requires a great deal of change in inputs—both internal and external. These changes must not only be implemented, but they must survive against the entrenched policies of the system. Inertia is a powerful force. Good intuitions for making a change in course must be backed up with persistence.

Combining the Forward and Backward Processes

To integrate "forward" and "backward" hierarchical planning one projects the likely future from present actions, adopts a desired future, designs new policies, adjoins them to the set of existing policies, projects a new future, and compares the two futures—the projected and the desired—for their main attributes. The desired future is modified to see what policy modification is again needed to make it become the projected future, and the process is continued. The basic process is shown in Figure 8.2.

Formulation of a planning process for an organization as boundary problem enables us to explicitly structure the decision framework. Using decision theory notions, we identify three basic variables: (1) planning policies available to the organization, (2) outcomes the organization may realize in the future, and (3) efficiencies that show the probabilistic relationship between planning policies and outcomes.

These three variables are common to all decision processes, but the relationship among them is different for all projected planning processes and the desired planning processes. For the projected process the policies are defined, the efficiencies are estimated, and the probable outcomes are deduced.

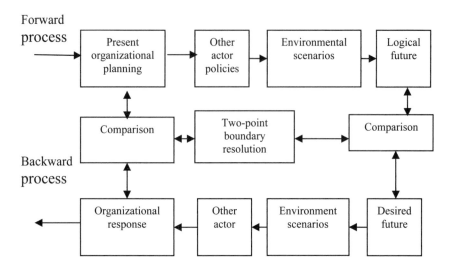

Figure 8.2 A Schematic Representation of the Basic Planning Orientation

For the desired process the outcomes are valued, the efficiencies are influenced, and the policies are developed. This difference is due fundamentally to the way the problem is organized in each case. The organizing principle in both processes is hierarchical, but the dominance relationships are reversed. Our purpose is to show that the use of hierarchies as an organizing principle for the two-point boundary planning problem enables rich solutions to be developed because directions of dominance are made explicit.

The Forward Process

The hierarchy of the forward or projected process may be characterized in the following sequence:

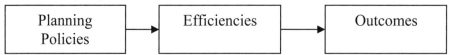

This process can be divided further by segmenting the efficiencies level into its two basic components: events caused by the purposeful behavior of other actors, and events caused by non-purposeful behavior (for example, by the weather). Purposeful behavior is itself a hierarchy, diagrammatically composed of the following elements:

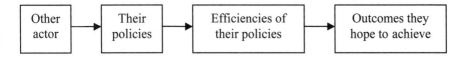

Some people have used the term transactional environment to describe other actors whose behavior directly affects organizational efficiencies. Such actors include suppliers, investors, customers, and the like. This analysis can, in turn, be expanded by adding another level to analyze the elements that contribute in the efficiency of the behavior of members of the transaction environment. Purposeful behavior of such actors has an indirect effect on the original organization; some use the term contextual environment to describe such effects

There are times when the elements (state variables) of the different outcomes are compatible and can thus be combined into a single composite outcome. From the pure outcomes of generating energy from nuclear power, fossil fuels, and solar energy one may use a strategy to combine all three outcomes. However, the outcomes may have incompatibilities that cannot be combined. For example, different plant site location outcomes cannot be combined to locate the plant in parts in each of them. Only one of the sites must be chosen.

The Backward Process

The hierarchy of the backward or desired process may be characterized in the following sequence:

The desired process begins where the projected process ends. The organization first examines the range of projected outcomes and determines the set of outcomes for which it desires to increase the likelihood of achievement and also the set of outcomes for which it is desired to minimize the likelihood of achievement. Then it works back to the efficiencies to identify the changes that are critical to the achievement of this goal. These changes must occur through planning policies adopted by the organization to influence the action of key actors in the transactional environment. Such policies, called counter-policies, are developed to make other policies more effective. These counter-policies can achieve their purposes by (1) instructing the actors to change their choice directly, (2) motivating them to change the values of the outcomes, or (3) inducing them to change their behavior by affecting the efficiencies of their choices. Inducement can, of course, take place by direct action of the organization if it has the power to affect efficiencies, or by instructing or motivating members of the contextual environment, who are part of the actors' transactional environment.

Note that the forward and backward hierarchic processes produce opposite effects. The projected process starts with a small number of planning policies and produces a large number of possible outcomes. The desired process starts with a small number of outcomes and produces a large number of policy options. Hence an interesting and highly relevant two-point boundary problem is raised: how do we reconcile into one integrated solution the large number of options that are created when each problem is defined separately? As we shall see in the examples that follow: the vehicle to accomplish this is the prioritization principle of the Analytic Hierarchy Process used by iteration of the forward and backward planning processes.

Summary of Forward-Backward Analysis

The mechanics of carrying out the forward-backward process of planning can be summarized as follows. Establish the forward process hierarchy by identifying the overall purpose of the planning exercise. It is the single element or focus of the hierarchy which occupies the top level. The second level should include the various forces, economic, political, social, which affect the outcome. The third level consists of the actors who manipulate these forces (sometimes it is possible to put the actors in the second level without any mention of the forces). In the fourth level one includes the objectives of each actor. The fifth level of the hierarchy is often optional and should include the policies that each actor pursues to fulfill his objectives. The sixth level is important. It involves the possible scenarios or outcomes that each actor is struggling to bring about as a result of pursuing his objectives (and applying his policies). The final level of the hierarchy is the composite outcome that is a result of all these different scenarios. After all, there is only one possible state of the world and it is a mixture of different people's attempts to shape it in a way which serves their interests. The composite scenario is also known as the logical outcome.

Because of the many and often conflicting interests that coalesce in this scenario, the result may be a dilution or weakening of what any of the actors' wishes to see as an outcome. As a result one or several of the actors may work to change some of their policies to bring about a new outcome that is closer to what they want to get. This calls for the backward process. In this process each actor identifies for his second level one or several desired scenarios he wishes to see take place and sets priorities for them as to how well he wishes to see them affect his overall desired future. The third level consists of problems and opportunities that prevent the attainment of the scenarios. The fourth level includes actors (whether mentioned in the forward process or not) who can influence solution of the problems. The fifth level includes these actor's objectives. The sixth level may or may not include their policies. The seventh level includes one particular actor's policies (or change in objectives) which if pursued can affect the attainment of the desired futures.

After prioritization of these policies (or objectives) in the backward process, only the most important ones are used in a second forward process. They are included with the previous forward policies of just those actors desiring change. Prioritization of the second forward process is revised only from the level of objectives or if there is a level of policies then from that level downward. Then one compares the priorities of the composite likely outcome of the second forward process with the priorities of the desired futures of the first backward process to see if the logical future is driven closer to the desired future. If not, a second iteration of the backward process is carried out by changing the priorities of the desired futures and/or examining new policies. Again the important ones are substituted in a third forward process and scenario priorities are calculated and compared with those of the second backward process. The procedure is repeated until one has fairly exhausted the possibilities in search of ways to improve the logical or likely outcome.

State Variables

There is an alternative way to use the weights assigned to the outcomes. A scenario describes a state of a system. In that state the system has a particular structure and flows. To characterize these meaningfully one uses a set of variables called state variables which specify the structure and flows of the system in that state. Thus a set of state variables may be defined and used to describe an outcome of a planning process. These variables may range over the different aspects of an outcome: political, economic, social, legal. Each of the basic scenarios may be described in terms of the change in each of these variables from the status quo. The intensity of variations above or below the status quo is indicated by a difference scale which ranges from - 9 to 9 (nine times below or nine times above).

An Example

Several years ago or we may say long ago since the 1973 fuel crisis, the federal government displayed an interest in cooperating with the private sector in the development of synthetic fuels [6]. The government, however, has not followed up very convincingly on its early initiatives and has yet to develop an explicit synthetic fuels (synfuels) policy. That was the thinking many years ago before ethanol came on the market in recent years. Ethanol requires a vast amount of land to grow corn (500 gallons of ethanol per acre with each acre yielding 200 bushels of corn or 2 and ½ gallons of ethanol per bushel), more than there is to cultivate enough corn and other cellulosic materials like wheat and rice straw and corn cobs, cardboard, wood and other fibrous plant materials (sugar cane in Brazil) to partly replace the 21 million barrels of oil the US consumes every day (6.6 billion barrels a year)-nearly a fourth of the entire world's consumption of oil. It is known that according to one estimate, a gallon of ethanol has 56% more energy than it takes to produce it.

Much of the US vast coal and shale reserves are located in the relatively sparsely settled West. In fact, some of the richest reserves are located in national parks and other protected areas, thereby setting the stage for a national debate on the trade-offs between ecological protection and energy independence. Thus, even on the tenuous assumption that the mass production of synthetic fuel is economically feasible, there is a thicket of regulations and environmental concerns that may impede progress in the synfuels industry.

Finally, the policies of the Oil and Petroleum Exporting Countries (OPEC) have an impact on the future of the synfuels industry. OPEC is interested in ensuring that the western industrialized nations (particularly the U. S. and Western Europe) remain dependent on Middle Eastern oil. A viable synfuels industry would enhance competition thus forcing OPEC to lower its prices in order to survive in the marketplace. OPEC may use its pricing policies to discourage investment in synfuels research and development. For example, it might temporarily stabilize oil prices in order to defuse the occasional clamoring for viable energy alternatives OPEC might then gradually increase its prices in order to continue to reap enormous profits. In this manner, the synfuels industry would become little more than a puppet with OPEC pulling the strings.

It is evident from the discussion above that the future of the synfuels industry in the United States with respect to transportation fuels is uncertain due to (1) the conflicting signals which the industry is receiving from the federal government; (2) the high cost of developing the synfuels industry, (3) the environmental concerns associated with the development of synthetic fuels, and, (4) the pricing policies of OPEC.

Where does the industry appear to be going and where should it go if the environment becomes more favorable? This problem was once approached from the standpoint of an energy company who, in the first forward process, attempts to envision what type of environment the synfuels industry will have to adapt to in the next 10 years. By "environment" we are referring to the general political, economic, technological and social milieu, within which the synfuels industry would develop or perhaps stagnate and die.

The First Forward Process

Figure 8.3 illustrates the hierarchy for the first forward process. The focus or objective is to portray the likely environment facing the synfuels industry in the U.S. in the next 10 years from when the study was done. Note that for purposes of this example for the synfuels industry pertains to transportation fuels, not fuels for industrial use, home heating, and the like.

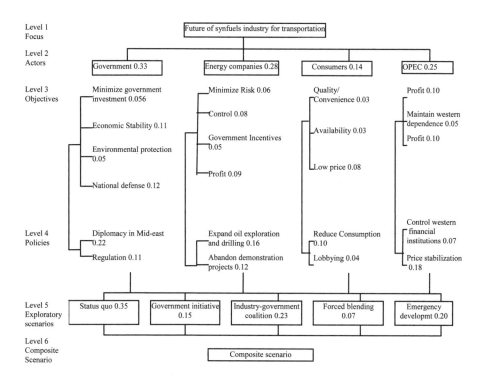

Figure 8.3 First Forward Planning Hierarchy

The main actors affecting the future of the synfuels industry are: (1) government; (2) energy companies; (3) consumers, and (4) OPEC. Each actor has certain objectives and is pursuing certain policies in order to fulfill those objectives. Finally, the hierarchy contains five exploratory scenarios which will comprise the composite scenario. The exploratory scenarios are briefly described below.

Status Quo: This scenario is characterized by continued government disinvestment in synfuels accompanied by reluctance on the part of the private sector to take the necessary risks to enhance the economic viability of the synfuels industry. The scenario assumes that OPEC oil prices will remain relatively stable thereby diminishing the attractiveness of alternative energy sources. Also there will be little or no change in the regulatory and environmental concerns which currently pose barriers to synfuel development.

Government Initiative: This scenario assumes that the federal government will act preemptively to minimize the capability of OPEC to once again bring the Western nations to their knees with an oil embargo. The scenario forecasts increased government involvement in and subsidization of synfuels research and development. Relatedly, the government will breathe new life into the synthetic Fuels Corporation, giving it the political mandate and financial resources necessary to design the research agenda and to develop a coherent national policy on synthetic fuels. The synfuels industry would be closely monitored and regulated in the same way that utility companies are controlled by government today. Finally, the scenario assumes that environmental concerns will be diminished by a combination of new technologies that will minimize adverse environmental effects and by the diminishing power of environmental interest groups.

Industry-Government Coalition: This scenario is similar to "Government Initiative" in that the federal government will take a renewed interest in synfuels research and will provide financial and technical support for those research efforts. The major difference is that the energy companies will control the research agenda and will maintain private ownership of demonstration plants, patents, and the like. Moreover, the industry will not be strictly monitored or controlled by government; rather, the free market system will prevail; therefore supply and demand patterns, not government regulations, will determine both the quantities of synfuels produced and the market price for those fuels.

Forced Blending: Some countries, such as Brazil, have implemented a policy of forced blending. In this scenario refineries are required to blend conventional fuels with prescribed percentages of synthetic fuels; the prescribed percentage increases over time. The policy would be analogous to the government forcing industry to conform to air quality standards by a particular date. The burden of developing the appropriate technology falls, of course, on the energy and transportation companies alone with the government providing little or no assistance.

Emergency Development: This scenario portrays a repetition of the 1973-74 oil embargo. Increased military and political tensions in the Middle East combined with continuous U.S. support of Israel will prompt retaliatory action by OPEC. The U.S. will react with an emergency research and development program. A "crisis atmosphere" will prevail and, therefore, the research and development agenda will not be systematically planned or coordinated. Most social and environmental concerns will be ignored as the country makes a concerted effort to establish energy independence. Also, energy companies will be encouraged (or coerced), through government appeals to their patriotism, to temporarily abandon the profit motive as the driving force behind their research and development activities.

Table 8.1 illustrates the prioritization of the state variables. Note that the state variables and their associated priorities reflect the interests of the energy company since the planning exercise is being conducted from its perspective. Table 8.2 illustrates the calibration of the state variables with respect to the exploratory scenarios. The first forward process produced a composite measurement of (-.31).

Table 8.1 Priorities of State Variables

State variables	Priority
Control	.32
Government incentives	.16
Free Market	.28
Research funds	.15
Citizen support	.09

The First Backward Process

The first backward process hierarchy is illustrated in Figure 8.4. Note that, while "Status Quo" is projected to be the most likely scenario, "Industry-Government Coalition" is the desired scenario from the point of view of the energy companies. The fifth level of this hierarchy contains policies that are being considered by the energy companies. A brief explanation of those policies follows.

Industrial Consortium: The consortium would serve as an industry-wise advisory body which would present a unified voice to the federal government on matters pertaining to synfuels research and development. The consortium would be a strictly voluntary organization with no formal policy making authority; it would, therefore, not violate laws pertaining to restraint of trade. It would serve as an informal forum for industry-government planning. It is believed that such a forum would streamline patterns of communication between government and industry.

Laboratory Research and Development: Even small scale field demonstration, e.g., coal gasification plants, have proved to be extremely costly and thus far have offered little promise of short term or long term pay-offs. Some industry representatives believe that synfuels researchers should "go back to the drawing board" so to speak through intensified laboratory research which is relatively inexpensive compared with field demonstration projects. Only when such research produces highly promising results would the industry approach the federal government for direct financial assistance or indirect incentives to proceed with the construction of demonstration plants.

Table 8.2 State Variable Calibration

	Status quo (.35)	Government initiative (.15)	Coalition (.23)	Forced Blend (.70)	Emergency Development (.20)	First forward process
Control	0	-5	+4	-7	-7	-1.72
Government incentives	-3	+2	+5	+2	+5	1.54
Free market	0	-7	+3	-2	-4	-1.30
Research funds	-3	+5	+4	0	+6	1.82
Citizen support	0	+2	-2	+1	+5	91
Composite						-.31

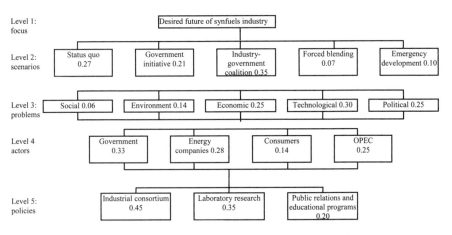

Figure 8.4 First Backward Planning Hierarchy

Public Relations and Educational Campaigns: It is suspected that the relatively stable oil prices combined with the disappointing performance of demonstration projects has produced widespread complacency and apathy toward synfuels research. A national media campaign would stress America's growing reliance on foreign oil, highlighting the politically volatile situation in the Mid-East and calling for long range planning to avoid a repetition of the 1973-74 embargo. In general, such a campaign would attempt to sway public opinion toward synfuels research.

Remark: At this point it should be noted that pair-wise comparison of the scenarios, with respect to the desired future (as was done in Table 8.3), is based on implicit assumptions of the scenarios without looking at the state variable values. Imprecision in judgment can be a result of lack of a more detailed understanding of the state variables whose values define each scenario. If we use the state variable priorities given in Table 8.1 and the state variable calibrations given in Table 8.2, a composite for each scenario in Table 8.2 can be obtained by multiplying the values of the state variables by their priorities. For example for the "status quo" we obtain
$(0)(0.32)+(-3)(0.16)+(0)(0.28)+(-3)(0.15)+(0)(0.09)=-0.93$
Doing this for the remaining four scenarios yields values of -2.31, 3.34, -2.39, and -1.21, respectively.

Here "coalition" with the only positive value (3.34) is the most favored future outcome, and "forced blend" is the least favorable one. The desired priorities of the exploratory scenarios for the backward planning hierarchy in Table 8.3 can then be adjusted relying in part on the magnitudes of these individual composites.

The Second Forward Process

The two high priority policies, Industrial Consortium and Laboratory Research, were introduced into the second forward process hierarchy as policies of the energy companies. The prioritization proceeded from the level of policies downward. The relative likelihood of "Industry-Government Coalition" (the desired scenario) occurring, improved somewhat from .23 to .29 as illustrated in Table 8.3. The "true" convergence, as determined by the composite measurement improved by nearly 100 from - .31 to - .003. Remember that a move toward zero in this case is a positive move. Table 8.4 illustrates the state variable calibrations and the composite measurement for the first and second forward processes.

Table 8.3 Second Forward Process — Relative Likelihood of Exploratory Scenarios

Scenarios	Relative likelihood
Status quo	.32
Government initiative	.13
Coalition	.29
Forced blending	.05
Emergency development	.21

Table 8.4 State Variable Calibrations for First and Second Forward Processes

State variables	First forward	Second forward
Control	-1.72	-1.31
Government incentives	1.54	1.90
Free Market	-1.30	-.98
Research funds	1.82	2.11
Citizen support	.91	.78

The Second Backward Process

Even though significant convergence was achieved, the future prospects for the synfuels industry do not appear very bright. It was determined, therefore, that another iteration of the forward-backward process was required. In the second backward process the planners decided to add a policy that would have a short term impact on shaping the future of the synfuels industry. "Industrial Consortium" and "Laboratory Research" would require time to produce meaningful results; the planners believed that the efficacy of these two policies might be enhanced if they were complemented with some policies that had positive impacts in the short term as well as long term. A second backward process hierarchy was constructed which was identical to that illustrated in Figure 8.2 (the first backward process) with one exception—a new policy ("Gasohol") was added and the weights of the three previous policies were adjusted to reflect the new alternative. A brief explanation of the new policy follows:

Gasohol: Alcohol may be produced from excess foodstuffs through fermentation and blended with gasoline to produce a fuel ("gasohol") suitable for use in conventional engines. At present, conventional engines can operate efficiently on fuel with up to a nine to one gas to alcohol ratio, above which there is a need to modify conventional engines. Also, large quantities of grain are required to produce relatively small quantities of alcohol. Despite these drawbacks the technology for producing gasohol is currently being used, with high consumer satisfaction, especially in the Mid-West States. Also, there are relatively few technological, social or environmental patterns associated with increasing its usage. While the long term prospects for gasohol may not be as promising as those for synfuels derived from shale, coal and other natural resources, it offers significant short-term potential. Specifically, if the energy companies can increase the short-term demand for gasohol, through price reductions, advertising campaigns, and the like, they may be more successful in gaining government and public support for long-term research and development efforts related to other synfuel technologies.

The Third Forward Process

In the third forward process hierarchy all four policies from the second backward process were included as policies of the energy companies. With the addition of short term as well as long-term policies, the perceived likelihood of "Industry-Government Coalition" (the desired scenario) increased again from .29 in the second forward process to .34 in the third forward process as illustrated in Table 8.5.

Table 8.5 Third Forward Process

Scenarios	Relative likelihood
Status quo	.31
Government initiative	.13
Coalition	.34
Forced blending	.01
Emergency development	.21

Table 8.6 illustrates the composite measurements for the first, second, and third forward hierarchies. Note that the convergence between the likely and desired futures improved rather significantly (186) between the first and third iterations. On the basis of this convergence, the planners recommended that the company pursue all four policies with emphasis corresponding to the priorities. A description of the scenario that will result from the implementation of these four policies follows:

Table 8.6 State Variable Calibrations for First, Second, and Third Forward Processes

State variables	First forward	Second forward	Third forward
Control	-1.72	-1.31	-.83
Government incentives	1.54	1.90	2.10
Free Market	-1.30	-.98	-.75
Research funds	1.82	2.11	2.34
Citizen support	.91	.78	.64
Composite	-.34	-.003	.269

It appears inevitable that the energy companies will lose a small amount of control over the synfuels industry by attempting to foster an industry-government coalition. Relatively, the free market forces of supply and demand will not be allowed to seek their true equilibrium point due to anticipated government intervention in the synfuels industry. On the positive side, however, government incentives to engage in synfuels research will be enhanced. Available research funds will increase slightly and public support for synfuels research will also increase slightly.

Conclusion

We have seen how to actualize our intuitive understanding of planning by successive iterations of the forward-backward process. The purpose is to decide on what is likely to happen, what we want, what we must control or bring about, and how effective this control is likely to be in directing the likely future towards the desired future. This approach not only unfolds our understanding but provides logical dynamics to test for promising alternatives. This kind of understanding must precede action. Before we proceed to alter the world we live in, with the hope that we can change it for the better, we need a means to test the soundness of our approach.

The complexity of the environment is increasing so rapidly that the impetus to plan and replan to keep up with change must always be present. As any plan is used to make a change, it must soon after be revised to incorporate the full impact of the change it has brought about. There are several reasons why no plan can be so fully dynamic that all aspects of change can be anticipated in it.

One is that we always plan for a part of our world, and occurrences elsewhere tend to overtake the system being planned for; hence the plan must be periodically revised. Another is that not all impacts can be anticipated, particularly those of a synergistic nature, which give rise to completely new entities that cannot be fully characterized in advance. This is true both of concrete physical constructions and of relations among people or among ideas. The close association of a few ideas could lead to the emergence of a new idea that is radically different from its constituent parts. The plan must now be rethought to take into consideration the new developments and their impacts.

Revising a plan may involve the addition or deletion of factors or preferably it can be restructured ab initio to incorporate subtleties that have come to light which cannot be easily accommodated in the older framework. We propose that in the process of implementing the composite scenario the plan should be revised periodically in periods ranging from 3 to 5 years: 3 years to allow the effects of actions to have sufficient time to become noticeable; 5 years to prevent the system from becoming too resistant to change. The ideas in the plan should be constantly reviewed and changed or interpreted on a daily basis as a means of tactical revision. But the structure and recommendations of the strategic plan, once adopted, should not be questioned every day.

The systems approach requires that a plan be approached as an organic whole, not in pieces. Thus major revisions must encompass the entire plan and not simply relate to some parts, leaving out others. This necessitates that not only the components of the plan but their interactions be studied and synthesized, that applications in one part be thought of in terms of their effect on the organization with regard to its structure and its function. Planning is more effective when practiced as an integrated whole.

References

1. Smets, P., Varieties of Ignorance and the Need for Well-Founded Theories, *Information Sciences*, 57-58, 135-144, 1991.

2. Ozdemir, M., and T.L. Saaty, The Unkown in Decision Making: What to do about it, *European Journal of Operational Research*, 174, 349-359, 2006.

3. O'Connor R.F., G.B. Williams, and A.W. Labib, An Effective Maintenance System Using Analytic Hierarchy Process, *Integrated Manufacturing Systems*, 9/2, 87-98, 1998.

4. Cooperrider, D.L. and D. Whitney, *Appreciative Inquiry: A positive Revolution in Change,* Berret-Koehler Publishers, 2005.

5. Emshoff, J. and T.L. Saaty, Applications of the Analytic Hierarchy Process to Long Range Planning Processes, *European Journal of Operational Research*, 10, 131-143,1982.

6. Saaty, T.L. and K. Kearns, *Analytical Planning*, Pergamon Press, Oxford, 1985, reprinted RWS Publications, 1991.

Chapter 9

Decisions with Dependence and Feedback
The Analytic Network Process

We said in Chapter 4 that a hierarchy is an efficient way to deal with complex systems, both structurally and functionally. However, a hierarchy assumes that the relative priorities of the elements in a higher level of the hierarchy are independent of those in the lower level. Structuring a problem as a hierarchy also requires one to understand the problem well to be able to locate clusters of elements in the right order from top to bottom. When one deals with an unstructured or a very complex problem, the systematic framework of a feedback network, which is a generalized form of a hierarchy, would be more appropriate. It involves cycles and feedback loops of influence between both elements and levels.

One had to overcome the limitation of linear hierarchic structures and the requirement that scales can be added and multiplied to deal with dependence and feedback using judgments about importance and preference along with, for example, measurements in the form of likelihood as probability. In addition the general theory of the ANP enables one to deal with the benefits, opportunities, costs, and risks (the BOCR merits) of a decision, by introducing the notion of negative priorities for C and R along with the rating of the top rated alternative for each of these four merits in terms of strategic criteria to enable one to combine the four values of each alternative into a single outcome. This chapter summarizes and illustrates the basic concepts of the ANP and shows how informed intuitive judgments can lead to real life answers that are matched by actual measurements in the real world [1, 2].

The AHP/ANP takes the descriptive rather than the normative or prescriptive approach to making decisions. In general it does not say one must do this or that but rather it helps people to lay out their perceptions in an organized way and provide their judgments as they do naturally. It is being used in practical applications in many places. For example, in making major national policy decisions, some military and government decisions and in corporations where project prioritization and resource allocation are pressing issues.

In making a decision, we need to distinguish between the goal-oriented hierarchic structures and the holistic and interactive network structures that we use to represent that decision problem. In a hierarchy we have levels arranged in a descending order of importance. The elements in each level are compared according to dominance or influence with respect to

hierarchies

the elements in the level immediately above that level. The arrows descend downwards from the goal pointing to where the influence originates from, which is a kind of service. The elements in lower levels contribute to or influence the well being and success of elements in higher levels. We can interpret the downward pointing of the arrows as a process of stimulating the influence of the elements in the lower level on those in the level above. In *networks* a network, the components (counterparts of levels in a hierarchy) are not arranged in any particular order, but are connected as appropriate in pairs with directed lines. Again an arrow points from one component to another to stimulate the influence of the elements of the second component on those in the first. The pairwise comparisons of elements in a component are made according to the dominance of influence of each member of a pair on an element in the same or in another component. Here again, influence may be evaluated in terms of importance, preference or likelihood. *attributes*

In addition, in a network, the system of components may be regarded as elements that interact and influence each other with respect to a criterion or attribute with respect to which the influences occurs. That attribute itself must be of a higher order of complexity than the components and a fortiori of higher order than the elements contained in the components. *control* We call such an attribute a control criterion. Thus even in a network, there is *criterion* a hierarchic structure that lists control criteria above the networks. For each of the four benefits, opportunities, costs and risks, known for brevity as BOCR merits we have a system of control criteria that we use to assess influence. The result is that such control criteria and/or their subcriteria serve as the basis for all comparisons made under them, both for the components and for the elements in these components. In a hierarchy one does not compare levels according to influence because they are arranged linearly in a predetermined order from which all influence flows downwards. In a network, the effect of the influence of different clusters of elements can differ from cluster to another cluster and hence they need to be weighted to incorporate the proportionality of their contributions. The criteria for comparisons are either included in a level, or more often implicitly replaced by using the idea of "importance, preference or likelihood" with respect to the goal, without being more finely detailed about what kind of importance it is. The control criteria for comparisons in a network are intended to be explicit about the importance of influence that they represent.

In a hierarchy, we ask the question for making a comparison, which of two elements is more dominant or has more influence (or in the opposite sense is influenced more) with respect to a certain element in the level above? In a network we ask, which of two elements is more dominant in influencing another element in the same or in another component with respect to a control criterion? In both hierarchies and networks the sense of

questions to rank hierarchies & networks

ANP vs. AHP — why they're different & how

→ ANP structure occurs by understanding the flow of influence

having influence or being influenced must be maintained in the entire analysis; the two should not be mixed together.

The ANP frees us from the burden of ordering the components in the form of a directed chain as in a hierarchy. We can represent any decision as a directed network. While the AHP has a visibly better structure that derives from a strict understanding of the flow of influence, the ANP allows the structure to develop more naturally, and therefore is a better way to describe faithfully what can happen in the real world. These observations lead us to conclude that hierarchic decisions, because of imposed structure are likely to be less accurate in representing a problem because it ignores dependence. By including dependence and feedback and by cycling their influence with the supermatrix, the ANP is more objective and more likely to capture what happens in the real world. It does things that the mind cannot do in a precise and thorough way. Putting the two observations together, the ANP is likely to be a strongly more effective decision-making tool in practice than the AHP.

ANP more realistic than AHP since AHP ignores dependence

three phase structure of ANP

In all we have a three phase structure of complex decisions: 1) The BOCR merits of the decision, their criteria and subcriteria known as control criteria in terms of which influence is evaluated, 2) The hierarchies or networks of influences and "objective" facts that make one alternative of the decision more desirable than another for each of the BOCR, and finally, 3) The system of strategic criteria in terms of which the top alternative of each of the BOCR merits must be rated by itself and whose ratings are then used to combine the weights of each alternative under all the four merits and obtain an overall synthesis. In each of these phases there are major concerns that are subdivided into less major ones and these in turn into still smaller ones. The entire set of three levels may sometimes be structured into a single network as we have done in some decision problems.

For an inconsistent matrix, the sum of all the dominances along paths of length 1, 2, and so on has a limit determined as a Cesaro sum. That limit is the principal eigenvector of the matrix of preferences. Let us develop these ideas in some detail. *Cesaro sum*

Let a_{ij} be the relative dominance of A_i over A_j. To simplify the notation, let the matrix corresponding to the reciprocal pairwise relation be denoted by $A = (a_{ij})$. The relative dominance of A_i over A_j along paths of length k is given by

inconsistent matrix

$$\frac{\sum_{j=1}^{n} a_{ij}^{(k)}}{\sum_{i=1}^{n}\sum_{j=1}^{n} a_{ij}^{(k)}}$$

where $a_{ij}^{(k)}$ is the (i,j) entry of the kth power of the matrix (a_{ij}). The total dominance $w(A_i)$, of alternative i over all other alternatives along paths of all lengths is given by the infinite series

$$w(A_i) = \sum_{k=1}^{\infty} \frac{\sum_{j=1}^{n} a_{ij}^{(k)}}{\sum_{i=1}^{n}\sum_{j=1}^{n} a_{ij}^{(k)}}$$

whose sum is the Cesaro sum

$$\lim_{M\to\infty} \frac{1}{M}\sum_{k=1}^{M} \frac{\sum_{j=1}^{n} a_{ij}^{(k)}}{\sum_{i=1}^{n}\sum_{j=1}^{n} a_{ij}^{(k)}}.$$

Cesaro sum explained ↓

Now we give some detail. Note that the sums of different sets with k numbers in each, determines their ranks according to their total value. The average of each sum is obtained by dividing by k. The averages give the same ranks because they only differ by the same constant from the original sums. Often the sum of an infinite series of numbers is infinite but if we form the average, that average as k tends to infinity may converge. In that case it converges to the same limit as that of the kth term of the infinite sum. Thus taking the limit of the averages gives us a meaningful ranking of the objects. This is a profound observation proved by the Italian Mathematician Ernesto Cesaro (1859-1906).

Cesaro Summability

Let us prove that if a sequence of numbers converges then the sequence of arithmetic means formed from that sequence also converges to the same limit as the sequence. This is known as Cesaro Summability.

Proof: Let s_n denote the nth term of the sequence and let $\sigma_n = \frac{s_1 + ... + s_n}{n}$, if

$\lim_{n\to\infty} \sigma_n = S$, then S is called the Cesaro sum of s_n. Let

$t_n = s_n - S, \tau_n = \sigma_n - S$, and thus $\tau_n = \frac{t_1 + ... + t_n}{n}$. We prove that $\tau_n \to 0$ as $n \to \infty$.

Choose $a > 0$, so that each $|t_n| < a$. Given $\varepsilon > 0$, now for $n > N$,

$$|\tau_n| \le \frac{|t_1|+...+|t_N|}{n} + \frac{|t_{N+1}|+...+|t_n|}{n} < \frac{Na}{n} + \varepsilon. \text{ Since } \varepsilon \text{ is arbitrary, it follows}$$

that $\lim_{n\to\infty} |\tau_n| = 0$ and $\sigma_n \to S$.

Cesaro summability ensures that

$$w(A_i) = \sum_{k=1}^{\infty} \frac{\sum_{j=1}^{n} a_{ij}^{(k)}}{\sum_{i=1}^{n}\sum_{j=1}^{n} a_{ij}^{(k)}} = \lim_{M\to\infty} \frac{1}{M} \sum_{k=1}^{M} \frac{\sum_{j=1}^{n} a_{ij}^{(k)}}{\sum_{i=1}^{n}\sum_{j=1}^{n} a_{ij}^{(k)}} = \lim_{k\to\infty} \frac{\sum_{j=1}^{n} a_{ij}^{(k)}}{\sum_{i=1}^{n}\sum_{j=1}^{n} a_{ij}^{(k)}}$$

This approach to the idea of derived overall dominance is a variant of the well-known theorem of Oskar Perron for positive matrices in which it is demonstrated that the limit converges to the principal right eigenvector of the matrix. Thus a reciprocal pairwise comparisons reciprocal matrix $A = (a_{ij})$, satisfies the system of homogeneous equations

$$\sum_{j=1}^{n} a_{ij} w_j = \lambda_{max} w_i, i = 1,...,n$$

where λ_{max} is the principal eigenvalue of the matrix A and w is its corresponding principal right eigenvector.

Mathematics of the Analytic Network Process

The Supermatrix of a Feedback System

Assume that we have a system of N clusters or components, whereby the elements in each component interact or have an impact on or are themselves influenced by some or all of the elements of that component or of another component with respect to a property governing the interactions of the entire system, such as energy or capital or political influence (Saaty, 2001). Assume that component h, denoted by C_h, $h = 1, ..., N$, has n_h elements, that we denote by $e_{h_1}, e_{h_2}, ..., e_{h_{n_h}}$. A priority vector derived from paired comparisons in the usual way represents the impact of a given set of elements in a component on another element in the system. When an element has no influence on another element, its influence priority is assigned (not derived) as zero.

The priority vectors derived from pairwise comparison matrices are each entered as a part of some column of a supermatrix. The supermatrix represents the influence priority of an element on the left of the matrix on an element at the top of the matrix. A supermatrix along with an example of one of its general entry i, j block are shown in Figure 9.1. The component C_i alongside the supermatrix includes all the priority vectors derived for nodes that are "parent" nodes in the C_i cluster. Figure 9.2 gives the supermatrix of a hierarchy along with its supermatrix. The entry in the last row and column of the supermatrix of a hierarchy is the identity matrix I.

Feedback Network with components having
Inner and Outer Dependence among Their Elements

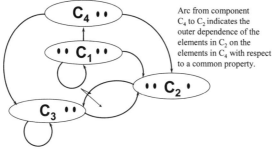

Arc from component C_4 to C_2 indicates the outer dependence of the elements in C_2 on the elements in C_4 with respect to a common property.

Loop in a component indicates inner dependence of the elements in that component with respect to a common property.

$$W = \begin{array}{c} \\ C_1 \\ \\ C_2 \\ \\ \\ C_N \end{array} \begin{bmatrix} W_{11} & W_{12} & \cdots & W_{1N} \\ W_{21} & W_{22} & \cdots & W_{2N} \\ \vdots & \vdots & \cdots & \vdots \\ W_{N1} & W_{N2} & \cdots & W_{NN} \end{bmatrix}$$

$$\mathbf{W}_{ij} = \begin{bmatrix} W_{i1}^{(j_1)} & W_{i1}^{(j_2)} & \cdots & W_{i1}^{(jn_j)} \\ W_{i2}^{(j_1)} & W_{i2}^{(j_2)} & \cdots & W_{i2}^{(jn_j)} \\ \vdots & \vdots & \cdots & \vdots \\ W_{in_i}^{(j_1)} & W_{in_i}^{(j_2)} & \cdots & W_{in_i}^{(jn_j)} \end{bmatrix}$$

Figure 9.1 The Structure and Supermatrix of a Network and Detail of a Matrix in it

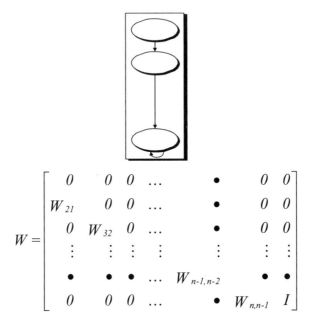

$$W = \begin{bmatrix} 0 & 0 & 0 & \cdots & \bullet & 0 & 0 \\ W_{21} & 0 & 0 & \cdots & \bullet & 0 & 0 \\ 0 & W_{32} & 0 & \cdots & \bullet & 0 & 0 \\ \vdots & \vdots & \vdots & \vdots & \vdots & \vdots & \vdots \\ \bullet & \bullet & \bullet & \cdots & W_{n-1,n-2} & \bullet & \bullet \\ 0 & 0 & 0 & \cdots & \bullet & W_{n,n-1} & I \end{bmatrix}$$

Figure 9.2 The Structure and Supermatrix of a Hierarchy

The Need for Powers of the Supermatrix to Represent Transitivities of all Order

According to Cesaro summability we only need to raise the supermatrix to limiting powers to capture the overall priorities of the elements. But there are different forms of the limit depending on the multiplicity of its principal eigenvalue, which as we shall see below must be equal to one or is a complex root of one, and on whether the matrix is reducible and cycles or not. We do not have sufficient room here to detail all these cases. It is sufficient to say that mostly the Cesaro sum is taken for the limits when they are not unique. The following is well known in algebra [1]. According to J. J. Sylvester one can represent an entire function of a (diagonalizable) matrix W whose characteristic roots are distinct as:

$f(W) = \sum_{i=1}^{n} f(\lambda_i) Z(\lambda_i)$, where $Z(\lambda_i) = \prod_{j \neq i}(\lambda_j I - W) / \prod_{j \neq i}(\lambda_j - \lambda_i)$. The $Z(\lambda_i)$ can

be shown to be complete orthogonal idempotent matrices of W; that is, they

have the properties $\sum_{i=1}^{k} Z(\lambda_i) = I$, $Z(\lambda_i) Z(\lambda_j) = 0$, $i \neq j$, $Z^2(\lambda_i) = Z(\lambda_i)$, where I

and 0 are the identity and null matrices, respectively. Thus for example if one raises a matrix to arbitrarily large powers, it is enough to raise its

[handwritten margin note: limits that are not unique]

eigenvalues

eigenvalues to these powers and form the above sum involving the sum of polynomials in W. Because the eigenvalues of a stochastic matrix are all less than one, when raised to powers they vanish except when they are equal to one or are complex conjugate roots of one. Because here the eigenvalues are assumed to be distinct, we have the simplest case to deal with, that is $\lambda_{max} = 1$ is a simple eigenvalue. Formally, because the right hand side is a polynomial in W multiplying both sides by W^∞ each term on the right would be a constant multiplied by W^∞ and the final outcome is also a constant multiplied by W^∞. Because we are only interested in the relative values of the entries in W^∞ we can ignore the constant and simply raise W to very large powers which the computer program SuperDecisions does in this case of distinct eigenvalues.

Next we consider the case where $\lambda_{max} = 1$ is a multiple eigenvalue. For that case we have what is known as the confluent form of Sylvester's theorem:

Sylvester's theorem

$$f(W) = \sum_{j=1}^{k} T(\lambda_i) = \sum_{i=1}^{k} \frac{1}{(m_i - 1)!} \frac{d^{m_i-1}}{d\lambda^{m_i-1}} f(\lambda)(\lambda I - W)^{-1} \frac{\prod_{i=1}^{n}(\lambda - \lambda_i)}{\prod_{i=m_{i+1}}^{n}(\lambda - \lambda_i)}\Bigg|_{\lambda - \lambda_i}$$

where k is the number of distinct roots and m_i is the multiplicity of the root λ_i. However, as we show below, this too tells us that to obtain the limit priorities it is sufficient to raise W to arbitrarily large power to obtain a satisfactory decimal approximation to W^∞.

The only possible nonzero survivors as we raise the matrix to powers are those λ's that are equal to one or are roots of one [2]. If the multiplicity of the largest real eigenvalue λ_{max} is n_1, then we have

$$W^\infty = n_1 \frac{\dfrac{d^{(n_1-1)}}{d\lambda^{(n_1-1)}}\left[(\lambda I - W)^{-1}\Delta(\lambda)\right]}{\Delta^{(n_1)}(\lambda)}\Bigg|_{\lambda=1}$$

where one takes derivatives of the characteristic polynomial of the matrix W, and $\Delta(\lambda) = \det(\lambda I - W) = \lambda^n + p_1\lambda^{n-1} + ... + p_n$. Also $(\lambda I - W)^{-1} = F(\lambda)/\Delta(\lambda)$ and $F(\lambda) = W^{n-1} + (\lambda + p_1)W^{n-2} + (\lambda^2 + p_1\lambda + p_2)W^{n-3} + ... + (\lambda^{n-1} + p_1\lambda^{n-2} + ... + p_{n-1})I$ is the adjoint of $(\lambda I - W)$.

Now the right side is a polynomial in W. Again, if we multiply both sides by W^∞, we would have on the right a constant multiplied by W^∞ which means that we can obtain W^∞ by raising W to large powers.

Sylvester's theorem
explained

For the cases of roots of one when $\lambda_{max} = 1$ is a simple or a multiple root let us again formally see what happens to our polynomial expressions on the right in both of Sylvester's formulas as we now multiply both on the left and on the right first by $\left(W^c\right)^\infty$ obtaining one equation and then again by $\left(W^{c+1}\right)^\infty$ obtaining another and so on c times, finally multiplying both sides by $\left(W^{c+c-1}\right)^\infty$. We then sum these equations and take their average on both sides. The left side of each of the equation reduces to W^∞ and the average is $\frac{1}{c}W^\infty$. On the right side the sum for each eigenvalue that is a root of unity is simply a constant times the sum $\left(W^c\right)^\infty + \left(W^{c+1}\right)^\infty + \cdots + \left(W^{c+c-1}\right)^\infty$. Also, because this sum is common to all the eigenvalues, it factors out and their different constants sum to a new constant multiplied by $(1/c)$. This is true whether one is a simple or a multiple eigenvalue because the same process applies to accumulating its constants. In the very end we simply have

$$\frac{1}{c}\left[\left(W^c\right)^\infty + \left(W^{c+1}\right)^\infty + \cdots + \left(W^{c+c-1}\right)^\infty\right] = \frac{1}{c}\left(1 + W + \cdots + W^{c-1}\right)\left(W^c\right)^\infty \quad c \geq 2 \quad, \text{ which}$$

amounts to averaging over a cycle of length c obtained in raising W to infinite power. The cyclicity c can be determined, among others, by noting the return of the form of the matrix of powers of W to the original form of blocks of zero in W.

Applications (Single Network)

ANP example

Market Shares for the Cereal Industry (2002)

The following is one of numerous validation examples done by graduate students in business most of whom work at some company. Many of the examples are done in class in about one hour and without access to data. The answer is only found later on the Internet. The example below was developed by Stephanie Gier and Florian John in March 2002. They write: To become familiar with the SuperDecisions software we have chosen to estimate the market shares for the Ready-to-Eat breakfast cereal industry. This idea was born after a delicious breakfast of Post's OREO O's. To see how good our assumptions were, we compare our calculated results with the market shares of 2001. First we created the model. We identified 6 major competitors in the ready to eat cereal market, Kellogg, General Mills, Post, Quaker, Nabisco and Ralston as our alternatives. There were more companies in this market having an actual cumulative market share of roughly about 6% that it turned out later that we had left out. Since we were only concerned with deriving relative values, the relative shares of other residual companies do not matter.

- Major impacts on the companies' market shares are:
- Price of the products offered (named cost for the consumer)
- Advertising / Sales Ratio (how much money is spend for advertising)
- Shelf Space (places where the products are located in the stores)
- Tools (Selling Tools used to increase sales and market shares)
- Distribution / Availability (major distribution channels used to sell the product)

These five major impacts (clusters) are further divided in the following nodes:

Tools: (Coupons, trade dealing, in-pack premiums, vitamin fortifications)
Distribution: (Supermarket Chains, Food Stores, Mass Merchandiser)
Shelf Space: (Premium Space, Normal Space, Bad Space)
Cost: (Expensive, Normal, Cheap)
Advertising: (<15%,<14%,<13%,<12%,<11%,<5%)

Their interactions are depicted in Figure 9.3. Second we carried out comparisons and performed calculations to obtain the final result (see later). Third we compared our calculated market shares with the real market shares for 2001. Table 9.1 lists estimated market share values and the actual ones taken from the website of the International Data Corporation.

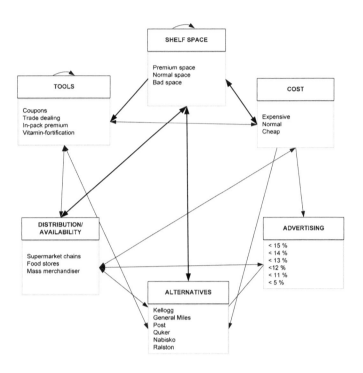

Figure 9.3 Cereal Industry Market Share

Table 9.1 Overall-Results, Estimated and Actual

Alternatives	Kellogg	General Mills	Post	Quaker	Nabisco	Ralston
Estimated	0.324	0.255	0.147	0.116	0.071	0.087
Actual	0.342	0.253	0.154	0.121	0.057	0.073

The compatibility index value for the estimated versus actual values was 1.01403 which is considered very good. A compatibility index of 1.000 would mean they were exactly the same. It is obtained by multiplying element-wise the matrix of ratios of one set of data by the transpose of the matrix of ratios of the other set, adding all the resulting entries and dividing by n^2 and requiring that this ratio not be more than 1.1.

Let us describe the calculations needed to derive the result in the "Estimated" column of Table 9.1. From the pairwise comparison judgments we constructed a super matrix, done automatically by the software Super Decisions. Then we weighed blocks of the supermatrix by the corresponding entries from the matrix of priority vectors of paired comparisons of the

results [handwritten annotation in left margin]

→ *details on creating the table* [handwritten annotation at bottom]

influence of all the clusters on each cluster with respect to market share shown in Table 9.2. This yielded the weighted supermatrix that is now stochastic as its columns add to one. We raised this matrix to limiting powers to obtain the overall priorities of all the elements in Figure 9.3.

Table 9.2 Cluster Priority Matrix

	Advertising	Alternatives	Cost	Distrib./ Availability	Shelf Space	Tools
Advertising	0.000	0.184	0.451	0.459	0.000	0.000
Alternatives	0.000	0.000	0.052	0.241	0.192	0.302
Cost	0.000	0.575	0.000	0.064	0.044	0.445
Distribution /Availability	0.000	0.107	0.089	0.000	0.364	0.159
Shelf Space	0.000	0.071	0.107	0.084	0.297	0.000
Tools	0.000	0.062	0.302	0.152	0.103	0.095

Market Shares for the Airline Industry (2001)

James Nagy did the following study of the market share of eight US airlines. Nowhere did he use numerical data, but only his knowledge of the airlines and how good each is relative to the others on the factors mentioned below. Note that in three of the clusters there is an inner dependence loop that indicates that the elements in that cluster depend on each other with respect to market share. Figure 9.4 shows the clusters and their inner and outer dependence connections. Table 9.3 gives final estimated and actual relative values that again are very close. Nagy writes: "I initially chose the airline industry for the assignment because I was a frequent traveler. My study group at Katz helped me make the comparisons between airlines that I did not have first hand experience as a passenger. Otherwise, I used my personal experience and perception of consumer sentiment towards the airlines to make the comparison. I was equally surprised at the results. In fact, I initially questioned how they could be so close. I would like to see the results of a study using today's consumer perception. A lot has changed in the industry since the 9/11 tragedy in the year 2001. You could divide the class up into 4 to 5 small groups and let them do the comparisons as individual groups and compare the results."

airline example with interdependence loops

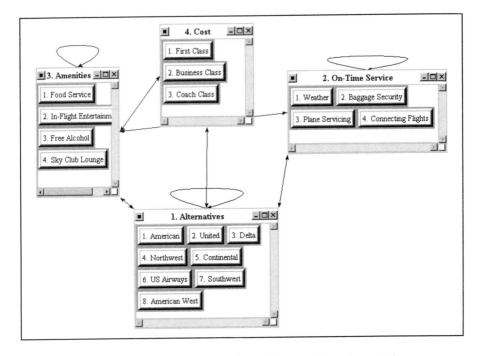

Figure 9.4 Airline Model from the ANP SuperDecisions Software

Table 9.3 Market Share of Airlines, Actual and Predicted

Airlines	Actual (yr 2000)	Model Estimate
American	23.9	24.0
United	18.7	19.7
Delta	18.0	18.0
Northwest	11.4	12.4
Continental	9.3	10.0
US Airways	7.5	7.1
Southwest	5.9	6.4
American West	4.4	2.9

Benefits, Opportunities, Costs, and Risks

We have seen from examples given before that market share or economic benefits is a control criterion that shapes our thinking when we deal with one kind of influence among competitors and their activities. There can be several control criteria or subcriteria of each control criterion in the complete analysis of a decision and some may have different merits: benefits (B), opportunities (O), costs (C) and finally risks (R). For each control criterion of these B, O, C, and R, one derives priorities for the alternatives of a decision

BOCR described

with respect to all the significant influences that cause some alternatives to have higher priority than others. One then combines the weights of the alternatives according to the weights of the control criteria of each of the B, O, C and R assessed in terms of strategic criteria. Strategic criteria are basic criteria used by individuals and groups such as corporations and governments to assess whether they should make any of the many decisions they face in their daily operations, and if they do which alternative's merits serve those criteria best. They do not depend on any particular decision for their priorities but are assessed in terms of the goals and values of the individual or the organization. Finally one rates (not compares) the top alternative for each B, O, C and R with respect to the strategic criteria and uses the resulting weights to combine the values of each alternative to determine the best one overall.

control criterion

We have seen from examples given before that market share or economic benefits is a control criterion that shapes our thinking when we deal with one kind of influence among competitors and their activities. There can be several control criteria or subcriteria of each control criterion in the complete analysis of a decision and some may have different merits: benefits (B), opportunities (O), costs (C) and finally risks (R). For each control criterion of these B, O, C, and R, one derives priorities for the alternatives of a decision with respect to all the significant influences that cause some alternatives to have higher priority than others. One then combines the weights of the alternatives according to the weights of the control criteria of each of the B, O, C and R assessed in terms of strategic criteria. Strategic criteria are basic criteria used by individuals and groups such as corporations and governments to assess whether they should make any of the many decisions they face in their daily operations, and if they do which alternative's merits serve those criteria best. They do not depend on any particular decision for their priorities but are assessed in terms of the goals and values of the individual or the organization. Finally one rates (not compares) the top alternative for each B, O, C and R with respect to the strategic criteria and uses the resulting weights to combine the values of each alternative to determine the best one overall ([2],[3]).

The synthesized results for each of the four control B, O, C and R merits can be combined to obtain a marginal outcome by taking the quotient of the benefits times the opportunities to the costs times the risks for each alternative (BO/CR). The results may be normalized but that does not change the ranks of the alternatives. This formula is only useful when one is certain that the relative measurements are commensurate that is of the same order of magnitude. In other words it is meaningless to divide thousands of dollars for benefits, by pennies for costs. As described above, they are also combined to obtain the total outcome by rating, one at a time instead of comparing, the top ranked alternative for each of the B, O, C and R with respect to strategic criteria that are needed to determine the merits of any decision. From this rating one then obtains normalized respective weights, b, o, c and r and computes the total outcome bB+oO-cC-rR for each alternative. Note in evaluating the benefits (opportunities) the paired comparisons judge responds to the question of dominance: which alternative contributes the most benefits (opportunities), whereas for costs (risks) one responds to the question which alternative costs (is subject to greater risks) more, which is opposite in sense to the benefits and opportunities and must be subtracted from them which may turn out to be negative [3]. It is known that the ranks obtained from ratio and total syntheses need not coincide.

Note that there is no advantage in using the weight b, o, c and r in the formula (BO/CR) because we would be multiplying the result for each alternative by the same constant bo/cr. Because all values lie between zero and one, we have from the series expansions of the exponential and logarithmic functions the approximation:

$$\frac{bBoO}{cCrR}=\exp(\log bB+\log oO-\log cC-\log rR)\approx 1+(\log bB+\log oO-\log cC-\log rR)+...\approx$$

$$1+(bB-1)+(oO-1)-(cC-1)-(rR-1)=1+bB+oO-cC-rR$$

Because the constant one is added to the overall value of each alternative we can eliminate it. The approximate result is that the ratio formula is similar to the total formula with equal weights assumed for the B, O, C, and R.

✗ Outline of the Steps of the ANP

① Make sure that you understand the decision problem in detail, including its objectives, criteria and subcriteria, actors and their objectives and the possible outcomes of that decision. Give details of influences that determine how that decision may come out.

② Determine the control criteria and subcriteria in the four control hierarchies, one each for the benefits, opportunities, costs and risks of that decision and obtain their priorities from paired comparison matrices. You may use the same control criteria and perhaps subcriteria for all of the four merits. If a control criterion or subcriterion has a global priority of 3% or less, you may consider carefully eliminating it from further consideration. The software automatically deals only with those criteria or subcriteria that have subnets under them. For benefits and opportunities, ask what gives the most benefits or presents the greatest opportunity to influence fulfillment of that control criterion. For costs and risks, ask what incurs the most cost or faces the greatest risk. Sometimes (very rarely), the comparisons are made simply in terms of benefits, opportunities, costs, and risks by aggregating all the criteria of each BOCR into their merit.

3 Determine a complete set of network clusters (components) and their elements that are relevant to each and every control criterion. To better organize the development of the model as well as you can, number and arrange the clusters and their elements in a convenient way (perhaps in a column). Use the identical label to represent the same cluster and the same elements for all the control criteria.

4 For each control criterion or subcriterion, determine the appropriate subset of clusters of the comprehensive set with their elements and connect them according to their outer and inner dependence influences. An arrow is drawn from a cluster to any cluster whose elements influence it.

5 Determine the approach you want to follow in the analysis of each cluster or element, influencing (the suggested approach) other clusters and elements with respect to a criterion, or being influenced by other clusters and elements. The sense (being influenced or influencing) must apply to all the criteria for the four control hierarchies for the entire decision.

6 For each control criterion, construct the supermatrix by laying out the clusters in the order they are numbered and all the elements in each cluster both vertically on the left and horizontally at the top. Enter in the appropriate position the priorities derived from the paired comparisons as subcolumns of the corresponding column of the supermatrix.

7 Perform paired comparisons on the elements within the clusters themselves according to their influence on each element in another cluster they are connected to (outer dependence) or on elements in their own cluster (inner dependence). In making comparisons, you must always have a criterion in mind. Comparisons of elements according to which element influences a third element more and how strongly more than another element it is compared with are made with a control criterion or subcriterion of the control hierarchy in mind.

8 Perform paired comparisons on the clusters as they influence each cluster to which they are connected with respect to the given control criterion. The derived weights are used to weight the elements of the corresponding column blocks of the supermatrix. Assign a zero when there is no influence. Thus obtain the weighted column stochastic supermatrix.

9 Compute the limit priorities of the stochastic supermatrix according to whether it is irreducible (primitive or imprimitive [cyclic]) or it is reducible with one being a simple or a multiple root and whether the system is cyclic or not. Two kinds of outcomes are possible. In the first all the columns of the matrix are identical and each gives the relative priorities of the elements from which the priorities of the elements in each cluster are normalized to one. In the second the limit cycles in blocks and the different limits are summed and averaged and again normalized to one for each cluster. Although the priority vectors are entered in the supermatrix in

normalized form, the limit priorities are put in idealized form because the control criteria do not depend on the alternatives.

Synthesize the limiting priorities by weighting each idealized limit vector by the weight of its control criterion and adding the resulting vectors for each of the four merits: Benefits (B), Opportunities (O), Costs (C) and Risks (R). There are now four vectors, one for each of the four merits. An answer involving ratio values of the merits is obtained by forming the ratio BO/CR for each alternative from the four vectors. The alternative with the largest ratio is chosen for some decisions. Companies and individuals with limited resources often prefer this type of synthesis. Governments prefer this type of outcome

Determine strategic criteria and their priorities to rate the four merits one at a time. Normalize the four ratings thus obtained and use them to calculate the overall synthesis of the four vectors. For each alternative, subtract the costs and risks from the sum of the benefits and opportunities. At other times one may add the weighted reciprocals of the costs and risks. Still at other times one may subtract the costs from one and risks from one and then weight and add them to the weighted benefits and opportunities. In all, we have four different formulas that we can use to synthesize.

Perform sensitivity analysis on the final outcome and interpret the results of sensitivity observing how large or small these ratios are. Can another outcome that is close also serve as a best outcome? Why? By noting how stable this outcome is. Compare it with the other outcomes by taking ratios. Can another outcome that is close also serve as a best outcome? Why?

Examples of Complex Network BOCR Decisions

Legalizing Gambling in Pennsylvania

Should the state of Pennsylvania legalize gambling? If they do, what types? The analysis was done by Eric Williams, Mike Zowacki, and Eric Zubovic (April 2004). They formulated a complex decision making model using the SuperDecisions software for the ANP to answer these questions from the viewpoint of the Governor of Pennsylvania. A complex decision has a Benefits, Opportunities, Costs and Risks (BOCR) model with 3 layers of networks: the BOCR nodes in the top level network, their control criteria hierarchies in the second layer, and, in the third layer, for the selected important control criteria there are decision subnets that contain the alternatives of the decision. In this decision there were eleven high priority nodes selected from the four control criteria subnets to become the control criteria. They are listed in Table 9.4. Their priorities were obtained by renormalizing their original priorities in the control criteria. For each of these a decision subnet was built, as shown in Figure 9.5. The results from the decision subnets are shown in Table 9.4. Figure 9.5 is an example of using a network for one benefits control criterion. The alternatives included the following: no gambling, slots only, slots and riverboat gambling, and all forms of gambling. No gambling meant that the state would not legalize any type of slot machine or table games. Slots only meant that the state would legalize only slot machines. Slots and riverboat gambling meant that the state would legalize slots and table games as long as they were housed on a riverboat of some sort. All forms of gambling allowed meant slots and table games anywhere in the state.

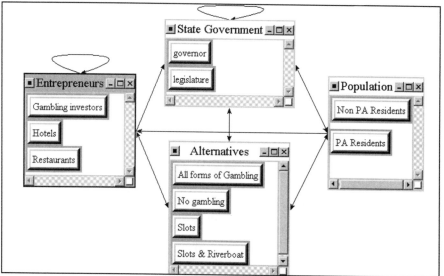

Figure 9.5 Example of a Decision Subnet

The BOCR model is used to evaluate the alternatives based on the specific factors involved in the decision problem. Recognizing that in many decisions the BOCR are not equally important, a second model is used to prioritize them. A hierarchy of a goal and the strategic criteria is structured and the strategic criteria are prioritized through pairwise comparison. The decision maker's personal strategic criteria must be satisfied regardless of the decision being made and are external to the particular decision problem being considered. The strategic criteria are used to rate the BOCR by first identifying the top priority alternative for Benefits, then using it as the representative for rating benefits for that alternative on each of the strategic criteria in Figure 9.6. The end result of the strategic model is the prioritization of the BOCR. These priorities are used in a formula to combine the results for the alternatives under the BOCR.

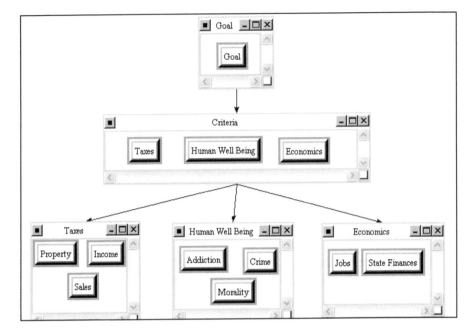

Figure 9.6 Strategic Criteria

Table 9.4 Ideal Ranking of Alternatives with Respect to BOCR Control Criteria and their Syntheses

	Benefits				Opportunities			
	State Revenue	Public Image	Help Unempl.	Benefit Synthesis	State Revenue	Demogr. Improvement	Tourism	Opportunities Synthesis
	0.315	0.274	0.411		0.131	0.321	0.548	
All Forms	1.000	1.000	1.000	1.000	1.000	1.000	1.000	1.000
No Gambling	0.124	0.070	0.106	0.102	0.066	0.116	0.352	0.239
Slots	0.269	0.232	0.261	0.255	0.210	0.261	0.508	0.389
Slots & R.Boats	0.403	0.452	0.448	0.435	0.402	0.442	0.685	0.570

	Costs			Risks			
	Bureaucr. Increase 0.249	Loss of Lottery Income 0.751	Costs Synthesis	Increased Unemployment 0.254	Companies Leaving 0.540	Lose Election 0.206	Risks Synthesis
All Forms	0.685	1.000	0.921	1.000	1.000	1.000	1.000
No Gambling	1.000	0.973	0.980	0.118	0.345	0.169	0.251
Slots	0.499	0.726	0.669	0.292	0.694	0.336	0.518
Slots & River Boats	0.516	0.824	0.747	0.530	0.538	0.454	0.519

Table 9.5 Verbal Ratings of the BOCR on the Strategic Criteria

	Addiction	Crime	Income	Jobs	Morality	Property	Sales	State Finan~
Priorities	0.029	0.127	0.063	0.089	0.013	0.291	0.034	0.355
Benefits	V.Low	V.Low	Low	V.High	Low	High	Low	V.High
Opport~	V.Low	V.Low	V.Low	V.High	V.Low	V.High	Medium	High
Costs	Medium	High	V.Low	V.Low	V.High	Medium	Low	Medium
Risk	High	V.High	Low	V.Low	High	V.Low	V.Low	Low

Numerical values corresponding to ratings: Very High (1.000), High (0.478), Medium (0.247), Low (0.121) and Very Low (0.068).

Table 9.5 shows the verbal ratings assigned to the BOCR for the strategic criteria. The purpose is to find out their priorities, recognizing that in a particular decision the merits are not equally weighted: benefits, for example, might be much more important to the decision maker than the costs.

The values associated with the ratings are shown in Table 9.6. The same ratings values were used for each strategic criterion in this case, though in general they would not be the same.

Table 9.6 Verbal Ratings Replaced by Values

	Addic-tion	Crime	Income	Jobs	Morality	Property	Sales	State Finan~	Weighted Sum	Normal-ized
	0.029	0.127	0.063	0.089	0.013	0.291	0.034	0.355	1.000	
Benefits	0.068	0.068	0.121	1.000	0.121	0.478	0.121	1.000	0.606	0.365
Opport~	0.068	0.068	0.068	1.000	0.068	1.000	0.247	0.478	0.573	0.345
Costs	0.247	0.478	0.068	0.068	1.000	0.247	0.121	0.247	0.255	0.154
Risks	0.478	1.000	0.121	0.068	0.478	0.068	0.068	0.121	0.226	0.136

The ratings in Table 9.6 are weighted by the priorities of the strategic criteria and summed, then normalized to give the priorities of the BOCR in this problem. The best alternative is then determined by using two formulas, the multiplicative ratio benefits to costs formula and the additive overall formula as shown in Table 9.7.

Table 9.7 Overall Synthesis using Two Different Formulas

	Benefits	Opportun-ities	Costs	Risks	Ratio Synthesis BO/CR (Normalized)	Overall Synthesis (bB+oO-cC-rR)
Synthesis of Alternatives	0.365	0.345	0.154	0.136		
All Forms	1.000	1.000	0.921	1.000	0.514	0.432
No Gambling	0.102	0.239	0.98	0.251	0.047	-0.065
Slots	0.255	0.389	0.669	0.517	0.136	0.054
Slots & River Boats	0.435	0.570	0.747	0.519	0.303	0.170

Legalizing all forms of gambling in Pennsylvania is shown to be the best option from the perspective of the Governor, regardless of which formula was used to synthesize. Slots and riverboat gambling came in second while slots only and no gambling were way behind. The benefits and opportunities outweigh the risks and costs.

When sensitivity analysis was performed with respect to benefits, all forms of gambling is always the best alternative. No gambling is the worst alternative. Sensitivity analysis with respect to costs shows that no gambling is always the worst decision no matter what the priority of costs is. Below 65%, all forms of gambling is the best alternative. When the priority of costs is between 65% and 70%, all gambling alternatives are relatively equal. Once costs go above 70%, slots only, is the best alternative. Sensitivity analysis with respect to risks shows that allowing all forms of gambling is the best alternative until the priority of risks reaches 48%. Between 48% and 56%, slots and riverboat gambling were the best alternatives. From 56% upwards, no gambling was the best alternative.

Best Alternative to Reduce the Effects of Gasoline Price Volatility for Automobiles in the US

The US economy has been continually growing and there has also been an increasing demand for oil. Our transportation systems are almost entirely dependent on fuels derived from conventional petroleum. Nearly all transportation modes, including air, rail, and highway, became much more energy efficient after the energy crisis in the early 1970's. However, in the past 15 years, demand for improved fuel efficiency has decreased due to lower gasoline prices. This has shifted vehicle purchase in recent years towards less fuel-efficient vehicles (pickups, minivans, and sport utility vehicles). Manipulation of oil prices by OPEC has been doing significant harm to the U.S. economy. In the past 30 years, every major oil price shock was followed by a recession and every major recession was preceded by an oil shock. In the last year there has been a lot of volatility in the price of gasoline from very low to quite high. What is the best policy the U.S. can adopt: ensure plenty of oil supplies, increase research into hybrid cars, increase the availability of public transportation, or increase research into alternative fuels? Who influences the decisions regarding reducing the effects of gasoline price volatility? These are the questions that are addressed in an effort to determine the best alternative for reducing volatility. The results are summarized below along the same lines as in the previous example. The strategic criteria (and subcriteria), all generically referred to as strategic criteria, are shown in Figure 9.7. The analysis was made in 2001 by Tina Owens and Danda Zhao.

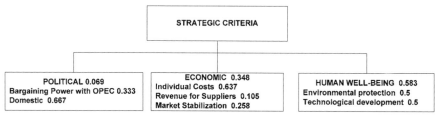

Figure 9.7 Strategic Criteria for BOCR Ratings

In Table 9.8 the best alternative for each of the BOCR merits was rated for how it impacted the six strategic subcriteria. These ratings were then multiplied by the priority of the respective strategic subcriteria and added and normalized at the end to obtain the priorities of the BOCR.

Table 9.8 Rating the BOCR Merits against the Strategic Criteria Corresponding Numerical Values for Ratings

Very High (0.45), High (0.30), Medium (0.14), Low (0.07), Very Low (0.04)					
		Benefits	Opportun-ities	Costs	Risks
Criteria	Subcriteria				
Political 0.069	Bargaining power with OPEC 0.333	Very High	High	Low	Medium
	Domestic 0.667	Medium	High	Medium	Low
Economic 0.348	Individual costs 0.637	High	Medium	Medium	High
	Revenue for suppliers 0.105	High	High	Medium	High
	Market stabilization 0.258	Very High	High	Low	Very Low
Human Well-Being 0.583	Environmental protection 0.5	Very High	Very High	High	Low
	Technological development 0.5	High	Very high	High	Medium
Priorities of the BOCR Merits		0.327	0.328	0.208	0.137

In Table 9.9 the conclusion, using either the ratio or overall synthesis, is that the best alternative is to Fund research into hybrid vehicles. The second and third ranked alternatives are Increase research into alternative fuels and Increase U.S. oil supplies respectively. As discussed earlier, the

U.S. has already initiated a directive toward increasing U.S. oil supplies. However, due to environmental activists and the risks associated with increasing U.S. oil supplies, the President may opt to increase funding into a hybrid vehicle, and in fact recently did so.

Table 9.9 Overall Outcomes for Solving Gas Price Volatility

Alternatives	Benefits 0.327	Oppor- tunities 0.208	Costs 0.328	Risks 0.137	Ratio Synthesis BO/CR	Overall Synthesis bB + oO –cC – rR
Increase U.S. oil supplies	1.000	0.951	1.000	1.000	0.250	0.690
Fund research into hybrid vehicle	0.694	1.000	0.555	0.329	1.000	1.000
Increase public transportation	0.601	0.454	0.469	0.755	0.203	0.334
Increase research into alternative fuels	0.774	0.845	0.747	0.337	0.683	0.819

The control criteria and their priorities are listed in Table 9.10. Figure 9.7 shows, for each merit, the control criteria hierarchical structure, the decision networks and their particular connections, associated with each of their selected control criteria. Only the highest priority control criteria are selected to have decision networks built for them. Figure 9.10 shows the clusters and the elements in each.

Table 9.10 23 Control Criteria and Subcriteria and their Priorities

BOCR Rating	Criteria	Sub-Criteria	Overall Priority of Control Criteria
Benefits	Economic(*0.571*)	US Agriculture *0.075*	*0.043*
		US Auto Industry *0.167*	*0.095*
		US Job Market *0.664*	*0.379*
		US Oil Industry *0.094*	*0.054*
	Reduce Reliance on OPEC (*0.143*)		*0.143*
	Technology (*0.286*)	Technology Innovator *0.333*	*0.095*
		Technology Leadership *0.667*	*0.190*
Opport~	Environmental Protection (*0.24*)		*0.240*
	Increase US exports (*0.21*)		*0.210*
	Political (*0.55*)	Bargaining Power with OPEC *0.333*	*0.183*
		Credibility of Bush Admin. *0.667*	*0.367*
Costs	Investment Cost(*0.8*)	Continual Future Costs *0.368*	*0.294*
		Educational Costs *0.082*	*0.066*
		Sunk Costs *0.55*	*0.440*
	Relations with Saudi Arabia (*0.2*)		*0.200*
Risks	Environmental Damage (*0.23*)		*0.230*
	International Opinion of Bush Administration (*0.4*)		*0.400*
	Protest/Riot (*0.123*)		*0.123*
	US technology Failure (*0.247*)		*0.247*

For more details about what is in the networks and the clusters, see Table 9.11.

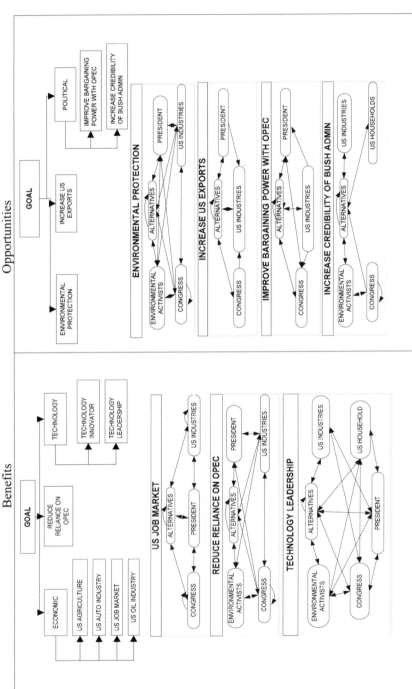

Figure 9.7 Control Criteria and Decision Networks

Table 9.11 Clusters in the Decision Networks and Elements in the Clusters

BOCR Control Criteria		Clusters	Elements
Benefits	Reduce reliance on OPEC	Environmental Activists	Environmental activists
		President	President
		US Industries	Agriculture, Auto industry, Oil industry
		Congress	Democrats, Republicans
	US job market	President	President
		US Industries	Agriculture, Auto industry, Oil industry
		Congress	Democrats, Republicans
	Technology leadership	Environmental Activists	Environmental activists
		President	President
		US Industries	Agriculture, Auto industry, Oil industry
		Congress	Democrats, Republicans
		US Households	High income, Low-income, Medium income
Opportunities	Environmental protection	Environmental Activists	Environmental activists
		President	President
		US Industries	Agriculture, Auto industry, Oil industry
		Congress	Democrats, Republicans
	Increase US exports	President	President
		US Industries	Agriculture, Auto industry, Oil industry
		Congress	Democrats, Republicans
	Improve bargaining power with OPEC	President	President
		US Industries	Agriculture, Auto industry, Oil industry
		Congress	Democrats, Republicans
	Increase credibility of Bush administration	Environmental Activists	Environmental activists
		US Industries	Agriculture, Auto industry, Oil industry
		Congress	Democrats, Republicans
		US Households	High income, Low-income, Medium income
Costs	Continual future costs	Environmental Activists	Environmental activists
		US Industries	Agriculture, Auto industry, Oil industry
		Congress	Democrats, Republicans
		US Households	High income, Low-income, Medium income
		Government	Department of energy, President
	Sunk costs	US Industries	Agriculture, Auto industry, Oil industry
		Congress	Democrats, Republicans
		President	President
Risks	International opinion of Bush administration	Congress	Democrats, Republicans
		President	President
All networks		Alternatives	**Increase U.S. oil supplies, Increase funding for Hybrid vehicle research, Increase availability of public transportation, Increase funding for alternative fuel research.**

References

1. Horn, R.A., and C.R. Johnson, *Matrix Analysis*, Cambridge University Press, NewYork, 1985.
2. Saaty T.L., *Theory and Applications of the Analytic Network Process*, RWS Publications, Pittsburgh, 2005.
3. Saaty, Thomas.L. and M. Ozdemir, Negative priorities in the Analytic Hierarchy Process, *Mathematical and Computer Modeling*, Vol. 37, pp1063-1075, 2003.

PART III: Conflict Resolution

When people have a common underlying set of objectives as in an organizational setting, they can work together to make group decisions. We have shown in Part II how the AHP helps such a group to produce a collective decision. Conflict can be seen as competition with incompatible potential future positions in which each party's objective is to occupy such a position. Groups in conflict who agree to work together may resolve their conflict constructively or rationally, but those who want to hurt each other follow a retributive way to resolve their conflict. The desire for retribution may be so great that a group may be willing to make ultimate sacrifices through self destruction in order to incur more hurt and damage to the other side. These are the ideas that we tackle in the next two chapters.

Chapter 10

Constructive Conflict Resolution

Conflict resolution today has to be the most important subject for those who think about it and more urgently by those who deal with it as a practical matter on a daily basis [1]. The subject has been a main occupation in the first author's career, from his days of working in disarmament in Washington, to teaching and writing [2,3] about the theory of games as a way to deal with conflicts, to many studies involving real political conflicts. Examples are Vietnam [2], terrorism in the Olympics [4], the conflict in Northern Ireland [5,6,7], the Middle East conflict, involving intensive meetings and discussions in Cairo, Egypt [8], in the early 1970s, the U.S.-OPEC energy conflict [9], and analysis of the conflict in South Africa in the 1980s [10], spurred by a conference in Pretoria in 1986 [11] resulting in a detailed analysis about the resolution of the conflict, commissioned by a government institute concerned with strategic studies. We need a practical quantitative approach that enables one to synthesize payoffs on different criteria. It delves in greater depth into the fine structures of strategies according to their merits and weaknesses when confronted with those of the opponent than does a game theoretic approach. It makes it possible for the parties to recognize and account for the strengths and weaknesses (political, military, social and so on) of their strategies against those of the opposition. The parties can work together through their representatives (perhaps often through the UN and in the presence of other parties to mitigate exaggerations and excessive claims) or do the analysis on their own with their own judgments partly imputed to what they think the opposition desires. In the absence of one party the judgments are surmised by the analyst from publicly declared positions and subjected to sensitivity analysis in case of uncertainties. In this manner one can evaluate the strategies of each party according to its merits against the strategies of the opponent(s) to improve the parties' understanding of the conflict in which they are involved. This type of analysis involves multi-criteria decisions with intangible payoffs derived from paired comparisons of the relative merits of the strategies against each of the opponent's strategies and then synthesizing the outcome across all merits and weaknesses, analyzed in short, medium and long range time frames.

Traditionally, conflicts have been analyzed quantitatively, using the normal form of a game, with payoffs of different strategies all played at the same time that often need to be measured in different ways [12]. We have a choice to make among the numbers we use to represent these payoffs [13]. Commonly, because of the complexity entailed in different kinds of measurement, ordinal numbers are used to indicate only that one payoff is larger than another [14]. But we can use stronger numbers, cardinal numbers, whose relative magnitudes are meaningful, particularly those used to measure priorities among the things that are traded off. These numbers can be used to measure different things and are then synthesized into a single overall outcome. Theoretical considerations and calculations which appear impossible with ordinal numbers become possible with cardinal numbers. The preliminary steps to understanding the nature of a particular conflict are: 1. Identify the parties to the conflict. 2. Identify the objectives, needs, and desires of each of the parties. 3. Identify possible outcomes of the conflict and possible "solutions." 4. Clarify the assumptions about the way in which each party views its objectives and, in particular, its view of the relative importance of these objectives and the varying, possibly multidimensional, payoffs for these objectives. 5. Set out these assumptions so each party can view the outcomes and the way in which a given outcome might meet their objectives. This seemingly simple set of steps presents some difficulties, since the perceptions of different parties may differ sharply. "One of the very interesting problems in the study of "perception" and one which is still largely unsolved is of the conditions under which "perceptions" of different individuals converge under the impact of symbolic communication and the conditions under which they diverge" [15].

In practice, as part of the negotiating tactic, parties often do not like to sit facing each other and cooperate to resolve the conflict. This is often a consequence of the fear that they might reveal something that gives the other side an advantage. This, of course, need not always be an issue for representatives of nations in conflict, as their decisions can be vetoed by their leaders back home. More important, mediators and arbitrators are frequently used as buffers who can convey a most agreeable attitude in explaining a tough line or laying out the opening position of each party. Most non-cooperative conflicts are helped by the presence of a third party or organization called in to assist. The mediators' concern with balancing and creating a fair result should outweigh their strict concern for impartiality. The mediators must be careful that their impartiality does not lead them to play into the hands of the stronger party and, similarly, an analyst who desires to model a current conflict and who seeks information from concerned parties runs the risk of allowing his or her formulation to be biased by his understanding of the situation. Even apparently unbiased observers tend to have a slanted view.

Another problem that arises with regard to actual measurement on different scales is how to make comparable assessments made by different players. The relative values obtained for one individual may not be commensurate with the relative values obtained by another individual and the solution then would be to embed the two individuals in a larger framework to determine the commensurability of their relative values. This problem of embedding is a special case of considering both individuals in a single framework with feedback that makes it possible to combine their separate beliefs and influences to obtain a single best outcome in which the question of commensurability is now no longer a pressing issue. Within that framework it is possible to assess the relative importance of the individuals according to various criteria of influence, and also by considering the priorities of their interactions, and the relative importance of their value systems. The outcome is then the one that is best in taking into account their separate points of view.

Thus a major problem in analyzing conflicts in quantitative terms is how to deal with the measurement of intangible factors that arise in a conflict. Analysis of equilibria in game theory is based on ordering pairs of strategies according to preference and assigning ordinal numbers accordingly. Often the ordinals are assigned intensities to indicate the degree of preference of one strategy, an intangible, over another, hoping to approximate to a cardinal expression of preference. However assigning such numbers is a fairly arbitrary and intuitive process that leaves one asking, is there a more scientific way to derive numbers to strategies that accords them a more accurate representation of an individual's preferences? The Analytic Hierarchy Process is a proven way to represent such a cardinal preference. The question now becomes how to apply it to represent payoffs in game theory, and how the analysis of equilibria would be theoretically different?

Professor Michael Maschler the renowned game theorist and one of the editors of the International Journal of Game Theory recently wrote the author: "People simply do not possess a utility function, or make mistakes when reporting their priorities. If you ask enough questions they will even state priorities that are not transitive. Thus, you cannot even determine a useful ordinal utility function. I do not know how to alleviate this difficulty. Therefore, at present, non-cooperative game theory can at best shed some insight on the real-life situation but usually it is not capable of suggesting definite recommendations (except for simple cases)".

Using ordinal payoffs in conflict resolution runs the risk of being arbitrary, because it attempts to summarize in a one step many differing payoffs on different dimensions into a single ordinal number for each party and, in general, that is impossible to do, whether each payoff is expressed with cardinal (ratio scale) numbers or with ordinal numbers on the different dimensions. This is very similar to the problem of multi-criteria decision-making that deals with combining measurements of both tangible and intangible criteria, and we propose an extension of how we deal with it in decision-making theory to conflict resolution.

Conflict Resolution as a Multi-Criteria Process

The complexity of negotiating conflicts is attributable to the fact that it is a multiobjective, multicriteria decision problem involving many intangible goals, criteria and alternatives. It cannot be reasoned one factor at a time and then implemented by putting the pieces together. Doing one thing in one place affects things everywhere else. Our usual method of logical reasoning generates linear chains of syllogisms. It is better suited for simple problems which deal with one factor at a time. It is not very effective in application to a complex problem involving many factors without having to make numerous assumptions which in the end give rise to a solution best characterized as a good guess. Such a solution often is acceptable to one side but not to the other because no collaborative reasoning can be adequately factored into the solution. This lack may also be the reason why the people in diplomacy and political science find it difficult to apply formal models to resolve conflicts.

What is needed here is a multicriteria decision approach that enables one to deal with the complexity as a whole, incorporating judgments and making trade-offs for all the parties involved with their participation in the process. Examples are given in my book with J. Alexander on conflict resolution [3].

The power of a nation cannot be ignored in conflict resolution. That power is what it and the rest of the world perceive its capabilities to be. To judge the relative power of nations we need to identify a set of factors that any nation assumes to be important. The relative power is then developed by first setting priorities on the factors followed by paired comparisons of the influence of the nations being considered. The synthesized result is a relative index of power for these nations.

The stability of the outcome of a conflict depends on the overall behavior of the parties and not just on the payoffs resulting from the strategies of the particular conflict. When the resolution of a conflict derives its principles simply from the local conditions of that conflict, it is possible and likely that in the global context with its many interactions, the outcome would not make sense, nor would the rationality [16] ascribed to the payoffs of the local conflict. Rationality applied in a narrow sense needs to be moderated or modified according to the larger context of global rationality. This is done by examining the relative merits, strengths and weaknesses of the parties, not just in that conflict, but in general. The ability and willingness to take and give are deduced from the large to the small and not vice versa - otherwise the outcome would appear to be incongruous and would not be honored.

We must involve the parties and, if they are unwilling to participate, then conjecture effectively best and worst scenarios for them and the outcome of confrontation resulting from these scenarios. We need to also look at the capabilities and history of the parties beyond the existing conflict, something which none of the quantitative theories of conflict resolution has taken into account so far.

To diminish negative feelings towards an opponent, the opponent must visibly take actions to improve expectations. Continued frustration in expectations increases hostility. One way to diminish frustration is to genuinely express good feelings and intentions towards the opponent. Another is to take unilateral actions indicating one's good intentions. Still a third is for the two sides to work together on some project which benefits both or benefits a third party to which the two sides are committed. Visits, contacts, and improved socialization are useful ways to decrease suspicion through exposure.

The difficulty with scientific, formal or technological problem solving is that it puts the greatest faith in the expert's understanding of the problem. Strategic analysis of conflicts is only one sociological way to look at things and is colored by the perceptions of the analysts who formalize them.

The Decomposition of Issues

What we must do is to unfold the complexity of conflicts as perceived by all sorts of thinking people. We then need to use our scientific approach to deal with them by first breaking them down into steps surmised to be essential in conflict resolution together with the dilemmas or anomalies associated with them. Factors that should be considered are cultural, social and psychological. We need to distinguish between types of conflicts and types of dispositions of the actors involved. We also need to develop different ways to assist in conflict resolution at each stage and then also as a whole. These steps may first be decoupled for better understanding and then brought together for a total solution. The origin of the conflict should be actually a part of the formulation of the problem together with a background on the parties, their needs and requirements and how willing they are to solve the problem. The formulation should also mention the means the parties are likely to follow to obtain resolution, and how likely they are to implement it and stick with the outcome. Only then may we really believe that we have an operationally useful approach to conflict resolution.

The process requires decomposing complexity according to different points of view, providing value judgments as to the importance of the factors involved in this decomposition, and then bringing together the different decompositions and judgments into a single overall framework, and finally synthesizing the diversity in a unified but rich and comprehensive understanding. This understanding can then be used to search for ways to narrow the differences and accelerate the process of conflict resolution, having employed the thinking and judgments of the same individuals or groups charged with the responsibility for action.

Comparing Apples and Oranges - Trading Off Intangibles

We use the Analytic Hierarchy Process to make the assessment of how much one set of concessions, some of which may be intangible, is worth against another set, often with the help of a negotiator.

Alternatives for negotiation have been observed in the literature to include the following categories:

1. Things: Territory, Money, Property
2. Concessions and recognition of rights
3. Weapon agreements
4. Trade and other material exchange
5. Ideological designs
6. Human rights and democracy
7. Cease bad propaganda
8. Compete successfully and enviably
9. Openness for movement
10. Share wealth and knowledge
11. Cultural exchange
12. Integrity and honesty in dealings
13. Motives for making policies and taking actions
14. Threats

It is important to note that incomplete information plays an important role in conflict resolution. One must use whatever information is available and keep revising the outcome with the arrival of new information.

An important factor in conflict resolution is that each party's conception of value is usually different. To align their value systems the parties may be able to find something which they agree on as a common frame of reference for making trade-offs. Alternatively, a mediator is invited to interrogate the parties and come to an understanding of worth between them. Such understanding is much more difficult to accomplish when there are several parties, each of whom may be reluctant to reveal anything about its values, for then the opponent may decide to ask for more. The less known the values and possessions of a party the more room that party has to negotiate and to offer concessions. Even divulging information to a negotiator can be done piecemeal so that it would not be easy to infer how much is available for exchange.

If one party is short on useful concessions to make in order to get concessions from the other, it can instead make credible threats to force the other side to make available more concessions for negotiation. It can also offer future concessions and extended cooperation. If one side holds back alternatives that the other side thinks should be in the negotiation set, the other side can refuse to negotiate or it must force the opponent with threats and sanctions to bring them into the set. Finally, it could offer such attractive concessions to cause the opponent to relax his tight hold. Conflicts do get resolved or forgotten. They get resolved by the threat of the use of force, by mediation, arbitration or by negotiation.

The benefit/cost framework of AHP in conflict resolution indicates that unless B can offer benefits to A to exchange for concessions it wants or unless it has threats that can incur valuable costs to A, A would not be willing to make concessions. The real situation strongly suggests that to avoid the use of force in society we need many more bodies for mediation and arbitration than we have.

The Quantitative Approach to Conflict Resolution

Decision making and conflict resolution are intimately related. The first deals with best choices by reconciling the multiple values of a single individual and the second by finding an agreed upon outcome to reconcile the values of many. In both cases one seeks the best outcome. The best-known quantitative approach for reconciling the different values of the parties in order to produce a fair resolution to a conflict is the theory of games, which is an abstract approach in search of equilibria for conflicts studied in terms of opposing strategies of several players [17].

The payoffs are usually represented by a single number for each party. These numbers are given by the parties (or assigned by the analyst) as rough estimates for opposing strategies matched in pairs and laid out in a matrix, mostly using ordinal numbers, particularly when dollars or other types of cardinal numbers are unavailable or not easily known. The purpose is to find a strategy that is overall optimal for all the parties, that is finding a cell in the matrix such that if either party moves to a different cell by changing strategy, the opponent can also change strategy to make the first party's payoff less [18]. The strategy oriented *normal form* of a game – a single matrix of pairs of numbers – over the more complex extensive form gives the mathematician an easy notation for the study of *equilibria* problems, because it bypasses the question of how *strategies* are put together, i.e. how the game is actually played. The concept of Nash equilibrium falls in this class of equilibria for non-cooperative games. John Nash made significant contributions to both non-cooperative game theory and to bargaining theory. He proved the existence of a strategic equilibrium for non-cooperative games – the Nash equilibrium – and proposed the "Nash program", in which he proposed dealing with cooperative games via their reduction to non-cooperative form. In his papers on bargaining theory, he founded axiomatic bargaining theory, and proved the existence of the Nash bargaining solution that was the first execution of the Nash program.

There have not been any other effective quantitative ways to analyze conflicts outside the ordinal equilibrium concepts of game theory [19]. When diverse multi-criteria measurements are available, they are assigned to the payoffs by the parties who have their own value systems. When the parties cooperate they can conceivably align their values (one of yours is worth two of mine). Is there any other way to obtain a best solution? One needs a credible way to combine the payoffs using cardinal measurements into a single overall outcome for each party.

For emphasis, we note again that if there are payoffs that result from a complexity of combinations of different components on different scales of measurement (as a payoff may be composed from factors that have different scales of measurement such as a war that involves money, the lives of people, cultural and social and political influences), it would generally not even be possible to combine them if one were to use ordinals, a question not addressed by game theory, which assumes that a wholesale hypothetical ordinal number can be assigned as the payoff. The idea of equilibrium would undoubtedly involve greater refinement if it were possible to use cardinal instead of ordinal numbers. The question then is what is gained from using cardinal numbers that is stronger than simply using equilibrium solutions. Were one to use cardinal instead of ordinal payoffs, can one obtain a better concept of solution other than the usual game theoretic one with ordinal payoffs? How would the solution be derived and its stability tested in that case?

We will elaborate respectively on Game Theory with its ordinal approach to equilibrium and the AHP with its cardinal multicriteria approach.

The Theory of Games; a Normative Theory of Conflict Resolution

The major normative, what-should-be theory that deals with a formalization of the resolution of conflicts is the theory of games. It offers solutions that are thought to be mathematically best in some sense. It is concerned with games of strategy, a well-known rational way to deal with only certain kinds of conflict. Not all conflicts can be formalized as games of strategy and resolved normatively. Its approach requires that strategies be identified in order to think about how to resolve conflicts.

Game theory studies conflict and cooperation by considering the number of players, their strategies and payoffs [20, 21]. Games have been classified as cooperative and non-cooperative and analyzed according to the degree of information available to the players. A game is played with pure and with randomized strategies. The players seek to maximize the expected value of their payoffs. For non-cooperative games the Von Neumann minimax theorem for two-person zero-sum games proves that every finite zero-sum two-person game has a solution in mixed strategies. In 1950 John F. Nash extended this theorem to the existence of a solution of an n-person constant sum game in mixed strategies as a Nash Equilibrium solution. The Prisoner's Dilemma and Chicken are two non-cooperative games that do not yield satisfactory equilibrium solutions, and thus more than the existing concepts of equilibrium is still needed to obtain a good solution for them.

For cooperative games, von Neumann and Morgenstern introduced the idea of a characteristic function of a game and of the worth achievable by a coalition of some of the players independently of the remaining players [12]. A solution is called a stable set with which is associated a core. The core may not always exist. But when it does, it can have a nucleolus, all of which contain the idea of solution to the cooperative game. Many alternative solution concepts have been proposed to deal with coalitions. The Shapley value is another approach to solving a cooperative game. This value sometimes belongs to the core of the game. How to calculate an equilibrium solution can involve nonlinear techniques that may be approximate.

Payoff and expected payoff are central concepts in game theory. But payoff is measured according to what and whose values? How are the values obtained, and are they unique or are there other measures of payoff and do they all yield the same solution? Is it possible to resolve conflicts by other theoretical means that do not parallel the game theoretic approach with multi-dimensional measurements?

An intriguing problem in game theory is the assumption that it is possible to estimate payoffs for strategies in a game before the strategies of one player have been matched against those of the opponent in actual competition. Except for the simplest and most transparent situations it is impossible to spell out all the moves and tactics of a real-life strategy to really get a good idea of how well it would fare in competition. Some broad qualities of a strategy may be known, but exact prescriptions of its effectiveness may encounter such unanticipated problems in practice that it may be difficult to get a "good" estimate of its worth when compared with other strategies.

A Descriptive Theory of Conflict Resolution; AHP/ANP

Our mind interacts with the real world in two different quantitative ways of measurement. The first is simple and easier to do and that is to determine which of two elements *A* and *B* has a property more than the other and simply indicate for example that *B* has it more than *A* [22]. In addition if there are several such elements and one wishes to rank them one may use ordinal numbers of any magnitude to indicate their order. There is the possibility that one may make an error in such estimates and thus the outcome may not be exactly as it is in reality. The second relies on our ability to differentiate between magnitudes when the elements are closer with respect to the property and say with a fair amount of certainty approximately how many times more one element has the property than the other (the lesser one used as the unit). This is a much more difficult task that has many uncertainties. However, if one were to use the judgment of someone who has long term familiarity with the elements, an "expert", one may wish to take that cardinal route simply to see what kind of outcome it leads to and how reliable it is. That approach is no longer simply a less reliable way of guessing at numbers. It is now a well grounded querie that has been developed in considerable mathematical depth and applied to numerous real life situations, and one might add successfully.

Conflict resolution can be regarded as a multiparty, muticriteria and multiperiod (short medium and long term outcomes) decision-making process that involves use of prioritization in the context of benefits, opportunities, costs and risks. From the field of behavioral economics that imports insights from psychology into economics, one learns that conflict resolution is also an evolutionary process of learning [23] to enrich the structure of factors included in the framework of analysis and the interaction and influence of these factors on the outcome with the passing of time. There are many conflict situations in which the grievance that a party has against another party or parties cannot be described in terms of strategies and in terms of responses to these strategies. A helpless person may have many creative and rational complaints against society but has no meaningful strategy to act on his/her grievances if indeed he/she who may also be crippled and inarticulate can. In other words not every wrong in the world can be formed as a game of strategy. Thus conflicts that can be formalized in terms of opposing strategies are a special case of conflicts in general. It is known that non-cooperative games do not always have an equilibrium solution for all the parties involved and these are the most intractable and pressing kinds of conflict including terrorism as a special case. The question is whether there is a way to formalize conflicts rationally in order that one may consider their solution without recourse to the idea of strategy where there may be no strategy, or when there is one, to analyze it as a particular case of a more general concept? It is easy to give examples of conflicts where no solution is possible. In a hungry society with little food to go around, the hungry would be opposed to the well fed for the threat of their survival. With increasing population and despite creativity and progress it may be that the world would reach a point where not all essential amenities would be potentially available to every one.

We will explore a different way of conflict resolution by giving examples that use network structures with dependence and feedback to derive different kinds of payoffs involving benefits, opportunities, costs and risk and then combine them into an overall payoff used to determine the best strategy to follow or to tradeoff different moves in a strategy to benefit the parties according to balance between their own value systems rather than according to an overall abstract strategic equilibrium.

Conflict Resolution with Benefits, Opportunities, Costs, and Risks

We study conflicts not in terms of equilibria but in terms of criteria and their priorities that help the players determine what the best tradeoffs to make within the framework of their relative position. Our first example performs global analysis of strategies using prioritization to determine the action that would lead to the best outcome for all the parties involved in the Israel-Palestinian Middle East conflict. The second example is a more detailed analysis of the best combination of moves to make for each of the parties that would facilitate negotiating resolution of the conflict in South Africa.

In his book Evolutionary Dynamics and Extensive Form Games, Ross Cressman writes, "My own personal experience is that much of human behavior involves interactions between people who have a long sequence of encounters. It is inconceivable that current decisions do not depend in an intricate manner on choices made in previous encounters, a feature that is contained in the concept of a history of an extensive form game but not explicitly revealed by the normal form,... where all the strategies are played at the same time by players who do not meet." Our approach using cardinal payoffs is illustrated with one example by a normal form application. The other applications use structures that are similar to the extensive form of a game.

Global Analysis of Conflicts — The Middle East

In this section we have taken a broad long term view of the conflict in the Middle East to determine the single best outcome that can lead to long term stability of that conflict [24]. We use four different merit structures: benefits, opportunities, costs, and risks (BOCR) to derive and synthesize priorities. The best outcome at first seems difficult to implement but in fact, but fortuitously, as reported on at the end is being pursued by people who in principle one might think should oppose the idea. What is the best long term strategy for Israel to pursue with the Palestinians regardless of what the Palestinians do or don't do?

Our analysis is carried out in three steps: (1) First, we identify criteria at the top often with subcriteria to study the different kinds of influences e.g. economic, social, political and so on for each of the BOCR. They are called control criteria because they control the thinking and judgments we provide to analyze the problem. We then select only the high priority ones for which we continue the analysis. Sometimes we use all of the control criteria. With respect to each of these, we create a network of clusters and elements in each cluster and their interconnections that interact with respect to that kind of influence, always including the alternatives in each network. The objective is to derive priorities for the alternatives in terms of that control criterion. Second, we compare the control criteria to derive priorities for them for each merit and use these priorities to weight and add the priorities of the alternatives with respect to each control criterion, thus obtaining a final overall outcome for the alternatives for each BOCR merit. Thus we have four priority vectors, one for each merit.

To combine them into a single vector, we identify strategic criteria used to evaluate the plausibility of taking any decision in that area of concern because analyzing any decision with alternatives only tells us which alternative is best but not whether the decision should in the end be taken. We prioritize the strategic criteria or subcriteria. We then create a rating scale for each of them. Often this rating scale is the same for all the criteria. We then rate the top alternative of each merit with respect to the strategic criteria. This gives us priorities for the BOCR merits that are then used to weight and combine the four vectors into a single outcome. We add the weighted benefits and opportunities and subtract from the outcome the sum of the weighted costs and risks because with respect to the latter two we provide judgments in response to the question which is more costly and which is more risky, thus generating priorities that are opposite to those we obtain for benefits and opportunities. This approach yields valid results when for example dollar or other values from known scales are used. We also simply form benefit to cost ratios including opportunities and risks in the answer. The two outcomes do not always lead to the same best alternative. In general it is the first formula that is the more reliable one. The second deals with marginal type of concern.

Structure of the Decision Problem — The Four Merits and Their Priorities

First we provide a list of all the control criteria. They are then compared as to their importance for each merit and in turn each subcriterion for each criterion. From the results we have kept the fourteen high-priority ones in bold in the right column of Table 10.1.

A. Benefits Subnets
- Economic Benefits
    - *Arms Control: Economic benefits derived from arms reduction
    - Economic Support from International Organizations: Economic support from the UN or IMF will be forthcoming for peace settlement
    - Revitalization of Trade: Benefits from trade between Arab/Israel, Arab/US and Israel/US
- Political Benefits

- *Leadership: Building strong political leadership within each country
- Support from Other Countries: Political support from other countries will increase as efforts are made to resolve the conflict
- Social Benefits
  - Improving understanding between Islam and Christianity: Increase the possibility of better understanding and sharing some religious values and rationalizing differences between Islam, and the Christian right with its cataclysmic belief in the second coming and the role Israel would play in that vision and how all that influences the sympathies of millions of Americans
  - *Social Integration: Building consensus on the issues through the incorporation of diverse public opinions and interests

B. Opportunities Subnets

- Economic Opportunities
  - Economic Development of the Middle East: Opportunity for economic development of the Middle East increases with resolution of the conflict
  - Revitalization of Oil Industry: Reduction of the threat of using oil as a weapon and integrating it long-range as a more dependable industry in globalization
- Political Opportunities
  - *Agreement on Establishing a fully Independent Palestinian State
  - Protection of Allies: Better to create and maintain friendly alliances with other countries in the region
  - *Security of Israel: Guaranteeing the security and survival of Israel
- Social Opportunities
  - *Peace Settlement: Contribution to peace settlement in the Middle East
  - Possibility of Jewish Capital Investment: Opportunity to invest in the development of the Middle East through single-minded Jewish driven leadership and capital

C. Costs Subnets

- Economic Costs
  - *Decrease in Defense Industry: Decrease expenditures on defense and save the large resources currently being spent on weapons and defense
  - Resettlement Costs: Expenses for resettling or vacating Israeli settlements

- Political Costs
    - *Acknowledgement of Palestinian Rights: Political costs in achieving political mood change for acknowledgement of Palestinian rights
    - *Foreign Relations: Costs of improving politics in the region
    - Peace Treaty: Costs of maintaining a peace treaty
- Social Costs
    - *Availability of Jewish Capital: Costs of obtaining Jewish capital now primarily invested in western countries
    - *Public Support Costs: Costs of obtaining support of public opinion in all countries involved

D. Risks Subnets
- Economic Risks
    - Environmental Concerns: Risks of damage to people and the environment in case of continued conflict
    - Opposition to the flow of Jewish Capital
- Political Risks
    - *Split of Allies: Risks of split among allies that could change the balance
    - *Terrorism: Risks of escalating terrorism as a habit around the world
- Social Risks
    - Religious Conflict: Risks of intensified long-range religious conflict between Islam and Christianity

*Split of Public Opinion: Possibility of split in public opinion on the issues that could force change in policy

The priorities in Table 10.1 were derived from a pairwise comparisons matrix. Let us take as an example, the political costs criterion, and consider how to derive the priorities of its three subcriteria: Acknowledgement of Palestinian Rights, Foreign Relations, and Peace Treaty as in the matrix in Table 10.2.

Table 10.1 Control Criteria and Their Priorities

Merits	Criteria	Subcriteria	Local Priorities	Global Priorities	Normalized Priorities
Benefits	Economic	Arms Control	0.651	**0.080**	**0.418**
	0.444	Economic Support from Int'l Org.	0.137	0.017	-
		Revitalization of Trade	0.212	0.026	-
	Political	Leadership	0.716	**0.043**	**0.222**
	0.215	Support from Other Countries	0.284	0.017	-
	Social	Improve Understanding between Islam and Christianity	0.273	0.026	-
	0.342	Social Integration	0.727	**0.069**	**0.360**
Opport~	Economic	Economic Development of Middle East	0.649	0.022	-
	0.197	Revitalization of Oil Industry	0.351	0.012	-
	Political	Agreement on Establishing Palestinian State	0.368	**0.031**	**0.288**
	0.500	Protection of Allies	0.098	0.008	-
		Security of Israel	0.534	**0.045**	**0.417**
	Social	Peace Settlement	0.625	**0.032**	**0.295**
	0.302	Possibility of Jewish Capital Investment	0.375	0.019	-
Costs	Economic	Decrease in Defense Industry	0.618	**0.034**	**0.122**
	0.170	Resettlement Costs	0.382	0.021	-
	Political	Acknowledgement of Palestinian Rights	0.557	**0.094**	**0.332**
	0.512	Foreign Relations	0.294	**0.049**	**0.175**
		Peace Treaty	0.149	0.025	-
	Social	Availability of Jewish Capital	0.319	**0.033**	**0.118**
	0.318	Public Support Costs	0.681	**0.071**	**0.252**
Risks	Economic	Environmental Concerns	0.314	0.012	-
	0.168	Opposition to flow of Jewish Capital	0.686	0.026	-
	Political	Split of Allies	0.371	**0.042**	**0.256**
	0.506	Terrorism	0.629	**0.072**	**0.435**
	Social	Religious Conflict	0.306	0.023	-
	0.326	Split of Public Opinion	0.694	**0.051**	**0.309**

Table 10.2 Political Costs Criteria's Pairwise Comparison Matrix

	Acknowledgement of Palestinian Rights	Foreign Relations	Peace Treaty	Normalized Priority
Acknowledgement of Palestinian Rights	1	2	4	0.557
Foreign Relations	1/2	1	2	0.294
Peace Treaty	1/4	1/2	1	0.149

Because of the possibility of inconsistent judgments and the opportunity to improve them, it can be proved mathematically that the principal eigenvector of the matrix (shown in normalized from on the right) as the unique way to drive the priorities. The process is applied in a similar way to making all the comparisons and in the end weighting and adding is used to combine priorities derived locally into global priorities.

Next we create one network with appropriate connections for each of these control criteria. Figure 10.1 shows a sample of two such networks. The outcomes cluster includes the following set of alternative.

Alternative Outcomes

We consider five potential outcomes to determine which has the greatest likelihood of long-term success according to the projected ability of the parties to exert the influences needed to bring them about. Our analysis includes the following options:

- Interminable Confrontation: This is the ongoing confrontation and conflict as we know it today through military and other actions of bloodshed.
- Enforcement & Supervision of Settlement: This is to supervise negotiation between Israel and the Palestinians by international organizations, and enforce implementation of the agreements.
- Strict & Legal Settlement without Enforcement: This is to force both Israel and the Palestinians to observe their mutual agreement by legal means, by the UN, and by world public opinion.
- Good Faith Settlement as in the Rabin era: This is to maintain or establish a peace treaty designed to avoid military confrontations through carrying it out in a friendly way only between Israel and the Palestinians.
- Economic Assistance to the Palestinians: This is to help the Palestinians with economic development, education, and planning a promising future.

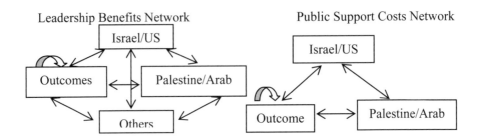

Figure 10.1 Two Networks

The priorities derived from these networks for the control criteria and their syntheses into a final outcome for each merit are shown in Tables 10.3 to 10.6. The top rated final alternative outcome in each of these four tables is rated in Table 10.7 with respect to the strategic criteria shown in Figure 10.2 along with their priorities. This yields the desired priorities for the four BOCR merits given in normalized form at the bottom of Table 10.7.

Table 10.3 Benefits' Overall Results

Alternatives	Arms Control (0.418)	Leadership (0.222)	Social Integration (0.360)	Final Outcome
Interminable Confrontation	0.235	0.251	0.212	0.230
Economic Assistance to Palestinian	1.000	1.000	1.000	1.000
Enforcement & Supervision of Settlement	0.717	0.752	0.707	0.721
Good Faith Settlement	0.365	0.396	0.315	0.354
Strict & Legal Settlement	0.498	0.527	0.455	0.489

Table 10.4 Opportunities' Overall Results

Alternatives	Agreement on Establishing Palestinian State (0.288)	Security of Israel (0.41	Peace Settlement (0.295)	Final Outcome
Interminable Confrontation	0.215	0.206	0.187	0.203
Economic Assistance to the Palestinians	1.000	1.000	1.000	1.000
Enforcement & Supervision of Settlement	0.298	0.701	0.670	0.576
Good Faith Settlement	0.388	0.324	0.288	0.332
Strict & Legal Settlement	0.194	0.463	0.433	0.377

Table 10.5 Costs' Overall Results

Alternatives	Decrease in Defense Industry (0.122)	Acknowledgement of Palestinian Rights (0.332)	Foreign Relations (0.175)	Availability of Jewish Capital (0.118)	Public Support Costs (0.253)	Final Outcome
Interminable Confrontation	1.000	1.000	1.000	1.000	1.000	1.000
Economic Assistance to Palestinians	0.230	0.283	0.241	0.243	0.251	0.256
Enforcement & Supervision of Settlement	0.343	0.384	0.334	0.363	0.362	0.362
Good Faith Settlement	0.738	0.744	0.703	0.714	0.751	0.734
Strict & Legal Settlement	0.521	0.550	0.513	0.529	0.550	0.538

Table 10.6 Risks' Overall Results

Alternatives	Split of Allies (0.256)	Terrorism (0.435)	Split of Public Opinion (0.309)	Final Outcome
Interminable Confrontation	1.000	1.000	1.000	1.000
Economic Assistance to the Palestinians	0.476	0.466	0.536	0.490
Enforcement & Supervision of Settlement	0.549	0.577	0.630	0.586
Good Faith Settlement	0.845	0.851	0.883	0.859
Strict & Legal Settlement	0.643	0.705	0.730	0.697

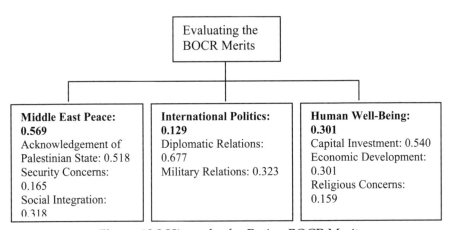

Figure 10.2 Hierarchy for Rating BOCR Merits

The four BOCR merits are rated according to five intensities listed in Table 10.7 below along with their priorities.

Finally these BOCR priorities are used to first weight the four final outcome vectors in Tables 10.3 to 10.6 to yield the four weighted outcomes in Table 10.8 and the final outcome in Table 10.9.

Table 10.7 Priority Ratings form the Merits: Benefits, Opportunities, Costs and Risks

Very High (0.42), High (0.26), Medium (0.16), Low (0.1), Very Low (0.06)

		Benefits	Opportunities	Costs	Risks
Middle East Peace	Acknowledgement of Palestinian State	Very High	High	Very High	High
	Security Concerns	Low	Low	High	High
	Social Integration	High	Medium	High	Medium
International Politics	Diplomatic Relations	High	Low	Very High	High
	Military Relations	Medium	Very Low	Medium	Medium
Human Well-Being	Capital Investment	High	Medium	Very High	High
	Economic Development	High	Medium	High	Medium
	Religious Concerns	Medium	Low	Medium	Medium
Priorities		0.278	0.169	0.328	0.226

Sensitivity Analysis

Benefits and Opportunities

This study infers that the policy of the economic assistance to the Palestinians is the most beneficial to all actors. In order to make sure how stable the outcome of the analysis, sensitivity analysis is conducted. First, we increase and decrease one of the four BOCR merits, keeping the others proportionally the same. If benefits increase from its original priority 0.278 to 0.5, and the sum of the other three merits composes the rest of 0.5, the economic assistance outcome is still preserved as the best policy among the five alternatives. Thus, as the priority of benefits increases, the best policy turns out to be the economic assistance policy. Enforcement & supervision of settlement outcome continues as the second best policy as the benefits priority increases. Additionally, interminable confrontation still becomes the least desirable policy.

Similarly, if opportunities increase from its original priority 0.169 to 0.5, the economic assistance policy is preserved as the best policy as well. Also, enforcement & supervision of settlement still turns out to be the second best policy and interminable confrontation is expected to be the least recommendable policy. Consequently, we find that no matter how much we increase or decrease the priorities of benefits and opportunities, the overall rank of the final outcome is preserved, although these experiments change the magnitudes of the superiority of the best alternative.

Table 10.8 Weighted BOCR Outcomes

Alternatives	Benefits		Opportunities		Costs		Risks	
	0.278	weighted	0.169	weighted	0.328	weighted	0.226	weighted
	CC Sum(from vectors)	(x .278)	CC Sum(from vectors)	(x .169)	CC Sum(from vectors)	(x .328)	CC Sum(from vectors)	(x .226)
Interminable Confrontation	0.230	0.064	0.203	0.034	1.000	0.328	1.000	0.226
Economic Assistance to Palestinian	1.000	0.278	1.000	0.169	0.256	0.084	0.490	0.111
Enforcement & Supervision of Settlement	0.721	0.200	0.576	0.097	0.362	0.119	0.586	0.132
Good Faith Settlement	0.354	0.098	0.332	0.056	0.734	0.241	0.859	0.194
Strict & Legal Settlement	0.489	0.136	0.377	0.064	0.538	0.176	0.697	0.157

All Idealized columns include a value of 1, so no need to re-idealize

Table 10.9 Final Outcome

Final Results:

Middle East Conflict

Alternatives	BO/CR (from unweighted columns in table above)	Normalized	bB+oO-cC-rR (from weighted col's in table above)	(Unitized by dividing each by the number with smallest absolute value)
Interminable Confrontation	0.047	0.004	-0.456	-9.695
Economic Assistance to Palestinian	**7.957**	**0.748**	**0.252**	**5.364**
Enforcement & Supervision of Settlement	1.956	0.184	0.047	0.990
Good Faith Settlement	0.186	0.017	-0.281	-5.971
Strict & Legal Settlement	0.492	0.046	-0.134	-2.855

Costs and Risks

Additionally, if costs priority increases from its original priority 0.328 to 0.5, the economic assistance policy still turns out to be the best policy to deal with. It is found that the overall rank of the five alternatives is preserved although the magnitudes of the priorities slightly change. Similarly, as the priority of risks increases from its original priority 0.226 to 0.5, the economic assistance policy is still preserved as the best policy although its superiority decreases gradually. However, we find that the overall rank of the five alternatives never changes although the magnitudes of the priorities change to some extent.

The final outcome suggests that the best policy to mitigate the Middle East Conflict is to provide the Palestinians with economic assistance. As of now, this policy has never been considered to be essential in resolving the conflict by any of the actors. It turns out to be critical in our analysis of the negotiations but not how to implement it in practice. We believe that traditional negotiations have not moved to the conflict closer to resolution because of lack of a strong recognition of the need to give the Palestinians compensation for at least the loss of their homes and property to grow food on and perhaps make sure that matters have been evenly balanced as far as they feel their rights are concerned. Furthermore, this kind of resolution does not focus as much on land, territory, and military action as much as it does on humane values and long term future relations.

The need for a peace settlement is as strong as ever. Admitting that the Palestinians are fighting for freedom and independence, economic assistance must be provided in a way that ultimately ensures Palestinian self-sufficiency and sustainability. This alternative has to be based on a great deal of collaboration among Israel, the Palestinians, the U.S., Arab and other countries. Assistance must be provided both for economic development and for education to help the Palestinians move into the future.

For nearly four years after the foregoing analysis was made one finds in the Economist, August 4, 2005, that "Sir Ronald Cohen" the chairman of the Portland Trust, called a "compassionate capitalist" by the Economist, who among other things, is promoting economic development in Palestine. *Sir Ronald believes that economic growth for the Palestinians is crucial if there is to be lasting peace with Israel.*

A Consensus Agreement for a Middle East Conflict Resolution (Oct 2006)

The Middle East conflict is not a series of wars tending toward peace, but a state of continued belligerency interrupted by war. It is not a single isolated problem to be solved but a system of people with conflicting aspirations [25]. Physically, the problem is geographic with two parties desiring the same piece of land, but its origins are deeply rooted in people's beliefs and in their attachments to a land consecrated by their great religions. There are claims made by these people of rights to live in the land and to have a state to maintain an identity. The problem is greatly compounded by widespread activities in the area, to include arms supply, cause support and the development of vested interests, thereby placing the problem in a complex global framework. Although one might expect that the global framework might accelerate a solution, in fact it complicates it due to the diversity of each participant's interests. Hence, a solution has eluded the global community. The Israeli-Palestinian conflict continues to plague the Middle East and threaten stability, not just regionally, but also globally by inciting some terrorist claims. Despite the best efforts of diplomats and world leaders, a satisfactory resolution has not emerged. Hence, it is with some degree of hubris that we present a solution that we expect will outperform other efforts. What we suggest is a holistic model that explores feedback from various criteria and input from key constituents.

Peace is almost always secured through accommodation, bargaining, and compromise – even after an overwhelming victory is obtained by one side. Our approach utilizes the Analytic Network Process, because it fits the realism in eliciting and capturing the intensity of judgments regarding the dominance of some factors over other factors, the synthesis of group judgments, and the performance of sensitivity analysis for the stability of the outcome. The study involved a mixed group of Palestinians, knowledgeable pro-Israeli experts, and others from the outside, like Saudi Arabia, Turkey, China and the US.

Over a three day period, the panel structured the problem, defined the constituents and developed several potential alternatives. The process was not without conflict and negotiation of its own. At times, the panel differed on various definitions, on the structure of the model, and on the potential solutions. However, there was nearly always unanimous agreement on the nature of the conflict, with little debate within either side about the underlying concerns or where the power and influence belonged that could bring about termination of a 58 year old confrontation. Similarly, there was practically no problem in identifying the key constituents. However, since the beginning of the conflict, leaders and others have proposed many alternatives solutions. These influenced the perception of the participants in regard to potential alternatives. In fact, one person suggested that the participants could have difficulty "thinking outside the box." He thought that the group was so influenced by previous attempts that they experienced difficulty in conceptualizing 'creative' alternatives that had not been proposed previously.

What follows is a brief account of the method employed, the model, the structure of the problem as a decision with benefits, opportunities, costs and risks and how comparisons were made in the analysis of the outcomes, recommendations for implementation, summary, and recommendations for getting others to look at the problem in this integrated and comprehensive framework.

Structuring the ANP Model for the Middle East Conflict Resolution

The problem was defined as an attempt to understand what forces and influences, because of their relative importance, would implicitly drive the outcome towards a consensus peace accord for the conflict between Israel and the Palestinians. To accomplish this task, a panel of 8 individuals was assembled to represent a cross section of people: international thinking representatives (3), Israeli thinking representatives (2), a Palestinian (1) and Muslim thinking representatives (3). In most cases, the individuals crossed the various categories and interests and did not fall into discrete separate groups. It was recognized that the panel did not represent a valid cross-sample or that the size of the panel was adequate to represent the different population sizes involved. It was agreed that the work is exploratory in nature, intended to demonstrate how the method can be used over a short period of time to arrive at a reasonable solution that is not outlandish to any of the sides.

It was agreed by all participants that no part of the decision would be done without consensus agreement whether it is what to add or delete from the model or to make or not make comparison judgments on low priority criteria in order to save time to arrive at an answer in three days. It was justified to do that because it was clear that such factors and their contributing judgments were not worth the effort. It was the role of the moderator to facilitate the process and ensure that all parties agreed before moving on to the next step in the process. However, the moderator made no contribution to the agreement but facilitated mutual understanding among the participants. Since pairwise comparisons are made in the prioritization stage of the ANP, it is critical that all parties understand the definitions of the terms used. Moreover, as illustrated later in the chapter, many questions about what dominated what with respect to a certain factor and how strongly it dominated it was often difficult to understand and even more difficult to conceptualize in practice. Hence, many of the questions were developed at length and repeatedly until they were well understood by all. This underscores the specific nature of the Middle East conflict and the necessity for consensus. Language and understanding the matter!

To ensure mutual understanding, the moderator needed to track the events on a screen projected for the participants and to use an additional measure to track the questions that were currently under consideration. In addition, the moderator maintained on the first screen the following items:

1) The software used for the ANP model;
2) Documentation of the definitions, terms and criteria agreed upon;
3) Notes on the 'process' and the steps taken to reach consensus;
4) Agenda.

Although the level of detail and effort taken to document the process seemed excessive at first, it was clear from the start that not only were the initial steps taken helpful but they had to be augmented further. The augmentation included the use of other visualization tools in order to gain consensus. Hence, the steps taken to document the panel's efforts are a nontrivial event. In fact, the use of the various 'tools' were necessary on multiple occasions to overcome objections. We believe that without these various tools, the group would have experienced greater hardships in reaching consensus.

As mentioned above, at no point in the development and evaluation of the problem was the process easy and we caution against the belief that this was anyone's intention. In fact, the "purpose" of the exercise was not easily agreed upon and on several occasions in the three days over which the panel met, the question about the purpose of the exercise was repeatedly readdressed. The panel agreed that its goal was to move toward a consensus agreement for what outcome is the best resolution of the Middle East Conflict. The group looked at the purpose of the project from various perspectives. First, the panel suggested that potential definitions for the panel's purpose could include:

- Peace in the region;
- Impact on global peace;
- Recognition of defined borders;
- Long-term future stability.

It was also recognized that there is an equally legitimate claim to view the problem from the vantage point of a more extremist Palestinian whose goals might include:

- Let them return (the Israelis) to where they came from;
- Right to return that creates a Palestinian majority;
- Allocation of natural resources including land;
- Infiltration of patriots - 'terrorists';
- Elimination of Israeli nuclear threat.

Finally, one might take the position of more extremist Israeli views whose goals might include:

- Status quo; Palestinians remain squeezed into small territories with restricted movement;
- Deport all Palestinians;
- Continued control of all resources;
- NO pro-Palestinian country should be able neutralize Israel's nuclear power.

After considerable discussion and we overly compress the process here, the panel agreed that any resolution is a process that requires consensus and it is consensus "buy-in" that encourages participation of all constituents.

Agreement on the 'purpose' of the panel was not the only portion of the model that needed some dialogue. In fact, every step along the 'process' required negotiation and consensus. Several ways were proposed within the panel about how to construct the model and develop the issues. It was agreed that any solution would have benefits, opportunities, costs and risks (BOCR). However, it was not as easy for the panel to agree on the strategic criteria in terms of which they would evaluate and synthesize.

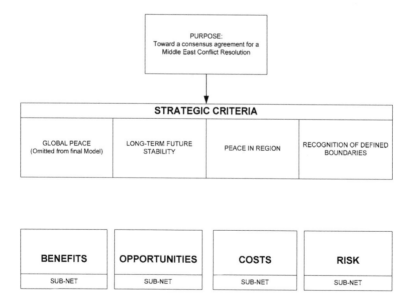

Figure 10.3 The ANP Main Top-level Structure for the Middle East Conflict Resolution model

The Strategic Criteria used to evaluate the BOCR are representative of the impact that a selected alternative would have on Global Peace, Long-

Term Stability, Peace in the Region, and Recognition of Defined Boundaries. Although the panel selected the four strategic criteria in Figure 10.3, they later agreed that Global Peace should be removed from the comparisons since stability and regional peace are believed to be strongly correlated with Global Peace.

While the strategic criteria and their meanings were still fresh and prior to moving into the development of the BOCR sub-networks (subnets), the panel evaluated the Strategic Criteria with respect to the purpose of the undertaking. The results of the comparisons are shown later under Prioritization. However, we believe that it is useful to detail the nature of the comparison for the Strategic Criteria at this point in order to mirror the efforts and document the methodology that we used in this case. The panel was presented with the pairwise comparisons of the four Strategic Criteria with the following questions involving pairs of criteria: "Which factors contribute more strongly and how much more strongly to resolving the conflict in the Middle East according to the desire of all the parties for 1) Global Peace or for Long-Term Future Stability in the Region, 2) Global peace or Peace in Region, 3) Global Peace or Recognition of Defined Boundaries, 4) Long-Term Future Stability or Peace in Region, 5) Long-Term Future Stability or Recognition of Defined Boundaries and finally 6) Peace in Region or Recognition of Defined Boundaries? Because Global Peace was eliminated, only the last three comparisons were made.

Figure 10.4 represents a sample of how the software package structures the comparison between the importances of Figure 10.4 Strategic Criteria Questionnaire

Comparisons wrt "Goal" node in "Strategic Criteria" cluster
Peace in Region is moderately more important than Recognition of Defined Borders

1.	Long-term future stability	>=9.5	9	8	7	6	5	4	3	2		2	3	4	5	6	7	8	9	>=9.5	No comp.	Peace in Region
2.	Long-term future stability	>=9.5	9	8	7	6	5	4	3	2	1	2	3	4	5	6	7	8	9	>=9.5	No comp.	Recognition of Defined Borders
3.	Peace in Region	>=9.5	9	8	7	6	5	4	3	2		2	3	4	5	6	7	8	9	>=9.5	No comp.	Recognition of Defined Borders

Figure 10.4 Strategic Criteria Questionnaire

Returning to our conflict problem, the top-level structure has the four Benefits/Opportunities/Costs/Risks (BOCR) merits and their sub criteria shown in Figure 10.3 which represents the total initial model. Some of the nodes in both the Strategic Criteria and the subordinate networks of the BOCR were eliminated after the initial ratings due to the level of insignificant contributions that they added to the overall result because of their low priorities as compared with the other factors. The subnets under each of the four BOCR merits were developed independently. The benefits and costs were conceptualized as the short-term or internal aspects of the alternative evaluation while the opportunities and risks were thought of as those elements that have long-term influences.

The Benefits Subnet: benefits are defined as the short-term gains that any group might experience given the criteria below.

- *Economic Status* in this network is defined as the short-term potential gains that might be realized given the implementation of one of the alternatives.
- *Human Rights* are defined as the short-term improvements in how the United Nations state what constitutes basic human liberties / freedoms.
- *Safeguard the oil supply* is defined as the incremental stability to the consistent delivery of oil; i.e. limited disruption to oil production.
- *Saves Lives* is defined as the reduction in the loss of lives.
- *Standard of Living* is defined as the incremental improvement for overall living conditions.

In the initial phases of developing the model, the panel faced the challenge to build a 'robust' model that includes all the criteria that they felt were important to accurately reflect those elements that would be important to reach a resolution. With respect to the short-term gains that might be realized by the constituents, the foregoing five criteria are the full set of short-term benefits necessary to realize a full benefits model. As the panel developed the connections among the various nodes in the cluster, they reached a consensus that not all five of the nodes were essential. *Economic Status* and *Human Rights* were retained, but it was believed that *Saves Lives* and *Standard of Living* were subsumed under them. *Safeguarding the oil supply* was not a valid criterion for the benefits network. In addition, the model provided legitimacy for what the members of the panel felt intuitively; the two excluded criteria were not significant to the model. In fact at first the two deleted criteria were included and were omitted after their priorities turned out to be very low in relation to the other three criteria.

The Benefits subnet is shown in Figure 10.5 as a sample of what the subnets under the BOCR model look like. The circular arrow shown in Figure 10.5 represents the fact that the "Constituents" cluster has feedback within the cluster. The implication of feedback within the alternative cluster is that each of the various constituents within this cluster influences the others within the cluster. For instance, a decision made by one party in the cluster influences the other parties in that cluster so that a movement toward peace by the Israelis and the Palestinians for example would have positive implications for both the United States and 'Others'. More detail about the implications of feedback and dependency will be discussed in the findings section of the chapter.

The Costs Subnet represents the short-term expenses and pains incurred by the constituents.

- *Arms industry* includes those costs that would be experienced by the arms industries through either loss of income or additional limitations to trade / sale placed on suppliers.
- *Internal chaos in Israel* is the attempt to capture the 'price' paid for disruption to lives that may be realized through the selection of any resolution alternative.
- *Making sacrifices* identifies the real expense incurred through both monetary and non-monetary forfeitures that may be incurred through any one of the various alternatives.
- *Relocation / dislocation* node represents the real expense of dislocation caused by the option of any one of the alternatives.
- *Reparations* are the price that would need to be paid for conciliatory actions.

The panel used the same process for the Costs subnets that they used for the Benefits subnet. Once the initial comparisons were made, the *Arms Industry* and *Relocation / Dislocation* were omitted since these two criteria accounted for insignificant priorities. The two omissions are not surprising since *Relocation* was captured by the *Reparations* criteria and the costs to the *Arms industry* are significantly outweighed by the potential costs of the other criteria.

The Opportunities Subnet is the long-term positive potentials that exist for the constituents.

- *Global Stability* is the opportunity for greater stability throughout the world in order to foster a secure environment.
- *Regional Stability* focuses on the regional stability surrounding the immediate parties to the conflict.
- *Return 'home'* represents the right of return for all displaced parties.
- *Safeguard the oil supply* refers to the long-term safety to the global distribution of oil.

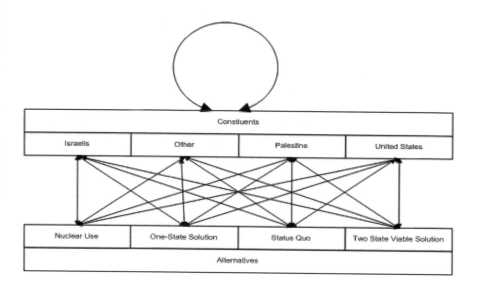

Figure 10.5 Benefits Subnetwork

The panel went through similar efforts in the Opportunities subnet as they did with the Benefits subnet. In the initial development of this subnet, four criteria were included as given above; the final model only contained *Regional Stability* and *Return 'home'*. Once again, *Safeguard the oil supply* was not deemed appropriate for the final consideration due to its low priority.

The Risk Subnet

- *'Wrong' people return* is the risk that the people who would return under the right to return option will be subversive types looking to incite further disruption instead of the type who want to foster a *sensus communitas*.
- *Further increase in radicalism* is the risk that selection of any one of the alternatives would lead to an increase in radical activities.
- *Further instability in region* is the potential of an alternative to lead to increased instability via continued fighting.
- *Limited longevity that promotes return to conflict* refers to the fact that an alternative, if opted for, may not be viable for long-term. Hence, the probability that it returns to a state of conflict may increase the problem since it may be seen as a continued failures of the leadership to implement a resolution.

Under the Risk subnet, only *'Wrong' people return* had sufficiently low priority to delete it from the model; the remaining criteria were maintained throughout the analysis.

Figure 10.6 summarizes the BOCR merits networks. In other words, it highlights both the short-term and long-term aspects of the model as well as the gains and loses that impact the alternatives.

Each of the criteria in Figure 10.5 under the BOCR merits model was evaluated with respect to the various constituents that influence the outcome of the model. Figure 10.7 illustrates the network of the various constituents. The constituent network captures the feedback and interdependence among the various parties. Although it may appear intuitive that choices made by Israel impact the Palestinians, the nature of the feedback and dependence involving the other parties (the U.S., Arabs, Muslims and the rest of the world) was not adequately understood until implemented in the model. The outcome of the dynamics between the various constituents is further explored below.

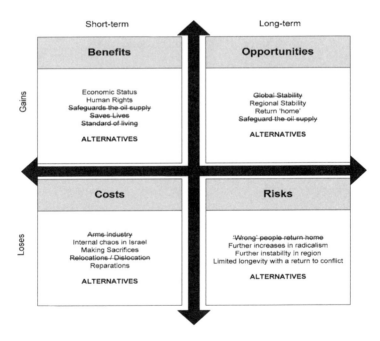

Figure 10.6 Summary of the Merits Networks

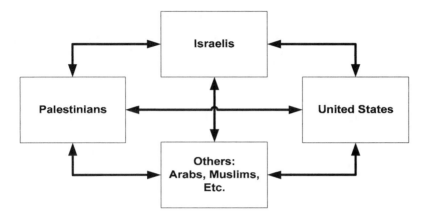

Figure 10.7 Constituent Network

Alternatives

The panel had to consider not only those initiatives that are 'popular' but also to develop 'creative' alternatives that may not have been explored or even present novel approaches. Furthermore, the group was instructed to think of alternatives as if there were no limits or boundaries. However, it was not easy to develop novel alternatives because of the enduring nature of the conflict and because of the scope of alternatives that have been developed thus far.

The full list of alternatives considered is as follows:

- **Status Quo**
- **Two-viable-state solution**
- **Nuclear use**
- **One-state solution**
- Legal solution enforced by the U.N.
- Two-viable-state solution (Positive initiative by Israel, economic contribution, etc…)
- Two-viable-state solution (Change in U.S. policy)
- Two-viable-state solution (Saudi initiative (2002) / Beirut Declaration).
- United Nations partition (1947)
- Jewish state

We consider the four bullets in bold above as the final alternatives to determine which has the greatest likelihood of long term success according to the projected ability of the parties to exert the influences needed to bring them about. The most significant part of the 'process' to note is that reducing the list to a select few options was the result of the group negotiating an agreement. The panel came to a consensus that the various two-viable-state solutions could be captured under one alternative with the understanding that the details of implementation would be worked out as part of the long-term process. The Two-viable-State Solution captures the various forms that include the Bush Model, or the Saudi Initiative. This model recognizes the various independent states as autonomous.

The threat of Nuclear Use captures the potential of a party in the conflict using a nuclear device to influence the outcome. The threat of use means Israel's possession of nuclear weapons as a deterrent for other groups to use but it also captures a potential radical group's ability to obtain and utilize nuclear weapons. Of all of the alternatives, this was the most difficult one to conceptualize when assessing the priorities in the evaluation process. In general, the group agreed that this was the least likely alternative but that it was necessary to include in the model since the threat exists and remains an option.

One-state solution combines both the Palestinians and the Israelis into a single unified state that recognizes all individuals as politically and socially equal as in a democracy. Status Quo is a continued condition that has periodic rises in hostility and warfare. To make this alternative sound plausible, one of the Palestinian participants humorously suggested that the most rapid way to resolve the conflict is for all Palestinians to convert to Judaism; he was told by an Israeli friend that many Russians had been brought into Israel and later converted to Judaism.

Prioritization

Strategic Criteria and Their Priorities

As explained above, the three strategic criteria were evaluated and their priorities shown below were used as the guiding factors of the BOCR merits. A sample of the questionnaire that uses the fundamental scale of absolute numbers and questions is shown in Figure 10.4 Strategic Criteria Questionnaire and the results of those comparisons are shown in Figure 10.8 and explained below.

Long-Term Future Stability captures the belief of the panel that any alternative that does not address and promote continuous stability in the region may contribute more harm than benefit. Additionally, the panel's consensus is that economic, political, and social developments in the region are dependent upon the 'stability' of the environment.

Peace in Region identifies the panel's conviction that economic, social, and political growth in the region are dependent upon long-term peace. Hence, any alternative must be evaluated against the potential of the choice to promote regional peace.

Recognition of Defined Boundaries was identified by the panel as a strategic criterion because agreed upon boundaries are a necessary component in selecting a resolution alternative.

Among the three strategic criteria to evaluate the BOCR merits, Peace in the Region has the highest priority (0.634) in contrast with Recognition of Defined Borders (0.192) and Long-Term Future Stability of (0.174). Therefore, we can qualify these priorities with the observation that any alternative selected must contribute to the long-term future stability of the region. The significant difference in the priorities underscores the overall importance that the panel attributed to long-term stability since economic, social, and political development in the region depend on stability.

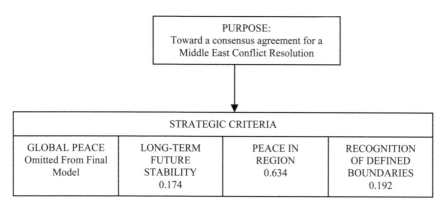

Figure 10.8 Hierarchy for Rating the BOCR Merits

BOCR Merits and Their Priorities

The importance of the four BOCR merits with respect to the strategic criteria is determined by prioritizing them according to the following five intensities and their priorities derived through pairwise comparisons are shown in Table 10.10.

Table 10.10 Priorities of Intensities

Intensities	Very High 0.42	High 0.26	Medium 0.16	Low 0.10	Very Low 0.06

Application of these intensities to rate the BOCR merits is shown in Table 10.7.

The rating outcome and final weights for each of the four merits are summarized in Table 10.11. These values are used as default values in an additive formula in developing the ANP model later on. For example, we asked the question for each of the merits: "what is the 'merit' of the top alternative under Benefits with respect to each of the Strategic Criteria?" This process was carried out in a similar way for Opportunities, Costs, and finally Risks. For instance, it was observed that there is a very high potential Benefits with respect to the first strategic criterion, i.e., Long-Term Future Stability. Once consensus was reached on the ratings for each of the merits, the resultant weights of the merits were derived as given in column 6 of Table 10.11.

Table 10.11 Priority Ratings for the Merits: Benefits, Opportunities, Costs and Risks with respect to the Strategic Criteria

Merit	Long-Term Future Stability 0.174	Peace in Region 0.634	Recognition of Defined Boundaries 0.192	Sum of Weighted Values	Normalized
(1)	(2)	(3)	(4)	(5)	(6)
B	Very High	High	Medium	0.64	0.20
O	High	High	High	0.61	0.19
C	Very High	Very High	Very High	1	0.31
R	Very High	Very High	Very High	1	0.31

Decision Networks

Considerable time was invested in defining terms, constructing the model, and reaching agreement on various aspects of the pairwise comparisons made in the evaluation of the BOCR merits. Substantial use of the various media was made during this portion of the evaluation in order to reach consensus. Figure 10.9 shows a sample of the ratings that the panel used to reach a consensus. Note that each of the numbers entered into the comparison sheet was agreed on by the group. At times, the discussion that ensued from the nature of the question was lengthy. Conversely, there were some questions on which the group was able to reach immediate agreement.

Comparisons wrt "One-state Solution" node in "Constituents" cluster Palestinians is equally to moderately more important than U.S.																					
1. Israelis	>=9.5	9	8	7	6	5	4	3	**2**	2	3	4	5	6	7	8	9	>=9.5	No comp.	Other
2. Israelis	>=9.5	9	8	7	6	5	4	3	2	2	3	**4**	5	6	7	8	9	>=9.5	No comp.	Palestinians
3. Israelis	>=9.5	9	8	7	6	5	4	3	2	2	**3**	4	5	6	7	8	9	>=9.5	No comp.	U.S.
4. Other	>=9.5	9	8	7	6	5	4	3	2	2	3	4	5	**6**	7	8	9	>=9.5	No comp.	Palestinians
5. Other	>=9.5	9	8	7	6	5	4	3	2	2	**3**	4	5	6	7	8	9	>=9.5	No comp.	U.S.
6. Palestinians	>=9.5	9	8	7	6	5	4	3	**2**	2	3	4	5	6	7	8	9	>=9.5	No comp.	U.S.

Figure 10.9 Sample Fundamental Scale of Absolute Numbers Questionnaire

Ten decision networks were created, one for each of the surviving BOCR criteria. As explained earlier each decision network contains the cluster of alternatives in addition to a cluster of the constituents. Table 10.12 shows each of a total 10 ratings for the BOCR constituents prioritized by pairwise comparisons and its corresponding value in relation to the criteria whose priorities were also obtained through pairwise comparisons. Both the local and global priorities are shown with respect to the various merits in the model. The values of global priorities were obtained as the product of BOCR rating (Table 10.11) times the corresponding local priority times the priority of its constituent.

Benefits

Among the two benefits criteria, the human rights criterion has the highest priority of 0.9 as compared with the economic benefits criterion of 0.1. Among the benefits criteria, the highest priority given by those representing the Palestinians with respect to human rights is (0.340). Interpretation of the priorities suggests that with respect to benefits, the Palestinians have the most to gain in the short run due to immediate improvement in human rights.

Although the United States has the next highest priority under economic benefits in Table 10.12, it also had the next highest priority for human rights since under the benefits node, human rights has the highest priority and the global rating for the United States is higher under this cluster. We interpret the United State's high rating under the benefits cluster to be indicative of public perception and political motivation. The overall results of the Benefits subnets are given in Table 10.13.

Table 10.12 Criteria and Their Priorities

Merits	Criteria	Constituents	Local Priorities	Global Priorities
Benefits	Human Rights 0.90	Israelis Palestinians United States Others	0.141 0.340 0.300 0.218	0.025 0.061 0.054 0.039
	Economic Status 0.10	Israelis Palestinians United States Others	0.154 0.274 0.310 0.263	0.003 0.005 0.006 0.005
Opportunities	Regional Stability 0.50	Israelis Palestinians United States Others	0.340 0.232 0.268 0.159	0.032 0.022 0.025 0.015
	Return Home 0.50	Israelis Palestinians United States Others	0.141 0.507 0.112 0.240	0.013 0.048 0.011 0.023
Costs	Internal Chaos In Israel 0.12	Israelis Palestinians United States Others	0.460 0.397 0.058 0.084	0.017 0.015 0.002 0.003
	Making Sacrifices 0.74	Israelis Palestinians United States Others	0.395 0.392 0.099 0.114	0.091 0.090 0.023 0.026
	Reparations / Relocations 0.15	Israelis Palestinians United States Others	0.253 0.336 0.201 0.210	0.012 0.016 0.009 0.010
Risks	Further Increase in Radicalism 0.46	Israelis Palestinians United States Others	0.421 0.332 0.125 0.122	0.058 0.046 0.017 0.017
	Further Instability in Region 0.34	Israelis Palestinians United States Others	0.277 0.330 0.110 0.282	0.028 0.024 0.011 0.029
	Limited Longevity that Promotes Return to Conflict 0.21	Israelis Palestinians United States Others	0.493 0.318 0.079 0.111	0.031 0.020 0.005 0.007

Table 10.13 Benefits' Overall Results

Criteria / Alternatives	Economic Status 0.10	Human Rights 0.90	Final Outcome
Nuclear Use	0.113	0.111	0.111
One-state Solution	0.944	0.960	0.959
Status Quo	0.633	0.588	0.592
Two-viable-state Solution	1	1	1

Opportunities

Within the opportunities cluster, both criteria had the same weighting which demonstrates that both regional stability and the right to return home have equal weights (0.50). However, it is interesting to note that within the regional criterion, the Israelis have the greatest weight (.340) while in returning home (0.507), the Palestinians have the greatest weight. In the long run, the Israelis perceive the greatest opportunity in the region's stability whereas the Palestinians believe that they have the greatest opportunity with the right to return home. Further, given that the Palestinians have the greatest global weight (0.048), suggests that overall the Palestinians' right to return home has the greatest global opportunity within the model. Table 10.14 presents the overall ranking of the alternatives with respect to opportunities.

Table 10.14 Opportunities' Overall Results

Criteria / Alternatives	Regional Stability 0.5	Return Home 0.5	Final Outcome
Nuclear Use	0.32	0.13	0.23
One-state Solution	0.96	0.55	0.76
Status Quo	0.54	0.16	0.35
Two-viable-state Solution	1	1	1

Costs

Among the three costs criteria, the Making Sacrifices costs criterion has the highest priority of 0.74 compared with the Reparations/Relocations costs criterion of 0.15 and the internal chaos costs criterion of 0.12. Among the costs constituents, the highest priority emerged from the rather evident conviction that both the Palestinians (0.392) and the Israelis (0.395) would have to make many sacrifices in the short run. Given that the global ratings of the other constituents on the other cost criteria are relatively low, we believe that implementation of a best alternative to a peace agreement will need to pay attention to the short term sacrifices that both groups will have to make. Table 10.15 shows the overall results of the alternatives with respect to the costs.

Table 10.15 Costs' Overall Results

Criteria ⟍ Alternatives	Internal Chaos in Israel 0.12	Making Sacrifices 0.74	Reparations / Relocations 0.15	Final Outcome
Nuclear Use	1	1	1	1
One-state Solution	0.38	0.38	0.26	0.36
Status Quo	0.56	0.71	0.16	0.61
Two-viable-state Solution	0.30	0.31	0.44	0.32

Risks

Among the three risk criteria, the criterion Further Increase in Radicalism has the highest priority of 0.46 compared with Further Instability in the Region (0.34) and with Limited Longevity with a Return to Instability (0.21). Interpretation of the results given in the risks merit is that the greatest long-term risk is that a selected alternative might result in an increase in radicalism that would further promote conflict in the region. This is followed by the risk that there might be an increase in instability due to implementation of one of the alternatives. Among the risks constituents, the highest priority is Israel's for both Increase in Radicalism (0.421) and for Limited Longevity with a Return to Instability (0.493). The findings presented here suggest that the Israelis are most concerned with the long-term risk of violence in the region (0.058). Similarly, with respect to the global priorities, we see that the Palestinians are also concerned with Long-Term Violence in the region (0.046). The final outcome for risks is given in Table 10.16.

It is worth noting that the local and global priorities are significant from a conflict resolution management perspective. These outcomes provide leaders with information important to overcoming obstacles toward a consensus agreement for a Middle East Conflict Resolution. For instance, the panel's evaluation under Benefits indicates that Human Rights have the higher of the two priorities. Furthermore, the Local Priorities under Human Rights suggests that both the Palestinians and the United States are fairly equal. Therefore, those leaders managing the process will know that with respect to Benefits (i.e. short-term gains); one ought to focus on the two groups with the highest ratings in order to ensure success. The remaining entries in Table 10.12 may be used similarly.

Table 10.16 Risks' Overall Results

Criteria / Alternatives	Further Increase In Radicalism 0.46	Further Instability In Region 0.34	Limited Longevity with Return to Conflict 0.21	Final Outcome
Nuclear Use	0.60	1	1	1
One-state Solution	0.40	0.24	0.43	0.43
Status Quo	1	0.55	0.76	0.98
Two-viable-state Solution	0.35	0.17	0.37	0.36

Synthesis of the BOCR Merits

The results obtained from the rating system (Table 10.11) and the over all results of the BOCR Merits are normalized and synthesized in order to capture the final outcome of the entire process in Table 10.17. For our purpose, we used the multiplicative power weighted formula which is expressed as $((Bb)(Oo))/((Cc)(Rr))$. For the Additive synthesis, we used the negative formulation expressed as $((Bb)+(Oo)-(Cc)-(Rr))$. Multiplicative synthesis illustrates which of the alternatives is preferable in the short term given all of the criteria under consideration; the additive synthesis illustrates the alternative that is preferable in the long term. We see that under both short and the long term the Two-State option is the best alternative.

Table 10.17 Synthesis of the Alternatives (Over all results)

Alternatives	Benefits 0.196	Opportunities 0.190	Costs 0.307	Risks 0.307	Multiplicative Synthesis	Additive Synthesis
Nuclear Use	0.11	0.23	1.00	0.82	0.00	(0.49)
One-state Solution	0.96	0.76	0.36	0.35	0.34	0.11
Status Quo	0.59	0.35	0.61	0.80	0.26	(0.25)
Two-viable-state Solution	1.00	1.00	0.32	0.29	0.62	0.20

After three days of discussion, analysis and evaluation, it turned out that the best alternative is a Two-state Solution and this was neither voiced nor explicitly subscribed to in advance. Recall that the group defined the Two-state solution to include the various forms suggested through the years which includes for example the rather well-known Bush Model, or the Saudi Initiative which also recognizes two independent autonomous states. The priorities also highlight points to keep in mind in the process of reaching agreement on a solution to resolve the Middle East Conflict where 'trouble' might arise and give leaders prior indication in order to avoid those pitfalls.

The results shown in Table 10.17 suggest also that the One-state Solution may be a viable option but with nearly half the priority of the best alternative. Recall that the One-state Solution was defined by the panel as the commingling of both the Palestinians and the Israelis under one unified state structure that recognizes all individuals as politically and socially equal under the generally understood notion of democracy. Given the relative nearness of the outcomes, leaders will need to monitor the process to gain insight into which direction seems more likely to succeed.

It is the Two-state-viable solution that comes out as the best alternative under all situations. Table 10.17 demonstrates that under both the multiplicative and the additive forms of synthesis, the Two-state solution is the best alternative.

There are far reaching implications for both the decision and implementation of the alternative derived in the model. Given that the Status Quo and the Nuclear Use options come out as clear negatives in the long run, we conclude that under no circumstance should either option be considered. This seems intuitive for the nuclear use option but may not have appeared so for the status quo. However, it is not difficult to determine that the current situation is not working given the periodic unrest in the Middle East and hence a negative outcome arises in the model that the panel put together.

Interpretation of the difference between the one-state solution and the two-state solution needs further elaboration. In Table 10.17, we see that there is a sizable difference between the one-state and the two-state solutions. One might expect that the one-state solution is a more viable option given the efficiencies that might arise from the two peoples coming together and in the integration of the land. However, given the BOCR results above, we see that there is greater B and O and less C and R in the two-state solution than there is in the one-state solution; this provides some insight into where our investigation into the management of resolving the conflict ought to begin. For instance, Table 10.12 shows that the Israelis could have the greatest 'risk' of increased radicalism and limited longevity whereas for the Palestinians the greatest risk is that there will be greater instability in the region. When we consider it along with the results presented in Table 10.16 Risks' Overall Results), we conclude that for the panel the concern was that the One-state solution poses the greatest risk for an increase in radicalism and limited longevity for the Israelis whereas for the Palestinians there is a concern that this solution will promote an increase in regional instability.

The major difficulty that we experience when we attempt to reach a conflict resolution roadmap in a conventional way is that it is difficult to keep all of the alternatives in mind at once in order to evaluate them. It is even more difficult to maintain cognitive attention of all of our judgments simultaneously in order to measure the importance of the alternatives with respect to the criteria that one puts forth. The outcome would be a matter of which of the highly respected or dominant participants puts forth the best argument that captures the minds of the others. The result of dominance over rational participation as described in this chapter is that one of the parties does not have a buy-in to the solution. A program such as the Analytic Network Process facilitates the cognitive mapping, simultaneous prioritization, and participation that make 'buy-in' possible. Further, what was once viewed as an esoteric prioritization process of the decision makers is now reduced to codified decisions by all the parties. The result of the codification process is joint-agreement and documentation for future review and follow-up.

Sensitivity Analysis

An interesting aspect of the model is that no matter how the criteria are adjusted or perturbed, the outcome remains stable. The sensitivity results from this model suggest that the two-state solution is always the best, followed by the one-state solution.

Conclusions

The final outcome suggests that the best policy to resolve the Middle East Conflict is to establish a two state solution. Since there is more than one proposal on the details of such solution, it is equally important to develop each proposed model in such a way that address a given set of criteria that would guarantee the long term stability and peace in the region. Only then another ANP model must be developed to evaluate each proposal against its criteria to select the most viable one that will serve the ultimate goal of this project. The authors agree that this work should be expanded to explore the opinions of those who are living in the region, regardless of their ethnic background or religion. An ANP based questionnaire might have an interesting result for academia and politicians as well. Such investigation should cover this phase of the research and the second one regarding the best outcome.

The model and the results given in this chapter suggest a variety of ways to manage the conflict resolution process and the implementation. The work presented here provides the reader with areas of potential concern for the leaders that must address the concerns of the various constituents and the people who must live in the environment. The most significant results of the model do not come from the numbers that are generated form the process, but rather the efforts and road-map that are generated. The results suggest that in order for any solution to work, the Israelis must recognize the Palestinians and their cause as an independent people with certain rights and concerns and the Palestinians will need to recognize Israel as an independent people with certain rights and concerns. The priorities generated reinforce the need for both parties (Israelis and Palestinians) to embrace the Middle East resolution as the leaders of the process in order to facilitate the development of *communitas* toward the resolution.

References

1. Rapoport, A., *Fights, Games and Debates*, University of Michigan Press, 1960.
2. Saaty, T.L., *Mathematical Models of Arms Control and Disarmament*, (translated to Russian), John Wiley and Sons, 1968. - 1
3. Saaty, T.L and J.M. Alexander, *Conflict Resolution: The Analytic Hierarchy Approach*, Praeger, New York, 1989.
4. Bennett, J.P. and T.L. Saaty, Terrorism: Patterns for Negotiation; A Case Study Using Hierarchies and Holarchies, *Terrorism: Threat, Reality, Response*, by Kupperman, R. and D. Trent, Hoover Press 1979.
5. Alexander, J.M. and T.L. Saaty, Stability Analysis of the Forward-Backward Process: Northern Ireland Case Study, *Behavioral Science*, **22**, pp375-382, 1977.
6. Alexander, Joyce M. and Thomas L. Saaty, "The Forward and Backward Processes of Conflict Analysis", *Behavioral Science* **22**, pp87-98. 1977.
7. Alexander, Joyce M. and Thomas L. Saaty, "An Analysis of Scotch-Irish Perceptions of the Northern Ireland Conflict", *Journal of Scotch-Irish Studies*, **2**(1), pp95-130, 2004.
8. Saaty, T.L., *Topics in Behavioral Mathematics*, Mathematical Association of America, Washington, D.C., 1973.
9. Saaty, T.L., The U.S.-OPEC Energy Conflict; The Payoff Matrix by the Analytic Hierarchy Process, *International Journal of Game Theory*, 1979.
10. Tarbell, D. and T.L. Saaty, The Conflict in South Africa, *Conflict Management and Peace Science*, Vol. 4, No. 2, pp. 151-168, 1980.
11. Saaty, T.L., The Conflict in South Africa, *Orion*, Vol. **4**, No. 1, pp. 3-25, 1988.
12. Von Neumann, J. and O. Morgenstern, *Theory of Games and Economic Behavior*, Princeton University Press, 1944.
13. Barash, D. P., *The Survival Game: How Game Theory Explains the Biology of Cooperation and Competition*, Owl Books, reprint 2004.

14. Myerson, R.B., *Game Theory: Analysis of Conflict*, Harvard University Press 1991.

15. Axelrod, R., *The Evolution of Cooperation*, Basic Books, 1984.

16. Elster, J., *Solomonic Judgements: Studies in the Limitations of Rationality*, Cambridge University, 1990.

17. Luce, R. D., and H. Raiffa, *Games and Decisions: Introduction and Critical Survey*, Wiley, 1957.

18. Isaacs, R., *Differential Games a Mathematical Theory with Applications to Warfare and Pursuit, Control and Optimization*, Dover Publications, 1999.

19. Weibull, J. W., *Evolutionary Game* Theory, MIT Press, 1995.

20. Brams, S. J., *Theory of Moves*, Cambridge University, 1994.

21. Ritzberger, K., *Foundations of Non-Cooperative Game Theory*, Oxford University Press, 2002.

22. Saaty, T.L., *Theory and Applications of the Analytic Network Process: Decision Making with Benefits, Opportunities, Costs, and Risks*, RWS Publications, Pittsburgh, PA, 2005.

23. Fudenberg D., and D. K. Levine, *The Theory of Learning in Games*, The MIT Press, 1998.

24. Saaty, T. and H. Chang, The Most Hopeful Outcome in the Middle East Conflict: The Analytic Network Process Approach, Chapter 10, in *Decision making with the Analytic Network Process: Economic, Political and Technological Applications with Benefits, Opportunities, Costs and Risks*, (T. Saaty and L. Vargas eds.), Springer International Series, 2006.

25. Bahurmoz, A. M. Hamid, M. Minutolo, T. Saaty and J. Zoffer, Synthesis of Complex Decision making: A Case Towards a Consensus Agreement for a Middle East Conflict Resolution, Working Paper, February, 2007.

Chapter 11

Retributive Conflict Resolution — the Desire to Hurt the Opponent

In constructive conflict resolution, each party identifies its demands and it is assumed that a way can be found to satisfy both parties' demands fairly. Fairly here means that each party forms a ratio of its benefits to those of the opponent and attempts to satisfy its own needs at least as much as its perceived evaluation of the opponent's benefits because the values may be interpreted differently by the two sides [1].

The second kind of conflict is *retributive* [2] with one or both parties harboring ill will towards the other. The idea is particularly relevant in long drawn-out conflicts which in the end fester and create almost ineradicable resentments. Here a party may be willing to give up much of its demands if misfortune can be brought to its opponent through some means, including justice as dispensed by the court system. Should the enemy die, they may forgive and forget, or sometimes they may be resentful because they have not extracted their pound of flesh.

The Allies' demand for unconditional surrender in World War II is an example. The object was to annihilate a hated opponent. If some German general had taken over and impaled Hitler in a vengeful way like the Italian patriots did to Mussolini, the end of the war with Germany may have come earlier. Until today there is resentment that Hitler, by eliminating himself, cheated those who wanted to deal him justice.

In Saudi Arabia the justice system allows a murderer to negotiate for his life with the surviving members of the family by paying them a large sum of money; hence cost to the defendant is turned into a material benefit to the plaintiff. The family members may reject this and demand his life. Finally, terrorists work to extract benefits by making the costs to their opponent sufficiently high to induce him to trade off such pains by offering them some benefits.

Most conflicts are easier to solve if they are nipped in the bud early. If they are delayed, the parties often become frustrated and angry and get to believe there is malice and dirty work that is prolonging their pain. This rankling increases the grievance, not only by insisting on unreasonable terms, but also by a hidden desire to inflict pain on the opponent to even things out. This hidden desire does not surface in the emotional way it developed because of the demand that people appear rational and interested in maximizing their own gain, rather than concentrating on incurring losses to the opponent. To love one's enemy and bless him becomes increasingly more difficult as time lapses and people start doing mean things to each other.   The parties could become malicious and apply themselves persistently to hurt each other. Our world is not so civilized as to rule out this possibility and its frequency. While earlier a party would have been willing to settle for its benefits, now in an implicit way that party wishes to get even with the opponent by causing him pain. In this case gain to a party is a combination (or product) of its benefits and its opponent's costs, pains or losses. This loss component meets emotional needs. Sometimes it can be bought off with additional benefits, but not always. The opponents suspect everything, including rationality, even when in principle it is supposedly serving the interests of both sides.

Thus in negotiations, each party not only calculates the incremental benefits it gets, but also the costs to its opponent. The more of either, the greater is the gain. Gain is the product of the benefits to the party and the costs (whose aim may also be long-run benefits) to the opponent. Each side must calculate what it estimates to be the opponent's gain as a product of benefits to the opponent and costs to itself and make sure that the ratio of its gain to the opponent's gain which it considers as a loss is greater than unity or not less than what the opponent is perceived to get. Thus each party is concerned with maximizing its gains via its benefits and the costs to the opponent and also by negotiating to increase this gain and decrease its loss (which is the gain to the opponent).   When several concessions are considered simultaneously, sums of the products of benefits and costs must be taken. We have the following ratios for the two parties A and B:

(as perceived by A)

$$\text{A's ratio:} \quad \frac{\text{gain to A}}{\text{A's perception of gain to B}} = \frac{\sum \text{A's benefits} \times \text{B's costs}}{\sum \text{B's benefits} \times \text{A's costs}} = \frac{\text{gain to A}}{\text{loss to A}}$$

where Σ is the sum taken over all concessions by B in the numerator and by A in the denominator. A's perceived ratio for B is the reciprocal of the above.

(as perceived by B)

$$\text{B's ratio:} \quad \frac{\text{gain to B}}{\text{B's perception of gain to A}} = \frac{\sum \text{B's benefits} \times \text{A's costs}}{\sum \text{A's benefits} \times \text{B's costs}} = \frac{\text{gain to B}}{\text{loss to B}}$$

where Σ is the sum taken over all concessions by A in the numerator and by B in the denominator. B's perceived ratio for A is the reciprocal of the above.

If each of the ratios is perceived by the corresponding party to be less than unity, the problem is to alter these perceptions so that both parties think that they are equally treated. By looking at its own ratio and the opponent's perceived ratio, that party will argue as follows: "Look what I am giving up. He gets high benefits and the costs to me are very high. He should be happy. On the other hand, look at what he is offering me. My benefits are low and the costs to him are very low. It is not a fair deal. He is not hurt enough by what he is offering me."

Note that constructive conflict resolution is a special case of retributive conflict resolution whereby the costs to the opponent are assigned a unit value. Each party assumes that the opponent is paying the full cost and concentrates on maximizing his own benefits. He cannot incur any further costs on the opponent.

In many instances where the parties feel that an essential part of the conflict arises from their disparity in relative power, it would be appropriate to weight the ratio of each party by its proportion of perceived power computed for both from appropriate hierarchies of influence as has been done in many examples. In that case, to equalize the two expressions becomes a more difficult task. By accepting guaranteed concessions, the weaker party may become stronger and its perceived power may change accordingly. It is exactly because of such possible changes that some long-standing conflicts should not be negotiated as a one-shot affair, but dealt with in terms of short, medium and long-range objectives.

A mediator works with each party to evaluate the priority of what it says it is giving up and what it is receiving based on its declared values (benefits and costs). The mediator then attempts to obtain convergence in a way which shows each party that the outcome is fair - i.e., that both their ratios are close. The mediator must substitute each party's perception of benefits and costs to the other by what he knows about the other party's values, avoiding exaggerations and distortions.

Unilateral concessions are actions taken by a single party evaluated in terms of their benefits to the acting party and their costs to that party. By forming the ratio of benefits to costs, those actions would be evaluated by the party to determine whether it is to its advantage to make such concessions.

Bilateral concessions are taken by both parties and may be evaluated in terms of their benefits to the party and the costs to the opponent. To make a trade-off they are compared with what it is estimated that the opponent would get. There are two outcomes, one for the party and one for the opponent. Concessions are sought to both obtain a certain level of gains to each side and also attain a fair ratio for both.

Multilateral concessions are based on comparisons made when there are several parties. In this case we use for each party the sum of the relative benefits times the relative costs for that party with every other party.

The Conflict in South Africa

The first author, during an invited visit to South Africa in 1986 where he gave workshops on the AHP, was asked by a high ranking official who worked for a strategic studies organization of the government and later paid, to do a detailed analysis of the South African conflict, using the AHP. It took several months to learn about the conflict and gather useful information about studies done by others. With assistance by his student V.J. Sethi, they structured and analyzed the conflict as a retributive one because of the kind of hostilities between the whites and the black at the time [3]. The report of that analysis was included as chapter 11 in the first author's coauthored book with Joyce Alexander on Conflict Resolution published by Praeger in 1989. We give here many of the highlights of that study many of whose conclusions, we observe, were implemented rather methodically. Our purpose is to show how some of the major steps of the analysis of what was considered as a retributive conflict were carried out.

For the South African conflict, for both the white government and the black majority, four hierarchies each were developed to calculate the above-described benefits and costs. In all, therefore, there were eight hierarchies constructed: four for the whites and four for the black majority, as shown in Figures 11.1 and 11.2. A list of seventeen concessions was clustered into six groups for the white government and eighteen concessions were clustered into another six groups for the blacks. These concessions formed the alternatives or bottom level of the hierarchy. One hierarchy in Figure 11.1 is shown in detail together with the accompanying calculations to illustrate the general method employed. The list of concessions for the black majority and the white government and the justification for choosing these concessions are discussed in Table 11.1. The first hierarchy in Figure 11.1 represents the white government's estimate of its benefits from black majority concessions. Comparative judgments were made at each level and for what it is worth, we show the judgments for level 1 in the hierarchy in Table 11.1:

Table 11.1 First judgment matrix for white government benefits

	AW	MP	EC	GS	DR	BP	Relative Weight
Appease White community (AW)	1	1/2	5	6	4	3	.291
Maintain power (MP)	2	1	4	5	5	6	.377
Improve economy (R)	1/5	1/4	1	7	4	3	.155
Gain sympathy (GS)	1/6	1/5	1/7	1	1/6	1/3	.032
Decrease retaliation (DR)	1/4	1/5	1/4	6	1	1	.078
Formulate acceptable Black policy (BP)	1/3	1/6	1/3	3	1	1	.067

The white government would benefit if (1) the white community is appeased, (2) the whites maintain their rule, (3) the economy improves, (4) the white government gains sympathy from the Western World, (5) the threat of retaliation against the whites by the blacks decreased, and (6) the white government creates an acceptable policy for the independence of the blacks. While some benefits, such as Appease Whites, Gain Sympathy, Improve Economy, were further subdivided, others led straight to the leaf nodes consisting of the list of black concessions. Comparative judgments were made at each level.

It is believed that maintenance of their rule is the main objective of the white government and is thus much more important than the other objectives. The second most important concern of the white government is to appease the white community. The white community pressured President P. W. Botha to declare a state of emergency (Newsweek, August 5, 1985). Its discontent has also led to the rise of the Afrikaaner-led Reconstituted National Party, which is threatening Botha's ruling Nationalist Party. Improving the economy was considered more important than gaining sympathy, and gaining sympathy was considered more important than decreasing the threat.

Similar subjective judgments were made at each level to complete the hierarchy. The results were aggregated to calculate the white government's benefits from each of the black concessions. While the preceding hierarchy demonstrates the calculation of benefits, the calculation of costs can be done in a similar fashion. All the results from the eight hierarchies, four in Figures 11.1a and 11.1b, and four in Figures 11.2a and 11.2b are shown in Table 11.3 and 11.4. Columns 3 and 6 in Table 11.3 show the total white losses and total black gains from the white government's concessions. Column 3 is the product of column 1, the costs to whites, and column 2, perceived benefits to blacks; column 6 is the product of column 4, the benefits to blacks, and column 5, perceived costs to whites. Similarly, in Table 11.4 columns 3 and 6 show respectively from the blacks' perspectives the total gain to whites and the total loss to blacks from blacks' concessions. Again column 3 is the product of columns 1 and 2, and column 6 is the product of columns 4 and 5.

These estimates of gains and losses are used by each party in deciding whether it should make a concession in return for a concession by the other party. For instance, the total white losses from the white government's concession of Release Nelson Mandela have the value of 1,860 (column 3, Table 11.3), The white government will agree to make this concession in exchange for any concession by the black majority that will give the white government gains greater than 1,860. A list of black concessions satisfying this criterion (from column 3, Table 11.3) is shown in Table 11.5. But the black majority will agree to make any of the concessions identified in Table 11.5 if, and only if, the gain to them from the white concession Release Nelson Mandela of 561 (column 6, Table 11.3) is greater than their loss from making any of the 6 black concessions. As shown in Table 11.5, the black losses from any of the black concessions are always greater than 561. The ratios of gains to losses are also calculated by each party and for this particular case are shown in Table 11.5. As can be seen, while this ratio is always greater than 1 for the whites, it is less than 1 if the blacks exchange any of their concessions of Table 11.5 with the white concession Release Nelson Mandela. Thus, the black majority would not agree to this exchange. This impasse is reached because each party wants its gains to be greater than its losses. The ratio of gains to losses is less than 1 for the blacks; thus, negotiation is needed for reconciliation, for otherwise the blacks may attempt to raise the cost for the whites.

Negotiation uses the various estimates of the gains and losses by the conflicting parties to analyze what sets of concessions, in terms of exchanges of particular black concessions with particular white concessions, might be acceptable to both parties. The objective of the negotiation is to ensure that each party's gain-loss ratio is greater than 1 and that one party does not perceive the other party's ratio to be much greater than its own. Here, they need to make the gain-loss ratio of the black, majority comparable with that of the white government on at least one black concession.

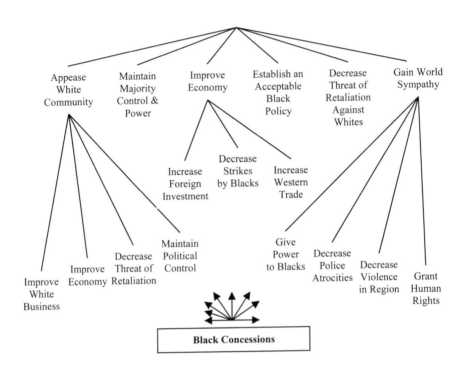

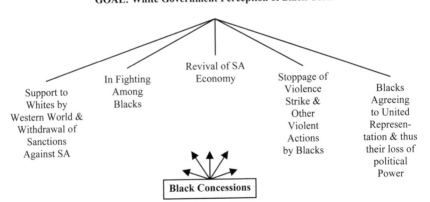

Figure 11.1a Hierarchies for Calculating Whites' Ratio

White Government Perception of Black Benefits

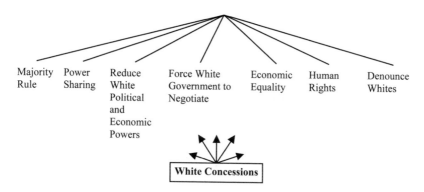

White Costs from Their Own Concessions

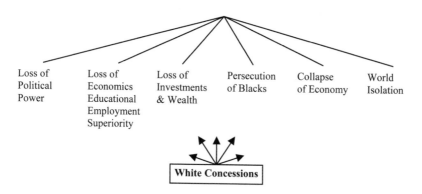

Figure 11.1b Hierarchies for Calculating Whites' Ratio

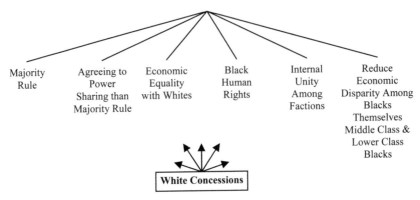

Black majority Benefits from White Concessions

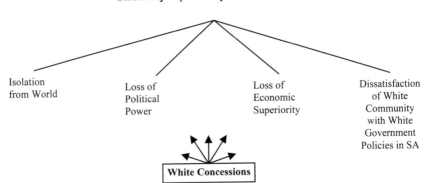

Black Majority's Perception of White Costs

Figure 11.2a Hierarchies for Calculating Blacks' Ratio

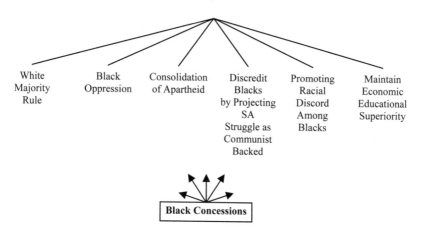

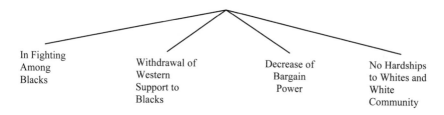

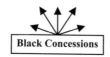

Figure 11.2b Hierarchies for Calculating Blacks' Ratio

Table 11.2 White and Black Concessions

Concessions by the white government

(1) Release political prisoners:
As of March 1986, this concession can be further subdivided into (a) Release only Nelson Mandela and (b) Release all prisoners.

(2) Draw up an agenda for a national convention (The Economist, July 27, 1985):
  (a) Invite all leaders including those from the banned African National Congress (ANC).
  (b) Invite only Bishop Tutu.
  (c) Invite all but Nelson Mandela unless he condemns violence.

(3) Maintain Neo-Apartheid: Defined by Martin and Johnson (1985) as meaning "the weakening of classical apartheid through economic change, the dismantling of some bits of petty apartheid and the extension of limited political rights to the coloreds and Indians coupled with the retention of a racially biased franchise, harsh implementation of influx control through forced removals and continued restrictions governing where people work and live," This concession was further subdivided into
  (a) Remove petty apartheid (in buses, for example).
  (b) Remove restrictions at beaches.
  (c) Make other cosmetic changes.

(4) Abandon the proposal of new regional councils; it consists of (Slabbert, 1983):
  (a) Give local government in black areas more autonomy and money.
  (b) Accept the reality of urban migration and develop a rational urbanization policy.
  (c) Abolish forced removals of people and the break-up of family life.

(5) Decentralize industries to black areas and black education:
  (a) Decentralize industries to black homelands.
  (b) Promote black education (government spending on education is $87 per pupil for blacks and $659 per pupil for whites).
  (c) Grant greater money for black improvement in the budget.

(6) Make a declaration of intent that will grant full citizenship, under one constitution, to all people of color:
  (a) Within one year.
  (b) Between one to two years.
  (c) In greater than two years.

Black majority concessions

(1) Decrease Western pressure:
  (a) Persuade the United States against disinvestment (without foreign investment only a growth rate of 3.5 percent compared to 5.5 percent otherwise will be managed).
  (b) Lift United States military sanctions (South Africa critically needs missile guidance systems, airplane and helicopter spares, reconnaissance aircraft, and ultimately a new generation of fighter bombers).
  (c) Lift Western trade barriers.
  (d) Abandon United States corporations' involvement through acts like Sullivan principles in South Africa's internal affairs.

(2) Abandon violence:
  (a) Nelson Mandela appeals to his followers to stop violence.
  (b) All leaders In South Africa appeal for abandoning violence.
  (c) ANC agrees to end violence.

(3) Stop strikes and boycotts:

(a) Stop the boycott of white businesses.
(b) Stop all strikes.
(c) Stop school boycotts by students.
(d) Stop the threat of unions making political demands (such as those by the Congress of South Africa Trade Unions (COSATU), which has about 500,000 members. Black membership in trade unions has increased threefold from 1980 to 1983).
(4) Protect white interests in the future:
(a) Protect white political power.
(b) Protect white investments.
(c) Agree to make a peaceful transition of power without any violent retaliations against whites.
(5) Agree to a sharing of political power rather than majority rule:
(a) Sharing of power to start immediately.
(b) A gradual evolution to power sharing within two years.
(6) Cooperate with the white government for economic growth,

Table 11.3 White Concessions

(1)	White Costs (2)	White Perception of Black Benefits (3)	Total White Loss (4)	Black Benefits (5)	Black Perception of White Costs (6)	Total Black Gain (7)
1(a) Release All Prisoners	.036	.019	684	.01	.02	200
1(b) Release Only Mandela	.060	.031	1 860	.017	.033	561
2(a) Invite All	.056	.056	3 136	.044	.037	1 628
2(b) Invite only Tutu	.008	.008	64	.006	.005	30
2(c) All but Mandela	.027	.027	729	.021	.018	378
3(a) Remove Apartheid In Buses, Trains	.013	.011	143	.006	.008	48
3(b) At Beaches	.013	.011	143	.006	.008	48
3(c) Others	.065	.054	3 510	.031	.041	1 271
4(a) More Autonomy	.109	.147	16 023	.102	.126	12 852
4(b) Solve Urban Black	.022	.029	638	.02	.025	500
4(c) No Relocation	.022	.029	638'	.02	.025	500
5(a) Decentralize Industry	.042	.063	2 646	.051	.047	2 397
5(b) Black Education	.012	1018	216	.015	.013	195
5(c) Give greater Money In Budget	.088	.132	11 616	.106	.097	10 282
6(a) Give Citizenship Shortly	.206	.175	36 050	.262	.238	62 356

| 6(b) | In 1 - 2 years | .174 | .148 | 25 752 | .221 | .201 | 44 421 |
| 6(c) | In > 2 years | .049 | .042 | 2 058 | .062 | .057 | 3 537 |

Table 11.4 Black Concessions

(1)	White Benefits (2)	White Perception of Black Costs (3)	Total White Gain (4)	Black Costs (5)	Black Perception of White Benefits (6)	Total Black Loss (7)
1(a) No Trade Barriers	.047	.097	4 559	.124	.069	8 556
1(b) No Military Sanctions	.020	.042	840	.053	.03	1 590
1(c) No Disinvestment,	.117	.242	28 314	.309	.173	53 457
1(d) No Sullivan Principles	.008	.018	144	.022	.013	286
2(a) Mandela Appeal for Non-Violence	.034	.029	986	.022	.021	462
2(b) All Leaders Appeal for Non-Violence	.170	.147	24 990	.110	.106	11 660
2(c) ANC Agrees to Non-Violence	.034	.029	986	.022	.021	462
3(a) Stop Boycott of Rent & Business	.088	.078	6 864	.058	.043	2 494
3(b) No Strikes	.026	.023	598	.017	.013	221
3(c) Stop School Boycotts	.025	.022	550	.016	.012	192
3(d) No Threats by Unions	.041	.037	1 517	.027	.020	540
4(a) Protect White Political Rights	.066	.037	2 442	.044	.016	704
4(b) Protect White Investments	.016	.009	144	.010	.038	380
4(c) Peaceful Transition	.019	.01	190	.012	.045	540
5(a) Agree to Power Sharing	.034	.017	578	.029	.007	203
5(b) Gradually	.034	.017	578	.029	.007	203
6(a) Co-operate for Economic Growth	.188	.129	24 252	.068	.215	14 620

Table 11.5 Gains and Losses

Black Concessions	White gains (Col 1)	Black losses (Col 2)	White ratio: gain/loss (Col 1/1860)	Black ratio. gain/loss (561/Col 2)
(1)	(2)	(3)	(4)	(5)
1(a). Induce Western world to lift trade barriers against SA:				
	4559	8556	2.45	0.065
1(c). Pressure US against any form of disinvestment:				
	28314	53457	15.22	0.01
2(b). All SA leaders appeal for non-violence:				
	24990	11660	13.43	0.048
3(a). Stop all boycotts:				
	6864	2494	3.69	0.225
4(a). Agree to White political rights in future:				
	2442	704	1.31	0.79
6(a). Cooperate for economic growth:				
	24252	14620	13.03	0.038

The numbers in Columns 1 and 2 of Table 11.5 are priorities that have been multiplied by 100 000.

As can be seen from Table 11.5, the white government's gain-loss ratio is smallest for the black concession of agreeing to white political power in the future and the black majority's gain-loss ratio for this alternative is 0.79. The blacks may reason that this is the only feasible concession that would cost the least and would agree to white political power in return for the whites to release Mandela. Otherwise they could iterate the process to either decrease the white ratio or increase the black majority's ratio which is discussed in more detail in the book *Conflict Resolution - The Analytic Hierarchy Approach*.by Saaty and Alexander.

References

1. Lehrer, K. and C. Wagner, *Rational Consensus in Science and Society. A Philosophical and Mathematical Study*, D. Reidel Publishing Company, Boston, 1981.

2. Saaty, T.L., Resolution of Retributive Conflicts, in: *Contributions of Technology to International Conflict Resolution*, H. Chestnut (ed.), Pergamon Press, 1986.

3. ------------- and J. Alexander, *Conflict Resolution - The Analytic Hierarchy Approach.* Praeger, New York, 1989.

Part IV: Addressing Significant Issues

There are three important concerns that cannot be addressed without the use of technical terms and some mathematics. They have to do with the rank mentioned in Chapter 2, the dispersion of the judgments of the individuals that make up the group and to what extent their judgments are still meaningful when aggregated, and finally the very essence of the ideas in this book providing a mathematical proof of the possibility of combining or aggregating individual judgments expressed as intensities of dominance into a group judgment. The next three chapters deal respectively with rank, dispersion, and possibility of group social function.

Chapter 12

Fundamentals of Comparisons, Rank Preservation and Reversal

Theme (*Weak version*): The rank of a given set of independent alternatives with respect to several criteria must stay the same if new alternatives are added or old ones deleted unless adding or deleting alternatives introduces or deletes criteria and changes judgments.

Theme (*Strong version*): Replace the word rank by priority with the added condition that the ratios of the priorities of the original alternatives must be the same before and after deleting old alternatives or adding new ones.

Rank preservation and reversal are important subjects in multicriteria decision-making particularly if a theory uses only one of two ways of creating priorities: rating alternatives one at a time with respect to an ideal or standard, or comparing them in pairs. It is known that our minds can do both naturally and without being tutored. When rating alternatives, they must be assumed to be independent and rank should be preserved. When comparing alternatives, they must be assumed to be dependent and rank may not always be preserved. However, even in making comparisons rank can be preserved if one uses idealization instead of normalization with the original set of alternatives and preserves that ideal from then on unless that ideal itself is deleted for some reason [1]. So often it is a matter of judgment as to whether it is desirable to force rank preservation or allow rank to adjust as necessary. Examples are given to illustrate the foregoing ideas.

As mentioned in Chapter 1, there are two types of judgment: "*Comparative judgment* and *absolute judgment*" [2]. In the Analytic Hierarchy Process (AHP) we call the first *relative measurement* and the second *absolute measurement*. In relative measurement we compare each alternative with many other alternatives and in absolute measurement we compare each alternative with one ideal alternative we know of or can imagine, a process we call *rating alternatives*. The first is descriptive and is conditioned by our observational ability and experience and the second is normative, conditioned by what we know is best, which of course is relative. Comparisons must precede ratings because ideals can only be created through experience using comparisons to arrive at what seems best. It is interesting that in order to rate alternatives with respect to an ideal as if they are independent can only be done after having made comparisons that involve dependence to create the ideal or standard in the first place. Making comparisons is fundamental and intrinsic in us. They are not an intellectual invention nor are they something that can be ignored.

The tradition of measurement makes one think that there is only one way to measure things and that is on a physical scale to assign values to them one at a time. We have been in the habit of creating scales and waiting for things to arrive to be measured on these scales as needed. A unique value is assigned to each thing or element from a scale. The value assigned to an element is unconditional, as it does not depend on the measurements of other elements. That is not the case with scales derived from paired comparisons. Unlike measurement on traditional scales, these scale values exist only after one has the objects or criteria to compare. In addition the values derived for each element are relative to what other values it is compared with, and thus each time an element is compared with other elements it has a different value. The values derived are conditional. Derived relative scales need not have a unit, but they can after they are derived by dividing by the value of one of them if desired. In addition it is possible to create an ideal after a first set is chosen and compare every element that is added thereafter with respect to the ideal with its unit value and allow it to become larger than that unit or smaller as needed. Relative scales of measurement derived from a fundamental scale of paired comparisons with values that belong to an absolute scale (invariant under the identity transformation) themselves belong to an absolute scale. One can see from the literature of scales that scales derived as in the AHP are a new paradigm in measurement that many people do not understand well even after a degree of exposure. But numerous examples show that it has useful characteristics not available in existing measurement particularly with regard to the measurement of intangibles, and with using judgment and understanding within a sizeable structure to examine possible future happenings. Usually we have been led to believe that intuition is unreliable because single hunches are usually inaccurate. We have found that intuition is very reliable when a knowledgeable person provides judgments that are many and well integrated within an organized structure. Because comparisons are our biological inheritance, and also because experience and judgment are what distinguishes the expert from the non-expert, it appears that we need to formalize our understanding within a transparent and justifiable scientific framework like the AHP to make it more reliable and usable.

There is no objectivity apart from human values that leads to the ranking of alternatives. Nature has no predetermined rank of alternatives on specially chosen criteria of its own. It is people who establish the criteria and their perceived rankings on these criteria.

When alternatives are thought to be independent of one another they are rated one at a time. In that case one must be able to say how high or how low an alternative rates on a criterion. To do that one must have something in mind called an ideal so that one gets the feeling about how close or far that alternative is from the ideal and allocates it to one of various intensity slots of ranking such as very high, high, medium, low, poor and so on. These intensity slots must themselves be compared pairwise to obtain numerical priorities for them that would be associated with the alternatives. One more thought here is that these intensities may fall in different order of magnitude. In this situation one needs to do groupings linked by a pivot so that an alternative can be honestly placed in one or the other of these groups as with the blueberry and the watermelon example shown in Chapter 2.

How really good an alternative is to serve our value system depends on what other alternatives there are. Even when we have measurements to apply to the alternatives, how effective that measurement is to help us choose that alternative depends on what other choices we have. It may be possible to decide how good an alternative is on its own independently of any prior knowledge and experience with other possibilities, but that is a rare occurrence. We assume alternatives to be completely independent of one another for convenience and not for scientific reasons. When we assume that alternatives are independent, we cannot compare them, but must rate them one at a time having an ideal in mind. This is a degenerate case of comparisons in which all the alternatives are compared with just one alternative, the ideal. That way we assign each a value relative to the ideal. Our arithmetic scheme for weighting the criteria and the alternatives and combining their weights to produce an overall result must reflect this. Introducing a new alternative or deleting an old one must have no effect on the outcome. But even when alternatives are assumed to be independent, having too many copies of an alternative or having too many alternatives, can influence our opinion of how good or bad any alternative is. We can cope with few law violations, but not as easily with many and let people out with a lighter sentence when there are many. This dependence on the number and on the quality of what other alternatives there are can have a substantial effect on our decisions. Number cannot be included as a criterion because indirectly, it implies dependence among the alternatives. Thus we cannot always rate alternatives one at a time ignoring what other alternatives there are even when they are functionally independent of each other. Performing pairwise comparisons takes into consideration the quality and number of the alternatives considered. Pairwise comparisons can be converted to treat alternatives as if they are independent and thus preserving rank by using idealization, assigning a unit value to the best alternative for each criterion, called the ideal, and proportionately to the others for the entire set of alternatives. Any new alternative is only compared with the ideal as in the ratings case and may obtain a value that is more than one, thus going above the ideal. This process would not show the effect of the influence of the number of alternatives on the outcome. If as often we must, we need to consider the natural influence of alternatives on others in the evaluation, we need to use the distributive not the ideal mode of normalization. The rank order produced by the two methods for the top alternatives have been experimentally found to agree in more than 90% of the cases.

Let us restate the ideas. When the criterion is intangible the alternatives of necessity are compared on a scale with respect to an ideal (the best conceivable alternative) one has in mind for that criterion. An ideal is understood or imagined by examining many diverse alternatives. Thus rating with respect to an ideal involves indirect dependence among the alternatives whether present or absent. The excellence of the ideal changes more and more when more is learned about a new and superior alternative; no matter how much imagination is applied, new alternatives that could not be imagined previously will come along and change the excellence of the old ideal to a new ideal. There is never a sure ideal that is permanent. Strictly speaking rating alternatives always compares them indirectly with other alternatives from which an ideal inherits its superior status and hence there is indirect dependence among all the alternatives all the time which implies the possibility of change in rank when alternatives are added or deleted. To preserve rank is to find a way to enforce its staying the same when new alternatives are added or old ones deleted. When alternatives are rated one at a time their scores are created independently and their ranks are always preserved. When they are compared, their ranks depend on each other and these ranks are no longer independent of one another. In that case to preserve rank, one takes the given set of alternatives and divides their priorities under each criterion by the largest priority among them so that the alternative with the largest value becomes the ideal among them. Any new alternative is only compared pairwise in a 2 by 2 matrix with the ideal alternative for that criterion and if better than that ideal, its priority becomes more than one and stays that way. In this case there can be no rank reversal.

There are situations in life when alternatives are mutually exclusive and exhaustive and no new alternatives can be added or existing ones deleted. The ranking of such alternatives differs from rankings that involve more and more alternatives, decisions in which the number of alternatives is open.

In paired comparisons, the ideal is used for each criterion when the alternatives are mutually exclusive and exhaustive. Otherwise the distributive mode is used and the ideal is formed at the end for further use as for example in BOCR. Thus BOCR answers can be of two kinds: One is for mutually exclusive and exhaustive alternatives with the ideal done for each criterion and one for dependent alternatives that can be increased by adding others or decreased by taking out some. In this case the ideal is formed from the distributive mode at the end. BOCR generally assumes the independence of the four merits. Otherwise they would be included in a single network to indicate their interdependence.

In practice we want to preserve rank to maintain order and reduce the complexity of the operational consequences to deal with rank changes. Thus the situation in which rank needs to be preserved must be specified. The best that one can say about them is that they invite attention when there are many alternatives over whose presence we have no control such as admitting students to a university, patients to a hospital, promoting military personnel, and so on, and the idea of fairness (first-come first-served) in ranking them seems to be the motivation to preserve their ranks. In all situations where we have control over what alternatives to consider, it seems reasonable to allow rank to change because their quality in our mind depends on what other alternatives we consider.

Structural and Functional Dependence

Unlike rating alternatives where we compare them to the best possible standard or ideal alternative, in the comparative judgment process we compare each alternative with some or all of the other alternatives. In that case an alternative that is poor on an attribute could have a relatively high priority when compared with still poorer alternatives on that attribute but have low priority on another attribute where it is compared with better-valued alternatives. Thus the final rank of any alternative depends on the quality of the other alternatives with which it is compared. Hence in making comparisons among alternatives, the priority of any alternative is influenced not only by how many alternatives it is compared with but by their quality.

In general increasing copies of an alternative indefinitely so that the universe is full of them tends to depreciate their value unless there is synergy among them so that the whole is more than the sum of its parts. Synergy happens when the copies support each other's functions, so that they tend to increase each other's value. The first, depreciation of value, is due to structural dependence and the second, appreciating value, is due to functional dependence in which the alternatives directly depend on each other like some industries do.

How do we determine whether alternatives are dependent? We compare them in pairs to see how strongly more a member of a pair influences a third alternative with respect to a common criterion. That is what we do in the ANP to derive dependence priorities. If there is no influence for any such comparison, the alternatives are independent.

We note that the ANP automatically takes into consideration the quality and number of alternatives with its interdependence. There are numerous occasions where for simplicity people try to force rank preservation and get wrong rankings for alternatives that should be ranked as if they are structurally dependent. Thus it is useful in practice to carry out both kinds of rankings. When one obtains different answers one needs to think about whether one wants to be normative and prevent rank reversal for some justifiable reason, or allow it to reverse for some practical and desirable reason related to relative performance rather than ideal performance. The president of a developing country was once told by an interviewer that according to the US Congress his country was not doing well. He said our progress should not be measured by the ideal standards of the most developed country but relative to how we were last year and where we are now. That is the difference between the two modes.

We describe the Corbin and Marley [3] example of the lady who shopped for hats and found two hats in Chapter 2. Assume that instead of the hats it was computers. In that case she would not change her mind and buy the better computer regardless how many of it there are. The judgments are identical in both cases yet the decision is different. What criterion can one use to account for the difference without violating independence? To say that the hats and computers are independently evaluated one by one prevents one from recognizing that there are many others, yet number has an effect and any criterion that takes it into consideration makes the alternatives dependent because of number. Changing one's preference because of knowledge that there are many of the same alternative, assumes there is dependence among the alternatives. It appears that whether number should or should not influence the outcome is up to the decision maker.

We see that there are three kinds of relations among alternatives: independence, conditional independence and functional dependence. Most multicriteria decision making (MCDM) literature is concerned with independent alternatives. Together with dependence that requires a network structure, conditional independence that is a special case of networks, but occurs in hierarchic structures, involves paired comparisons and uses normalization in deriving priorities. The alternatives are dependent if when comparing them pairwise, some are perceived to influence a third alternative with respect to a given attribute more than others. Otherwise they are independent but conditionally so if pairwise compared.

Normative Versus Descriptive Theories

In MCDM a theory can be normative or it can be descriptive. For example Utility Theory (MAUT, MAVT) is a normative theory whereas the AHP and

ANP are descriptive. A descriptive or positive statement is a statement about what is that contains no indication of approval or disapproval (e.g., this paper is white; cows eat vegetables). It is clear that a positive statement can be wrong. A normative, or prescriptive "what ought to be" statement tells us how things should be (e.g., people ought to be honest). There is no way of disproving this statement. If one disagrees with it, he has no sure way of convincing someone who believes the statement that he is wrong unless one goes out to take samples of what is actually happening and show that the assertions made do not conform to reality. Religion is normative (categorical) about what should be, science is descriptive about what is. In nature that has no judgments to make or criteria to add or delete, the presence of many alternatives, that are otherwise independent of each other, can reduce or increase the survivability and thus also the priority of other living things. How anyone living at a certain time in human progress can believe that they know everything so well that they then set down a criterion of rationality for all time illustrates why utility theory has had profound intellectual problems.

The attention given to rank has been a subject of debate for a long time. In the book by Luce and Raiffa, Games and Decisions [4], the authors present four variations on the axiom about whether rank should or should not be preserved with counterexamples in each case and without concluding that it always should and why.

They write:

"Adding new acts to a decision problem under uncertainty, each of which is weakly dominated by or is equivalent to some old act, has no effect on the optimality or non-optimality of an old act."

and elaborate it with

"If an act is non optimal for a decision problem under uncertainty, it cannot be made optimal by adding new acts to the problem."

and press it further to

"The addition of new acts does not transform an old, originally non-optimal act into an optimal one, and it can change an old, originally optimal act into a non-optimal one only if at least one of the new acts is optimal. ".

and even go to the extreme with:

"The addition of new acts to a decision problem under uncertainty never changes old, originally non-optimal acts into optimal ones."

and finally conclude with:

"The all-or-none feature of the last form may seem a bit too stringent ... a severe criticism is that it yields unreasonable results."

These authors clearly sensed that it is not reasonable to force rank preservation all the time.

Utility theory with its interval scale outcomes, and interval scales that cannot be summed, assumes the strict independence of alternatives and therefore ignores situations that its methodology cannot handle such as the dependence of alternatives on alternatives either in number and kind or in function (as happens in paired comparisons) or criteria on alternatives. In utility theory alternatives are only rated one at a time and even then people noticed with examples that rank should not always be preserved [see references]. But multi-attribute utility advocates thought that with multi-criteria decision-making this is no longer a problem. To explain why ranks were reversing, they thought that there has to be new criteria or change in judgments. But that is not enough as we have seen. Keeney and Raiffa in their book [5] on page 272, in referring to their scaling constants k_y and k_z say that "If we assessed $k_y = .75$ and $k_z = .25$ we cannot say that Y is three times more important as Z. In fact we cannot conclude that attribute Y is more important than Z. Going one step further it is not clear how we would precisely define the concept that one attribute is more important than another." The methodological approach of utility theory has had intrinsic problems and paradoxes like those studied by the Nobel laureate Maurice Allais, and by Daniel Ellsberg. In its original form multi-attribute utility theory (MAUT) banned comparisons of criteria but took up doing that after the AHP showed how and a new theory appeared with the name multi-attribute value theory (MAVT).

If one can compare criteria one can with greater ease also compare alternatives and there is no need for utility functions assumed to exist to use in all decisions. Measurement derived from paired comparison in the AHP is needed in the general framework of the ANP to handle these cases. The new paradigm of relative measurement allows one to include these previously ignored dependencies.

Need for Normalization when an Existing Unit of Measurement is Used for all the Criteria

When there is a single unit of measurement for all the criteria, normalization is important for converting the measurements of alternatives to relative values and synthesizing in order to obtain the right answer. Let us see first what happens when we go from scale measurements to relative values with respect to two criteria by using the same kind of measurement such as dollars for two criteria and give the measurements of three alternatives for each. We then add them and then normalize them by dividing by their total with respect to both criteria as in Table 12.1 to obtain their relative overall outcome.

Table 12.1 Scale Measurement Converted to Relative Measurement

Alternatives	Criterion C_1	Criterion C_2	Sums	Relative Value of Sums
A_1	1	3	4	4/18 = .222
A_2	2	4	6	6/18 = .333
A_3	3	5	8	8/18 = .444

Normalization is Basic in Relative Measurement

To obtain the relative values in the last column of this table, given that the numbers in the two columns under the criteria are represented in a form relative to each other, the AHP requires that the criteria be assigned priorities in the following way. One adds the measurement values under each criterion and divides it by the sum of the measurements with respect to all the other criteria measured on the same scale. This gives the priority of that criterion for that unit of measurement. Multiplying the relative values of the alternatives by the relative values of the criteria, and adding gives the final column of Table 12.2. Each of the middle three columns in Table 12.2 gives the value and the value normalized (relative value) in that column.

Table 12.2 Scale Measurement Converted to Relative Measurement

Alternatives	Criterion C_1 Normalized weight= 6/18		Criterion C_2 Normalized weight=12/18		Sums and Normalized Sums		AHP Synthesized Weighted Relative Values
A_1	1	1/6	3	3/12	4	4/18	4/18 = .222
A_2	2	2/6	4	4/12	6	6/18	6/18 = .333
A_3	3	3/6	5	5/12	8	8/18	8/18 = .444

The outcome in the last column coincides with the last column of Table 12.1, as it should. More generally, normalization is always needed when the criteria depend on the alternatives as in the ANP.

One thing we learn from this example is that if we add new alternatives, the ratios of the priorities of the old alternatives remain the same. Let us prove it for example in the case of two criteria C_1 and C_2. We begin with two alternatives A and B, whose priorities under C_1 and C_2 are respectively, a_i and b_i $i = 1, 2$ which in relative form are

$$a_i / \sum_{i=1}^{2} a_i \text{ and } b_i / \sum_{i=1}^{2} b_i.$$

The weights of C1 and C2 are respectively

$$\sum_{i=1}^{2} a_i / (\sum_{i=1}^{2} a_i + \sum_{i=1}^{2} b_i), \sum_{i=1}^{2} b_i / (\sum_{i=1}^{2} a_i + \sum_{i=1}^{2} b_i).$$

Synthesizing by weighting and adding yields for the overall priorities of A and B respectively

$$(a_1 + b_1) / (\sum_{i=1}^{2} a_i + \sum_{i=1}^{2} b_i), \text{ and } (a_2 + b_2) / (\sum_{i=1}^{2} a_i + \sum_{i=1}^{2} b_i).$$

The ratio of these priorities is $(a_1 + b_1)/(a_2 + b_2)$ which only depends on their values and not on the priorities of the criteria. We note that the sum of the values of the alternatives is used to normalize the value of each alternative by dividing by it. But this value is also the numerator of the priority of that criterion and cancels out in the weighting process leaving the sum of the values of the alternatives under both criteria in the denominator of the final result. This sum in turn cancels in taking the ratio of the priorities of A and B. Now it is clear that if we add a third alternative C, this ratio of the priorities of A and B remains unaffected by the change in the priorities of the criteria due to C. We conclude that in this case where the priorities of the criteria depend on the alternatives, the ratio of the priorities of the alternatives is invariant to adding a new alternative. This invariance should also hold in the stronger case when the criteria are independent of the alternatives, but the alternatives themselves are structurally independent of one another. When proportionality is not maintained because of structural dependence for each criterion, rank can reverse. Thus when the ideal mode is used the ideal must be preserved so that when new alternatives are added, they are compared with the old ideal allowing values to go above one, and thus the ratios among the existing alternatives can be preserved.

One can say that there is a natural law that binds absolute measurement to relative measurement on several criteria and that law is normalization. However, normalization loses information about the original measurements, the original unit of measurement and its associated zero. For example, normalizing measurement in pennies and corresponding values of measurement in dollars yield the same relative values, losing the information that they come from different orders of magnitude and have different units.

Examples of Justified Rank Reversals

Now we will discuss two examples.

A First Example — Phantom Alternatives as used in Marketing

The following example illustrates an interesting and real occurrence in the world of marketing. A phantom alternative A_3 is publicized in the media to deliberately cause rank reversal between A_1 and A_2 with the ideal mode. We begin with A_1 dominating A_2. Introducing A_3 we obtain reversal in the rank of A_2 over A_1 once with A_3 between A_1 and A_2 and once ranking the last of the three. This is the case of a phantom alternative (a car) A_3 that is more expensive and thus less desirable but has the best quality in terms of efficiency. People bought A_1 because it is cheaper but A_2 is a much better car because of its efficiency. Knowing that a (considerably) more expensive car A_3 will be on the market that also has only slightly better efficiency than A_2 makes people shift their preference to A_2 over A_1, without anything happening that causes them to change the relative importance of the criteria: efficiency and cost. Car A_3 is called a phantom because it is never made, it is proposed in advertising in a way to induce people to change their overall choice, although their preferences remain the same as before. Note that we already showed that with consistent judgments that preserve proportionality among the old alternatives, rank reversal could take place with no change in the weights of the criteria. With inconsistency proportionality is no longer preserved and rank reversal is even more natural. We recall that when dealing with intangibles, judgments are rarely consistent no matter how hard one tries unless they are forced to be consistent afterwards through number crunching.

The following example shows that one can preserve the old judgments, but if the new alternatives have slightly different judgments, the rank will change with the ideal mode when the alternative that is ideal is changed. In Part A of the example, on introducing A3, the ideal changed from A2 to A3 under the second criterion and A3 has the value .2 under the first criterion. In Part B of the example, the only difference is that A3 has the value .3 under the first criterion. The upshot is A2 is the best choice in both after introducing the phantom, but in the first case A2 > A3 > A1 while in the second case A2 > A1 > A3.   As the phantom A3 becomes more costly (Example – Part B) it becomes the least desirable. Note   that   because   of idealization, as A3 assumes values closer to those of A2, A1 would remain the more desired of the two alternatives A1 and A2.

Example - Part A

$$
\text{Cost} \quad
\begin{array}{cc} A_1 & A_2 \end{array}
\qquad
\begin{array}{c} A_1 \\ A_2 \end{array}
\begin{pmatrix} 1 & 2.5 \\ 1/2.5 & 1 \end{pmatrix}
$$

$$
\text{Efficiency} \quad
\begin{array}{cc} A_1 & A_2 \end{array}
\qquad
\begin{array}{c} A_1 \\ A_2 \end{array}
\begin{pmatrix} 1 & 1/9 \\ 9 & 1 \end{pmatrix}
$$

$$
\text{Cost} \quad
\begin{array}{ccc} A_1 & A_2 & A_3 \end{array}
\qquad
\begin{array}{c} A_1 \\ A_2 \\ A_3 \end{array}
\begin{pmatrix} 1 & 2.5 & 3\frac{1}{3} \\ \frac{1}{2.5} & 1 & 1\frac{1}{3} \\ \frac{1}{3\frac{1}{3}} & \frac{1}{1\frac{1}{3}} & 1 \end{pmatrix}
$$

$$
\text{Efficiency} \quad
\begin{array}{ccc} A_1 & A_2 & A_3 \end{array}
\qquad
\begin{array}{c} A_1 \\ A_2 \\ A_3 \end{array}
\begin{pmatrix} 1 & 1/9 & \frac{1}{9.4737} \\ 9 & 1 & \frac{1}{1.0526} \\ 9.4737 & 1.0526 & 1 \end{pmatrix}
$$

Alternatives	Cost 0.55	Efficiency 0.45	Composition	Normalized Weights	
A1	1	0.111111	0.6	0.8955224	A1>A2
A2	0.4	1	0.67	0.1044776	
			1.27		

Alternatives	Cost 0.55	Efficiency 0.45	Composition	Normalized Weights	
A1	1	0.105556	0.5975	0.3212366	
A2	0.4	0.95	0.6475	0.3481183	A2>A3>A1
A3	0.3	1	0.615	0.3306452	
			1.86		

Example – Part B

Cost $\quad A_1 \quad A_2$

$$
\begin{array}{c}
A_1 \\
A_2
\end{array}
\begin{pmatrix}
1 & 2.5 \\
1/2.5 & 1
\end{pmatrix}
$$

Efficiency $\quad A_1 \quad A_2$

$$
\begin{array}{c}
A_1 \\
A_2
\end{array}
\begin{pmatrix}
1 & 1/9 \\
9 & 1
\end{pmatrix}
$$

Cost $\quad A_1 \quad A_2 \quad A_3$

$$
\begin{array}{c}
A_1 \\
A_2 \\
A_3
\end{array}
\begin{pmatrix}
1 & 2.5 & 5 \\
\frac{1}{2.5} & 1 & 2 \\
\frac{1}{5} & \frac{1}{2} & 1
\end{pmatrix}
$$

Efficiency $\qquad A_1 \qquad A_2 \qquad A_3$

$$
\begin{array}{c}
A_1 \\
A_2 \\
A_3
\end{array}
\begin{pmatrix}
1 & 1/9 & \frac{1}{9.4737} \\
9 & 1 & \frac{1}{1.0526} \\
9.4737 & 1.0526 & 1
\end{pmatrix}
$$

	Cost	Efficiency		Normalized	
Alternatives	0.55	0.45	Composition	Weights	
A1	1	0.111111	0.6	0.8955224	A1>A2
A2	0.4	1	0.67	0.1044776	
			1.27		

	Cost	Efficiency		Normalized	
Alternatives	0.55	0.45	Composition	Weights	
A1	1	0.105556	0.5975	0.3310249	
A2	0.4	0.95	0.6475	0.3587258	A2>A1>A3
A3	0.2	1	0.56	0.3102493	
			1.805		

A Second Example

We begin with two alternatives A and B. We have on pairwise comparing them in Table 12.3 with respect to the criteria Efficiency and Cost whose priorities are .5 each:

Table 12.3 Example of Rank Reversal with Change in Ideal

	Efficiency (.5)				Cost (.5)					Composite Ideal	
	A	B	Norm	Ideal	A	B	Norm	Ideal	Comp Dist	Comp	Renorm.
A	1	3	0.75	1	1	0.5	0.33	0.5	0.542	0.75	0.5294
B	0.333	1	0.25	0.333	2	1	0.67	1	0.458	0.6667	0.4706
								1		1.6458	1

The question above is whether to normalize by dividing the weights of the alternatives by their sum (distributive mode) or idealize by dividing by the weight of the largest alternative (ideal mode). The distributive mode gives A = .54 and B = .46 while the normalized ideal mode gives A = .53 and B = .47. Now, if we add C that is a relevant alternative under efficiency, because it dominates both A and B we obtain as in Table 12.4:

Table 12.4 Example of Rank Reversal with Change in Ideal

	Efficiency (.5)					Cost (.5)						Composite Ideal	
	A	B	C	Norm	Ideal	A	B	C	Norm	Ideal	Comp Dist	Comp	Renorm.
A	1	3	0.5	0.3	0.5	1	0.5	4	0.308	0.5	0.3038	0.500	0.304
B	0.333	1	0.167	0.1	0.17	2	1	8	0.615	1	0.3577	0.583	0.354
C	2	6	1	0.6	1	0.25	0.13	1	0.077	0.125	0.3385	0.563	0.342
				3.25	1.63	13				1		1.6458	1

The distributive mode gives A = .30, B = .36 and C = .34 with rank reversal between A and B, and the normalized ideal mode gives A = .30, B = .35 and C = .34 again with rank reversal. There is rank reversal with both the distributive and ideal modes because C is dominant with respect to efficiency. Now the old ranks of A and B can be preserved if we maintain the original ideals under each criterion and for each criterion we compare the new alternatives only with the ideal, allowing its value to go above its value of one if necessary. One can even compare it with several of the old alternatives, preserving their relative values but improving any inconsistency only with respect to these values and in view of that adopting a final scale value for the new alternative. In that case we have for the above example the following (Table 12.5):

Table 12.5 Preserving Rank in the Second Example with no Change in Ideal

	Efficiency (.5)				Old		Cost (.5)					Composite		Ideal
	A	B	C	Norm	Ideal		A	B	C	Norm	Ideal	Comp Dist	Comp	Renorm.
A	1	3	0.5	0.3	1	A	1		0.5	4	0.308	0.5	0.3038	0.75	0.3024
B	0.333	1	0.167	0.1	0.333	B	2		1	8	0.615	1	0.3577	0.6667	0.2689
C	2	6	1	0.6	2	C	0.25	0.125	1	0.077	0.125	0.3385	1.0625	0.4285
							3.25	1.63	13		1		2.4792	1

Here there is no rank reversal. In this case we have idealized only once by using the initial set of alternatives but never after so that rank would be preserved from then on unless the ideal alternative is deleted in which case we idealize again. Which is the situation in real life? Not that it should but that it turns out that way. How would we know if it is right or not? We know it by experiencing regret. Do we eliminate the regret if we idealize once or many times, most likely not. We would feel that we did not choose correctly. But that would always be the case because process theory teaches us that change is always happening and we can at best always sub-optimize in the face of new alternatives (not just new criteria).

Negative Priorities

In this section we wish to give the reader an idea about thinking that extends applications of the AHP to negative numbers which also has an effect on rank and its preservation and reversal. It is just another indication that preserving rank is often a forcing of the alternatives to conform to one's expectations so one can track them for some kind of convenience, than a natural process that must comply with a general theorem proven with mathematical rigor. It also casts a shadow on the belief that rank preservation is an easy principle to advocate, and that advocating and practicing it can lead to harmful outcomes in the real world of which we may not be aware of.

Negative numbers on a Cartesian axis are a result of interpreting negative numbers in an opposite sense to the numbers that fall on the positive side. How we make this interpretation is important. Not long ago, Euler believed that negative numbers were greater than ⊚ and mathematicians of the sixteenth and seventeenth century did not accept them as numbers, although Hindu mathematicians had invented and used them long before. In the AHP we deal with normalized or relative numbers that fall between zero and one. They behave somewhat like probabilities. In practice, probabilities are obtained through counting frequencies of occurrence. In the AHP the numbers are priorities that are obtained by paired comparisons. One often derives probabilities from paired comparisons in response to the question: "Of a pair of events, which is more likely to occur". Thus the AHP enables one to derive not only probabilities but also more general scales that relate to importance and to preference in terms of higher-level criteria.

Although one does not speak of negative probability, even as one may subtract a probability value from another as in subtracting probabilities from one, often one needs to use negative priorities [6]. While it is true that at first glance ranking a set of objects: first, second, third and so on, negative priorities do not appear to contribute much to this idea of rank, positive and negative numbers together give us a cardinal basis for ranking in terms of positive and negative, favorable and unfavorable measurements.

In their paper on the Performance of the AHP in Comparison of Gains and Losses, Korhonen and Topdagi [7]] who were not concerned with the use of negative numbers but only with "when the utility of the objects cannot be evaluated on the same ratio scale," conclude that " the AHP was able surprisingly well to estimate the reasonable utility values for objects. The origin separating utility and disutility scales was estimated as well."

Relative measurements are derived as ratio scales and then transformed through division by their sum or by the largest of their values to absolute numbers like probabilities on an absolute scale. Negative priorities can be derived from positive dominance comparisons and from ratings just as positive priorities are, except that the sense in which the question is asked in making the comparisons is opposite to that used to derive positive numbers. For example, to derive a positive scale we ask which of two elements is larger in size or more beautiful in appearance. To derive negative priorities we ask: which of two elements is more costly or which of two offenses is a worse violation of the law. We cannot ask which is less painful because in paired comparisons we need the lesser element to serve as the unit of comparison and must estimate the larger one as a multiple of that unit. In a decision, one may have a criterion in terms of which alternatives are found to contribute to a goal in a way that increases satisfaction, and other alternatives contribute in a way that diminishes satisfaction. Here there is symmetry between positive and negative attributes. Some flowers have a pleasant fragrance and are satisfying whereas other flowers have an unpleasant smell and are dissatisfying; hence a need for negative numbers to distinguish between the two types of contribution. Because they are opposite in value to positive priorities we need a special way to combine the two. When several criteria are involved, an alternative may have positive priorities for some as in benefits and opportunities and negative priorities for others as in costs and risks. These are treated separately in four different hierarchies in the AHP. Alternatively, one can use the ANP with numerous networks involving influence control criteria that enable one to ask the right question in making paired comparisons particularly among clusters. They are then combined in a particularly practical way using the top ranked ideal alternative for each of the benefits, opportunities, costs and risks (BOCR) to rate (not compare) them one at a time with respect to strategic criteria that one uses to evaluate whether any decision on any matter should be made and if so which alternative is overall the best one to adopt. These four rating priorities are then used to synthesize the priorities of each alternative evaluated within the BOCR framework. The benefits opportunities results are added and from their sum one subtracts the weighted sum of the costs and risk. The outcome may be negative.

Conclusions

This chapter demonstrates that with relative measurement, conditional independence or structural dependence plays an important role in influencing the rank of the outcome. Economic theory, used to control and forecast downturns in economies, needs relative measurement to do its calculations. The different up and down economic fluctuations can be better accounted for by including the effects of both structural and functional dependence. The ANP is a useful tool for doing that as I have shown in several works coauthored with economists. These works were published in journals but are available in electronic form by email if you will contact me. In this book we have shown how to formulate the problem of phantoms that has been raised by utility theorists who have no way to account for it, we also need to formulate decoys and others discussed in reference [8] in the context of the paradigm of paired comparisons rather than in the old paradigm of one at a time rating of alternatives.

In this regard it may be worth noting that the only other theory that purports to measure intangibles which is utility theory assumes that a utility function takes on a certain definite "approximate" form of a curve or function derived by considering a few alternatives that a new alternative would also fall near that curve. But what if it does not? Will it then be used to revise the curve and what if there is yet another alternative that does not fall on the new curve? The problem remains unsolved in the same way that in dealing with rank one has to consider different orders of magnitude for different dimensions of measurement. The fundamental problem remains as to how to generalize a preference function to cover all possible alternatives.

References

1. Saaty, T.L., *Fundamentals of Decision Making with the Analytic Hierarchy Process*, RWS Publications, Pittsburgh, PA, 1994, revised 2000.
2. Blumenthal, A., *The Process of Cognition*, Prentice-Hall, Inc., Englewood Cliffs, New Jersey, 1977.
3. Corbin, R. and A.A.J. Marley, Random Utility Models with Equality: An Apparent, but Not Actual, Generalization of Random Utility Models, *Journal of Mathematical Psychology* 11, 274-293, 1974.
4. Luce, R.D. and H. Raiffa, *Games and Decisions: Introduction and Critical Survey*, Dover Publications, Reprint 1989.
5. Keeney, R.L. and H. Raiffa, 1976, *Decisions with Multiple Objectives: Preference and Value Tradeoffs*, Wiley, New York, 1976.
6. Saaty, T.L. and M. Ozdemir, Negative priorities in the Analytic Hierarchy Process, *Mathematical and Computer Modelling*, Vol. 37, pp1063-1075, 2003.
7. Korhonen, P. and H. Topdagi, Peformance of the AHP in Comparison of Gains and Losses, Helsinki School of economics, 2002, unpublished.
8. Farquhar, P.H. and A.R. Pratkanis, 1993, "Decision Structuring with Phantom Alternatives", Management Science 39(10), p. 1214-1226.

Additional Readings

Buede, D. and D.T. Maxwell, Rank Disagreement: A Comparison of Multi-criteria Methodologies, Journal of Multi-Criteria Decision Analysis, Vol. 4, 1-21, 1995.

Bunge, M., Treatise on Basic Philosophy, *Vol. 7 of Epistemology and Methodology III: Philosophy of Science and Technology Part II: Life Science, Social Science and Technology.* D. Reidel Publishing Company, Boston, 1985.

Freeman, K.M., A.R. Pratkanis and P.H. Farquhar, Phantoms as Psychological Motivation: Evidence for Compliance and Reactance Processes, University of California, Santa Cruz and Carnegie Mellon University, 1990.

Grether, D.M. and C.R. Plott, Economic Theory of Choice and the Preference Reversal Phenomenon, *The American Economic Review* 69(4), 623-638, 1979.

Kahneman, D. and A. Tversky, Prospect Theory: An Analysis of Decision Under Risk, *Econometrica* **47**, pp. 263-291, 1979.

McCardle, K.F. and R.L. Winkler, Repeated Gambles, Learning, and Risk Aversion, *Management Science* **38**(6), 1992.

McCord, M. and R. de Neufville, Empirical Demonstration that Expected Utility Decision Analysis is Not Operational, Chapter in *Foundation of Utility and Risk Theory with Applications*, Stigun Wenstop (ed.), Reidel Publishing Company, Boston, pp. 181-200, 1983.

Pommerehne, W.W., F. Schneider, and P. Zweifel, Economic Theory of Choice and the Preference Reversal Phenomenon: A Reexamination, *American Economic Review* **72**(3), pp. 569-573, 1982.

Saaty, T. L., and I. Millet, On the relativity of relative measures – accommodating both rank preservation and rank reversals in the AHP, *European Journal of Operational Research*, **121** (2000), pp. 205-212, 2000.

Saaty, T.L. and L.G. Vargas, Experiments on Rank Preservation and Reversal in Relative Measurement, *Mathematical and Computer Modelling* **17**(4-5), 13-18, 1993.

Saaty, T.L., Rank Generation, Preservation, and Reversal in the Analytic Hierarchy Decision Process, *Journal of the Decision Sciences Institute*, Vol. **18**, No. 2, 1987.

Tversky, A. and D. Kahneman, Judgment under Uncertainty: Heuristics and Biases, *Science*, V. **185**, pp. 1124-1131, 1974.

Tversky, A. and I. Simonson, Context-dependent Preferences, *Management Science* **39**(10), pp. 1179-1189, 1993.

Tversky, A., P. Slovic and D. Kahneman, The Causes of Preference Reversal, *The American Economic Review* **80**(1), 204-215, 1990.

Tyszka, T., Contextual Multiattribute Decision Rules, *Human Decision Making*, Sjoberg, L., T. Tyszka and J.A. Wise (eds.), Doxa, Bodafors, Sweden, 1983.

Zeleny, Milan, 1982, *Multiple Criteria Decision Making*, McGraw-Hill, New York, 1982.

Chapter 13

Dispersion of Group Judgments

To achieve a decision with which the group is satisfied, the group members must accept the judgments, and ultimately the priorities. This requires that (a) the judgments be homogeneous, and (b) the priorities of the individual group members be compatible with the group priorities. There are three levels in which the homogeneity of group preference needs to be considered: (1) for a single paired comparison (monogeneity), (2) for an entire matrix of paired comparisons (multigeneity), and (3) for a hierarchy or network (omnigeneity). In this chapter we study monogeneity and the impact it has on group priorities.

In all facets of life groups of people get together to make decisions. The group members may or may not be in agreement about some issues and that is reflected in how homogeneous the group is in its thinking. In the AHP groups make decisions by building a hierarchy together and providing judgments expressed on a 1 to 9 discrete scale having the reciprocal property. Condon et al. [1] mentioned that there are four different ways in which groups estimate weights in the AHP: "…consensus, vote or compromise, geometric mean of the individual judgments, and weighted arithmetic mean." The first three deal with judgments of individuals while the last deals with the priorities derived from the judgments.

To achieve a decision with which the group is satisfied, the judgments, and ultimately the priorities, must be accepted by the group members. This requires that (a) the judgments be homogeneous, and (b) the priorities of the individual group members be compatible with the group priorities.

There are three levels in which the homogeneity of group preference needs to be considered: (1) for a single paired comparison (monogeneity), (2) for an entire matrix of paired comparisons (multigeneity), and (3) for a hierarchy or network (omnigeneity). Monogeneity relates to the dispersion of the judgments around their geometric mean. The geometric mean of group judgments is the mathematical equivalent of consensus if all the members are considered equal. Otherwise one would use the weighted geometric mean. Aczel and Saaty [2] showed that the only mathematically valid way to synthesize reciprocal judgments preserving the reciprocal condition is the geometric mean. If the group judgments for a single paired comparison are too dispersed, i.e., they are not close to their geometric mean, the resulting geometric mean may not be used as the representative judgment for the group.

Multigeneity relates to the compatibility index of the priority vectors. The closeness of two priority vectors $v = (v_1,...,v_n)^T$ and

$w = (w_1, ..., w_n)^T$ can be tested through their compatibility index (Saaty, [3]) given by $\frac{1}{n^2} e^T V \circ W^T e$, where $\circ$ is the Hadamard or elementwise product, $V = (v_i/v_j)$ and $W = (w_i/w_j)$. Note that for a reciprocal matrix $A = (a_{ij})$ with principal eigenvalue λ_{max} and corresponding right eigenvector $w = (w_1, ..., w_n)$, $\frac{1}{n^2} e^T A \circ W^T e = \lambda_{max}/n^2$.   Thus, one can test the compatibility of each individual vector with that derived from the group judgments. A homogeneous group should have compatible individuals. It is clear that homogeneity at the paired comparisons level implies compatibility at the group level, but the converse is not always true. At the hierarchy or network level, it appears that it is more meaningful to speak of compatibility than of homogeneity. The main thrust of this chapter is to study monogeneity.

Dispersion in judgments leads to violations of Pareto Optimality at both the pairwise comparison level and/or the entire matrix from which priorities are derived. Ramanathan and Ganesh [4] explored two methods of combining judgments in hierarchies but they violated the Pareto Optimality Principle for pairwise comparisons [5], and hence, they incorrectly concluded that the geometric mean violates Pareto Optimality. Pareto Optimality at the pairwise level is not sufficient to ensure Pareto Optimality at the priority level. Fundamentally, Pareto Optimality means that if all individuals prefer A to B then so should the group. The group may be homogeneous in some paired comparisons and heterogeneous in others thus violating Pareto Optimality. The degree of violation of Pareto Optimality can be measured by computing compatibility along the rows, which yields a vector of compatibility values. What does one do when a group is not homogeneous in all its comparisons? Lack of homogeneity (heterogeneity) on some issues may lead to breaking up the group into smaller homogeneous groups. How should one separate the group into homogeneous subgroups? Since homogeneity relates to dispersion around the geometric mean, and dispersion itself involves uncertainties, how much of the dispersion is innate and how much is noise that when filtered one can speak of true homogeneity? In other words, how does one separate random considerations from committed beliefs?

Dispersion at the single paired comparison level affects the priorities obtained by each group member individually and could lead to violating Pareto Optimality. Should one combine or synthesize the priorities of the individuals to obtain the group priority or should one combine their judgments?

Here we develop a way to test monogeneity, i.e., how homogeneous the judgments of the members of a group are for each judgment they give in response to paired comparisons. This is done by deriving a measure of the dispersion of the judgments based on the geometric mean. Computing the dispersion around the geometric mean requires a multiplicative approach rather than the usual additive expected value used to calculate moments around the arithmetic mean. This leads to a new multiplicative or geometric expected value used to define the concept of geometric dispersion. The geometric dispersion of a finite set of values is given by the geometric mean of the ratios of the values to their geometric mean, if the ratio is greater than 1, or the reciprocal, if the ratio is less than or equal to 1. This measure of variability or dispersion of the judgments around the geometric mean allows us to (a) determine if the geometric mean of the judgments of a group can be used as the synthesized group judgment, (b) if the geometric mean cannot be used, divide the group into subgroups according to their geometric dispersion, and (c) measure the variability of the priorities corresponding to the matrix of judgments synthesized for the group.

In general, unless a group decides through consensus which judgments to assign in response to a paired comparison, the individual members may give different judgments. We need to find if the dispersion of this set of judgments is a normal occurrence in the group behavior. To do this, we compare the dispersion of the group with the dispersion of a group providing random responses to the paired comparison. Thus, we assume that an individual's pairwise comparison judgments about homogeneous elements is considered random, and expressed on a discrete $1/9, \ldots, 1/2, 1, 2, \ldots, 9$ scale of seventeen equally likely values. A sample consists of a set of values selected at random from the set of seventeen values, one for each member of the group. It is the dispersion of this sample of numbers around its geometric mean that concerns us. This dispersion can be considered a random variable with a distribution. Because treating the judgments as discrete variables becomes an intractable computational problem as the group size increases, we assume that judgments belong to a continuous random distribution. For example, if there are five people each choosing one of 17 numbers in the scale $1/9, \ldots, 1, \ldots, 9$, there are $17^5 = 1,419,857$ possible combinations of which 20,417 are different. Thus, the dispersion of each sample from its geometric mean has a large number of values for which one needs to determine the frequency and thus the probability distribution. To deal with this complexity, we use the continuous generalization instead. This allows us to fit probability distributions to the geometric dispersion for groups of arbitrary size. Once we have the continuous distribution of the geometric dispersion, the parameters that characterize this distribution are a function of the number of individuals, n in the group.

To use the geometric mean to synthesize a set of judgments given by several individuals in response to a single pairwise comparison, as the representative judgment for the entire group, the dispersion of the set of judgments from the geometric mean must be within some prescribed bounds. To determine these bounds, we use the probability distribution of the sample geometric dispersion mentioned above. We can then find how likely the observed value of the sample geometric dispersion is. This is done by computing the cumulative probability below the observed value of the sample dispersion in the theoretical distribution of the dispersion. If it is small then the observed value is less likely to be random, and we can then infer that the geometric dispersion of the group is "small" and the judgments can be considered homogeneous or α-cohesive at that specified α level. On the other hand, if the dispersion is unacceptable, then we could divide the group of individuals into subgroups representing similarity in judgment.

The remainder of the chapter is structured as follows. In the next section we give a summary of the geometric expected value concept and its generalization to the continuous case that leads to the concept of product integral. In the section that follows, we define the geometric dispersion of a positive random variable and apply it to the judgments of groups. In the section after this we approximate the distribution of the group geometric dispersion. Then we sketch how groups could be divided into subgroups if the geometric dispersion is large, and in the last section we show the impact of the dispersion of a group's judgments on the priorities associated with their judgments.

Generalization of the Geometric Mean to the Continuous Case

Let X be a random variable. Given a sample from this random variable $\tilde{x} = (x_1,...,x_n)$, the sample geometric mean is given by $\bar{x}_G \equiv \prod_{i=1}^{n} x_i^{1/n}$. Let us assume that not all the values are equally likely, and their absolute frequencies are equal to $m_1,...,m_k$ with $\sum_{i=1}^{k} m_i = n$.

Then, the sample geometric mean is given by: $\bar{x}_G \equiv \left[\prod_{i=1}^{k} x_i^{m_i} \right]^{1/n} = \prod_{i=1}^{k} x_i^{m_i/n}$.

An estimate of the probabilities $p_i = P[X = x_i]$ is given by $\hat{p}_i = \dfrac{m_i}{n}$. Thus the geometric expected value of a discrete random variable X is given by:

$$E_G[X] = \prod_{\forall x_i} x_i^{P[X=x_i]} = e^{\left\{ \sum_{\forall x_i} P[X=x_i]\ln x_i \right\}} = e^{E[\ln X]} \qquad (1)$$

In the continuous case, because $P[X = x] = 0$ for all x, we need to use intervals rather than points, and hence, we obtain:

$$E_G[X] = \lim_{\Delta x \to 0} \prod_{\forall x} x^{P[x < X \le x+\Delta x]} = \prod_{\forall x} x^{f(x)dx} \qquad (2)$$

Equation (2) is known as the product integral [6]. If X is defined in the interval (s,t], we have

$$\ln E_G[X] = \lim_{\Delta x \to 0} \sum_{s \le x \le t} P[x < X \le x+\Delta x]\ln x_i = \int_{(s,t]} f(x)\ln x\,dx \quad .$$

In general, we have

$$E_G[X] = \prod_{\mathfrak{D}(X)} x^{f(x)dx} = e^{\mathfrak{D}(X)} = e^{\{E[\ln X]\}} \tag{3}$$

where $\mathfrak{D}(X)$ is the domain of the variable X and $\int_{\mathfrak{D}(X)} f(x)dx = 1$.

The Geometric Dispersion of a Positive Random Variable

Using the geometric expected value, we define a measure of dispersion similar to the standard deviation. Let σ_G be the geometric dispersion of a positive random variable X given by $\sigma_G(X) = E_G\left[\left|\frac{X}{\mu_G}\right|_G\right]$, where

$$|x|_G = \begin{cases} x & \text{if } x>1 \\ \frac{1}{x} & \text{if } x\leq 1 \end{cases}. \quad \text{For } |\ln x| = \begin{cases} \ln x, & x>1 \\ \ln\frac{1}{x}, & x\leq 1 \end{cases}, \quad \text{then } e^{|\ln x|} = \begin{cases} x, & x>1 \\ \frac{1}{x}, & x\leq 1 \end{cases} \text{ and}$$

$\sigma_G(X) = \exp\left\{E[|\ln\frac{x}{\mu_G}|\right\} = \mu_G^{2F(\mu_G)} \exp\left\{-2\int_0^{\mu_G}(\ln x)f(x)dx\right\}$. It is possible now

to write $x = \mu_G\omega^{\sigma_G}$, where the variable ω has a geometric mean equal to 1 and a geometric dispersion equal to $e^{-2\int_0^1 \ln x f(x)dx}$.

Geometric Dispersion of Group Judgments

Let X_k, $k=1,2,...,n$ be the independent identically distributed random variables associated with the judgments. Let $\{X_k, k=1,2,...,n\}$ be continuous random variables distributed according to a reciprocal uniform $RU[\frac{1}{9},9]$, i.e., the variable $Y_k = \ln X_k$ is a uniform random variable defined in the interval $[-\ln 9, \ln 9]$. The probability density function (pdf) of Y_k is given by $g(y) = \frac{1}{2\ln 9}I_{[-\ln 9,\ln 9]}(y)$, and hence, the pdf of X_k is given by $f(x) = \frac{1}{2\ln 9}\frac{1}{x}I_{[\frac{1}{9},9]}(x)$.

The sample geometric dispersion is given by:

$$s_G(x_1,...,x_n) = \left[\prod_{k=1}^{n}\left|\frac{x_k}{\bar{x}_G}\right|_G\right]^{1/n} = \left[\prod_{k=1}^{n}e^{\left|\ln\frac{x_k}{\bar{x}_G}\right|}\right]^{1/n} \tag{4}$$

Let $(x_{[1:n]},...,x_{[n:n]})$ be the order statistics corresponding to the sample $\{x_k, k=1,2,...,n\}$, i.e., $x_{[h:n]} \leq x_{[k:n]}$ if $h\leq k$. Let n_1 be a value for which $x_{[k:n]} \leq \bar{x}_G$ for $k=1,2,...,n_1$. We have

$$\ln s_G(x_{[1:n]},...,x_{[n:n]}) = \frac{1}{n}\sum_{k=1}^{n}\ln\left|\frac{x_{[k:n]}}{\overline{x}_G}\right| = \frac{2n_1}{n}\left[\ln\overline{x}_G - \ln\overline{x}_{[n_1:n]}^G\right]$$

and hence, we obtain

$$s_G(x_1,...,x_n) = s_G(x_{[1:n]},...,x_{[n:n]}) = \left(\overline{x}_G/\overline{x}_{[n_1:n]}^G\right)^{2n_1/n}.$$

For a group consisting of n individuals, the distribution of $S_G(X_1,...,X_n)$ is given by

$$P[S_G \le s] = \sum_{n_1=1}^{n} P\left[\left[\frac{\overline{X}_G}{\overline{X}_{[n_1:n]}^G}\right]^{2n_1/n} \le s \,\Big|\, \upsilon_n = n_1\right] P[\upsilon_n = n_1]$$

where $\upsilon_n = \upsilon_n(A,\overline{x}_G)$ represents the number of occurrences of the event $A \equiv \{X_k \le \overline{x}_G\}$, and it is also equal to the index of the largest order statistic less than or equal to the sample geometric mean [7]. Let $\quad S_{k,n}(\overline{x}_G) = \sum_{1\le i_1 < i_2 < \cdots < i_k \le n} P[X_{i_1} \ge \overline{x}_G, X_{i_2} \ge \overline{x}_G,..., X_{i_k} \ge \overline{x}_G]\quad$.   Since

$$S_{k,n}(\overline{x}_G) = \sum_{r=k}^{n}\binom{r}{k}P[\upsilon_n = r], \text{ and } P[\upsilon_n = r] = \sum_{k=0}^{n-r}(-1)^k\binom{k+r}{r}S_{k+r,n} \text{ we have}$$

$$P[S_G \le s] = \sum_{t=1}^{n} P\left[\left[\frac{\overline{X}_G}{\overline{X}_{[t:n]}^G}\right]^{2t/n} \le s \,\Big|\, \upsilon_n = t\right]\sum_{k=0}^{n-t}(-1)^k\binom{k+t}{t}S_{k+t,n}.$$

Thus, the density function is given by:

$$f_{GD}(s) = \sum_{t=1}^{n} f_{GD}(s \,|\, t)\sum_{k=0}^{n-t}(-1)^k\binom{k+t}{t}S_{k+t,n} \tag{5}$$

that is a convex combination of density functions of variables of the form

$$\left(\prod_{k=1}^{n}(X_k)^{1/n}\Big/\prod_{h=1}^{n_1}(X_h)^{1/n_1}\right)^{2n_1/n}, \text{ i.e., the ratio of products of reciprocal}$$

uniform variates.   These density functions are of the form

$$\frac{1}{z}(a_0 + a_1\ln[z]+\cdots+a_{n-1}\ln[z]^{n-1})$$
.

There are closed form expressions for the density function of the geometric dispersion for a group consisting of three or less individuals, but for groups larger than three, it is cumbersome and not much precision is gained from it.   Instead, we approximate them using simulation.

Approximations of the Geometric Dispersion of Group Judgments

We computed the geometric dispersion of randomly generated samples of size 20,000 under the assumption that the judgments are distributed according to a continuous reciprocal uniform distribution $RU[\frac{1}{9},9]$.   We did this for groups consisting of 4, 5,..., 15, 20, 25, 30, 35, 40, 45, and 50 individuals.   We found that as the group size increases, the geometric dispersion tends to become gamma distributed. The parameters of these gamma distributions with location parameter equal to 1 are given in Table 13.1. To extend these models to groups of any size, we fit regression models to the parameters of the gamma distributions. Regression models of the shape (α) and the scale (β) parameters versus n appear to be surprisingly robust:

α(shape) = -3.48226 + 1.40829*n   (R-squared = 99.9741)
β(scale) = 0.897865 + 0.504361*n   (R-squared = 99.981)

In addition, the average and variance of the geometric dispersion can also be estimated from the parameters of these models:

mean = exp(1.03505 – 1.01298/n)   (R-squared = 99.8463)
variance = 7.23275*$n^{-1.0664}$ (R-squared = 99.9706)

Note that as n tends to infinity, the average geometric dispersion tends to 2.81524 (99% C.I. (2.79228,2.8384)) and the variance tends to zero (99% C.I. (1.44E-9, 2.31E-9)).

Table 13.1 Gamma Distribution parameters ($\gamma = 1$)

$$Gamma(\alpha, \beta, \gamma) = \frac{\beta^{\alpha}}{\Gamma(\alpha)} (x - \gamma)^{\alpha-1} e^{-\beta(x-\gamma)}$$

n	Shape α	Scale β
4	2.80051	1.27561
5	4.03976	1.76548
6	5.40204	2.27523
7	6.55616	2.69154
8	7.67909	3.1141
9	9.29459	3.68852
10	10.4217	4.08574
11	11.8255	4.59905
12	13.0628	5.04772
13	14.4586	5.55345
14	16.0157	6.10734
15	17.4963	6.65405
20	24.2381	9.02191
25	31.4048	11.6058
30	38.5573	14.1547
35	45.6409	16.6991
40	53.1646	19.3885
45	60.1011	21.8493
50	67.254	24.429

We now have the basis for a statistical test to decide if the dispersion of a group can be considered larger than usual, i.e., that the probability of obtaining the value of the sample geometric dispersion of the group is greater than a pre-specified significance level (e.g., 5 percent) in the distribution of the group geometric dispersion. For example, for a group of size 6, whose judgments on a given issue are equal to $\{2, 3, 7, 9, 1, 2\}$, the geometric dispersion of the group is equal to 1.9052169. The average geometric dispersion is estimated to be equal to $\exp(1.03505 - 1.01298/6) = 2.378$. Taking the usual significance level of 5 percent, we observe that $P[S_G(6) < 1.9052169] = 0.0376176 < 0.05$. Thus, the p-value corresponding to the sample geometric dispersion indicates that it seems rare to observe values of the geometric dispersion smaller than the sample geometric dispersion, and hence, the geometric dispersion of the group is not unusually large, which in turn implies that the geometric mean can be used as the representative preference judgment for the entire group.

Group Member Classification by the Geometric Dispersion

Let us assume that $\{x_k, \ k = 1, 2, ..., n\}$ is a group of judgments and let $\{x_{[k:n]}, \ k = 1, 2, ..., n\}$ be their order statistics. If

$F_{GD}[s_G(x_1, ..., x_n)] \equiv P[S_G(X_1, ..., X_n) \le s_G(x_1, ..., x_n)] < \alpha$ (where α is usually taken to be equal to 0.05) then the geometric mean can be used as a representative of the group judgment. On the other hand, if $F_{GD}[s_G(x_1, ..., x_n)] \equiv P[S_G(X_1, ..., X_n) \le s_G(x_1, ..., x_n)] > \alpha$ then the group needs to discuss the paired comparisons further in an attempt to reach consensus. To determine which members of a group disagree the most and hence make the geometric dispersion large, we find the p-values corresponding to the geometric dispersions of the groups of judgments given by: $\{x_{[1:n]}, x_{[2:n]}\}$, ..., $\{x_{[1:n]}, x_{[2:n]}, ..., x_{[k:n]}\}$, ..., $\{x_{[1:n]}, x_{[2:n]}, ..., x_{[n:n]}\}$.

Let $s_G(k) = s_G(x_{[1:n]}, ..., x_{[k:n]})$, $k = 2, ..., n$. We give without proof because of space limitations the following results.

Lemma 1: $s_G(k) = s_G(x_{[1:n]}, ..., x_{[k:n]})$ is a non-decreasing function of k, i.e., $s_G(k) \ge s_G(k-1)$.

Theorem 1: Given a set of judgments $\{x_{[k:n]}, \ k = 1, 2, ..., n\}$ with corresponding ordered geometric dispersions $\{s_G(k), \ k = 1, 2, ..., n\}$, if for any k, $P[S_G(k) \le s_G(k)] \le \alpha$ then $P[S_G(k-1) \le s_G(k-1)] \le \alpha$.

Definition: A group of judgments $\{x_k, \ k = 1, 2, ..., n\}$ is said to be α-cohesive if $P[S_G(n) \le s_G(n)] \le \alpha$.

Definition: A member of a group of α-cohesive judgments is said to be a liaison of the group if the group is not α-cohesive after the elimination of the corresponding judgment from the set of judgments.

The Liaison Theorem: Given a group of n α-cohesive judgments, a liaison does not exist if and only if all subgroups of cardinality (n-1) are α-cohesive.

The existence of a liaison means that we may be able to divide a group into two subgroups whose preferences differ, and for which the geometric mean cannot be used as the representative group judgment. This is the subject of further study.

Geometric Dispersion and Priority Variation

To study the relationship that exists between the geometric dispersion of a group and the dispersion of the corresponding eigenvectors, we find the range of variability of each component of the eigenvector for given sets of group judgments. This is done by first finding the distribution of the eigenvector components for random reciprocal matrices whose entries are distributed according to reciprocal uniform distributions $RU[l_{ij}, u_{ij}]$.

Theorem 2: For a random reciprocal matrix $X = (x_{ij})$ with entries distributed according to a reciprocal uniform distribution, $x_{ij} \sim RU[l_{ij}, u_{ij}]$, the components of the random variable $w = (w_1, ..., w_n)^T$ corresponding to the principal right eigenvector are distributed according to a beta, $\dfrac{w_i - \underline{w}_i}{\overline{w}_i - \underline{w}_i} \square Beta(\alpha_i, \beta_i)$, where $\underline{w}_i = \min\{w_i\}$ and $\overline{w}_i = \max\{w_i\}$, and the principal right eigenvector of the reciprocal matrix whose entries are given by the geometric mean of its entries, $E_G[x_{ij}]$, is given by:

$$(E[w_1], ..., E[w_n])^T = \left(\frac{\alpha_1}{\alpha_1 + \beta_1}(\overline{w}_1 - \underline{w}_1) + \underline{w}_1, \cdots, \frac{\alpha_n}{\alpha_n + \beta_n}(\overline{w}_n - \underline{w}_n) + \underline{w}_n \right)^T .$$

Let $x_{ij} = \mu_{ij} w_{ij}^{\sigma_{ij}}$ where $\mu_{ij} = \sqrt{l_{ij} u_{ij}}$ is the geometric mean and σ_{ij} is the geometric dispersion of $x_{ij} \sim RU[l_{ij}, u_{ij}]$. By definition, $\mu_{ji} = 1/\mu_{ij}$ and $\sigma_{ji} = \sigma_{ij}$. Thus, we have $w_{ji} = 1/w_{ij}$. Let us assume that the reciprocal matrix of geometric means is consistent, i.e., $\mu_{ij}\mu_{jk} = \mu_{ik}$. Then the principal right (pr-) eigenvector of the matrix $(x_{ij} = \mu_{ij} w_{ij}^{\sigma_{ij}})$ is given by the Hadamard product of the pr-eigenvector of the matrix (μ_{ij}), μ_w, and the pr-eigenvector of the matrix $(w_{ij}^{\sigma_{ij}})$. The entries of this matrix are random reciprocal uniform variables $RU[l_{ij}/\mu_{ij}, u_{ij}/\mu_{ij}]$ whose geometric dispersion is given by $\left(u_{ij}/l_{ij}\right)^{1/4}$. Since the geometric dispersion of the variables x_{ij} and that of the variables $w_{ij}^{\sigma_{ij}}$ is the same, because $x_{ij}/\mu_{ij} = w_{ij}^{\sigma_{ij}}$, we have $\sigma_{ij} = \left(u_{ij}/l_{ij}\right)^{1/4}$. Thus, bounding the dispersion of the entries of the matrix $(w_{ij}^{\sigma_{ij}})$ bounds the dispersion of the entries of the matrix $(x_{ij} = \mu_{ij}w_{ij}^{\sigma_{ij}})$.

Consider a group of five people who provide the judgments given in the following matrix:

$$\begin{pmatrix} 1 & (2,3,4,5,6) & (1/2,2,1,1/3,4) & (3,4,1/2,2,8) \\ & 1 & (1,2,3,4,5) & (5,4,3,2,1) \\ & & 1 & (1/4,1/3,1,2,5) \\ & & & 1 \end{pmatrix}$$

The geometric dispersion of each group and their corresponding p-values (see Table 13.2) that the judgments (1, 3), (1, 4) and (3, 4) have large geometric dispersion. This leads to large dispersion on the values of the eigenvector components (See Table 13.3) and a violation of Pareto Optimality. Reducing the dispersion of the judgments as in the matrix below, for example,

$$\begin{pmatrix} 1 & (2,3,4,5,6) & (2,2,1,1,2) & (3,4,3,2,8) \\ & 1 & (1,2,3,4,5) & (5,4,3,2,1) \\ & & 1 & (1,2,1,2,5) \\ & & & 1 \end{pmatrix}$$

leads to less dispersed eigenvectors that satisfy Pareto Optimality (See Table 13.4).

Table 13.2 Geometric dispersions and p-values

GD	1	1.399306	2.194046	2.586241
	1.399306	1	1.63026	1.63026
	2.194046	1.63026	1	2.62424
	2.586241	1.63026	2.62424	1

p-value	0	0.005	0.157	0.3
		0	0.025	0.025
			0	0.315
				0

Table 13.3 Individual Eigenvectors and Eigenvector of the Geometric Mean

	P1	P2	P3	P4	P5	GM
w1	0.288293	0.460725	0.267140199	0.351129	0.581191	0.41676
w2	0.301287	0.274057	0.283579312	0.281388	0.207615	0.266142
w3	0.201647	0.116421	0.135419348	0.273203	0.136396	0.178548
w4	0.208772	0.148798	0.313861141	0.09428	0.074798	0.138551

Table 13.4 Individual Eigenvectors that satisfy Pareto Optimality

	P1	P2	P3	P4	P5	GM
w1	0.401242	0.473463	0.439457696	0.438378	0.535109	0.471061
w2	0.295662	0.268317	0.269969347	0.265162	0.227089	0.253814
w3	0.187044	0.172147	0.17688459	0.184266	0.161707	0.176787
w4	0.116052	0.086073	0.113688366	0.112194	0.076095	0.098339

Conclusions

In this chapter we put forth a framework to study group decision-making in the context of the AHP. A principal component of this framework is the study of the homogeneity of judgments provided by the group. We developed a new measure of the dispersion of a set of judgments from a group for a single paired comparison, and illustrated the impact that this dispersion has on the group priorities. A subject of future research is the study of the relationship between dispersions on the individual paired comparisons in the entire matrix, the consistency of judgments, the compatibility of the priority vectors and the measurement of the violation of Pareto Optimality.

References

1. E. Condon, B. Golden and E. Wasil, Visualizing Group Decisions in the Analytic Hierarchy Process. *Computers and Operations Research,* (2003). **30**: 1435-1445.
2. J. Aczel, T.L. Saaty, Procedures for synthesizing ratio judgments. *Journal of Mathematical Psychology,* (1983). **27**: 93-102.
3. T.L. Saaty, Fundamentals of Decision Making. Pittsburgh, PA: RWS Publications, 1994.
4. R. Ramanathan and L.S. Ganesh, Group preference aggregation methods employed in the AHP: An evaluation and an intrinsic process for deriving member's weightages. *European Journal of Operational Research,* (1994). **79**: 249-269.
5. T.L. Saaty and L.G. Vargas, *The Possibility of Group Choice: Pairwise Comparisons and Merging Functions.* 2003, The Joseph M. Katz Graduate School of Business: University of Pittsburgh, Pittsburgh, PA.
6. R.D. Gill, S. Johansen, A survey of product-integration with a view toward application in survival analysis. *The Annals of Statistics,* (1990). **18**(4): 1501-1555.
7. J. Galambos, The Asymptotic Theory of Extreme Order Statistics. New York: J. Wiley, 1978.

Chapter 14

Possibility of Group Choice

An earlier version of this chapter, coauthored by Thomas Saaty and Luis Vargas, was published in the International Journal of Information Technology & Decision Making (IJITDM) and received the Herbert Simon Award for Outstanding Contribution in Information Technology and Decision Making in January 2012.

1. INTRODUCTION

Preferences in Arrow's conditions are ordinal. Here we show that when intensity of preference represented by reciprocal pairwise comparisons is considered, it is always possible to construct an Arrowian social welfare function using a two-stage social choice process. In stage 1 the individual pairwise relations are mapped into a social pairwise relation. In stage 2 the social pairwise relation is used to generate a cardinal ranking and this ranking is then used to select a particular member of the choice set.

A social welfare function is an aggregation of individual choice functions. According to Arrow, for a group to agree unanimously on a choice, their preferences must be the same as the preferences of one of the members of the group, the dictator. He assumes that people indicate their preferences by saying "I like *a* better than *b* or *b* better than *a*" without expressing the intensity or strength of those preferences, for example, "I like *a* much more than *b*." Clearly, what "much more" means needs to be defined. In this context the preferences are ordinal. In an example at the end of the chapter we illustrate that group decision making situations often require expressing the intensity of preferences.

Instead of using individual binary relations on the feasible set X as the input, we use individual judgments. A judgment is a comparison of two elements. Consider an individual comparing n objects according to some criterion. Let us also assume that there exists a scale that can be used to measure the criterion value for these objects and let the measurements be $x_1, x_2, ..., x_n$. The relative magnitude or intensity of the criterion for two arbitrary objects i and j could be written as the ratio of the measurements x_i and x_j, i.e., $a_{ij} \equiv x_i / x_j$. If the vector of measurements $\mathbf{x}$ is unknown to the individual making the comparisons, then the relative paired comparisons would have to be estimated by an experienced judge using judgments for each pair. That is, when the exact value a_{ij} is not known, we obtain an approximation to it, $\hat{a}_{ij}$, made by judgment. The estimate $\hat{a}_{ij}$ is a pairwise judgment, and the set of individual pairwise judgments represents an individual pairwise relation. Note that the pairwise judgments a_{ij} satisfy the conditions $a_{ij}a_{jk} = a_{ik}$ for all i, j and k (consistency) and $a_{ji} = a_{ij}^{-1}$ for all i and j (reciprocal). The set of judgments a_{ij} represents a consistent pairwise relation. The set of judgments $\hat{a}_{ij}$ represents a reciprocal pairwise relation. All consistent pairwise relations are reciprocal pairwise relations but the converse is not true.

The social choice process is a two-stage one. In stage 1 the individual pairwise relations are mapped into a social pairwise relation. In stage 2 the social pairwise relation is used to generate a cardinal ranking of the members of X and this ranking is then used to select a particular member of X. Thus, to decide that alternative i is preferred to alternative j we need to derive a cardinal preference relation from the reciprocal pairwise relations.

2. PAIRWISE COMPARISONS AND ARROW'S CONDITIONS

In this section we show that the geometric mean aggregation procedure of the judgments of the individuals in a group, represented by reciprocal pairwise comparisons, satisfies Arrow's conditions.

Let $\mathfrak{A} = \{A_i\}_{i=1}^n$ denote a *finite* set consisting of at least three alternatives or outcomes, and let $\mathfrak{M}$ be a set of m individuals whose ordinal preferences (e.g., *a* preferred to *b* but not by how much) on $\mathfrak{A}$ form a *weak order*. Let $\mathfrak{F}$ denote the set of mappings from $\mathfrak{A} \times \mathfrak{A}$ to the set of positive real numbers $\mathbb{R}^+$. When a pairwise relation P is

applied on a set of elements (alternatives), e.g., $P(A_i, A_j)$, it is referred
to as a *pairwise comparison* or *judgment* in which the (pairwise)
dominance of A_i over A_j or A_j over A_i is expressed numerically on an
absolute scale. A *reciprocal pairwise relation* P over $\mathfrak{A} \times \mathfrak{A}$ is an
element of $\mathfrak{F}$ that satisfies the following conditions:

a. For all $A_i \in \mathfrak{A}$, $P(A_i, A_i) = 1$.

b. For   all $A_i, A_j \in \mathfrak{A}, i \neq j$, $P(A_i, A_j)P(A_j, A_i) = 1$,   i.e.,
    $P(A_j, A_i) = 1/P(A_i, A_j)$.

Definition: A reciprocal pairwise relation P is said to be *consistent* if
and   only   if   for   all i, j and s the   relationship
$P(A_i, A_j)P(A_j, A_s) = P(A_i, A_s)$ holds.

Definition: The reciprocal pairwise relation P is said to satisfy
pairwise preference of alternative A_i over alternative A_j if and only if
$P(A_i, A_j) > 1$.

Let $\mathfrak{P}$ be the set of all reciprocal pairwise preference
relations. There are $n(n-1)/2$ paired comparisons $P(A_i, A_j)$ of n
elements that define these relations. Denote by P_k the reciprocal
pairwise relation associated with the kth member of a group $\mathfrak{M}$ of m
members. A *reciprocal pairwise profile* is given by the sets of
reciprocal pairwise preference relations $\mathbf{P} = (P_1, P_2, ..., P_m) \in \mathfrak{P}^m$. In
general, two members of the group would have different judgments,
i.e., for any two alternatives i and j, $P_h(A_i, A_j) \neq P_k(A_i, A_j)$ for $h \neq k$.
A procedure for aggregating or synthesizing pairwise preference
relations is by definition a mapping f from a subset of the m-fold
Cartesian product $\mathfrak{P}^m$ to $\mathfrak{P}$, i.e., $f(\mathbf{P}) = f(P_1, ..., P_m) = P$. We denote
$\mathbf{P}|_A$ as the restriction of the reciprocal pairwise profile $\mathbf{P}$ to a subset $\mathbf{A}$
of $\mathfrak{A}$. For reciprocal pairwise profiles not all aggregation procedures
are valid. We would like the aggregation procedure to preserve the
reciprocal property. Aczel and Saaty (1983) proved that the only
aggregation procedure f that satisfies:

a. separability: $f(x_1, ..., x_m) = g(x_1) \circ \cdots \circ g(x_m)$,

b. unanimity: $f(x, ..., x) = x$,

c. homogeneity: $f(\lambda x_1, \ldots, \lambda x_m) = \lambda f(x_1, \ldots, x_m)$, $\lambda > 0$, and

d. the reciprocal property: $f(1/x_1, \ldots, 1/x_m) = 1/f(x_1, \ldots, x_m)$,

is the geometric mean. The geometric mean is given by

$$f(\mathbf{P})(A_i, A_j) = \left[\prod_{k=1}^{m} P_k(A_i, A_j) \right]^{\frac{1}{m}}.$$

We can now introduce *Arrow's conditions* for pairwise comparisons.

Unrestricted Domain: A pairwise preference aggregation procedure is said to satisfy the condition of *unrestricted domain* if its domain is all of $\mathfrak{P}^m$.

Pareto Principle: A pairwise preference aggregation procedure $f : \mathfrak{P}^m \to \mathfrak{P}$ satisfies *pairwise unanimity* if and only if for some pair A_i and A_j of $\mathfrak{A}$ and any reciprocal pairwise profile $\mathbf{P}$, $P_k(A_i, A_j) > 1$ for all $k \in \mathfrak{M}$, implies $P(A_i, A_j) > 1$, where $P = f(\mathbf{P})$.

Pairwise Cardinal Independence from Irrelevant Alternatives: A pairwise aggregation procedure f is said to satisfy *pairwise cardinal independence from irrelevant alternatives* (PCIIA) if for any subset $\mathbf{A}$ of $\mathfrak{A}$ with three elements and for any two reciprocal pairwise profiles $\mathbf{P}$ and $\mathbf{Q}$ such that $\mathbf{P}|_\mathbf{A} = \mathbf{Q}|_\mathbf{A}$ then $f(\mathbf{P})|_\mathbf{A} = f(\mathbf{Q})|_\mathbf{A}$.

Not all aggregation procedures satisfy PCIIA. For example, map each individual weak order R_k on $\mathfrak{A}$ generated by $P_k(A_i, A_j)$ into a utility representation, $u_k = u(R_k)$, such that $A_i \succ A_j$ if and only if $u_k(A_i) > u_k(A_j)$, and then set $P(A_i, A_j) = \dfrac{\sum\limits_{k \in \mathfrak{M}} u_k(A_i)}{\sum\limits_{k \in \mathfrak{M}} u_k(A_j)}$. This procedure violates PCIIA.

Non-Dictatorship: A pairwise aggregation procedure f is said to be *pairwise cardinally non-dictatorial* if there is no group member $d \in \mathfrak{M}$ such that for all $\mathbf{P} \in \mathfrak{P}^m$, $f(\mathbf{P}) = P_d$.

Theorem 1: The geometric mean aggregation procedure $f : \mathfrak{P}^m \to \mathfrak{P}$ satisfies (i) unrestricted domain, (ii) pairwise unanimity, (iii) pairwise cardinal independence from irrelevant alternatives and (iv) pairwise cardinal non-dictatorship.

Proof:

(i)　　The condition of unrestricted domain is automatically satisfied because the aggregation procedure is defined on all pairwise reciprocal profiles without restriction.

(ii)　　Given $\mathbf{P} \in \mathfrak{P}^m$ such that for any pair A_i and A_j of $\mathfrak{A}$,

$P_k(A_i, A_j) > 1$ for all $k \in \mathfrak{M}$, then by definition,

$$f(\mathbf{P})(A_i, A_j) = \left[\prod_{k=1}^{m} P_k(A_i, A_j) \right]^{\frac{1}{m}} > 1$$

and f satisfies pairwise unanimity.

(iii)　　Let $\mathbf{P}$ and $\mathbf{Q}$ be two reciprocal pairwise profiles. Let $a_{ijk} \equiv P_k(A_i, A_j)$ and $b_{ijk} \equiv Q_k(A_i, A_j)$. Let $\mathbf{A} = \{A_i, A_j, A_l\} \subset \mathfrak{A}$. If $\mathbf{P}|_{\mathbf{A}} = \mathbf{Q}|_{\mathbf{A}}$, then $a_{ijk} = b_{ijk}$, $a_{ilk} = b_{ilk}$ and $a_{jlk} = b_{jlk}$, for all k, and $f(\mathbf{P})|_{\mathbf{A}} = f(\mathbf{Q})|_{\mathbf{A}}$ follows.

(iv)　　In general, the geometric mean of a set of (positive) numbers is not equal to any one of these numbers, and hence, it is non-dictatorial.

Thus, the geometric mean gives rise to an aggregate (*social*) reciprocal pairwise relation that satisfies all four of Arrow's conditions. Here we assumed that all members of the group have the same importance. However, when the individuals have different importance, Aczel and Alsina (1986) extended the foregoing Aczel and Saaty (1983) result.

Using paired comparisons to represent intensity of preference has not been used very often in social choice. Barrett et al. (1992) used ordinal pairwise fuzzy relations as representations of intensity of preference, and they concluded that under several alternative transitivity conditions the power of the group is restricted to a coalition or the group is indecisive. A transitivity condition they explore is known as quasitransitivity. In terms of our reciprocal pairwise comparisons it would be written as follows: if for all $A_i, A_j, A_s \in \mathfrak{A}$, $P(A_i, A_j) > 1 > P(A_j, A_i)$ and $P(A_j, A_s) > 1 > P(A_s, A_j)$ then $P(A_i, A_s) > 1 > P(A_s, A_i)$. This condition holds if the reciprocal pairwise comparisons are consistent;

i.e., $P(A_i, A_k) = P(A_i, A_j)P(A_j, A_k)$, for all i and j.

Consistency implies quasitransitivity, but the converse is not true.

To make group decisions it is not enough to only use pairwise comparisons, because the order implied by $A_i \succsim A_j$ if and only if (the geometric mean) $f(\mathbf{P})(A_i, A_j) \geq 1$ may not be acyclic. That is, the utility representation w generated by $f(\mathbf{P})(A_i, A_j)$ may be such that $A_i \succ A_j$ because $f(\mathbf{P})(A_i, A_j) > 1$, but $w(A_j) > w(A_i)$. Thus to decide that $A_i \succ A_j$, we need to derive a cardinal preference relation from the reciprocal pairwise relations.

3. CARDINAL PREFERENCE RELATIONS

To define cardinal preference relations we need to introduce the concept of a scale. A scale is a triple $(\mathfrak{A}, \mathbb{R}, w)$ where $\mathfrak{A}$ is a set of objects, $\mathbb{R}$ is a set of numbers and w is a mapping from the objects to the numbers, $w: \mathfrak{A} \to \mathbb{R}$, that must be invariant under transformation (Krants et al. 1971, Roberts 1979). The type of transformation defines the type of scale. Ordinal, interval, ratio and absolute scales are invariant under monotone, affine (positive linear), similarity (multiplication by a positive constant) and identity transformations, respectively. There are many other scales of which a well-known one, that is too weak to be useful in this study, is the nominal scale that is invariant under one-to-one correspondence. Let

$\mathfrak{C}$ denote the set of all possible functions from $\mathfrak{A}$ to the set of real numbers $\mathbb{R}$, $\mathfrak{C} = \{w \mid w : \mathfrak{A} \to \mathbb{R}\}$.

In the economics literature a *cardinal preference relation* over $\mathfrak{A}$ is a subset W of $\mathfrak{C}$ of utility functions such that if f belongs to W then so does $\alpha + \beta f$ for every real number α and every positive real number β, and if f and g both belong to W there is some real number α and some positive real number β such that $g = \alpha + \beta f$. This definition can be easily extended to a set of transformations T such that if f belongs to W then so does $\phi(f)$ for every ϕ in T, and for any two members f and g of W there is some ϕ in T such that $g = \phi(f)$. ϕ is called an invariance transformation that defines the kind of scale used.

If ϕ is any monotone transformation the scale is ordinal. Goodman and Markowitz (1952) assumed that preferences are expressed by means of a value function invariant under monotone transformations. They showed that if ϕ is also linear, then no social welfare function is possible. However, if ϕ is a positive similarity transformation then the only possible social welfare function is the product of the welfare functions of the individuals.

If ϕ is an affine transformation (i.e., a similarity transformation followed by a translation) then interval scales are used. Samuelson (1967) conjectured that Arrow's impossibility theorem should hold when individuals and the group express their "cardinal" preferences by the von-Neumann-Morgenstern (v-NM) utility functions known to belong to an interval scale. Campbell (1973) made a convincing case for the possibility of using intensity of preference in the formulation of the impossibility theorem, but he did not specify the type of function to be used. Kalai and Schmeidler (1977) proved Samuelson's conjecture: *If the set of alternatives contains 4 or more elements, then an aggregation procedure is continuous, satisfies cardinal independence from irrelevant alternatives and also satisfies unanimity if and only if it is cardinally dictatorial.* Later Hylland (1980) proved that the continuity condition is not necessary.

If ϕ is a similarity transformation then the scales involved are ratio scales. By assuming that individual utility functions belong to the same ratio scale, a restriction known as ratio scale full comparability (RSFC), Kevin Roberts (1980) showed that if a social welfare function satisfies the conditions of unrestricted domain, independence from irrelevant alternatives, the weak Pareto condition of strict preference, and invariance under positive similarity transformations, then there exists a social welfare function that preserves positive proportionality known as *homothetic* (i.e., $f(x) \geq f(y) \Leftrightarrow f(\lambda x) \geq f(\lambda y)$ for all $\lambda > 0$) that is not dictatorial.

The main theme emerging from these works is that in order for a non-dictatorial social function to exist, it must at least be invariant under similarity transformations, i.e., belong to a ratio scale.

In the traditional social choice literature (Kalai and Schmeidler 1977, Keeney 1976) a procedure for aggregating cardinal preferences is by definition a function φ from an m-fold Cartesian product of $\mathfrak{C}$ to $\mathfrak{C}$, i.e., $\varphi : \mathfrak{C}^m \to \mathfrak{C}$, a *social welfare function*. A *cardinal profile* is given by $W = (W_1, ..., W_m) \in \mathfrak{C}^m$. For a nonempty subset $\mathbf{A}$ of $\mathfrak{A}$ and W in $\mathfrak{C}$, $W|_{\mathbf{A}}$ denotes the cardinal preferences induced by W in $\mathbf{A}$. Arrow's conditions can now be stated as follows.

Unrestricted Domain: An aggregation procedure φ is said to satisfy the condition of *unrestricted domain* if its domain is all of $\mathfrak{C}^m$.

Pareto Principle: An aggregation procedure $\varphi : \mathfrak{C}^m \to \mathfrak{C}$ satisfies *unanimity* if and only if for any pair A_i and A_j of $\mathfrak{A}$ and any cardinal profile $W = (W_1, ..., W_m) \in \mathfrak{C}^m$, if $W_k(A_i) \geq W_k(A_j)$ for all $k \in \mathfrak{M}$ then $W(A_i) \geq W(A_j)$, where $W \equiv \varphi(W)$.
Note: $W_k(A_i) \geq W_k(A_j)$ if and only if $w_k(A_i) \geq w_k(A_j)$ for all $w_k \in W_k$.

Independence from Irrelevant Alternatives: An aggregation procedure is said to satisfy *cardinal independence from irrelevant* *alternatives* (CIIA) if for any subset **A** of $\mathfrak{A}$ with three elements, and for any two cardinal profiles W and V: $W|_\mathbf{A} = V|_\mathbf{A}$ implies $\varphi(W)|_\mathbf{A} = \varphi(V)|_\mathbf{A}$.

Non-Dictatorship: An aggregation procedure φ is *cardinally non-dictatorial* if there does not exist a member of the group, $d \in \mathfrak{M}$, such that for all the cardinal profiles $W \in \mathfrak{C}^m$, $\varphi(W) = W_d$, i.e., φ is the projection of W on the dth coordinate.

We are interested in a very specific type of cardinal preference relations, absolute cardinal preference relations, because the unidimensional scale derived from the pairwise comparisons (i.e., the principal right eigenvector) is an absolute ratio scale, i.e., a ratio scale with 1 as multiplier.

4. ABSOLUTE CARDINAL PREFERENCE RELATIONS

In this section we show that if the cardinal preferences of the individuals were to be represented by numbers from an absolute scale, and instead of just one comparison, several are considered, and each comparison by many individuals is aggregated by using the geometric mean from which then a group function is derived, then that function satisfies Arrow's conditions, both when the judgments of each individual are consistent and when they are not consistent.

We have seen in Section 3 that a cardinal preference relation is associated with some type of invariance transformation that defines the scale in which the intensity of preference is measured. If the invariance transformation is the identity, then the intensity of preference is measured on an absolute scale. Let $\mathcal{W}$ denote the set of all absolute cardinal preference relations over $\mathfrak{A}$. An *absolute cardinal preference relation* W over $\mathfrak{A}$ is a subset of $\mathcal{W}$ such that:

1. W is nonempty; and
2. If $w, v \in W$ then for all $A_i \in \mathfrak{A}$, $v(A_i) \equiv w(A_i)$, i.e., W contains one element.

Traditionally, the social choice literature has studied the aggregation of these individual cardinal preference functions, i.e., a social welfare function is a mapping from W^m to W. We instead study the aggregation of judgments from which an Arrowvian social welfare function can be derived. Thus, we establish a mapping from the set of reciprocal pairwise profiles $\mathfrak{P}^m$ to the set of absolute cardinal preference relations W through the set of reciprocal pairwise relations $\mathfrak{P}$, i.e., $\mathfrak{P}^m \rightarrow \mathfrak{P} \rightarrow W$. We distinguish between two cases, consistent and inconsistent reciprocal pairwise relations. Let $\mathfrak{P}_C$ and $\mathfrak{P}_I$ denote the sets of consistent and inconsistent reciprocal pairwise relations, respectively. Reciprocal pairwise relations can be represented using matrix notation. Let

$$
A = \begin{bmatrix}
\dfrac{x_1}{x_1} & \dfrac{x_1}{x_2} & \cdots & \dfrac{x_1}{x_n} \\[2mm]
\dfrac{x_2}{x_1} & \dfrac{x_2}{x_2} & \cdots & \dfrac{x_2}{x_n} \\[2mm]
\vdots & \vdots & \ddots & \vdots \\[2mm]
\dfrac{x_n}{x_1} & \dfrac{x_n}{x_2} & \cdots & \dfrac{x_n}{x_n}
\end{bmatrix}
$$

be a consistent pairwise relation. The entries of the matrix A satisfy the properties: $a_{ij} a_{jk} = a_{ik}$ and $a_{ij} a_{ji} = 1$ or $a_{ji} = a_{ij}^{-1}$. The former is known as the consistency property (Saaty 1977) and the latter as the reciprocal property . Conversely, if the matrix A is consistent, then its coefficients have the form $a_{ij} \equiv \dfrac{x_i}{x_j}$. Thus, by multiplying the matrix A of pairwise comparisons by the vector of measurements $\mathbf{x} = (x_1, x_2, ..., x_n)^T$ we have $A\mathbf{x} = n\mathbf{x}$. Since $\text{Trace}(A) = n$, the $\text{Trace}(A)$ is equal to the sum of the eigenvalues of A, and the rank$(A) = 1$, it follows that n is the only non-zero eigenvalue of A, and the vector $\mathbf{x}$ is its associated (principal) right eigenvector. Therefore, to recover the measurements from the matrix when it is consistent it is sufficient (but not necessary) to solve an eigenvalue problem. In this simple case, the principal right eigenvector is any column of A because an eigenvector is unique to within a multiplicative constant. We next show that it is both *necessary and sufficient* when the matrix is not consistent (inconsistent).

If the vector of measurements **x** is unknown then the relative paired comparisons would have to be estimated. That is, when the exact value $a_{ij} \equiv \dfrac{x_i}{x_j}$ is not known, we obtain an approximation to it made by judgment as $\hat{a}_{ij} = \left(\dfrac{x_i}{x_j}\right)\varepsilon_{ij}$. In that case $\hat{a}_{ji} = \left(\dfrac{x_j}{x_i}\right)\varepsilon_{ji}$ where the ε_{ij}'s are perturbations that satisfy $\varepsilon_{ij}\varepsilon_{ji} = 1$. A perturbation theorem (Saaty 1977) in matrix algebra assures us that to obtain an estimate $\hat{\mathbf{x}}$ of the vector **x** it is sufficient to solve the principal eigenvalue problem $\hat{A}\hat{\mathbf{x}} = \lambda_{\max}\hat{\mathbf{x}}$, where $\hat{A}$ is the n-by-n matrix of judgments $\hat{a}_{ij}$ (perturbations of the $a_{ij} = x_i / x_j$) and $\lambda_{\max}$ is its principal eigenvalue. It turns out that the principal eigenvector is also necessary because comparisons involve the concept of dominance which says how much one object is preferred over another. Transitivity requires considering paths of different lengths between the two objects and calculating the intensity of dominance along its arcs. Each of these lengths is given by the corresponding power of A. When A is consistent, $A^k = n^{k-1}A$, and thus, all order transitivity is obtained as a constant times A. That is not the case when A is inconsistent(i.e., reciprocal but not consistent). In that case one must consider all powers of A obtaining the vector of dominance from the normalized sum of its rows for each power of A. The average of these vectors in the limit coincides with the principal right eigenvector of A (Saaty 2001).

The absolute cardinal preference relation associated with a pairwise preference relation is the principal right eigenvector of the matrix of pairwise comparison judgments.

Suppose that the purpose of collective choice is the selection of one of the objects from among the n objects according to a criterion.

For example, the objects could be alternative health care policies, and the criterion could be the estimated cost of implementing each of them. Each individual k in the group would provide a matrix of pairwise comparisons A_k and the objective is to combine them to produce a single pairwise comparison matrix that would represent the preferences of the group. From this matrix we derive a relative scale of priorities as its principal right eigenvector. This scale is the social welfare function.

We can now approach the problem of constructing a social welfare function as depicted in the diagram given in Figure 14.1.

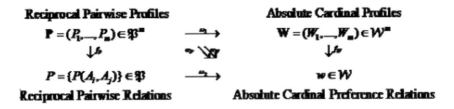

Figure 14.1 Mapping of priority and judgment spaces. The social welfare functions $\sigma_P = \omega_2 \circ f_P$ and $\sigma_W = f_W \circ \omega_1$

$\sigma_P = \omega_2 \circ f_P$ is the synthesis of f_P that first maps reciprocal pairwise profiles **P** to a reciprocal pairwise relation P, and ω_2 that maps a reciprocal pairwise relation P to a final cardinal preference relation w measured on an absolute scale. The traditional approach would be similar to the mapping $\sigma_W = f_W \circ \omega_1$ that first maps each individual reciprocal pairwise relation P_k to its individual absolute cardinal preference relation W_k and then maps all the individual cardinal relations to a cardinal preference relation w which in our case would be measured on an absolute scale. The two mappings σ_P and σ_W yield the same result when the number of alternatives n is equal to three, or when they are restricted to consistent pairwise profiles, but for $n \geq 4$ they may not coincide.

The social welfare function is given by the principal right eigenvector of the matrix associated with the mapping $\sigma_P = \omega_2 \circ f_P$ (Figure 14.2).

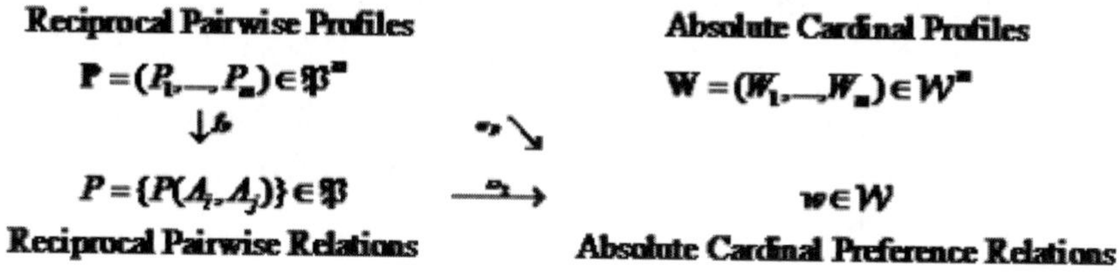

Reciprocal Pairwise Profiles

$\mathbf{P} = (P_1, \ldots P_m) \in \mathfrak{P}^m$

↓ f_P

$\mathbf{P} = \{P(A_i, A_j)\} \in \mathfrak{P}$

Reciprocal Pairwise Relations

Absolute Cardinal Profiles

$\mathbf{W} = (W_1, \ldots W_m) \in \mathcal{W}^m$

σ_P ↘

$\longrightarrow \omega_2$

$w \in \mathcal{W}$

Absolute Cardinal Preference Relations

Figure 14. 2 The social welfare mapping $\sigma_P = \omega_2 \circ f_P$

(Note here that in Figure 14.2 we have intentionally left out the arrows between $\mathfrak{P}^m$ and $\mathcal{W}^m$ and between $\mathcal{W}^m$ and $\mathcal{W}$ because there are no mappings.)

Formally, this can be summarized as follows. Let f_P be the geometric mean aggregation procedure from $\mathfrak{P}^m$ to $\mathfrak{P}$, i.e., $f_P(\mathbf{P}) = P$. Let ω_2 be a mapping from $\mathfrak{P}$ to $\mathcal{W}$ that assigns to each P in $\mathfrak{P}$ the principal right eigenvector w of the corresponding matrix $\{a_{ij} \equiv P(A_i, A_j)\}$, i.e. $\omega_2(P) \equiv w$. Let σ_P be the aggregation procedure from $\mathfrak{P}^m$ to $\mathcal{W}$. Note that σ_P assigns reciprocal pairwise profiles $\mathbf{P}$ to absolute cardinal relations w, i.e.;

$$\sigma_P(\mathbf{P}) = (\omega_2 \circ f_P)(\mathbf{P}) = \omega_2(f_P(\mathbf{P})) = \omega_2(P) = w.$$

We define Arrow's conditions for this mixed aggregation procedure as follows:

Unrestricted Domain: An aggregation procedure σ_P is said to satisfy the condition of *unrestricted domain* if its domain is all of $\mathfrak{P}^m$.

Pareto Principle: An aggregation procedure $\sigma_P : \mathfrak{P}^m \to \mathcal{W}$ satisfies *unanimity* if and only if for any pair A_i and A_j of $\mathfrak{A}$ and any reciprocal pairwise profile **P**, $P_k(A_i, A_j) \geq 1$ for all $k \in \mathfrak{M}$ implies $w(A_i) \geq w(A_j)$, where $w = \sigma_P(\mathbf{P})$.

Independence from Irrelevant Alternatives: An aggregation procedure σ_P is said to satisfy *cardinal independence from irrelevant alternatives* (CIIA) if for any subset **A** of $\mathfrak{A}$ with three elements and for any two reciprocal pairwise profiles **P** and **Q**: $\mathbf{P}|_\mathbf{A} = \mathbf{Q}|_\mathbf{A}$ implies $w|_\mathbf{A} = v|_\mathbf{A}$, where $w = \sigma_P(\mathbf{P})$ and $v = \sigma_P(\mathbf{Q})$.

Non-Dictatorship: A pairwise aggregation procedure σ_P is said to be *cardinally non-dictatorial* if there is no group member $d \in \mathfrak{M}$ such that for all $\mathbf{P} \in \mathfrak{P}^m$, $\sigma_P(\mathbf{P}) = w_d$.

We now show that this composite aggregation procedure $\sigma_P = \omega_2 \circ f_P$ in fact satisfies *Arrow's conditions*. We distinguish two mutually exclusive situations: consistent ($\mathfrak{P}_\mathfrak{C}^m$) and inconsistent ($\mathfrak{P}_\mathfrak{J}^m$) pairwise profiles, i.e. $\mathfrak{P} = \mathfrak{P}_\mathfrak{C}^m \cup \mathfrak{P}_\mathfrak{J}^m$.

4.1 Consistent profiles

Theorem 2: The aggregation procedure $\sigma_P : \mathfrak{P}_\mathfrak{C}^m \rightarrow \mathcal{W}$ defined on consistent pairwise profiles ($\mathfrak{P}_\mathfrak{C}^m$) satisfies unanimity, cardinal independence from irrelevant alternatives and it is non-dictatorial.

Proof: Let $\mathbf{P} = \left(P_k(A_i, A_j) \equiv \dfrac{w_{ik}}{w_{jk}}, k = 1, 2, ..., m \right)$ be a consistent pairwise profile. We have

$$\sigma_P(\mathbf{P}) = (\omega_2 \circ f_P)(\mathbf{P}) = \omega_2(P) = \omega_2 \left(P(A_i, A_j) = \dfrac{\prod\limits_{k=1}^{m} w_{ik}^{1/m}}{\prod\limits_{k=1}^{m} w_{jk}^{1/m}} \right).$$

$$= \left(\prod\limits_{k=1}^{m} w_{ik}^{1/m}, i = 1, ..., n \right) = w$$

Also, $\quad \sigma_W(\mathbf{P}) = (f_W \circ \omega_1)(\mathbf{P}) = f_W(\omega_1(P_1), ..., \omega_1(P_m)) = f_W(w_1, ..., w_m)$

where $\omega_1(P_k) = w_k = (w_{1k}, ..., w_{nk})^T$ and we have

$$\sigma_W(\mathbf{P}) = \left(\prod_{k=1}^{m} w_{1k}^{1/m}, ..., \prod_{k=1}^{m} w_{nk}^{1/m} \right)^T = w \quad \text{and} \quad \text{hence,} \quad \sigma_P = \sigma_W \text{ on}$$

consistent pairwise profiles. In addition, because we have shown that the geometric mean satisfies *Arrow's conditions*, it follows that $\sigma_P = \sigma_W$ also satisfies these conditions.

We note that σ_P defined on consistent profiles has the multiplicative form given by $\sigma_W(\mathbf{P}) = \left(\prod_{k=1}^{m} w_{1k}^{1/m}, ..., \prod_{k=1}^{m} w_{nk}^{1/m} \right)^T$. The social welfare functions developed by DeMeyer and Plott (1971) and Kaneko and Nakamura (1979) also have a multiplicative form. DeMeyer and Plott showed that for pairwise intensity of preferences given by ratios $\left\{ \dfrac{x_i^k}{x_j^k}, k = 1, ..., m \right\}$, rather than perturbations of ratios of the form $\left\{ \hat{a}_{ij}^k = \left(\dfrac{x_i^k}{x_j^k} \right) \varepsilon_{ij}^k, k = 1, ..., m \right\}$ as we assumed above, invariant under similarity transformations (i.e., multiplication by a positive constant), there exists a non-dictatorial social welfare function of the form $\prod_{k=1}^{m} (x_i^k)^K$, where K is a real number. DeMeyer and Plott's social welfare function is an extension of Nash's solution of the bargaining problem in which the welfare of a group is maximized by considering the payoffs resulting from the product of individual utilities (Nash 1950).

4.2 Inconsistent profiles

When σ_P is defined on inconsistent reciprocal pairwise profiles, unanimity and cardinal independence from irrelevant alternatives do not always hold. With consistency, if $P_k(A_i, A_j) \geq 1$ for all k, then $w(A_i) \geq w(A_j)$. However, with inconsistency unanimity may not be satisfied and we need to define conditions under which this also holds. One such condition is pairwise dominance.

Pairwise Dominance: A pairwise relation P_k is said to satisfy *pairwise dominance* if for all pairs of alternatives i and j, the following condition holds:
$$P_k(A_i, A_l) \geq P_k(A_j, A_l), \text{ for all } l \text{ or } P_k(A_j, A_l) \geq P_k(A_i, A_l), \text{ for all } l.$$

Pairwise dominance implies that given any two rows of the matrix associated with the pairwise relation $\{a_{ijk} \equiv P_k(A_i, A_j)\}$, one row always dominates the other, i.e., $a_{ilk} \geq a_{jlk}$, for all l, or $a_{jlk} \geq a_{ilk}$, for all l. Pairwise dominance implies transitivity, for then if row i dominates row j and row j dominates row k, then row i dominates row k.

Let P_k be a reciprocal pairwise relation that satisfies pairwise dominance. Let $w_k = \omega_2(P_k)$ be the corresponding absolute cardinal relation. By construction, if for a pair of alternatives i and j, we have $P_k(A_i, A_l) \geq P_k(A_j, A_l)$ for all l then the corresponding cardinal relation satisfies $w_k(A_i) \geq w_k(A_j)$.

A reciprocal pairwise profile satisfies pairwise dominance if all its reciprocal pairwise relations satisfy pairwise dominance. This means that if alternative i is preferred to alternative j then alternative i is preferred to the other alternatives more than alternative j is preferred to them. Using this condition the Pareto principle can now be modified as follows.

Pareto Principle with Pairwise Dominance: An aggregation procedure $\gamma_P : \mathfrak{P}^m \to \mathfrak{P}$ satisfies *strong unanimity* if and only if for any pair A_i and A_j of $\mathfrak{A}$ and any reciprocal pairwise profile $\mathbf{P}$,
$$P_k(A_i, A_l) \geq P_k(A_j, A_l) \quad \text{for} \quad \text{all} \quad l \quad \text{and} \quad \text{all } k \in \mathfrak{M}, \quad \text{implies}$$
$$P(A_i, A_l) \geq P(A_j, A_l) \text{ for all } l, \text{ where } \gamma_P(\mathbf{P}) = P \in \mathfrak{P}.$$

Note that for pairwise profiles, strong unanimity implies unanimity. To see this, we substitute $l = j$ in $P_k(A_i, A_l) \geq P_k(A_j, A_l)$, we have $P_k(A_i, A_j) \geq P_k(A_j, A_j) = 1$ for all k, and $P(A_i, A_j) \geq P(A_j, A_j) = 1$ follows.

Let $\mathfrak{P}_{\mathfrak{D}} \subset \mathfrak{P}$ be the set of reciprocal pairwise relations that satisfy pairwise dominance. Let $\sigma_P |_{\mathfrak{D}} : \mathfrak{P}_{\mathfrak{J}}^m \to W$ be the restriction of σ_P to $\mathfrak{P}_{\mathfrak{D}}^m \subset \mathfrak{P}_{\mathfrak{J}}^m$.

Theorem 3: The geometric mean aggregation procedure γ_P restricted to $\mathfrak{P}_{\mathfrak{D}}^m \subset \mathfrak{P}_{\mathfrak{J}}^m$ satisfies strong unanimity.

Proof: Let $\mathbf{P} = (P_1, ..., P_m) \in \mathfrak{P}_{\mathfrak{D}}^m \subset \mathfrak{P}^m$ be a reciprocal pairwise profile that satisfies pairwise dominance. Then, for any pair of alternatives i and j, $P_k(A_i, A_l) \geq P_k(A_j, A_l)$, for all l and k, we have

$$f_P(\mathbf{P})(A_i, A_l) = \left[\prod_{k=1}^m P_k(A_i, A_l) \right]^{\frac{1}{m}} \geq \left[\prod_{k=1}^m P_k(A_j, A_l) \right]^{\frac{1}{m}} = f_P(\mathbf{P})(A_j, A_l)$$

or
$P(A_i, A_l) \geq P(A_j, A_l)$ for all l
and the geometric mean satisfies strong unanimity.

Theorem 4: The aggregation procedure $\sigma_P |_{\mathfrak{D}} : \mathfrak{P}_{\mathfrak{J}}^m \to W$ satisfies unanimity, cardinal independence from irrelevant alternatives and it is non-dictatorial.
Proof: Let $\mathbf{P} = (P_1, ..., P_m)$ be a reciprocal cardinal profile. From Theorem 2, γ_P satisfies strong unanimity, i.e., for every pair of alternatives (i, j), $f_P(\mathbf{P})(A_i, A_l) \geq f_P(\mathbf{P})(A_j, A_l)$ for all l, or $a_{il} = P(A_i, A_l) \geq P(A_j, A_l) = a_{jl}$ for all l, and hence, by construction

$$\sum_{l=1}^n a_{il} w(A_l) \geq \sum_{l=1}^n a_{jl} w(A_l) \quad \text{or} \quad w(A_i) \geq w(A_j) \quad \text{and} \quad \sigma_P |_{\mathfrak{D}} \quad \text{satisfies}$$

unanimity.

Let **P** and **Q** be two reciprocal pairwise profiles and let w and v the corresponding absolute cardinal relations, respectively. If for any subset **A** of $\mathfrak{A}$ with three elements $\mathbf{P}|_{\mathbf{A}} = \mathbf{Q}|_{\mathbf{A}}$ is true, then by Theorem 1 the geometric mean aggregation procedure satisfies pairwise independence from irrelevant alternatives and hence $f_P(\mathbf{P})|_{\mathbf{A}} = f_P(\mathbf{Q})|_{\mathbf{A}}$. Let $f_P(\mathbf{P}) = P$ and $f_P(\mathbf{Q}) = Q$, and let $w = \omega_2(P)$ and $v = \omega_2(Q)$. We have

$$\sigma_P|_{\mathfrak{D}}(\mathbf{P})|_{\mathbf{A}} = (\omega_2 \circ f_P)(\mathbf{P})|_{\mathbf{A}} = \omega_2(f_P(\mathbf{P})|_{\mathbf{A}}) = \omega_2(f_P(\mathbf{Q})|_{\mathbf{A}}) =$$

$$\in (\omega_2 \circ f_P)(\mathbf{Q})|_{\mathbf{A}} = \sigma_P|_{\mathfrak{D}}(\mathbf{Q})|_{\mathbf{A}}$$

and thus $w|_{\mathbf{A}} = v|_{\mathbf{A}}$.

Let $\mathbf{P} = (P_1, ..., P_m) \in \mathfrak{P}_{\mathfrak{D}}^m$ and $w = \sigma_P(\mathbf{P}) \in \mathcal{W}$. $\sigma_P|_{\mathfrak{D}}: \mathfrak{P}^m \to \mathcal{W}$ is dictatorial if there is a member d of the group for which $\sigma_P(\mathbf{P}) = w_d$. For this to happen, the following must hold: $\sigma_P(\mathbf{P}) = \omega_2(f_P(\mathbf{P})) = \omega_2(P_d)$ and $w(A_i) = w_d(A_i)$ for all i. But by Theorem 1, the geometric mean aggregation procedure f_P is non-dictatorial, i.e., $f_P(\mathbf{P}) \neq P_d$, from which we have $\sigma_P(\mathbf{P}) = \omega_2(f_P(\mathbf{P})) \neq \omega_2(P_d)$ and hence, $\sigma_P|_{\mathfrak{D}}: \mathfrak{P}^m \to \mathcal{W}$ is non-dictatorial.

Note that although the aggregation procedure is defined on the set of reciprocal pairwise relations that satisfy pairwise dominance, the condition of unrestricted domain is not violated. Consider three individuals and three alternatives, $A_i, i = 1, 2, 3$, whereby the first person has the ordering $A_1 \succ A_2 \succ A_3$; the second person the ordering $A_2 \succ A_3 \succ A_1$; and the third person the ordering $A_3 \succ A_1 \succ A_2$. We show below that the ordering $A_1 \,\square\, A_2 \,\square\, A_3$ is possible.

Let $\{a_{ijk}, i, j, k = 1, 2, 3\}$ be their reciprocal pairwise preferences. To conform with these three different orderings along with pairwise dominance, these preferences must satisfy the following conditions:

Person 1: $A_1 \succ A_2 \succ A_3$ implies that the entries of the matrix

$$\begin{pmatrix} 1 & a_{121} & a_{131} \\ a_{121}^{-1} & 1 & a_{231} \\ a_{131}^{-1} & a_{231}^{-1} & 1 \end{pmatrix}$$ must satisfy $a_{121} > 1$, $a_{131} > a_{231}$, $a_{121}^{-1} > a_{131}^{-1}$ and

$a_{231} > 1$, i.e., pairwise dominance.

Person 2: $A_2 \succ A_3 \succ A_1$ implies that the entries of the matrix

$$\begin{pmatrix} 1 & a_{122} & a_{132} \\ a_{122}^{-1} & 1 & a_{232} \\ a_{132}^{-1} & a_{232}^{-1} & 1 \end{pmatrix}$$ must satisfy $a_{122}^{-1} > a_{132}^{-1}$, $a_{232} > 1$, $a_{232}^{-1} > a_{122}$ and

$a_{132} < 1$.

Person 3: $A_3 \succ A_1 \succ A_2$ implies that the entries of the matrix

$$\begin{pmatrix} 1 & a_{123} & a_{133} \\ a_{123}^{-1} & 1 & a_{233} \\ a_{133}^{-1} & a_{233}^{-1} & 1 \end{pmatrix}$$ must satisfy $a_{133} < 1$, $a_{233}^{-1} > a_{123}$, $a_{133} > a_{233}$ and

$a_{123} > 1$.

The social reciprocal pairwise relation is given by the matrix of geometric means

$$\begin{pmatrix} 1 & \prod_{k=1}^{3} a_{12k}^{-3} & \prod_{k=1}^{3} a_{13k}^{-3} \\ \prod_{k=1}^{3} a_{12k}^{3} & 1 & \prod_{k=1}^{3} a_{23k}^{-3} \\ \prod_{k=1}^{3} a_{13k}^{3} & \prod_{k=1}^{3} a_{23k}^{3} & 1 \end{pmatrix}$$

It is also known (Saaty 1980) that the principal right eigenvector of a 3-by-3 reciprocal matrix is given by the geometric mean of its rows. This is not true for higher order matrices. The ordering $A_1 \square A_2 \square A_3$ would be induced if the principal right eigenvector of the matrix of geometric means is the vector $\left(\dfrac{1}{3}, \dfrac{1}{3}, \dfrac{1}{3}\right)^T$. Thus, we must have

$$\left(\prod_{k=1}^{3} a_{12k}^{-3} \prod_{k=1}^{3} a_{13k}^{-3}\right)^{-3} = K, \qquad \left(\prod_{k=1}^{3} a_{12k}^{3} \prod_{k=1}^{3} a_{23k}^{-3}\right)^{-3} = K \qquad \text{and}$$

$$\left(\prod_{k=1}^{3} a_{13k}^{3} \prod_{k=1}^{3} a_{23k}^{3}\right)^{-3} = K \quad \text{which upon normalization to unity would}$$

yield the vector $\left(\dfrac{1}{3}, \dfrac{1}{3}, \dfrac{1}{3}\right)^{T}$. Note that $K=1$ because

$$\left(\prod_{k=1}^{3} a_{12k}^{3} \prod_{k=1}^{3} a_{23k}^{-3}\right)^{-3}\left(\prod_{k=1}^{3} a_{13k}^{3} \prod_{k=1}^{3} a_{23k}^{3}\right)^{-3} = K^{2} \text{ and}$$

$$\left(\prod_{k=1}^{3} a_{12k}^{3} \prod_{k=1}^{3} a_{23k}^{-3}\right)^{-3}\left(\prod_{k=1}^{3} a_{13k}^{3} \prod_{k=1}^{3} a_{23k}^{3}\right)^{-3} = \left(\prod_{k=1}^{3} a_{12k}^{3} \prod_{k=1}^{3} a_{13k}^{3}\right)^{-3} = 1/K \text{, and}$$

hence, we have $K^{2} = 1/K$ or $K^{3} = 1$. Since $K>0$, we have $K=1$ that

yields $\prod_{k=1}^{3} a_{12k}^{-3} = \prod_{k=1}^{3} a_{13k}^{3} = \prod_{k=1}^{3} a_{23k}^{-3} = a$, a positive constant. In sum, the

social pairwise preference relation is given by the matrix

$\begin{pmatrix} 1 & a & a^{-1} \\ a^{-1} & 1 & a \\ a & a^{-1} & 1 \end{pmatrix}$. This shows that the existence of such a social

reciprocal pairwise relation and the ensuing absolute cardinal relation
is not restricted by pairwise dominance. Of course, what is considered
a three way tie in an ordinal setting need not be when cardinal
intensity of preference is considered. For example, if the three people
had the reciprocal pairwise relations given by

$$A_1 \succ A_2 \succ A_3 \qquad\qquad A_2 \succ A_3 \succ A_1 \qquad\qquad A_3 \succ A_1 \succ A_2$$

$$Person\ 1: \begin{pmatrix} 1 & 2 & 4 \\ 1/2 & 1 & 3 \\ 1/6 & 1/2 & 1 \end{pmatrix}, \quad Person\ 2: \begin{pmatrix} 1 & 1/6 & 1/5 \\ 6 & 1 & 3 \\ 5 & 1/5 & 1 \end{pmatrix}, \quad \begin{matrix} Person\ 3: \end{matrix} \begin{pmatrix} 1 & 5 & 1/2 \\ 1/5 & 1 & 1/6 \\ 2 & 6 & 1 \end{pmatrix}$$

the social reciprocal pairwise relation would be given by

$$
\begin{pmatrix}
1 & \prod\limits_{k=1}^{3} a_{12k}^{-3} & \prod\limits_{k=1}^{3} a_{13k}^{-3} \\
\prod\limits_{k=1}^{3} a_{12k}^{3} & 1 & \prod\limits_{k=1}^{3} a_{23k}^{-3} \\
\prod\limits_{k=1}^{3} a_{13k}^{3} & \prod\limits_{k=1}^{3} a_{23k}^{3} & 1
\end{pmatrix}
=
\begin{pmatrix}
1 & \left(10/6\right)^{1/3} & \left(4/10\right)^{1/3} \\
\left(10/6\right)^{-1/3} & 1 & \left(9/6\right)^{1/3} \\
\left(4/10\right)^{-1/3} & \left(9/6\right)^{-1/3} & 1
\end{pmatrix}
$$

And the corresponding social absolute cardinal relation represented by the principal right eigenvector would be given by the vector $(0.3184, 0.3291, 0.3525)^{T}$ which yields the ordering $A_3 \succ A_2 \succ A_1$, which is not an ordering of any of the group members.

5. EXAMPLE

To illustrate our approach we have selected the House Appropriations Subcommittee on Defense of the United States House of Representatives. The subcommittee ranked not just the different objectives, the troops' well-being, weapon systems and fiscal responsibility, but also made tradeoffs among them to produce the set of allocations given in the Fiscal Year 2009 Defense Appropriations Bill. Thus, to make the type of tradeoffs the Appropriations Subcommittee made we need to express preferences with a degree of intensity, e.g., "the troops' well-being is moderately more important than weapons systems." This type of comparison is known as a cardinal pairwise comparison or judgment.

Let us assume that the Appropriations Subcommittee consists of five people and that they wish to distribute an additional budget amount of $99 billion among three "key investments" as they call them in (Juola 2008): Keeping our commitments to our troops and their families (Troops' Well-Being"), weapons programs ("Weapons Systems") and improving fiscal responsibility ("Fiscal Responsibility"). Each member of the subcommittee compares the three investments in pairs. In this case there are three pairs. For each pair, each member gives a judgment as to which investment is more important, and how much more important, in his/her opinion, to reach the goals mentioned above. For example, to attain the objectives, what is more important "Troops' Well-Being" or "Weapons Systems" and how much more important?

Judgments are translated into numerical values using the 1-9 scale in Figure 3. For theoretical and empirical **derivation** and **validation** of this scale with numerous examples see for example (Saaty 1980; 2000).

THE FUNDAMENTAL 1-9 SCALE FOR PAIRWISE COMPARISONS

Intensity of importance	Definition	Explanation
1	Equal importance	Two elements contribute equally to the objective
3	Moderate importance	Experience and judgment slightly favor one element over another
5	Strong importance	Experience and judgment strongly favor one element over another
7	Very strong importance	An activity is favored very strongly over another
9	Absolute importance	The evidence favoring one activity over another is of the highest possible order of affirmation
2, 4, 6, 8	Used for intermediate values	
Decimals	1.1, 1.2, 1.3, ...1.9	For comparing elements that are very close
Rational numbers	Ratios arising from the values above that may be greater than 9	In order to complete the matrix if consistency were to be forced based on an initial set of n numerical values
Reciprocals	If element i has one of the above nonzero numbers assigned to it when compared with element j, then j has the reciprocal value when compared with i	If the judgment is k in the (i, j) position in matrix A, then the judgment $1/k$ must be entered in the inverse position (j, i).

Figure 3 The 1-9 Scale

Using the summary of the 2009 appropriations subcommittee, in which they wrote (Juola 2008):

"The Defense Appropriations bill puts troops first, preparing them for whatever emergencies may arise, providing them with first class weapons and equipment, and ensuring that they and their families are well taken care of.

The bill makes critical investments into the health, well-being and readiness of our forces. These recommendations address issues raised by troops, their families and Department of Defense officials in testimony before the Congress, and discovered through visits to military bases across the United States and overseas.

At the same time, the bill realizes its obligation to meet the recent dependence on the use of contractors with increased support for their management and oversight. It likewise makes a commitment to fiscal responsibility."

we translated these writings (for illustrative purposes only) into judgments as given in Table 1. A pairwise comparison, for example, "Troops' Well-Being" versus "Weapons Systems", for an individual consists in identifying the "key investment" he prefers less, say "Weapons Systems", and estimating numerically how many times more important the more preferred investment ("Troops' Well-Being") is than the less preferred one ("Weapons Systems") using the scale in Figure 3 (Saaty 1977). Assume that the five committee members provided the judgments (2, 3, 2, 2, 2), respectively. The less preferred investment is then assigned the reciprocal value when compared with the more preferred one (i.e., 1/2, 1/3, 1/2, 1/2, 1/2). The comparisons are arranged in a three by three matrix as given in Table 1, matrix 1.

Table 1a Individual judgments

Goal: Strengthen US Armed Forces and US security

	Troops' Well-being	Weapons Systems	Fiscal Responsibility
Troops' Well-being	1	(2,3,2,2,2)	(5,5,2,4,4)
Weapons Systems	(1/2, 1/3, 1/2, 1/2, 1/2)	1	(2,3,3,3,1)
Fiscal Responsibility	(1/5, 1/5, 1/2, 1/4, 1/4)	(1/2, 1/3, 1/3, 1/3, 1)	1

Table 1b Geometric mean of individual judgments

Goal: Strengthen US Armed Forces and US security

	Troops' Well-being	Weapons Systems	Fiscal Responsibility
Troops' Well-being	1	2.1689	3.8073
Weapons Systems	1/2.1689	1	2.2206
Fiscal Responsibility	1/3.8073	1/2.2206	1

The individual judgments or pairwise comparisons are then synthesized by taking their geometric mean (Aczel and Saaty 1983) (see Table 1, matrix 2), and finally, a set of priorities is derived using the eigenvalue model (Saaty 1977) explained above. If all the decision makers agree on a numerical pairwise estimate, i.e., consensus is reached and there is no need for the geometric mean synthesis which of course if used, gives back the common value of the decision makers. Table 2 gives the committee's and estimated relative funding priorities resulting from this exercise. The priorities derived induce a ranking on the alternatives that are compared.

Table 2 Group funding priorities versus estimated priorities

	Committee	**Estimated**
Troops' Well-being	57.14%	57.42%
Weapons Systems	28.57%	28.63%
Fiscal Responsibility	14.29%	13.95%

Most collective choice problems have multiple criteria. Thus, in addition to having to aggregate judgments under each criterion, we also need to aggregate social choice functions across criteria. The theory that pulls all this together, on which the concepts of this chapter are based, is the Analytic Hierarchy Process (AHP) (Saaty 1977;

1980). It has been applied in a wide variety of settings (Saaty 2001; Saaty and Vargas 2006).

6. CONCLUSIONS

We have shown by construction that with reciprocal pairwise relations represented on an absolute scale and satisfying strong unanimity (i.e., pairwise dominance) and cardinal independence from irrelevant alternatives, a non-dictatorial social welfare function exists. One aspect that cardinal preferences bring out, that seems difficult to include in ordinal preferences, is the importance of the judges themselves. It is not at all clear how to include the importance of a judge with his ordinal preference judgments when combining them into priority functions, but it can be done with cardinal preferences (Aczel and Alsina 1986).

References

Aczel, J. and C. Alsina (1986). "On Synthesis of Judgments." <u>Socio-Economic Planning Sciences</u> **20**: 333-339.

Aczel, J. and T. L. Saaty (1983). "Procedures for Synthesizing Ratio Judgments." <u>Journal of Mathematical Psychology</u> **27**: 93-102.

Barrett, C. R., P. K. Pattanaik and M. Salles (1992). "Rationality and Aggregation of Preferences in an Ordinally Fuzzy Framework." <u>Fuzzy Sets and Systems</u> **49**: 9-13.

Campbell, D. E. (1973). "Social Choice and Intensity of Preference." <u>Journal of Political Economy</u> **81**(1): 211-218.

DeMeyer, F. and C. R. Plott (1971). "A Welfare Function Using "Relative Intensity" of Preference." <u>Quarterly Journal of Economics</u> **85**(1): 179-186.

Goodman, L. A. and H. Markowitz (1952). "Social Welfare Functions Based on Individual Rankings." <u>American Journal of Sociology</u> **58**(3): 257-262.

Hylland, A. (1980). "Aggregation procedure for cardinal preferences: A comment." <u>Econometrica</u> **48**(2): 539-542.

Juola, P. (2008). Summary: FY09 Defense Appropriations BIll, U.S. House of Representatives: Committee on Appropriations.

Kalai, E. and D. Schmeidler (1977). "Aggregation Procedure for Cardinal Preferences: A Formulation and Proof of Samuelson's Impossibility Conjecture." Econometrica **45**(6): 1431-1438.

Kaneko, M. and K. Nakamura (1979). "The Nash Social Welfare Function." Econometrica **47**(2): 423-436.

Keeney, R. L. (1976). "A Group Preference Axiomatization with Cardinal Utility." Management Science **23**(2): 140-145.

Krantz, D. H., R. D. Luce, P. Suppes and A. Tversky (1971). Foundations of Measurement Vol. I. New York, Academic Press.

Nash, J. (1950). "The Bargaining Problem." Econometrica **18**: 155-162.

Roberts, F. S. (1979). Measurement Theory with Applications to Decisionmaking, Utility and the Social Sciences. Encyclopedia of Mathematics and Its Applications, G.-C. Rota. Reading, MA, Addison-Wesley Publishing Company.

Roberts, K. W. S. (1980). "Interpersonal Comparability and Social Choice Theory." The Review of Economic Studies **27**(2): 421-439.

Saaty, T. L. (1977). "A Scaling Method for Priorities in Hierarchical Structures." Journal of Mathematical Psychology **15**: 234-281.

Saaty, T. L. (1980). The Analytic Hierarchy Process. New York, McGraw Hill.

Saaty, T. L. (2000). Fundamentals of Decision Making with the Analytic Hierarchy Process. Pittsburgh, PA, RWS Publications.

Saaty, T. L. (2001). The Analytic Network Process. Pittsburgh, PA, RWS Publications.

Saaty, T. L. and L. G. Vargas (2006). Decision Making with the Analytic Network Process. International Series in Operations Research and Management Science, F. E. Hillier, Springer.

Samuelson, P. (1967). Arrow's Mathematical Politics. Human Values and Economic Policy. S. Hook. New York, New Your University Press: 41-51.

Appendix

Inconsistency of Group Judgments

We have mentioned the need to accommodate inconsistency in human judgment within bounds to improve understanding when new information causes us to revise our thinking and beliefs about the world. The question now is: when individual judgments are aggregated by the geometric mean into group judgments, what can one say about the degree or of inconsistency of the group as it relates to the inconsistency of the individuals involved? Can it get to be wildly inconsistent so that its meaning is lost in the diversity of judgments used? This is undoubtedly an interesting and important question that has to be answered. That the inconsistency of the group cannot exceed the largest inconsistency of any of its members can be easily seen in the case of three alternatives and m individuals. Let

$$
\begin{bmatrix}
1 & a_{12k} & a_{13k} \\
1/a_{12k} & 1 & a_{23k} \\
1/a_{13k} & 1/a_{23k} & 1
\end{bmatrix}
$$

be the matrix of judgments of the kth individual. Its principal eigenvalue derived elsewhere, is known to be $\lambda_k = 1 + \left(a_{12k}a_{23k}a_{31k}\right)^{1/3} + \left(a_{13k}a_{32k}a_{21k}\right)^{1/3}$ [23]. Let

$$
\begin{bmatrix}
1 & a_{12} & a_{13} \\
1/a_{12} & 1 & a_{23} \\
1/a_{13} & 1/a_{23} & 1
\end{bmatrix}
$$
be the matrix of geometric means of the judgments where

$a_{ij} = \prod_{k=1}^{m} (a_{ijk})^{1/m}$. Writing the principal eigenvalue of this matrix as a function of

the geometric means of the judgments we obtain:

$$\lambda_k = 1 + \left(a_{12}a_{23}a_{31}\right)^{1/3} + \left(a_{13}a_{32}a_{21}\right)^{1/3}$$

$$= 1 + \left(a_{12}a_{23}a_{31}\right)^{1/3} + \left(a_{12}a_{23}a_{31}\right)^{-1/3}$$

$$= 1 + \left[\prod_k (a_{12k}a_{23k}a_{31k})^{1/m}\right]^{1/3} + \left[\prod_k (a_{12k}a_{23k}a_{31k})^{1/m}\right]^{-1/3}$$

$$= 1 + \left[\prod_k (a_{12k}a_{23k}a_{31k})^{1/3}\right]^{1/m} + \left[\prod_k (a_{12k}a_{23k}a_{31k})^{-1/3}\right]^{1/m}$$

$$\leq \prod_k \left[1 + (a_{12k}a_{23k}a_{31k})^{1/3} + (a_{12k}a_{23k}a_{31k})^{-1/3}\right]^{1/m}$$

$$= \prod_k (\lambda_k)^{1/m} \leq \max_k \{\lambda_k\}$$

having used the inequality of Holder $\sum \prod_k x_k \leq \prod_k \left(\sum (x_k)^m\right)^{1/m}$ that connects

sums of products to the products of sums, and the inconsistency of a group judging three alternatives cannot be greater than the inconsistency of the most inconsistent individual. Unfortunately, because of Galois Theory and the unsolvability of algebraic equations be extracting roots beyond quartics we do not have similar expressions to work with for the general case. So we follow an alternate route to prove:

Theorem (Bounded Inconsistency): For a group of nearly consistent individuals, the inconsistency of group judgments aggregated by the geometric mean from individual judgments is at most equal to the largest of the individual inconsistencies.

Proof: First we show that the inconsistency of a group along cycles of length three satisfies this theorem and is related to the inconsistency index given by

$$\mu_k \equiv \frac{\lambda^{(k)}_{\max} - n}{n-1} = -1 + \frac{1}{n(n-1)} \sum_{1 \leq i < j \leq n} \left(\varepsilon_{ijk} + \frac{1}{\varepsilon_{ijk}}\right)$$

where $\lambda^{(k)}_{\max}$ is the principal eigenvalue of the matrix $\left(a_{ijk} = \frac{w_{ik}}{w_{jk}} \varepsilon_{ijk}\right)$. Thus, we

have $\lambda^{(k)}_{\max} w_{ik} = \sum_j a_{ijk} w_{jk} = \sum_j \frac{w_{ik}}{w_{jk}} \varepsilon_{ijk} w_{jk} = w_{ik} \sum_j \varepsilon_{ijk}$ and $\lambda^{(k)}_{\max} = \sum_j \varepsilon_{ijk}$ for

all i.

Let $\left(a_{ijk} = \frac{w_{ik}}{w_{jk}} \varepsilon_{ijk}\right)$ $k = 1, 2, ..., m$ be the n-by-n matrices of pairwise

comparisons of m individuals. Let $\delta_{ijk} = \varepsilon_{ijk} - 1$. By definition inconsistency in the judgments of an individual means that $a_{ijk}a_{jlk} \neq a_{ilk}$ for at least some i, j and l. The inconsistency of a 3-cycle for the kth individual can be measured by $a_{ijk}a_{jlk}a_{lik}$. So, clearly, if these judgments were consistent $a_{ijk}a_{jlk}a_{lik} = 1$ for all i, j and l. Thus, inconsistency can be measured with an index that must exclude loops that only connect judgments with themselves preventing the formation of 3-cycles. We have

$$I_k(n,3) = \frac{1}{n(n-1)(n-2)} \sum_{i \neq j \neq l} a_{ijk}a_{jlk}a_{lik} = \frac{1}{n(n-1)(n-2)} \sum_{i \neq j \neq l} \varepsilon_{ijk}\varepsilon_{jlk}\varepsilon_{lik}$$

that is equal to one with consistency. The index corresponding to the matrix of geometric means for the group is given by

$$I(n,3) = \frac{1}{n(n-1)(n-2)} \sum_{i \neq j \neq l} \prod_k (a_{ijk}a_{jlk}a_{lik})^{1/m} \equiv \frac{1}{n(n-1)(n-2)} \sum_{i \neq j \neq l} a_{ij}a_{jl}a_{li}$$

$$= \frac{1}{n(n-1)(n-2)} \sum_{i \neq j \neq l} \varepsilon_{ij}\varepsilon_{jl}\varepsilon_{li} \equiv \frac{1}{n(n-1)(n-2)} \sum_{i \neq j \neq l} \prod_k (\varepsilon_{ijk}\varepsilon_{jlk}\varepsilon_{lik})^{1/m}$$

$$\leq \prod_k \left(\frac{1}{n(n-1)(n-2)} \sum_{i \neq j \neq l} (\varepsilon_{ijk}\varepsilon_{jlk}\varepsilon_{lik}) \right)^{1/m} = \prod_k [I_k(n,3)]^{1/m}$$

$$\leq \max_k \{I_k(n,3)\}$$

again having used Holder's inequality. *Thus, the 3-cycle inconsistency of a group does not exceed the 3-cycle inconsistency of the most inconsistent individual.* Now we show that $I_k(n,3)$ is analytically related to μ_k. It serves as the link to connect μ for the group to $\mu_1, \mu_2, ..., \mu_m$, the inconsistency measures of the individuals, so we can say how the inconsistency of individuals judgments affects the inconsistency of the geometric mean of these judgments, i.e., that $\mu \leq \max_k \{\mu_k\}$.

Substituting $1+\delta_{ijk}$ for ε_{ijk} we obtain

$$I_k(n,3) = \frac{1}{n(n-1)(n-2)} \sum_{i\neq j\neq l} (1+\delta_{ijk})(1+\delta_{jlk})(1+\delta_{lik})$$

$$= \frac{1}{n(n-1)(n-2)} \left[n(n-1)(n-2) + n\sum_{i\neq j}\delta_{ijk} + n\sum_{j\neq l}\delta_{jlk} + n\sum_{l\neq i}\delta_{lik} \right.$$

$$\left. + \sum_{i\neq j\neq l}\delta_{ijk}\delta_{jlk} + \sum_{i\neq j\neq l}\delta_{ijk}\delta_{jlk} + \sum_{i\neq j\neq l}\delta_{ijk}\delta_{jlk} + \sum_{i\neq j\neq l}\delta_{ijk}\delta_{jlk}\delta_{lik} \right]$$

$$= 1 + \frac{3}{(n-1)}\sum_{i\neq j}\delta_{ijk} + \frac{3}{n(n-1)(n-2)}\sum_{i\neq j\neq l}\delta_{ijk}\delta_{jlk} +$$

$$+ \frac{1}{n(n-1)(n-2)}\sum_{i\neq j\neq l}\delta_{ijk}\delta_{jlk}\delta_{lik}$$

In addition, $\lambda_{\max}^{(k)} = \sum_j (1+\delta_{ijk}) = n + \sum_j \delta_{ijk}$ and

$\mu_k \equiv \dfrac{\lambda_{\max}^{(k)}-n}{n-1} = \dfrac{1}{n-1}\sum_j \delta_{ijk}$. Note that for any $i, \delta_{iik} = 0$ for all k. In addition,

by summing over i we obtain $\mu_k = \dfrac{1}{n(n-1)}\sum_i\sum_j \delta_{ijk}$. We now write the index

$I_k(n,3)$ of the kth individual as a function of μ_k as follows:

$$I_k(n,3) = 1 + \frac{3}{(n-1)(n-2)}\sum_{i\neq j}\delta_{ijk} + \frac{3}{n(n-1)(n-2)}\sum_{i\neq j\neq l}\delta_{ijk}\delta_{jlk} +$$

$$\frac{1}{n(n-1)(n-2)}\sum_{i\neq j\neq l}\delta_{ijk}\delta_{jlk}\delta_{lik}$$

$$= 1 + \frac{3n}{(n-2)}\mu_k + \frac{3}{n(n-1)(n-2)}\sum_{i\neq j}\delta_{ijk}\sum_{l}\delta_{jlk} +$$

$$\frac{1}{n(n-1)(n-2)}\sum_{i\neq j\neq l}\delta_{ijk}\delta_{jlk}\delta_{lik}$$

$$= 1 + \frac{3n}{(n-2)}\mu_k + \frac{3\mu_k}{n(n-2)}\sum_{i\neq j}\delta_{ijk} + \frac{1}{n(n-1)(n-2)}\sum_{i\neq j\neq l}\delta_{ijk}\delta_{jlk}\delta_{lik}$$

$$= 1 + \frac{3n}{(n-2)}\mu_k + \frac{3(n-1)}{(n-2)}\mu_k^2 + \frac{1}{n(n-1)(n-2)}\sum_{i\neq j\neq l}\delta_{ijk}\delta_{jlk}\delta_{lik}$$

In a neighborhood of $\varepsilon_{ij}=1$ corresponding to near consistency we have

$$I_k(n,3) = 1 + \frac{3n}{(n-2)}\mu_k + o(\delta_{ijk})$$

and for the group index $I(n,3)$ by simply suppressing the subscript k above we have:

$$I(n,3) = 1 + \frac{3}{(n-1)(n-2)}\sum_{i\neq j}\delta_{ij} + \frac{3}{n(n-1)(n-2)}\sum_{i\neq j\neq l}\delta_{ij}\delta_{jl} +$$

$$\frac{1}{n(n-1)(n-2)}\sum_{i\neq j\neq l}\delta_{ij}\delta_{jl}\delta_{li}$$

$$= 1 + \frac{3n}{(n-2)}\mu + o(\delta_{ij}).$$

Thus, finally $I(n,3) = 1 + \frac{3n}{n-2}\mu + o(\delta_{ij}) \leq \max_k\left\{1 + \frac{3n}{n-2}\mu_k + o(\delta_{ijk})\right\}$ and

$$\mu \leq \max_k\{\mu_k\}.$$

It follows that for experts whose inconsistency is individually not too large, the group's inconsistency cannot be larger than that of the most inconsistent individual.

INDEX

List of Books on the AHP and ANP

Mathematical Principles of Decision Making: Generalization of the Analytic Network Process to Neural Firing and Synthesis

Thomas L. Saaty, 531 pp., RWS Publications, 2010, ISBN-10 1888603100 or ISBN-13 9781888603101, softcover.

In this book the theory of the analytic network process and analytic hierarchy process (AHP/ANP), developed by Saaty over the past 40 years, is summarized. AHP and ANP are based on a method for deriving measures for both tangibles and intangibles through paired comparisons using either human judgment or data and synthesizing the results to make the best choice. Saaty shows how the theory applies in complex decisions represented in hierarchic structures and in network structures that have dependence and feedback involving finite elements and clusters and then extends the ideas to neural forms involving a continuum number of comparisons. For finite structures the ideas are applied in the context of benefits, opportunities, costs and risks in many areas including resource allocation and conflict resolution. The generalization to continuous comparisons is shown to lead to the inverse square law in physics, to neural firings in the context of stimulus response, and to mathematical expressions for stimuli responses.

The Encyclicon

The *Encyclicon* is a multi-volume encyclopedia of Analytic Network Process applications that includes examples ranging from simple models with feedback involving single networks, such as those for estimating market share of companies based on soft notions like consumer perceptions, to complex decisions involving benefits, opportunities, costs and risks (BOCR). The decisions are categorized into business and trade, crime and terrorism, energy, government, military, health, industry and production, politics, public concern, sports, and career decisions. The SuperDecisions software for the AHP/ANP can be obtained from *www.superdecisions.com*.

(Encyclicon Vol. 1) A Dictionary of Decisions with Dependence and Feeback based on the Analytic Network Process

Thomas L. Saaty and Müjgan Özdemir, 292 pages, RWS Publications, Pittsburgh, PA, 2005, ISBN 1-888603-05-4, paperback.

RWS Publications

Specializing in Books on the AHP and ANP

4922 ELLSWORTH AVENUE, PITTSBURGH, PA 15213 USA

PHONE 412-414-5984; FAX 412-681-4510

SALES@RWSPUBLICATIONS.COM

This book includes a 28 page introductory chapter to the subject that begins with pairwise comparisons, hierarchies, eigenvectors and consistency, goes on to networks with dependence and feedback and gives a comprehensive illustration of a complex example with benefits, opportunities, costs and risks (BOCR) networks. It includes 100 examples from singles networks such as those used for estimating market share to complex BOCR examples with sub-networks.

(Encyclicon Vol. 2) A Dictionary of Complex Decisions using the Analytic Network Process

Thomas L. Saaty and Brady Cillo, 356 pages, RWS Publications, Pittsburgh, PA, 2008, ISBN 1-888603-09-7 or 978-1-888603-09-5, paperback.

Volume 2 has a 24 page appendix on the theory behind the AHP and ANP. It also includes a comprehensive illustration of a BOCR complex model in Chapter 1with the rest of the chapters of examples divided into: Business Strategy, Business Operations, Business Location Selection, National Government, State and Local Government, Social Policy, International Relations, International Affairs, Education and Career, Personal Investments, Sports.

(Encyclicon Vol. 3) A Dictionary of Complex Decisions using the Analytic Network Process

Thomas L. Saaty and Luis G. Vargas, 298 pages, RWS Publications, Pittsburgh, PA, 2011, ISBN 1-888603-11-9 or 978-1-886603-11-0, paperback.

In Volume 3, Chapter 1 has personal decision examples and the first of these is expanded to show the details of its complex benefits, opportunities, costs and risks decision structure. The other examples in the book are divided into chapters on micro policy decisions, strategy decisions, macro policy decisions, investment decisions and sports.

Theory and Applications of the Analytic Network Process: Decision Making with Benefits, Opportunities, Costs, and Risks

Thomas L. Saaty, 352 pp., RWS Publications, 2009 edition. ISBN 1-888603-06-2, softcover.

Updated book on the Analytic Network Process. It improves upon the 2001 edition and the 2005 edition by emphasizing more complex decisions in light of their benefits, opportunities, costs and risks (BOCR), and by showing how to include the decision maker's strategic criteria that must be satisfied regardless. The important background material from the earlier book on the analytic network process, published in 2001, is

---

RWS Publications

Specializing in Books on the AHP and ANP

4922 ELLSWORTH AVENUE, PITTSBURGH, PA 15213 USA

PHONE 412-414-5984; FAX 412-681-4510

SALES@RWSPUBLICATIONS.COM

included, but there are new examples of complex models that handle benefits, opportunities, costs and risks in subnets. For the accompanying SuperDecisions software and numerous applications, please go to www.superdecisions.com.

The Fundamentals of Decision Making and Priority Theory with the Analytic Hierarchy Process

Thomas L. Saaty, 478 pages, RWS Publications, Pittsburgh, PA, 2011 revision, ISBN 0-9620317-6-3, or 978-0-9620317-6-2, paperback.

This book is a comprehensive summary, primarily of the author's own thinking and research, of the Analytic Hierarchy Process (AHP) and decision making. It includes advanced mathematical theory, diverse applications, and new theoretical material not previously published elsewhere. It replaces the original book on the AHP, *The Analytic Hierarchy Process*, published by McGraw Hill in 1980.

Decision Making for Leaders, The Analytic Hierarchy Process for Decisions in a Complex World

Thomas L. Saaty, 343 pages, RWS Publications, Pittsburgh, PA, 2008, ISBN 0-9620317-8-X, or 978-0-9620317-8-6, paperback.

This book is a general introduction to the Analytic Hierarchy Process (AHP) for decision making and is intended for those who must set priorities and make decisions. It does not demand that the reader have a technical background but explains the philosophy and general approach to defining the problem and setting priorities. It is an appropriate book for college level courses on decision making with the AHP.

Creative Thinking, Problem Solving and Decision Making

Thomas L. Saaty, 267 pages, RWS Publications, Pittsburgh, PA, 2010 edition, ISBN-1-888603-03-8, hardcover.

In this new edition there are beautiful original color paintings that capture the essence of the creative process. The book has the same original rich collection of ideas: profiles of creative people, projects and products, theory, philosophy, physics and metaphysics...and jokes, and incorporates recent research from a growing body of academicians and practitioners about the essence of creativity. Exercises at the end of each chapter help the reader build creative "muscles" and develop confidence and new creative ability skills. It includes a chapter on decision making with the analytic hierarchy process.

RWS Publications

Specializing in Books on the AHP and ANP

4922 ELLSWORTH AVENUE, PITTSBURGH, PA 15213 USA

PHONE 412-414-5984; FAX 412-681-4510

SALES@RWSPUBLICATIONS.COM

AWARDS FOR THE IDEAS IN THE AHP/ANP
BOOKS
Thomas L. Saaty

This book contains a new chapter based on an award winning paper on the possibility of combining individual judgments into a representative group judgment by Thomas Saaty and Luis Vargas who were awarded the Herbert Simon Award for Outstanding Contribution in Information Technology and Decision Making in 2012 for their paper, published in 2005, in the International Journal of Information Technology & Decision Making (IJITDM). A different version of this paper also appeared in 2011 in the journal Social Choice and Welfare. In 2011 Thomas Saaty was awarded an honorary doctorate by Jagiellonian University in Krakow, Poland, for his contribution to the theory of decision making: the concepts of the analytic hierarchy process and the analytic network process. In 2008 The Institute of Operations Research and Management Science (INFORMS) recognized Saaty for his Analytic Hierarchy Process (AHP) by giving him its impact award: "The AHP has revolutionized how we resolve complex decision problems." In 2007 he was awarded the Akao Prize by the International Society of Quality Function Deployment. In 2005 he was elected to the US National Academy of Engineering for "the development and generalization of the analytic hierarchy process and the analytic network process in multi-criteria decision-making." In 2009 Thomas Saaty, who holds the Chair of Distinguished Professor at the University of Pittsburgh was awarded the Chancellor's Distinguished Research Award for his outstanding and continuing record of research and scholarly activity. In 2000 the International Society for Multi-criteria Decision Making awarded its Gold Medal to Professor Saaty for "the development of the analytic hierarchy process and the impact of his lifelong research on several disciplines."

RWS Publications

Specializing in Books on the AHP and ANP

4922 ELLSWORTH AVENUE, PITTSBURGH, PA 15213 USA

PHONE 412-414-5984; FAX 412-681-4510

SALES@RWSPUBLICATIONS.COM